Engd by A.H. Ritchie.

Harriet Beecher Stowe

MEN OF OUR TIMES;

OR

LEADING PATRIOTS OF THE DAY.

BEING NARRATIVES OF THE LIVES AND DEEDS OF

Statesmen, Generals, and Orators.

INCLUDING

BIOGRAPHICAL SKETCHES AND ANECDOTES

OF

LINCOLN, GRANT, GARRISON, SUMNER, CHASE, WILSON, GREELEY, FARRAGUT, ANDREW, COLFAX, STANTON, DOUGLASS, BUCKINGHAM, SHERMAN, SHERIDAN, HOWARD, PHILLIPS AND BEECHER.

BY

HARRIET BEECHER STOWE,

AUTHOR OF UNCLE TOM'S CABIN.

BEAUTIFULLY ILLUSTRATED

WITH EIGHTEEN STEEL PORTRAITS.

PUBLISHED BY SUBSCRIPTION ONLY.

HARTFORD PUBLISHING CO., HARTFORD, CONN.

J. D. DENISON, NEW YORK; J. A. STODDARD, CHICAGO, ILL.

1868.

Electrotyped by
LOCKWOOD & MANDEVILLE,
HARTFORD, CONN.

DEDICATION.

To the Young Men of America,

THESE RECORDS

OF THEIR ELDER BRETHREN IN THE REPUBLIC,

ARE INSCRIBED

BY THE AUTHOR.

LIST OF ILLUSTRATIONS.

PREFACE.

In these sketches of some of the leading public men of our times, the editor professes to give such particulars of their lives, and such only, as the public have a right to know.

Every such man has two lives, his public and his private one. The one becomes fairly the property of the public, in virtue of his having been connected with events in which every one has a share of interest; but the other belongs exclusively to himself, his family, and his intimate friends, and the public have no more right to discuss or pry into its details than they have into those of any other private individual.

The editor has aimed to avoid all privacies and personalities which might be indelicate in relation to family circles. She has indeed, in regard to all the characters, so far as possible, dwelt upon the early family and community influences by which they were formed, particularly upon the character and influence of mothers; but such inquiries relate for the most part to those long dead, and whose mortal history has become a thing of the past.

Whenever the means have been at hand, the family stock from which each man has been derived, has been minutely traced. The question of inherited traits is becoming yearly one of increasing interest, and most striking results come from a comparison of facts upon this subject. The fusion of different races is said to produce marked results on the characteristics of the human being. America has been a great smelting furnace in which tribes and nations have been melted together, and the result ought to be some new developments of human nature. It will always be both interesting and useful to know both the quality of the family stock, and the circumstances of the early training of men who have acted any remarkable part in life.

Our country has recently passed through a great crisis which has concentrated upon it for a time the attention of the civilized world. It has sustained a shock which the whole world, judging by past experience, said must inevitably shatter the republic to fragments, and yet, like a gallant ship in full sail, it has run down the terrible obstacle, and gone on triumphant, and is this day stronger for the collision.

This wonderful success is owing to the character of the people which a Christian Democracy breeds. Of this people we propose to give a specimen; to show how they were formed in early life, from the influences which are inherent in such a state.

We are proud and happy to know that these names on our list are after all but *specimens.* Probably every reader of this book will recall as many more whom he will deem equally worthy of public notice. There is scarcely one of them who would not say in reference to his position before the public, what Lincoln said: "I stand where I do because some man must stand there, but there are twenty others that might as well have been leaders as myself." On the whole, we are not ashamed to present to the world this list of men as a specimen of the graduates from the American school of Christian Democracy.

So far as we know, the American government is the only permanent republic which ever based itself upon the principles laid down by Jesus Christ, of the absolute equal brotherhood of man, and the rights of man on the simple ground of manhood. Notwithstanding the contrary practices of a section of the States united in the Union, and the concessions which they introduced into the constitution, nobody doubts that this was the leading idea of the men who founded our government. The declaration of American Independence crystalized a religious teaching within a political act. The constitution of the United States still further elaborates these principles, and so strong was the logic of ideas that the conflict of opinions implied in the incidental concessions to opposite ideas, produced in the government of the country a continual and irrepressible discord. For a while it seemed doubtful which idea would triumph, and whether the accidental parasite would not strangle and wither the great original tree. The late war was the outcome of the whole. The fierce fire into which our national character has been cast in the hour of trial, has burned out of it the last lingering stain of compromise with anything inconsistent with its primary object, "to ordain justice and perpetuate liberty."

These men have all been formed by the principles of that great Christian document, and that state of society and those social influences which grew out of it, and it is instructive to watch, in their early life, how a Christian republic trains her sons.

In looking through the list it will be seen that almost every one of these men sprang from a condition of hard-working poverty. The majority of them were self-educated men, who in early life were inured to industrious toil. The farm life of America has been the nursery of great men, and there is scarce a man mentioned in the book who has not hardened his muscles and strengthened his brain power by a hand to hand wrestle with the forces of nature in agricultural life. Frugality, strict temperance, self-reliance and indomitable industry have been the lessons of their early days.

Some facts about these specimen citizens are worthy of attention. More than one-half of them were born and received their early training in New England, and full one-third are direct lineal descendants of the Pilgrim fathers. All, so far as we know, are undoubted believers in the Christian religion—the greater proportion of them are men of peculiarly and strongly religious natures, who have been active and efficient in every peculiarly religious work. All have been agreed in one belief, that the teachings of Jesus Christ are to be carried out in political institutions, and that the form of society based on his teachings, is to be defended at any sacrifice and at all risks.

There is scarcely a political man upon this list whose early efforts were not menaced with loss and reproach and utter failure, if he advocated these principles in the conduct of political affairs. For these principles they have temporarily suffered buffetings, oppressions, losses, persecutions, and in one great instance, DEATH. All of them honored liberty when she was hard beset, insulted and traduced, and it is fit that a free people should honor them in the hour of her victory.

It will be found when the sum of all these biographies is added up that the qualities which have won this great physical and moral victory have not been so much exceptional gifts of genius or culture, as those more attainable ones which belong to man's moral nature.

Taken as a class, while there is a fair proportion both of genius and scholarship among them, yet the general result speaks more of average talent and education turned to excellent account, than of any striking eminence in any particular direction.

But we regard it as highest of all that they were men of good and honest hearts—men who have set their faces as a flint to know and do the RIGHT. All of them are men whose principles have been tried in the fire, men who have braved opposition and persecution and loss for the sake of what they believed to be true, and knew to be right, and for this even more than for their bravery in facing danger, and their patience and perseverance in overcoming difficulties, we have good hope in offering them as examples to the young men of America.

In respect to one of the names on the list, the editor's near relationship, while it gives her most authentic access to all sources of just information, may be held to require an apology. But the fashion of writing biographies of our leading men is becoming so popular that the only way in which a prominent man can protect himself from being put before the public by any hands who may think fit to assume the task, is to put into the hands of some friend such authentic particulars as may with propriety be recorded. Mr. Beecher has recently been much embarrassed by the solicitation of parties, who notwithstanding his remonstrances, announce an intention of writing his life. He has been informed by them that it was to be done whether he consented or not, and that his only choice was between furnishing these parties with material, or taking the risk of what they might discover in their unassisted researches.

In this dilemma, it is hoped that the sketch presented in this volume, as being undeniably authentic, may so satisfy the demand, that there may be no call for any other record.

H. B. STOWE.

HARTFORD, January, 1868.

CONTENTS.

CHAPTER VII.—HORACE GREELEY.

CHAPTER VIII.—DAVID G. FARRAGUT.

CHAPTER IX.—JOHN A. ANDREW.

CHAPTER X.—SCHUYLER COLFAX.

Engd by A H Ritchie.
A. Lincoln

CHAPTER I.

ABRAHAM LINCOLN.

The Men of our Time—Lincoln Foremost—The War was the Working-Man's Revolution—Abraham Lincoln's Birth and Youth—The Books he read—The Thirty Thousand Dollars for Tender—The Old Stocking of Government Money—A Just Lawyer; Anecdotes—His First Candidacy and Speech—Goes to Legislature and Congress—The Seven Debates and Campaign against Douglas in 1858—Webster's and Lincoln's Language Compared—The Cooper Institute Speech—The Nomination at Chicago—Moral and Physical Courage—The Backwoodsman President and the Diplomatists—Significance of his Presidential Career—Religious Feelings—His Kindness—"The Baby Did It"—The First Inaugural—The Second Inaugural, and other State Papers—The Conspiracy and Assassination—The Opinions of Foreign Nations on Mr. Lincoln.

Our times have been marked from all other times as the scene of an immense conflict which has not only shaken to its foundation our own country, but has been felt like the throes of an earthquake through all the nations of the earth.

Our own days have witnessed the closing of the great battle, but the preparations for that battle have been the slow work of years.

The "Men of Our Times," are the men who indirectly by their moral influence helped to bring on this great final crisis, and also those who, when it was brought on, and the battle was set in array, guided it wisely, and helped to bring it to its triumphant close.

In making our selection we find men of widely different spheres and characters. Pure philanthropists, who, ignoring all selfish and worldly politics, have labored against oppression and wrong; far-seeing statesmen, who could foresee the working of political causes from distant years; brave naval and military men, educated in the schools of our country; scientific men, who helped to perfect the material forces of war by their discoveries and ingenuity—all are united in one great crisis, and have had their share in one wonderful passage of the world's history.

Foremost on the roll of "men of our time," it is but right and fitting that we place the honored and venerated name of the man who was called by God's providence to be the leader of the nation in our late great struggle, and to seal with his blood the proclamation of universal liberty in this country—the name of

ABRAHAM LINCOLN.

The revolution through which the American nation has been passing was not a mere local convulsion. It was a war for a principle which concerns all mankind. It was the war for the rights of the working class of society as against the usurpation of privileged aristocracies. You can make nothing else of it. That is the reason why, like a shaft of light in the judgment day, it has gone through all nations, dividing the multitudes to the right and the left. *For* us and our cause, all the common working classes of Europe—all that toil and sweat, and are oppressed. *Against* us, all privileged classes, nobles, princes, bankers and great manufacturers, all who live at ease. A silent instinct, piercing to the dividing of soul and spirit, joints and marrow, has gone through the earth, and sent every soul with instinctive certainty where it belongs. The poor laborers of Birmingham and Manchester, the poor silk weavers of Lyons, to whom our conflict has been present starvation and lingering death, have stood bravely *for* us. No sophistries could blind or deceive *them;* they knew that *our* cause was *their* cause, and they suffered their part heroically, as if fighting by our side, because they knew that our victory was to be their victory. On the other side, all aristocrats and holders of exclusive privileges have felt the instinct of opposition, and the sympathy with a struggling aristocracy, for they, too, felt that our victory would be their doom.

This great contest has visibly been held in the hands of Almighty God, and is a fulfillment of the solemn prophecies with which the Bible is sown thick as stars, that He would spare the soul of the needy, and judge the cause of the poor. It was He who chose the instrument for this work, and He chose him with a visible reference to the rights and interests of the great majority of mankind, for which he stood.

Abraham Lincoln was in the strictest sense *a man of the working classes.* All his advantages and abilities were those of a man of the working classes, all his disadvantages and disabilities those of the working classes, and his position at the head of one of the most powerful nations of the earth was a sign to all who live by labor, that their day is coming. Lincoln was born to the inheritance of hard work, as truly as the poorest laborer's son that digs in our fields. He was born in Kentucky, in 1809. At seven years of age he was set to work, axe in hand, to clear up a farm in a Western forest. Until he was seventeen his life was that of a simple farm laborer, with only such intervals of schooling as farm laborers get. Probably the school instruction of his whole life would not amount to more than six months. At nineteen he made a trip to New Orleans as a hired hand on a flat-boat, and on his return he split the timber for a log cabin and built it, and enclosed ten acres of land with a rail fence of his own handiwork. The next year he hired himself for twelve dollars a month to build a flat-boat and take her to New Orleans, and any one who knows what the life of a Mississippi boatman was in those days, must know that it involved every kind of labor. In 1832, in the Black Hawk Indian war, the hardy boatman volunteered to fight for his country, and was unanimously elected a captain, and served with honor for a season in frontier military life. He was very popular with his soldiers for two reasons; the first was his great physical strength; the second, that he could tell more and better stories than any other man in the army. Odd constituents for a commander's character; but like everything else in Lincoln's life, the fact shows how wonderfully he represented, and therefore suited, the people. Some time after the war, the surveyor of Sangamon county, being driven with work, came to him to take the survey of a tract off from his hands. True, he had never studied surveying, but what of that? He accepted the job, procured a chain and a treatise on surveying, and *did the work.* Do we not see in this a parallel of the wider wilderness which in later years he was to undertake to survey and fit for human habitation, *without* chart or surveyor's chain?

After this, while serving as a postmaster, he began his law studies. He took the postmastership for the sake of reading all the papers that came into the town, at the same time borrowing the law books he was too poor to buy, and studying by the light of his evening fire. He soon acquired a name in the country about as a man of resources and shrewdness. He was one that people looked to for counsel in exigencies, and to whom they were ready to depute almost any enterprise which needed skill and energy, or patience and justice. "He was in great request," says one of his biographers, "by thick-headed people, because of his clearness and skill in narration." It might well have been added, because also of his kindness, patience and perfect justness of nature in listening, apprehending and stating.

Mr. Lincoln was now about twenty-three. His life thus far may perhaps be considered as his education; at any rate, it is the part of his life which answers to the school years, college course, and professional studies of a regularly educated lawyer at the East. It included, of actual "schooling," only the six months total already mentioned. Even then it was his mother who had taught him to read and write. Of the use of books of any kind, this backwoods graduate had little enough. His course of reading was a very thorough illustration of the ancient rule to "read not many but much." He read seven books over and over. Of three of them, the Bible, Shakspeare and Æsop's Fables, he could repeat large portions by heart. The other four were the Pilgrim's Progress, the Life of Washington, the Life of Franklin, and the Life of Henry Clay. It is a curious fact that neither then nor afterwards did he ever read a novel. He began Ivanhoe once, but was not interested enough to finish it. He was one of those men who have the peculiar faculty of viewing this whole world of men and things as a side spectator, and the interest of the drama of life thus silently seen at first hand, was to him infinitely more interesting than any second hand imitation. "My life is story enough," once said a person of this peculiar temperament, "what should I want to read stories for?" The interest he felt in human beings was infinitely stronger with him than the interest in artistic representation.

One of his biographers says that he "seldom bought a new book, and seldom read one," and he adds, with a good deal of truth, that "his education was almost entirely a newspaper one," and that he "was one of the most thorough newspaper readers in America."

But that which was much more the real essence of his self-education, was the never-ceasing and strenuous course of laborious thought and reasoning that he kept up, upon the meaning, the connection, the tendency, the right and wrong, the helps or remedies, of all the past facts he read of, or of the present facts that he experienced in life. And this education he not only began early and pursued effectively, but he never ceased it. All his life he maintained that course of steady labor after practical knowledge and practical wisdom. Whenever he could read a good book he did, and his practice for a long time was, after having finished it, to write out an analysis of it; a very fatiguing but very improving process. One of his companions while a young "hired man," described him in after years, as "the likeliest boy in God's world.

He would work all day as hard as any of us, and study by fire-light in the log house half the night, and in this way he made himself a thorough practical surveyor." Another man described him as he saw him while working for a living, in 1830, or thereabouts, "lying on a trundle-bed, with one leg stretched out rocking the cradle containing the child of his hostess, while he himself was absorbed in the study of English grammar."

The world has many losses that mankind are not conscious of. The burning of the Alexandrian library was an irreparable loss, but a greater loss is in the silence of great and peculiar minds. Had there been any record of what Lincoln thought and said while he thus hewed his way through the pedantic mazes of book learning, we might have some of the newest, the strangest, the most original contributions to the philosophy of grammar and human language in general that ever have been given. They would have savored very much of Beethoven's answer when the critics asked him why he would use consecutive octaves in music. "Because they sounded well," said the scornful old autocrat; and Lincoln's quiet perseverance in a style of using the English language peculiarly his own had something of the same pertinacity. He seemed equally amused by the critical rules of rhetoric, and as benevolently and paternally indulgent to the mass of eager scholars who thought them important, as he was to the turbulent baby whom he rocked with one leg while he pursued his grammatical studies. But after his own quaint, silent fashion, he kept up his inquiries into the world of book learning with remarkable perseverance, and his friend and biographer, Mr.

Arnold, says, became "thoroughly at home in all the liberal studies and scientific questions of the day." This is rather strongly put, and we fancy that Lincoln would have smiled shrewdly over it, but the specifications which Mr. Arnold adds are undoubtedly true. Mr. Lincoln "had mastered English, and made some progress in Latin, and knew the Bible more thoroughly than many who have spent their lives in its perusal."

But what book learning he obtained would never have made him a lawyer, not to say President. The education which gave him his success in life was his self-training in the ability to understand and to state facts and principles about men and things.

In 1836 our backwoodsman, flat-boat hand, captain, surveyor, obtained a license to practice law, and as might be expected, rose rapidly. One anecdote will show the esteem in which he was held in his neighborhood. A client came to him in a case relating to a certain land claim, and Lincoln said to him, "Your first step must be to take thirty thousand dollars and go and make a legal tender; it of course will be refused, but it is a necessary step." "But," said the man, "I haven't the thirty thousand dollars to make it with." "O, that's it; just step over to the bank with me, and I'll get it." So into the bank they went, and Lincoln says to the cashier, "We just want to take thirty thousand dollars to make a legal tender with; I'll bring it back in an hour or two." The cashier handed across the money to "Honest Abe," and without a scratch of the pen in acknowledgment, he strode his way with the money, all in the most sacred simplicity, made the tender, and brought it back with as much nonchalance as if he had been borrowing a silver spoon of his grandmother.

It was after he had been practicing law some time, that another incident took place, showing him as curiously scrupulous about small sums as he was trusty and trusted about large ones. When he left New Salem and went to Springfield, he was still so poor that he even found it difficult to procure the necessaries of life. For some years he struggled forward, when one day there came a post-office agent, who in pursuance of the routine business of the department, presented to the almost penniless and still struggling ex-postmaster a regulation draft for the balance due to the Washington office, in all $17.60. Dr. Henry, a friend of Mr. Lincoln's, happening to fall in with the agent, went along with him, intending to offer to lend the money, as it was about certain that he could have no such sum as that at his command. When the draft was presented, Lincoln asked the officer to be seated, sat down himself a few moments, looking puzzled; then asked to be excused for a little, stepped out to his boarding house and returned. He brought with him an old stocking, untied it, and poured out on the table a quantity of small silver coin and "red cents." These they counted; they amounted to $17.60, the precise amount called for by the draft. More than that—it was *the very money* called for by the draft, for at leaving his postmastership, the punctilious officer had tied up the balance on hand, and kept it by him, awaiting the legal call for it. At paying it over, he remarked that he *never used, even temporarily, any money that was not his.* This money, he added, he felt belonged to the government, and he had no right to exchange or use it for any purposes of his own.

His honesty, shrewdness, energy and keen practical insight into men and things soon made him the most influential man in his state, both as lawyer and politician. Of this influence, and most especially of its depending upon his wonderfully direct plain common sense, and the absolute honesty and utter justness of his mind, there are many anecdotes. In politics and in law alike, both the strength of his conscientiousness and the kind of yearning after a rounded wholeness of view which was an intellectual instinct with him, forced him habitually to consider all sides of any question. "For fifteen years before his election to the Presidency," says one writer, in striking illustration of this habit in politics, "he subscribed regularly to *The Richmond Enquirer* and *The Charleston Mercury*. He grew slowly, as public opinion grew; and as an anti-slavery man, was a gradual convert." Thus it resulted that "while Rhett and Wise, with slavery in full feather, wrote every day the inviolateness of secession and the divinity of bondage, these two Illinois lawyers, (Lincoln and his partner, Herndon,) in their little square office, read every vaunting cruel word, paid to read it, and educated themselves out of their mutual indignations."

In like manner he was fair and impartial in legal investigations. "The jury" says one account, "always got from him a fair statement of any case in hand, and years later it was remarked by the Chief Justice of Illinois that when Lincoln spoke, he argued both sides of the case so well that a speech in response was always superfluous."

Mr. Lincoln's fellow lawyers used to say that he was in professional matters, "perversely honest." He could not take hold heartily on the wrong side. He never engaged in it, knowingly; if a man desired to retain him whose cause was bad, he declined, and told the applicant not to go to law. A lady once came to him to have him prosecute a claim to some land, and gave him the papers in the case for examination, together with a retainer in the shape of a check for two hundred dollars. Next day she came to see what her prospects were, when Mr. Lincoln told her that he had examined the documents very carefully, that she "had not a peg to hang her claim on," and that he could not conscientiously advise her to bring an action. Having heard this judgment, the lady thanked him, took her papers, and was about to depart. "Wait a moment," said Mr. Lincoln, "here is the check you gave me." "But," said she, "Mr. Lincoln, I think you have earned *that.*" "No, no," he answered, insisting on her receiving it, "that would not be right. I can't take pay for doing my duty."

He was quite as prompt and just in accepting unprofitable duty as in declining its profitable opposite. During all the early part of his legal practice in Springfield, it was considered an unpopular and politically dangerous business for a lawyer to defend any fugitive slave on trial for surrender to the South, and even the brave Col. Baker, in those days also practicing there, on one occasion directly refused to defend such a case, saying that as a political man he could not afford it.

But the luckless applicant, having consulted with an abolitionist friend, went next to Lincoln, and got him. "*He's* not afraid of an unpopular case," said the friend; "when I go for a lawyer to defend an arrested fugitive slave, other lawyers will refuse me; but if Mr. Lincoln is at home, he will always take up my case."

On a few occasions after having even entered into the trial of a case, Mr. Lincoln would find that, as sometimes happens, he had been deceived by his own client, and that he really had not the right on his side. When this was the case, he could as it were be seen to wilt at once, and whatever further he might do in the case was only mechanical. In such a case, having an associate, and having refused to argue it, the associate argued the case *and won it*, and then offered to divide with Mr. Lincoln the fee of $900; but Lincoln would not take a cent. Once in defending a man sued for delivering lambs instead of sheep, the testimony clearly showed that such delivery had been made. Instead of trying to confuse the witnesses or becloud the evidence, Mr. Lincoln ascertained how many such lambs had been delivered, and quietly told the jury that they must give a verdict against his client. He simply cautioned them to be just in fixing the damages. When he had recovered a verdict against a railroad company, and a certain offset against his client was to be deducted, he interrupted the final decision just in time to have the offset *made larger* by a certain amount which he had just found out ought to be added to it. His careful and primitive scrupulousness was just as marked in dealing with any associates in a case. When he received a joint fee his invariable custom was to divide it properly, and tie up in a separate parcel each associate's part of *the very money received*, duly labelled and directed.

In 1841 Mr. Lincoln argued before the Supreme Court of Illinois, the case of Nance, a negro girl, who had been sold within the state. A note had been given in payment for her, and the suit was brought to recover upon this note. Mr. Lincoln, defending, proved that Nance was free, and that thus nothing had been sold; so that the note was void. The Court below had sustained the note, but the Supreme Court, in accordance with Mr. Lincoln's argument, reversed this judgment. The decision made Nance free, and put a stop to sales of human beings in Illinois.

Another remarkable case in which he was engaged, was, the defence of young Armstrong from a charge of murder. This Armstrong was the son of a man who had befriended and employed Mr. Lincoln in youth, and the present charge was, that he had killed a certain person who had unquestionably died from injuries received in a camp-meeting riot where young Armstrong was present. The father was dead, and the mother aged and poor; a chain of apparently perfectly conclusive circumstantial evidence had been forged, which had convinced the community of Armstrong's guilt; indeed, had he not been safely secured in a strong jail he would have been lynched. Neither the youth nor his old mother had any money. The people and the newspapers were furious against the prisoner; and his fate appeared absolutely certain even to himself, when Mr. Lincoln, hearing of the matter in some way, volunteered for the defence, and was gladly accepted. When the trial came on, the evidence for the prosecution was given, and constituted what appeared to the audience a perfectly conclusive proof of guilt. Lincoln cross-examined very lightly, only correcting up and ascertaining a few places and dates; and his own witnesses were only to show comparatively good previous character for the prisoner.

The prosecutor, sure of his prey, made only a short and formal argument. Mr. Lincoln followed for the defence. He began slowly, calmly, carefully. He took hold of the heart of the evidence for the state—that of the chief witness. He pointed out first one discrepancy, and then another, and then another. He came at last to that part of the evidence where this principal witness had sworn positively that he had been enabled by the light of the moon to see the prisoner give the fatal blow with a slung shot; and taking up the almanac he showed that at the hour sworn to on the night sworn to *the moon had not risen;* that the whole of this evidence was a perjury.

The audience, gradually stirred and changed in the temper of their minds by the previous series of skilfully displayed inconsistencies, rising from hate into sympathy, flamed suddenly up at this startling revelation, and the verdict of "not guilty" was almost visible in the faces of the jury. But this was not all. Turning upon the infamous man who had sought to swear away another's life, Mr. Lincoln, now fully kindled into his peculiarly slow but intensely fiery wrath, held him up to the view of court and jury and audience, in such a horrid picture of guilt and shame that the miserable fellow, stunned and confounded, actually fled from the face of the incensed lawyer out of the court room. And in conclusion, Mr. Lincoln appealed to the jury to lay aside any temporary prejudices, and to do simple justice. And he referred to the motive of his own presence there,—to his gratitude for the kindness of the prisoner's father in past years, in a manner so affecting as to bring tears from many eyes. In less than half an hour the jury returned a verdict of not guilty, and the young man was set free, his life saved and his character restored.

When he went for the second time into public life, on the passage of the Nebraska Bill in 1854, he was becoming eminent in the difficult and lucrative department of patent law. But his fellow lawyers used to call his fees "ridiculously small." Indeed, he never took but one large fee, and that his friends insisted on his taking. This was $5,000 from the Illinois Central Railroad Company, one of the richest corporations in the country, and for very valuable services in a very important case. Once before this he had received what he thought a large fee, and he made a good use of it. The sum was five hundred dollars, and a friend who called to see him the next morning, found him counting it over and over, and piling it up on the table to look at. "Look here," he said, "see what a heap of money I've got from the ——— case! Did you ever see anything like it! Why, I never had so much money in my life before, put it all together!" Then he added, that if he could only get another $250 to put with it, he would at once buy a quarter-section of land, and settle it on his old step-mother. This was an odd use to make of a man's first important gains in money, and his friend, who at once loaned him the required additional amount, tried to make him give the land for the old lady's life only. But Lincoln insisted on his own plan, saying, "I shall do no such thing. It is a poor return at the best, for all the good woman's devotion and fidelity to me, and there isn't going to be any half-way work about it."

Mr. Lincoln was a great favorite at the bar, his good nature, his kindness, and his unfailing flow of stories, making him a most welcome guest on every circuit.

He never took technical advantages, but on the other hand often showed an adversary some error in matter of form, and suggested to him how to cure it. His forensic habits were excessively simple, but very effective. The most telling of all of them was *to be in the right;* for when juries know that a lawyer habitually refuses to be on the wrong side, habitually breaks down if on that side, simply from consciousness of the fact, and habitually makes strong and clear arguments if on the right side, they are prepossessed in favor of that lawyer before he says a word. He did not make speeches to the jury, he talked with them; often in warm weather taking off his coat for coolness, selecting some intelligent looking juryman, reasoning with him until convinced, then taking another, and so on. He did not browbeat witnesses, but kept them comfortable and good humored. In short, Mr. Lincoln was decidedly and deservedly a powerful as well as a successful lawyer. He must have been of great professional powers to maintain himself, and rise to the leadership of the bar, with the competitors he had. Among these were Mr. Douglas, Secretary Browning, Senator Trumbull, Governor Yates, Judge Davis of the U. S. Supreme Court, Col. Baker, Gen. Hardin, Gov. Bissell, Gen. Shields, Senator Washburn, N. B. Judd, Gen. Logan, and others. He became recognized by his fellow-citizens as "the first lawyer in Illinois," and one of the judges on the bench described him as "the finest lawyer he ever knew," and another as "one of the ablest he had ever known."

Like so many of his profession, Mr. Lincoln was very early a politician. Indeed, his devotion to politics interfered very considerably with his gains, and delayed his eminence in his profession. The value to his fellow-countrymen of the political results which he was the means of bringing to pass, is, however, so infinitely beyond any money value, that no regret can be felt at his ambition.

Mr. Lincoln's popularity among his neighbors, his assiduous study of the newspapers, his intense and untiring meditations and reasonings on the political questions of the day, brought him into the political field pretty early and pretty well prepared. It was in 1832, when he was twenty-three years old, that his first candidacy and his first speech took place. The story and speech all together are so short that they can be inserted here in full. On the day of election, then, Mr. Lincoln's opponent spoke first, and delivered a long harangue of the regular political sort. Lincoln, who followed him, completed his oration in just seventy-nine words—less than one minute's talking. This is what he said: "Gentlemen, fellow citizens:—I presume you know who I am; I am humble Abraham Lincoln. I have been solicited by many friends to become a candidate for the Legislature. My politics can be briefly stated. I am in favor of a national bank, I am in favor of the internal improvement system, and a high protective tariff. These are my sentiments and political principles. If elected I shall be thankful, if not, it will be all the same."

He was beaten, however, in spite of his terseness. But in his own district he received all but seven out of 284 votes; and he was never beaten again in any election by the people.

His actual political career, not counting this defeat, began in 1834, when he was chosen member of the State Legislature, and being too poor to afford a horse, *walked* over a hundred miles to Vandalia to take his seat. He remained a member for four successive terms of two years each. Mr. Douglas became a member two years after him, in 1836; the two men quickly became party leaders on their respective sides of the house, and thus their political courses and their political rivalries began almost together. At the two latter of his four legislative terms, Mr. Lincoln was the Whig candidate for Speaker, and once lacked only one vote of being elected. Mr. Lincoln's eight years' service in the State Legislature was busy and useful, and gave him an assured and high position in his party. The work done was usually of a local character, of course, its most important departments being that of the improvement of internal communication by railroad and canal, and that of education.

But even on the question of slavery, the one significant occasion for utterance which arose was promptly improved, and in such a manner as to show both the settled feelings and convictions of Lincoln's mind on the subject, and his characteristic practice of restricting his official utterances strictly to the exigencies of the case. His dislike of slavery was not only the consequence of his inborn sense of justice and kindly feelings, but was his direct inheritance from his parents, who left Kentucky and settled in Indiana expressly to bring up their family on free instead of slave soil. In March, 1839, some strong pro-slavery resolutions were passed by the Legislature of Illinois, and by large majorities in both houses. This, the few anti-slavery members could not prevent. But Mr. Lincoln and Mr. Dan Stone took the most decided stand in their power on the other side, by putting on record on the House journals a formal protest against the resolutions. In this protest, they declared views that would to-day be considered very conservative, about legal or political interference with slavery; but they also declared in the most unqualified manner, and in so many words, their belief "that the institution of slavery is founded on both injustice and bad policy."

At the end of his fourth term, Mr. Lincoln declined a further nomination, finding it absolutely necessary to devote more time than hitherto to his own private affairs. When he thus left the Legislature of his own accord, he was virtually the leader of his party in the State, having reached that creditable and influential though unofficial position by his own good qualities, in the eight years of his life ending with his thirty-fifth. It was a great achievement for a man no older, and so destitute of outside help.

For four years Mr. Lincoln now remained a hard-working lawyer, although he did a good deal of political work besides, particularly in "stumping" Illinois and Indiana in the Presidential canvass of 1844. In this campaign Mr. Lincoln made many strong and effective speeches for Henry Clay, and though his candidate was beaten, his own reputation as a politician and speaker was much increased. In 1846 he was elected to Congress as a Whig, and his extreme popularity at home is shown by the fact that his own majority on this occasion was 1,511 in the Springfield district, while Mr. Clay's had been only 914.

During this congressional term, Mr. Lincoln met the grinding of the great question of the day—the upper and nether millstone of slavery and freedom revolving against each other. Lincoln's whole nature inclined him to be a harmonizer of conflicting parties, rather than a committed combatant on either side. He was firmly and from principle an enemy to slavery, but the ground he occupied in Congress was in some respects a middle one between the advance guard of the anti-slavery army and the spears of the fire-eaters. He voted with John Quincy Adams for the receipt of anti-slavery petitions; he voted with Giddings for a committee of inquiry into the constitutionality of slavery in the District of Columbia, and the expediency of abolishing slavery in that district; he voted for the various resolutions prohibiting slavery in the territories to be acquired from Mexico, and he voted forty-two times for the Wilmot Proviso. On one occasion, he offered a plan for abolishing slavery in the District of Columbia, by compensation from the national treasury, with the consent of a majority of the citizens. He opposed the annexation of Texas, but voted for the bill to pay the expenses of the war. He voted against paying for slaves as property, when that question came up in the celebrated Pacheco case, and thus recorded his denial of the right of owning men, or of its acknowledgment by the nation.

During this term of service in Congress, Mr. Lincoln was a laborious and faithful public servant; always present to vote, and always ready for business; and his speeches, homely and rough as they were, showed so much broad strong sense, natural rectitude, sincerity, and power of reasoning, as to give him a good position as a debater. He declined a re-election; tried for but did not obtain the commissionership of the Land Office at Washington; declined appointments as Secretary and as Governor of Oregon Territory; returned to his home and his work; was unsuccessful as candidate for the United States Senate in the Illinois Legislature of 1849–50; and labored industriously at his profession, until the repeal of the Missouri Compromise, the Kansas Nebraska Bill, and the violences and iniquities connected with them, called him once more into public life.

He now took the field, heart and soul against the plot to betray our territories into slavery, and to perpetuate the power of that institution over the whole country. Henceforth he was all his life a public man; first a prominent champion in the decisively important state of Illinois, and afterwards the standard bearer and the martyr of Freedom in America.

That contest in Illinois, in which the political doctrines of Mr. Douglas were the central theme of discussion, and in which he himself on one side and Mr. Lincoln on the other, were the leading speakers and the controlling minds, was an important act in that great drama of emancipation which culminated in the Rebellion. In Mr. Lincoln's life it was if possible still greater in comparative importance; for his debates with Douglas determined his reputation as a speaker and a public man, and lifted him to the position from which he stepped into the presidential chair.

During other previous and subsequent portions of his life, other traits of Mr. Lincoln's character were often and clearly exemplified. But at no time was he nearly as plainly and strikingly prominent as a power, as during his contest with that bold and energetic politician and remarkably ready and forcible debater, Stephen A. Douglas.

Their first great public duel, as it may be called, was at Springfield, in October, 1854, just after the passage of the Nebraska bill. The country was all aflame with excitement. Every fibre of justice, honor, honesty, conscience that there was in the community was in that smarting and vibrating state which follows the infliction of a violent blow, and Douglas had come back to his own state to soothe down the irritation and to defend his wicked and unpopular course before the aroused tribunal of his fellow citizens.

He was to defend his course and conduct to a great audience assembled at the State fair, and Mr. Lincoln was to answer him.

Never was there a greater contrast between two men. Douglas might be called a brilliant impersonation of all the mere worldly forces of human nature. He had a splendid physique, with all the powers of the most captivating oratory, the melody of a most astonishing voice which ran with ease through every gamut of human feeling, grave, gay, pathetic, passionate, enthusiastic; now rising with irresistible impetuosity, now mocking with gay and careless defiance, and with this voice and this person, he was master of all those shadings and delicacies of sophistry by which the worse can be made to appear the better reason. He knew well how to avoid answering a telling argument by a dazzling glitter of side issues—to make a plain man believe he had got his difficulty solved, when he had been only skilfully bewitched, and made to forget where it was. In a popular audience he had something for every one. Gaiety, gallantry and compliments for ladies, assured confidence for doubters, vehement assertions for timid people, stormy brow-beatings, and lion roars of denunciation, to finish with a grand sweep the popular impression which his sophistries and assertions had begun. Of truth, he made that very sparing use which demagogues always do. A little blue line of steel makes a whole heavy headed iron axe go through the wood,—and so Douglas just skilfully and artistically tipped the edges of heavy masses of falsehood with the cutting force of some undeniable truth.

Of moral sensibility Douglas had not enough in his nature, even to understand that kind of material in others, and to make allowance for it. Nothing could be more exactly the contrary of Lincoln's scrupulous careful self-education, in pure questions of the right and the wrong of things, than Douglas' glittering, careless, reckless, defiant mode of treating all these subjects. Lincoln had trained himself always to ask, What is it right to do? Douglas, What *can* I do? Lincoln, to enquire What course *ought* they to take? Douglas, What course can I make them take? Lincoln, to ask, What is the truth—Douglas, What can be made to *seem* truth. His life question was an inquiry, pure and simple, how much can I get, how much can I do, without losing my hold over men and being turned out of society?

The pure moral aspects of political questions, he flouted and scoffed at as unworthy the attention of a practical politician. The rights of human beings, the eternal laws of rectitude, he treated as a skilful conjurer treats so many gaily painted balls, which he throws up and tosses and catches, simply to show his own agility; he played with them when they came in his way, just as he thought he could make them most effective for his own purposes.

But if he did not understand or care for eternal principles, he was perfect master of all the weak and low and petty side of human nature. He knew how to stir up all the common-place, base and ignoble passions of man; to bring his lower nature into lively exercise.

The first day in the fair, the multitude was given up to him, and he swept and played on them as a master musician sweeps a piano, and for the hour he seemed to be irresistible, bearing all things in his own way.

Lincoln had this advantage, when his turn came, that he represented that higher portion of human nature, of which Douglas had little knowledge, and which his mode of treatment had left almost wholly untouched. We have spoken of the vast legal influence which Lincoln had gradually acquired in his own state, by the intense pertinacity with which he identified himself in every case with right and justice, so that the mere fact that he had accepted a cause was a strong reason in advance for believing it the true one.

The people had been excited, amused, dazzled and bewildered, and were tossing restlessly as the sea swells and dashes after a gale—when that plain man without outward "form or comeliness," without dazzle of oratory, or glitter of rhetoric, rose to give them in a fatherly talk, the simple eternal RIGHT of the whole thing.

It was, he felt, an hour of destiny, a crisis in the great battle to be fought for mankind for ages to come, and an eye witness thus describes the scene: "His whole heart was in the subject. He quivered with feeling and emotion; the house was as still as death." And another account describes how "the effect of this speech was most magnetic and powerful. Cheer upon cheer interrupted him, women waved their handkerchiefs, men sprung from their seats and waved their hats in uncontrollable enthusiasm." Mr. Douglas was present at this speech, and was the most uneasy auditor there. As soon as Mr. Lincoln had concluded, Mr. Douglas jumped up and said that he had been abused, "though," he added, "in a perfectly courteous manner." He went on with a rejoinder, and spoke for some time, but without much success. In fact, he was astounded and disconcerted at finding that there was so much to be said against him, and that there was a man to say it so powerfully. The self-confident and even arrogant tone in which he had opened the debate was gone. At closing, he announced himself to continue his remarks in the evening, but he did not do it. He had received a blow too tremendous even for his immense vigor, and from which he could not so quickly recover.

A little while afterwards, Douglas spoke again and Lincoln answered him again, at Peoria, and with a similar result. The vast positive will of the "Little Giant" could not stand up against the still loftier power with which Mr. Lincoln assailed him from the height of a moral superiority that irresistibly carried with it the best convictions of the whole community, and cowed the defiant wrong-doer. Mr. Lincoln was *right*. Mr. Douglas felt himself vanquished by a power incomprehensible to himself, and of which none of his political calculations ever took account.

But as regards the struggle at this time in Illinois, the fact that he felt himself over-weighted, was sufficiently proved by his declining, after the two duels at Springfield and Peoria, to proceed, as Mr. Lincoln invited him, with a series of such debates in other parts of the State.

Mr. Lincoln, having thus publicly shown himself far stronger than the strongest of his opponents, proceeded to show himself a man of kindly self-command, by foregoing the Republican nomination to the U. S. Senate, and giving it to Hon. Lyman Trumbull, in order to save the risk of admitting Matteson, the pro-slavery candidate. Unquestionably this conduct coincided with the shrewdest selfishness; but very few are the politicians from whom a selfishness small and near would not conceal the larger and further one. It was by earnest and assiduous personal influence that Mr. Lincoln secured Mr. Trumbull's election.

It is said of a certain great diplomatist, that he was so accustomed to dealing with men as knaves that when he had to do with an honest man he always blundered. Douglas' mistake and defeat were precisely of this kind. He had so little sense of conscience or moral feeling himself that he was perfectly unprepared for the uprising of these sentiments on the part of the people, and astonished at the power which a man might wield simply from addressing a class of sentiments which he habitually ignored.

So in Congress, when the petition of the three thousand clergymen was presented against the Kansas and Nebraska bill, he was in a perfect rage, and roared like a lion at bay. That this contemptible question of right and wrong should get up such an excitement and seriously threaten such a brilliant stroke of diplomacy as he meditated, seemed to him, in all sincerity, perfectly ridiculous—he could not sufficiently express his hatred and contempt.

Mere power as a debater, either in parliamentary assemblies or before popular meetings, has often existed, without any share of the calmer, and larger, and profounder, and more reflective abilities of the statesman. Mr. Lincoln possessed both, and in both, his methods were alike of an intuitively practical, and remarkably direct, simple and effective nature. Doubtless he had often given proofs of skill in practical politics, during his consultations of the preceding twenty years, with the leaders and managers of his party in Illinois. Obscure operations of local party organizations seldom make any record, or become visible at all on the surface of history. But the man who in an adverse hour, when all other counsellors have failed, can unite discordant elements into a new party, must be confessed to have statesmanlike skill. This is more peculiarly so when this party must be founded on a moral principle, and must be bounded and circumscribed in its working by moral rules and restraints. While unprincipled men can help themselves by any and all sorts of means, men of principle are confined to those within certain limits, and the difficulties of organization in such cases are vastly greater.

When in 1856 the Illinois convention met to choose delegates to the National Convention that nominated Fremont, there was in the political ocean a wild chaos of elements. Free Soil men, Anti-Nebraska men, Liberty Party men, Native Americans, Old Whigs and Old Democrats, and newly arrived emigrants of no party at all, mixed up in heterogeneous confusion, tossing and tumbling blindly about for a new platform to stand on. After long and vain discussion, the committee on a platform sent for Mr. Lincoln and asked for a suggestion. All the sections of the Convention were opposed to slavery extension, but in no other current political question were they at one. There was imminent danger of discord and division. Their calm adviser quietly said, "Take the Declaration of Independence, and Hostility to Slavery Extension. Let us build our new party on the rock of the Declaration of Independence, and the gates of hell shall not prevail against us." Mr. Lincoln's profound and unfailing moral sense had seized upon the relation between the heart of the United States and eternal right. His suggestion embodied the only doctrine that could have won in the coming battle. What he advised was done, and the party, on this platform, revolutionized Illinois, made Mr. Lincoln President, extinguished slavery, and reorganized the nation.

At Philadelphia, the same question came up again, and was solved by adopting the same principle. It was on this occasion that Mr. Lincoln's high position and important influence in the northwest received the first acknowledgement that he was obtaining a national reputation. He obtained a vote of one hundred and ten for the Vice Presidency on the preliminary or informal ballot.

The great effort, however, which finally and firmly established Mr. Lincoln's reputation as a speaker and statesman, was in 1858, when he and Douglas once more were brought to a face encounter before the people of Illinois, as opposing candidates for the U. S. Senate.

During the months of August, September and October, according to the honest western custom, these two opposing candidates stumped the State together, and presented their opposing claims and views in a series of public gatherings. These meetings were in consequence of Mr. Lincoln's invitation, but Mr. Douglas in accepting adroitly contrived to name terms that gave him the opening and the closing turns, not only of the whole series, but of four out of seven of the meetings.

In the June and July preceding, Mr. Lincoln made three other speeches, two at Springfield and one at Chicago, which may be considered a sort of preface to the great debates. The first of these, at Springfield, June 17, 1858, was in some respects the most remarkable of Mr. Lincoln's oratorical productions. It was made at the close of the Republican State Convention which nominated Mr. Lincoln a candidate for the U. S. Senate; and its opening paragraph is so remarkable for style, so heavy with meaning, and so instinct with political foresight, that it is worth quoting entire. It is as follows:

"Mr. President, and Gentlemen of the Convention:—If we could first know where we are, and whither we are tending, we could better judge what to do, and how to do it. We are now far into the fifth year since a policy was initiated with the avowed object and confident promise of putting an end to slavery agitation. Under the operation of that policy, that agitation has not only not ceased, but has constantly augmented. In my opinion it will not cease until a crisis shall have been reached and passed. 'A house divided against itself cannot stand.' I believe this government cannot endure permanently half slave and half free. I do not expect the Union to be dissolved—I do not expect the house to fall—but I do expect it will cease to be divided. It will become all one thing or all the other. Either the opponents of slavery will arrest the further spread of it, and place it where the public mind shall rest in the belief that it is in the course of ultimate extinction; or its advocates will push it forward, till it shall become alike lawful in all the States, old as well as new, North as well as South."

In this brief statement, Mr. Lincoln set forth the whole object of the southern and northern parties on the slavery question, and though he did not prophesy which way the contest would be decided, he did prophesy exactly the two alternatives to one of which the country was necessarily to advance. It is further noticeable here that Mr. Lincoln's statement includes exactly the same prophecy, only not so classically worded, as Mr. Seward's famous phrase, in his speech at Rochester, the following October, of "an Irrepressible Conflict." And once more; the opening sentence, as a writer upon Mr. Lincoln has shown, is in like manner curiously coincident in thought with the first sentence of another still more famous speech—Daniel Webster's reply to Hayne. Mr. Webster said:

"When the mariner has been tossed for many days in thick weather, and on an unknown sea, he naturally avails himself of the first pause in the storm, the earliest glance of the sun, to take his latitude, and ascertain how far the elements have driven him from his true course. Let us imitate that prudence, and before we float further, refer to the point from which we departed, that we may at least be able to conjecture where we now are."

That is a stately and sonorous opening, majestic and poetical. Now compare it with Mr. Lincoln's synonym: "If we could first know where we are, and whither we are tending, we could better judge what to do, and how to do it." The thing could not have been said more shortly, more directly, more clearly, more strongly in English. As the writer observes from whom this parallel is taken, Mr. Webster used eighty-two words, nearly a quarter of them having over one syllable; Mr. Lincoln only twenty-five, of which only three, or less than one-eighth, have more than one syllable. Counting still more closely, we find that Mr. Webster used 347 letters, to Mr. Lincoln's 88." In less than one-third the words, in just over one-fourth the letters, and without the least approach to a figure of speech, Mr. Lincoln said what Mr. Webster did. "This," to quote once more, "may seem a petty method of comparing orators; but it reveals a great secret of directness, clearness, simplicity and force of style; it goes far to explain how Mr. Lincoln convinced an audience."

"This speech," says Mr. Arnold, "was the text of the great debate between Lincoln and Douglas." It states the question in the United States as between slavery and freedom, with very great strength and plainness, and lays down the principles that apply to it with equal power. It had been carefully prepared beforehand, as a manifesto for which the times were ripe. For the first time it placed the speaker publicly upon advanced anti-slavery ground; and it is by no means improbable that in taking that ground, Mr. Lincoln had some secret conscious or half conscious feeling not only that he was marking out the place that his party must occupy in the coming struggle, but that in doing so he assumed the place of standard-bearer. He explained the doctrines of the Nebraska Act, and the Dred Scott decision; showed how the Democratic party had become ranged on the side of slavery; explained how the result of the Dred Scott decision, together with the indifferent policy so jauntily vaunted by Douglas, of "not caring whether slavery were voted up or down," must result in a final victory of slavery; and showed how Mr. Douglas' doctrines permitted and invited that final victory. And having thus showed "where we are, and whither we are tending," he ended with a solemn but cheering exhortation, "what to do and how to do it." "The result," he said, "is not doubtful. We shall not fail, if we stand firm we shall not fail. Wise counsels may accelerate, or mistakes delay it, but sooner or later, THE VICTORY IS SURE TO COME."

That is the language, not of a party politician, recommending expedient nostrums, but of a statesman who feels profoundly that his people are sound at heart, and will assuredly one day do full justice; who proclaims in advance the eternal victory of the right side, and boldly calls on all who hear him to advance up to the line of their own consciences.

Before delivering this speech, Mr. Lincoln locked himself into a room with his partner, Mr. Herndon, and read him the first paragraph of the speech. "What do you think of it?" said he. Herndon answered, "I think it is all true, but I doubt whether it is good policy to say it now." Mr. Lincoln replied, "That makes no difference; it is the truth, and the nation is entitled to it." This was both honest and politic; for if the ground of principle as against expediency had not been taken, there was none left to oppose the reasonings of Mr. Douglas, which were extremely adroit, and so far as expediency admitted, indeed unanswerable.

In the conduct of that remarkable campaign of 1858, Mr. Douglas was the advocate of expediency, Mr. Lincoln of principle. Mr. Douglas appealed to the prejudices of the white race against the black, and argued in favor of present ease and selfish indifference to justice in our conduct as a nation. Mr. Lincoln incessantly appealed to the consciences of his audience, to all that part of human nature which is kindly, which is just, which is noble; to the broad doctrines upon which our national freedom was originally based. It is true that along with these main currents of debate numerous minor questions and side issues came up; but such was the pervading color, the chief drift of the discussion. Over and over and over again, there sounds out among the words of Douglas, "This is a white man's government; the negro ought not to vote." And even more constant is the lofty reply, "I stand by the Declaration of Independence, and the everlasting rights of humanity. The negro is a man, and he ought to have all the rights of a man!"

Mr. Lincoln's speech at Springfield, on June 17th, has been briefly described. Mr. Douglas, coming home to his own State, to justify his course, and receive his re-election, answered him in his Chicago speech of July 9th, and Mr. Lincoln rejoined next day. Douglas spoke again, at Bloomington on the 16th, and at Springfield on the 17th, and on the latter day Mr. Lincoln spoke also at Springfield. In this speech he set forth a curious and characteristic contrast between himself and his opponent, in a grotesque and sarcastic manner that must have told sharply upon his western audience, while its comic surface is underlaid with the usual solid basis of conscious adherence to justice and principle. Mr. Lincoln said:

"Senator Douglas is of world-wide renown. All the anxious politicians of his party, or who have been of his party for years past, have been looking upon him as certainly, at no distant day, to be the President of the United States. They have seen in his round, jolly, fruitful face, post-offices, land-offices, marshalships and cabinet appointments, chargeships and foreign missions, bursting and sprouting out in wonderful exuberance, ready to be laid hold of by their greedy hands. And as they have been gazing upon this attractive picture so long, they cannot, in the little distraction that has taken place in the party, bring themselves to give up the charming hope; but with greedier anxiety they rush about him, sustain him, and give him marches, triumphal entries, and receptions beyond what even in the days of his highest prosperity they could have brought about in his favor. On the contrary, nobody has ever expected me to be President. In my poor, lean, lank face, nobody has ever seen that any cabbages were sprouting out. These are disadvantages, all taken together, that the Republicans labor under. *We* have to fight this battle upon principle, and upon principle alone. I am, in a certain sense, made the standard-bearer in behalf of the Republicans. I was made so merely because there had to be some one so placed—I being in no wise preferable to any other one of the twenty-five—perhaps a hundred, we have in the Republican ranks. Then I say I wish it to be distinctly understood and borne in mind, that we have to fight this battle without many

—perhaps without any—of the external aids which are brought to bear against us. So I hope those with whom I am surrounded have principle enough to nerve themselves for the task and leave nothing undone that can be fairly done, to bring about the right result."

Two years before, Mr. Lincoln had used even stronger terms in contrasting himself and his antagonist. In 1856 he said: "Twenty-two years ago, Judge Douglas and I first became acquainted; we were both young men—he a trifle younger than I. Even then we were both ambitious, I perhaps quite as much as he. With me, the race of ambition has been a failure —a flat failure. With him, it has been one of splendid success. His name fills the nation, and it is not unknown in foreign lands. I affect no contempt for the high eminence he has reached. *So reached that the oppressed of my species might have shared with me in the elevation*, I would rather stand on that eminence than wear the richest crown that ever pressed a monarch's brow."

Mr. Lincoln's exact position on the emancipation question at this time, is an interesting illustration of his firm adherence to principle, and at the same time of his extreme caution in touching established laws, and his natural tendency to give voice to the average public sentiment of his day, rather than to go beyond it, or to reprove that sentiment for not going further. He averred over and over again, that he was "not in favor of negro citizenship;" but he said "there is no reason in the world why the negro is not entitled to all the rights enumerated in the Declaration of Independence—the right of life, liberty and the pursuit of happiness. In the right to eat the bread without the leave of anybody else, which his own hand earns, he is my equal, and the equal of Judge Douglas, and the equal of every other man."

The same primary granite substratum of moral right, of everlasting justice, underlies all these speeches. It crops out here and there, in passages, a specimen of which is worth quoting, not merely for the sake of their aptness then or now; but also as excellent patterns for the application of moral principles to political practices—a lesson peculiarly important in a republic, simply because its diligent employment is the sole possible basis of national strength and happiness. In the debate at Quincy, October 13th, Mr. Lincoln stated a whole code of political ethics, along with its application to the case in hand, in one paragraph, as follows:

"We have in this nation this element of domestic slavery. It is a matter of absolute certainty that it is a disturbing element. It is the opinion of all the great men who have expressed an opinion upon it, that it is a dangerous element. We keep up a controversy in regard to it. That controversy necessarily springs from difference of opinion, and if we can learn exactly—can reduce to the lowest elements—what that difference of opinion is, we perhaps shall be better prepared for discussing the different systems of policy that we would propose in regard to that disturbing element. I suggest that the difference of opinion, reduced to its lowest terms, is no other than the difference between the men who think slavery a wrong and those who do not think it a wrong. The Republican party think it wrong—we think it is a moral, a social and a political wrong. We think it is a wrong not confining itself merely to the persons or the States where it exists, but that it is a wrong in its tendency, to say the least, that it extends itself to the existence of the whole nation. Because we think it wrong, we propose a course of policy that shall deal with it as a wrong. We deal with it as with any other wrong, in so far as we can prevent its growing any larger, and so deal with it that in the run of time there may be some promise of an end to it. We have a due regard to the actual presence of it amongst us and the difficulties of getting rid of it in any satisfactory way, and all the Constitutional obligations thrown about it. I suppose that in reference both to its actual existence in the nation, and to our Constitutional obligations, we have no right at all to disturb it in the States where it exists, and we profess that we have no more inclination to disturb it than we have the right to do it. We go further than that; we don't propose to disturb it where, in one instance, we think the Constitution would permit us. We think the Constitution would permit us to disturb it in the District of Columbia. Still we do not propose to do that, unless it should be in terms which I don't suppose the nation is very likely soon to agree to—the terms of making the emancipation gradual and compensating the unwilling owners. Where we suppose we have the Constitutional right, we restrain ourselves in reference to the actual existence of the institution and the difficulties thrown about it. We also oppose it as an evil so far as it seeks to spread itself. We insist on the policy that shall restrict it to its present limits."

Still more sharply and strongly he stated the question in the last debate, at Alton, as simply this: Is Slavery wrong?

"That is the real issue. That is the issue that will continue in this country when these poor tongues of Judge Douglas and myself shall be silent. It is the eternal struggle between these two principles—right and wrong—throughout the world. They are the two principles that have stood face to face from the beginning of time; and will ever continue to struggle. The one is the common right of humanity and the other the divine right of kings. It is the same principle, in whatever shape it develops itself. It is the same spirit that says, "You work and toil and earn bread, and I'll eat it." No matter in what shape it comes, whether from the mouth of a king who seeks to bestride the people of his own nation and live by the fruit of their labor, or from one race of men as an apology for enslaving another race, it is the same tyrannical principle."

With equal force he often exposed and rebuked the moral levity shown by his opponent—his affectation of indifference to all principle, his supercilious dazzling contempt of moral distinctions. In his last speech at Alton, he very fully reviewed the whole question, and Mr. Douglas' individual position before the country, with great breadth and power.

There was as striking a contrast between the externals of the two champions, as between their political doctrines. Douglas went pompously up and down the land, with special trains of railroad cars, bands of music, long processions, banners, cannon firing, and all the flourish and gaudy show of a triumphing conqueror; and he is said to have paid away half his fortune in securing this fatal victory. But Mr. Lincoln went about almost as frugally, as plainly, as quietly, as if he had been on one of his accustomed legal circuits, and reflected with a queer astonishment upon the trifling sum that he did actually expend. He said to a friend after the campaign was over, "I don't believe I have expended in this canvass one cent less than Five Hundred Dollars in cash!" He sometimes good humoredly alluded to these demonstrations. "Auxiliary to these main points," he says, "to be sure, are their thunderings of cannon, their marching and music, their fizzle-gigs and fire works; but I will not waste time with them, they are but the little trappings of the campaign." Mr. Townsend, a picturesque writer, thus contrasts the bearing of the two men: "Douglas was uneasily arrogant in Lincoln's presence; the latter, never sensitive nor flurried, so grew by his imperturbability that when he reached the White House, Mr. Douglas was less surprised than anybody else. The great senatorial campaign, in which they figured together, is remembered by every Springfielder. Douglas, with his powerful voice and facile energy, went into it under full steam. Lincoln began lucidly and cautiously. When they came out of it, Douglas was worn down with rage and hoarseness, and Lincoln was fresher than ever. He prepared all the speeches of this campaign by silent meditation, sitting or lying alone, studying the flies on the ceiling. "The best evidence of his superiority in this debate is the fact that the Republicans circulated both sets of speeches as a campaign document in 1860, but Mr. Douglas's friends refused to do so.

And Mr. Arnold, a personal friend of Mr. Lincoln's, attributes to Mr. Lincoln just that sort of superiority that comes from a consciousness of being on the right side and of having an antagonist in whose attitude there is reason for contempt. "He had one advantage," says Mr. Arnold, "over Douglas, he was always good humored; he had always an apt and happy story for illustration, and while Douglas was sometimes irritable, Lincoln never lost his temper." And Mr. Arnold says that when Lincoln and Douglas came to Chicago together just after the close of the seven debates, "Lincoln was in perfect health, his face bronzed by the prairie suns, but looking and moving like a trained athlete. His voice was clearer, stronger and better than when he began the canvass. Douglas was physically much broken. He was so hoarse that he could hardly articulate, and was entirely unintelligible in an ordinary tone."

But the circumstance that shows most clearly of all, how entirely Mr. Lincoln saw over, and through, and beyond his adversary, both as statesman and politician, how entirely he managed him, wielded him, used him, is the fearful grip into which he put the "Little Giant" on the question of the conflict between "Popular Sovereignty" and the Dred Scott decision. In return for a series of questions by Mr. Douglas, Mr. Lincoln, having answered them all categorically, prepared certain others to put to Mr. Douglas; and of these one was:

"Can the people of a United States Territory, in

any lawful way, against the wish of any citizen of the United States, exclude slavery from its limits prior to the formation of a State Constitution?"

When Mr. Lincoln consulted a friend upon this set of questions, the friend remonstrated against this one; saying in substance, "In answer, Mr. Douglas must either accept the Dred Scott decision as binding, which would lose him the election to the Senate in consequence of the popular feeling in Illinois against it, or else that he must assert that his doctrine of "squatter sovereignty" would enable the territory to keep slavery out, by "unfriendly legislation," contrary to the Dred Scott decision. And this," urged the friend, "he will do; it will satisfy Illinois, and give Douglas the senatorship. You are only placing the step for him to rise upon."

"That may be," said Mr. Lincoln, with a shrewd look, "*but if he takes that shoot he never can be President.*" This meant, that while the doctrine of legislating slavery out of a territory might satisfy Illinois, it would be odious and inadmissible to the whole South, and that it would therefore render Douglas' election to the Presidency impossible. And it came to pass exactly as Mr. Lincoln foretold at this time, and as he told "Billy" when he returned home at the end of the canvass. One of Mr. Lincoln's characteristic sentences afterwards summed all the contradiction of Douglas' position, in the statement that it was "declaring that a thing may be lawfully driven away from a place where it has a lawful right to go."

These seven debates were the most widely known of Mr. Lincoln's labors in this campaign, but he made about fifty other speeches in different parts of the State.

The result of this celebrated canvass was to return Douglas to the Senate, although the vote of the people was in favor of Lincoln. The Legislative districts in the State had been so arranged by the Democratic party as to secure their majority in the Legislature. But even if the popular majority had been with Douglas, Mr. Lincoln had won. He set out to lose the State; he set out to carry the nation; and he did it. It was the foresight of the statesman, contending with the cunning of the politician. It was part of the victory that he who really lost thought he had won. Mr. Herndon, Mr. Lincoln's law partner, told afterwards how Mr. Lincoln came home and said, "Billy, I knew I should miss the place, when I competed for it. *This defeat will make me President.*"

In the period between this canvass and the Presidential nomination at Chicago, Mr. Lincoln, while at work in his profession, did good service in the cause of freedom in several of the States, making a number of effective speeches in Ohio, Kansas, and particularly in New England and New York. His contest with Douglas had probably already made Mr. Lincoln the second choice of large numbers of Republicans for the nomination of 1860. His great speech at Cooper Institute in February, 1860, confirmed this choice, and enlarged those numbers.

The invitation which resulted in his great Cooper Institute speech was originally to give a lecture in Plymouth Church, in Brooklyn, and he was to receive $200 for it. After some delay, at last he agreed to speak on February 27th; but the three young men who had organized the course, thought the time late in the season, and began to fear that they would lose money. It sounds curious enough now, to think of a fear lest a speech by Mr. Lincoln should not refund $350 expenses, but so they thought. A political friend of his who had negotiated the engagement, at last assumed one fourth of the risk, and with a good deal of trouble, managed to have the speech at Cooper Institute, instead of Brooklyn. Attempts were vainly made to induce one and then another Republican club to assume the risk of the engagement. The New York Times, in announcing the lecture, kindly spoke of the speaker as "a lawyer who had some local reputation in Illinois."

The Cooper Institute speech was prepared with much care, and was a production of very great power of logic, history and political statement. It consisted of an exposition of the true doctrines of the founders of our nation on the question of slavery, and of the position of the two parties of the day on the same question. It was alive and luminous throughout with the resolute and lofty and uncompromising morality on principle, which had colored all his debates with Douglas, and made a very deep impression upon the audience present, and upon the far greater audience that read it afterwards.

Its close was very powerful. After showing that the demands of the South were summed up in the requirement that the North should call slavery right instead of wrong, and should then join the south in acting accordingly, he added:

"If our sense of duty forbids this, then let us stand by our duty, fearlessly and effectively. Let us be diverted by none of those sophistical contrivances wherewith we are so industriously plied and belabored—contrivances such as groping for some middle ground between the right and the wrong, vain as the search for a man who should be neither a living man nor a dead man—such as a policy of "don't care" on a question about which all true men do care—such as Union appeals, beseeching true Union men to yield to disunionists, reversing the Divine rule, and calling, not the sinners, but the righteous to repentance—such as invocations of Washington, imploring men to unsay what Washington said, and undo what Washington did. Neither let us be slandered from our duty by false accusations against us, nor frightened from it by menaces of destruction to the Government, nor of dungeons to ourselves. Let us have faith that right makes might, and in that faith let us, to the end, dare to do our duty, as we understand it."

The words are singularly plain, they are nakedly homely. But the thoughts are very noble and very mighty.

At the close of the speech, the same friend who had engineered it, made a few remarks, in which he prophesied. He said, "One of three gentlemen will be our standard bearer in the Presidential contest of this year; the distinguished Senator from New York—Mr. Seward; the late able and accomplished Governor of Ohio, Mr. Chase, or the unknown knight who entered the political list, against the Bois Guilbert of democracy, Stephen A. Douglas, on the prairies of Illinois, in 1858, and unhorsed him— Abraham Lincoln.

The narrator adds, "Some friends joked me after the meeting, as not being a good prophet. The lecture was over; all the expenses were paid; I was handed by the gentlemen interested, the sum of $4.25 as my share of the profits." It is worth adding that Mr. Lincoln observed to the same gentleman, after his subsequent tour further eastward, "when I was East, several gentlemen made about the same remark to me that you did to-day about the Presidency; they thought my chances were about equal to the best."

The story of the nomination at Chicago, of the election, of the perilous journey to Washington, need not be repeated. While the nominating convention was sitting, Mr. Lincoln's friends telegraphed to him that in order to be nominated he needed the votes of two of the delegations, and that to secure these, he must promise that if elected the leaders of those delegations should be made members of his Cabinet. He telegraphed at once back again; "I authorize no bargains and will be bound by none." The adoption of those ten words as a rule would go very far to purify the whole field of political party action.

Little did the convention that nominated Abraham Lincoln for President, know what they were doing. Little did the honest, fatherly, patriotic man, who stood in his simplicity on the platform at Springfield, asking the prayers of his townsmen and receiving their pledges to remember him, foresee how awfully he was to need those prayers, the prayers of all this nation and the prayers of all the working, suffering common people throughout the world. God's hand was upon him with a visible protection, saving first from the danger of assassination at Baltimore, and bringing him safely to our national capital.

Perhaps the imperturbable cool courage of Mr. Lincoln was the trait in him least appreciated in proportion to his share of it. He promptly and unhesitatingly risked his life to keep his Philadelphia appointment on the way to Washington, filling his programme, because it was his duty, without any variance for assassins. It should be here recorded, by the way, that the story that he fled from Harrisburg, disguised in a Scotch cap and cloak, which made so much noise in the country at the time, was a forgery, devised by a disreputable reporter. Mr. Lincoln never used any disguises, and it would have required more than one "Scotch cap" to bring his six feet four down to an average height.

He was so kind-hearted, so peaceable, so averse, either to cause or to witness controversy or wrath, that only the extremest need would force him to the point of wrath and of fighting. But when the need was real, the wrath and the fight came out. Whether moral or physical courage, upon a real demand for it, it never failed. On his flat boat trip to New Orleans in his youth, he and his mate, armed only with sticks of wood, beat off seven negro marauders who attacked and would have robbed their boat. When clerk in a country store he seized, flung down and subdued a bully who was insolent to some women, and what is more, the beaten bully became his friend. He once, alone, by suddenly dropping from a scuttle down upon the platform, kept off a gang of rowdies who were about to hustle his friend Col. Baker off the stand. He and Baker once, with no others, escorted to the hotel, a speaker who was threatened with violence by a Democratic crowd whom he had offended. When some Irishmen at Springfield once undertook to take possession of the poll and restrict the voting to their friends, Lincoln, hearing of it, stepped into the first store, seized an axe helve, and marched alone through the turbulent crowd up to the poll, opening the road as he went; and alone he kept the ballot-box free and safe until the foolish crowd gave up their plan. His anger sometimes—though very seldom—flamed up at ill usage of himself; but never so hotly as at ill usage to others. When a poor negro citizen of Illinois was imprisoned at New Orleans, simply for being a free negro from outside of Louisiana, and was about to be sold into slavery, to pay jail fees, Mr. Lincoln found that the Governor of Illinois could not help the poor fellow. When the fact became plain, he jumped up and swore, "By the Almighty," he said, "I'll have that negro back, or I'll have a twenty years' agitation in Illinois, until the Governor *can* do something in the premises!" Somebody sent money and set the man free; or else the twenty years' agitation would have begun, and finished too. An officer, a worthless fellow, after being dismissed and repeatedly trying to get back into the army, at last insolently told President Lincoln, "I see you are fully determined not to do me justice." Now this was just what he *was* determined to do him; and in righteous anger he arose, laid down his papers, collared the fellow, walked him to the door and flung him out, saying, "Sir, I give you fair warning, never to show yourself in this room again. I can bear censure, but not insult!"

In Mr. Lincoln's administration, the world has seen and wondered at the greatest sign and marvel of our day, to wit, a plain working man of the people, with no more culture, instruction or education than any such working man may obtain for himself, called on to conduct the passage of a great nation through a crisis involving the destinies of the whole world. The eyes of princes, nobles, aristocrats, of dukes, earls, scholars, statesmen, warriors, all turned on the plain backwoodsman, with his simple sense, his imperturbable simplicity, his determined self-reliance, his impracticable and incorruptible honesty, as he sat amid the war of conflicting elements, with unpretending steadiness, striving to guide the national ship through a channel at whose perils the world's oldest statesmen stood aghast. The brilliant courts of Europe levelled their opera glasses at the phenomenon. Fair ladies saw that he had horny hands and disdained white gloves; dapper diplomatists were shocked at his system of etiquette; but old statesmen, who knew the terrors of that passage, were wiser than court ladies and dandy diplomatists, and watched him with a fearful curiosity, simply asking, "*Will* that awkward old backwoodsman really get that ship through? If he does, it will be time for us to look about us." Sooth to say, our own politicians were somewhat shocked with his State papers at first. "Why not let *us* make them a little more conventional, and file them to a classical pattern?" "No," was his reply, "I shall write them myself. *The people will understand them.*" "But this or that form of expression is not elegant, nor classical." "*The people will understand it,*" was his invariable reply. And whatever may be said of his State papers, as compared with the diplomatic standards, it has been a fact that they have always been wonderfully well understood by the people, and that since the time of Washington, the State papers of no President have more controlled the popular mind. And one reason for this is, that they have been informal and undiplomatic. They have more resembled a father's talks to his children than a State paper. And they have had that relish and smack of the soil, that appeal to the simple human heart and head, which is a greater power in writing than the most artful clerices of rhetoric. Lincoln might well say with the apostle, "But though I be rude in speech yet not in knowledge, but we have been thoroughly *made manifest among you* in all things." His rejection of what is called fine writing, was as deliberate as St. Paul's, and for the same reason—because he felt that he was speaking on a subject which must be made clear to the lowest intellect, though it should fail to captivate the highest. But we say of Lincoln's writings, that for all true, manly purposes of writing, there are passages in his State papers that could not be better put —they are absolutely perfect. They are brief, condensed, intense, and with a power of insight and expression which make them worthy to be inscribed in letters of gold. Such are some passages of the celebrated letter to the Springfield convention, especially that masterly one where he compares the conduct of the patriotic and loyal blacks with that of the treacherous and disloyal whites. No one can read this letter and especially the passage mentioned, without feeling the influence of a mind both strong and generous. "Peace does not appear so distant as it did. I hope it will come soon and come to stay; and so come as to be worth the keeping in all future time. It will then have been proved that among freemen there can be no successful appeal from the ballot to the bullet, and that they who take such appeal are sure to lose their case and pay the cost. And then there will be some black men who can remember that with silent tongue, and clenched teeth, and steady eye, and well-poised bayonet, they have helped mankind on to this great consummation, while I fear there will be some white ones unable to forget that with malignant heart and deceitful speech they have striven to hinder it."

The lesson of Mr. Lincoln's career as President, is a manifold one. He was in a strangely full and close manner the exponent, the representative, the federal head, the voice, the plenary agent, of the people of the United States. As such, his life teaches what the war teaches, to wit; the strength and the magnificent morality of an intelligent people, trained in self-control, in thought, in the doctrines of justice and freedom, and in the fear of God.

As one man's life, the life of Mr. Lincoln after his election is simply the picture over again, on a gigantic scale, in stronger colors, in bolder relief, of the same courage, devotion, strength, industry, energy, sense, decision, kindness, caution, instinctive feeling of what was right and what was practicable, and deliberate execution of it, that had marked his career before, as the political leader in a great state controversy, and as a laborious lawyer at the bar. As he mounted upon a higher plane of action, his views became enlarged and elevated. Especially is it noticeable how as President, he was very much more open and specific in avowing an immediate dependence upon help higher than man's, in doing the work before him. Mr. Lincoln was naturally inclined to religious feelings. His habit of considering all the affairs of life from the religious point of view, at the tribunal of the laws of God, is clearly traceable in his private history and even in his political campaigns. He was not obtrusive nor unreasonable however in avowals of this feeling. It would have been out of place to request the prayers of his fellow citizens during the debates with Douglas, almost as much as to ask the prayers of the jury while arguing a case. But while placed at the head of his nation, during the vastest peril of its existence—while occupying the most prominent, the most powerful, the most responsible, the most difficult, and the most dangerous position upon the whole round world—while at the very front of the very vanguard of humanity in the great battle which was deciding whether good or evil should overcome—in such a position, no avowals of the need of Divine aid, no repetition of the consciousness of that need, no requests for the sympathy and the help of all good men's prayers, could be too frequent or too free. This profound sense of human weakness and of God's strength, and a distinct sentiment of mournful foreboding, give the whole coloring to the brief address in which he bade good bye to his neighbors at Springfield, at setting out for Washington in 1861.

This habit of religious feeling, and the avowal of it, remained a very marked one during all Mr. Lincoln's Presidency. Subordinate to this, the acts of his official life, his written and spoken utterances, and his personal conduct, were mainly marked by solicitous and extreme sense of duty, unfailing resolution, unerring tact and wisdom, and a kindness and patience entirely unparalleled in the history of governments. These traits were often hidden by his quaint modes of expression, by the wonderful flow of humorous anecdotes which he so constantly used in arguing, in answering, in evading, or for entertainment; and by his confirmed habit of arguing all questions against himself, against his own views, before coming to a conclusion. These externals often concealed him, often occasioned him to be misunderstood, distrusted, and opposed. It was only as time passed on, and his public acts gradually formed themselves into his history, that it was possible for those broad and massive characteristics to be seen in a just perspective. Now however, they are visible throughout all his life, whether traced in anecdote, in speech, in state papers, in cabinet debates, in intercourse with the representatives of bodies of the people, or in executive orders and acts.

Of all these traits, Mr. Lincoln's kindness was unquestionably the rarest, the most wonderful. It may be doubted whether any human being ever lived whose whole nature was so perfectly sweet with the readiness to do kind actions; so perfectly free from even the capacity of revenge. He could not even leave a pig in distress. He once on circuit, drove past a pig, stuck fast in a mud hole. Having on a suit of new clothes, he felt unable to afford them for the pig, but after going two miles, he could not stand it, turned and drove back, made a platform of rails, helped out the pig, spoiled his new clothes, and then went contentedly about his business. He used to help his poor clients with money—a ridiculous thing in a lawyer. He was quite as helpless about traitors and deserters and criminals, as about pigs; even when pardoning or non-retaliation was actually doing harm. The beseechings and tears of women, the sight of a little child, even a skilful picture of the sorrow of a scoundrel's friends, was almost certain to gain whatever favor they sought. It really sometimes seemed as if he was tenderer of individual lives than of multitudes of them, so nearly impossible was it for him to pronounce sentence of death or to forbear the gift of life. His doorkeeper had standing orders never to delay from one day to another any message asking for the saving of life. He undoubtedly did harm by giving life to deserters, and thus weakening army discipline. He heard a child cry in his anteroom one day, and calling his usher, had the woman that carried the child shown in. She had been waiting three days, by some mischance. Her husband was to be shot. She stated her case; the pardon was at once granted; she came out of the office praying and weeping; and the old usher, touching her shawl, told her who had really saved her husband's life. "Madam," said he, "the baby did it."

One of his generals once urgently remonstrated with him for rendering desertion safe, though it was seriously weakening the army. "Mr. General," said Mr. Lincoln, "there are already too many weeping widows in the United States. For God's sake don't ask me to add to the number, for I won't do it." Even to put a stop to the unutterable horrors which were slowly murdering our brave men in the rebel prisons, he could not retaliate. He said, "I can never, never starve men like that. Whatever others may say or do, I never can, and I never will, be accessory to such treatment of human beings." Once, after the massacre at Fort Pillow, he pledged himself in a public speech that there should be a retaliation. But that pledge he could not keep, and he did not.

His perfectly sweet kindness of feeling was as inexhaustible towards the rebels as such, as towards dumb beasts, or the poor and unfortunate of his own loyal people, and it was shown as clearly in his state papers and speeches as in any private act or word. That sentiment, and one other—the unconditional determination to adhere to the doctrines of the Declaration of Independence and to do his sworn official duty—colored the series of speeches which he made on his way to Washington. At Philadelphia, where he was especially impressed with associations about the old Independence Hall, he said, speaking of that edifice, and standing within the old Hall itself:

"All the political sentiments I entertain have been drawn, so far as I have been able to draw them, from the sentiments which originated in and were given to the world from this hall. I have never had a feeling, politically, that did not spring from the sentiments embodied in the Declaration of Independence."

Then he referred to the doctrine of freedom in that instrument; and he said:

"But if this country can not be saved without giving up that principle, I was about to say I would rather be assassinated in this spot than surrender it. * * * I have said nothing but what I am willing to live by, and if it be the pleasure of Almighty God, to die by."

These references to assassination and death, were no casual flourishes of oratory. They were deliberate defiances of the fate which had already been denounced against the speaker, in public and in private, which continued to be threatened during all the rest of his life, and which finally actually befel him, but the fear of which never made him turn pale nor waver in his duty. He began as soon as he was nominated, to receive anonymous letters from the South threatening him with death. They became so frequent that he kept a separate file of them. They continued to come, up to the year of his death. The first one or two, he said, made him "a little uncomfortable;" but afterwards he only filed them. The train on which he left home for the East, was to have been thrown off the track. A hand grenade was hidden in one of the cars. An association was known to exist at Baltimore for the express purpose of killing him. When therefore he spoke as he did at Philadelphia, it was doubtless with a feeling that some one concerned in these plans was probably hearing him, and understanding him. It was, no doubt, at the same time a sort of vow, taken upon himself under the feelings aroused by the birth-place of the Declaration which he had so often and so well defended. Whether a challenge, a vow, or a mere statement of principle, he kept his word. He lived by it, and he died by it.

The same mixture of firmness and kindness appears in the First Inaugural, and in this document there is also another most characteristic element;—circumspect adherence to the Constitution as he understood it, and most remarkable care and skill in the language used to interpret law, or to announce his own conclusions or purposes. Lover of freedom as he was, and believer in the rights of man, he had already been invariably careful not to demand from the masses of men whom he sought to influence, more than they could be expected to give. Now, he went even further. He expressly and clearly avowed his intention to execute all that he had sworn, even the laws most distasteful to any freeman. In speaking of the crisis of the moment, and after setting forth his doctrine of national sovereignty and an unbroken Union, he promised to maintain it as far as he could, and added:

"Doing this I deem to be only a simple duty on my part; and I shall perform it so far as practicable, unless my rightful masters, the American people, shall withhold the requisite means, or in some authoritative manner direct the contrary."

Then, as if to avert ill feeling if possible:

"I trust this will not be regarded as a menace, but only as the declared purpose of the Union, that it will constitutionally defend and maintain itself."

Then, with careful adherence to the mildest terms possible—could anything be a more peaceful assertion of national right than the simple "hold, occupy and possess"?—he says what the nation will do:

"In doing this there need be no bloodshed or violence, and there shall be none, unless it be forced upon the national authority. The power confided to me will be used to hold, occupy and possess the property and places belonging to the government, and to collect the duties and imposts; but beyond what may be necessary for these objects, there will be no invasion, no using of force against or among the people anywhere."

The remainder of the Inaugural is just such a kindly, homely, earnest, sincere, straight-forward appeal to the South, as he might have made in a country court-house in Illinois, "taking off his coat, leaning upon the rail of the jury box, and singling out a leading juryman and addressing him in a conversational tone." Having stated the case, and once more barely repeated that it was "his duty to administer the present government as it came to his hands, and to transmit it unimpaired by him to his successor," he then quietly but powerfully appeals to his own two life-long trusts, God Almighty, and the free people of America. He asks:

"Why should there not be a patient confidence in the ultimate justice of the people? Is there any better or equal hope in the world? In our present differences, is either party without faith of being in the right? If the Almighty Ruler of nations, with his eternal truth and justice, be on your side of the North, or on yours of the South, that truth and that justice will surely prevail, by the judgment of the great tribunal of the American people."

And the final paragraphs are sad and heavy with his

unutterable longings and yearnings for peace; so that the words, plain and simple as they are, are full of deep and melancholy music:

"You can have no conflict without being yourselves the aggressors. You have no oath registered in heaven to destroy the government, while I shall have the most solemn one, to 'preserve, protect and defend' it.

I am loth to close. We are not enemies, but friends. We must not be enemies. Though passion may have strained, it must not break our bonds of affection. The mystic cord of memory, stretching from every battle-field and patriot grave to every living heart and hearthstone all over this broad land, will yet swell the chorus of the Union, when again touched, as surely they will be, by the better angels of our nature."

As the war went on, the same unwavering decision, the same caution and kindness marked the whole action of the Executive. Especially were these traits exhibited in his dealings with the main question at issue, that of slavery.

On this point he bore a pressure such as it is safe to say no mortal son of earth ever bore before or since. The interests of the great laboring, suffering classes that go to make up human nature, were all at this period of history condensed into one narrow channel, like that below Niagara where the waters of all the great lakes are heaped up in ridges, and seem, in Scripture language, to "utter their voices and lift up their hands on high." Like the course of those heavy waters the great cause weltered into a place where its course resembled that sullen whirlpool below the falls where the awful waters go round and round in blindly, dizzy masses, and seem with dumb tossings and dark agonies to seek in vain for a clear, open channel. In this dread vortex, from time to time are seen whirling helplessly the bodies of drowned men, fragments of wrecked boats splintered and shattered, and trees torn to ghastly skeletons, which from time to time dart up from the whirling abyss with a sort of mad, impatient despair.

So we can all remember when the war had struggled on a year or two—when a hundred thousand men, the life and light and joy of as many families, who entered it warm with hope and high in aspiration, were all lying cold and low, and yet without the least apparent progress towards a result—when the resistance only seemed to have become wider, deeper, more concentrated, better organized, by all that awful waste of the best treasures of the nation; then was the starless night—the horror of the valley of the shadow of death. Above, darkness filled with whisperings, and jibes, and sneers of traitor fiends; on one side a pit, on the other a quagmire, and in the gloom all faces gathered blackness, and even friends and partisans looked strangely on each other. Confidence began to be shaken. Each separate party blamed the other as they wandered in the darkness. It was one of the strange coincidences which show the eternal freshness of Scripture language in relation to human events, that the church lesson from the Old Testament which was read in the churches the Sunday after the attack on Sumter, was the prediction of exactly such a conflict:

"Prepare war, wake up the mighty men, let all the men of war draw near; let them come up:

Beat your plough-shares into swords, and your pruning-hooks into spears: let the weak say, I *am* strong.

Assemble yourselves, and come, all ye heathen, and gather yourselves together round about: thither cause thy mighty ones to come down, O Lord.

Put ye in the sickle, for the harvest is ripe: the press is full, the fats overflow; for their wickedness *is* great.

Multitudes, multitudes in the valley of decision: for the day of the Lord *is* near in the valley of decision.

The sun and the moon shall be darkened, and *the stars shall withdraw their shining.* The Lord also shall roar out of Zion, and utter his voice from Jerusalem; and the heavens and the earth shall shake: but the Lord *will be* the hope of his people, and the strength of the children of Israel. So shall ye know that I am the Lord your God."

The repeated defeats, disasters, and distresses that had come upon the Union cause stirred the conscience of all the religious portion of the community. They remembered the parallels in the Old Testament where the armies of Israel were turned back before the heathen, because they cherished within themselves some accursed thing—they began to ask whether the Achan who had stolen the wedge of gold and Babylonish vest in our midst was not in truth the cause why God would not go forth with our armies! and the pressure upon Lincoln to end the strife by declaring emancipation, became every day more stringent; at the same time the pressure of every opposing party became equally intense, and Lincoln by his peculiar nature and habits, must listen to all, and take time to ponder and weigh all. In consequence there was a time when he pleased nobody. Each party was incensed at the degree of attention he gave to the other. He might say, in the language of the old prophet, at this time, "Woe is me, my mother, that thou hast borne me a man of strife, and a man of contention to the whole earth! I have neither lent on usury, nor men have lent to me on usury; *yet* every one of them doth curse me." He was, like the great Master whom he humbly followed, despised and rejected of men, a man of sorrows and acquainted with grief; we hid, as it were, our faces from him, he was despised, and we esteemed him not. Like the poor, dumb, suffering, down-trodden classes for whom he stood, he had no prestige of personal advantages, or of that culture which comes from generations of wealth and ease. His method of thought and expression had not the stamp of any old aristocratic tradition. He was a sign upon the earth—the sign and the leader of a new order of events in which the power and the prestige should be in the hands of the plain, simple common people, and not in those of privileged orders. But the time had not yet come, and now was their hour of humiliation, and while in England the poor operatives of Manchester bravely and manfully bore starvation caused by want of cotton, rather than ask their government to break the blockade and get it for them; while the poor silk weavers of Lyons, and the poorer classes all over Europe trembled, and hoped, and sympathised with the struggling cause and its unfashionable leader—all the great, gay, successful, fashionable world went the other way. Punch had his jolly caricatures of Lincoln's long, thin face, and anxious perplexities, and the caricatures of Paris were none the less merry. Even in America there was a time when some of his most powerful friends doubted his fitness for his position, and criticisms filled the columns of every newspaper. In Washington, every fop and every fool felt at liberty to make a jest at the expense of his want of dignity, and his personal awkwardness. He was freely called an ape, a satyr, a stupid blockhead, for even the ass can kick safely and joyfully at a lion in a net. Even his cabinet and best friends said nothing for him, and kept an ominous and gloomy silence.

Lincoln knew all this, and turned it over in the calm recesses of his mind, with a quiet endurance, gilded at times by a gleam of the grim, solemn humor peculiar to himself. "I cannot *make* generals," he said once, "I would if I could." At another, to an important man who had been pressing some of his own particular wisdom npon him, "Perhaps you'd like to try to run the machine yourself." Somebody gave him a series of powerful criticisms which a distinguished writer had just poured forth on him. "I read them all through," he said quaintly, "and then I said to myself, Well, Abraham Lincoln, are you a man, or are you a dog?"

No man in the great agony suffered more or deeper, but it was with a dry, weary, patient pain, that many mistook for insensibility. "Whichever way it ends," he said to the writer, on one occasion, "I have the impression that I shan't last long after it's over."

After the dreadful repulse at Fredericksburg, he is reported to have said, "If there is a man out of hell that suffers more than I do, I pity him." In those dark days, his heavy eyes and worn and weary air told how our reverses wore upon him, and yet there was a never failing fund of patience at bottom that sometimes rose to the surface in bubbles of quaint sayings or a story that forced a laugh even from himself. The humor of Lincoln was the oil that lubricated the otherwise dry and wiry machinery of his mind. The power of looking at men and things with reference to their humorous side, enabled him to bear without irritation many things in the political joltings and jarrings of his lot, which would have driven a more nervous man frantic. It is certainly a great advantage to be so made that one can laugh at times when crying will do no good, and Lincoln not only had his own laugh in the darkest days, but the wherewithal to bring a laugh from a weary neighbor. His jests and stories helped off many a sorry hour, and freshened the heart of his hearer for another pull in the galling harness.

He saw through other men who thought all the while they were instructing or enlightening him, with a sort of dry, amused patience. He allowed the most tedious talker to prose to him, the most shallow and inflated to advise him, reserving only to himself the right to a quiet chuckle far down in the depths of his private consciousness. Thus all sorts of men and all sorts of deputations saw him, had their talks, bestowed on him all their tediousness, and gave him the benefit of their opinions; not a creature was denied access, not a soul so lowly but might have their chance to bore the soul of this more lowly servant of the people. His own little, private, quiet, harmless laugh was his small comfort under all these inflictions. Sometimes the absolute confidence with which all contending sides urged their opinions and measures upon him, seemed to strike him with a solemn sense of the ludicrous. Thus when Dr. Cheever, at the head of a committee of clergymen, had been making a vigorous, authoritative appeal to him in Old Testament language, to end all difficulties by emancipation, Lincoln seemed to meditate gravely, and at last answered slowly, "Well, gentlemen, it is not very often that one is favored with a *delegation direct from the Almighty!*"

Washington, at this time, was one great hospital of wounded soldiers; the churches, the public buildings all filled with the maimed, the sick and suffering, and Lincoln's only diversion from the perplexity of state was the oversight of these miseries. "Where do you dine?" said one to him in our hearing. "Well, I don't dine, I just browse round a little, now and then." There was something irresistibly quaint and pathetic in the odd, rustic tone in which this was spoken.

Even the Emancipation Proclamation—that one flag stone in the wide morass of despondency on which the wearied man at last set firm foothold, did not at first seem to be a first step into the land of promise.

It was uttered too soon to please some parties, too late to please others. In England it was received in the face of much military ill success, with the scoffing epigram that the President had proclaimed liberty in the states where he had no power, and retained slavery in those where he had. It is true there was to this the sensible and just reply that he only gained the right to emancipate by this war power, and that of course this did not exist in states that were not at war; but when was ever a smart saying stopped in its course by the slow considerations and explanations of truth?

The battle of Gettysburg was the first argument that began to convince mankind that Mr. Lincoln was right. It has been well said, that in this world nothing succeeds but *success*. Bonaparte professed his belief that Providence always went with the strongest battalions, and therein he expressed about the average opinion of this world. Vicksburg and Gettysburg changed the whole face of the nation—they were the first stations outside of the valley of the shadow of death.

The nation took new courage—even the weary clamorers for peace at any price, began to shout on the right side, and to hope that peace might come through northern victory, and so it *did* come, they did not care how.

Whereas a few months before, Lincoln was universally depreciated, doubted, scoffed and scorned, now he found himself re-elected to the Presidential chair, by an overwhelming majority. It was in fact almost an election by acclamation. When the votes were being counted in New York late at night, and this victory became apparent, the vast surging assembly at the motion of one individual, uncovered their heads and sang a solemn Doxology—an affecting incident which goes far to show what sort of feelings lay at the bottom of this vast movement, and how profoundly the people felt that this re-election of Lincoln was a vital step in their onward progress.

At this hour the nation put the broad seal of its approbation on all his past course. At this moment she pledged herself to follow him and him alone to the end.

Perhaps never was man re-elected who used fewer of popular arts—made fewer direct efforts. He was indeed desirous to retain the place, for though he estimated himself quite humbly, still he was of opinion that on the whole his was as safe a hand as any, and he had watched the navigation so far as to come to love the hard helm, at which he had stood so painfully. In his usual quaint way he expressed his idea by a backwoods image. Alluding to the frequent fordings of turbulent streams that are the lot of the western traveller, he said, "It is'nt best to swap horses in the middle of a creek."

There was something almost preternatural in the calmness with which Lincoln accepted the news of his re-election. The first impulse seemed to be to disclaim all triumph over the opposing party, and to soberly gird up his loins to go on with his work to the end.

His last inaugural has been called by one of the London newspapers "the noblest political document known to history."

It was characterized by a solemn religious tone, so peculiarly free from earthly passion, that it seems to us now, who look back on it in the light of what has followed, as if his soul had already parted from earthly things, and felt the powers of the world to come. It was not the formal state-paper of the chief of a party in an hour of victory, so much as the solemn soliloquy of a great soul reviewing its course under a vast responsibility, and appealing from all earthly judgments to the tribunal of Infinite Justice. It was a solemn clearing of his soul for the great sacrament of death:

"*Fellow Countrymen*—At this second appearing to take the oath of the Presidential office, there is less occasion for an extended address than there was at the first. Then a statement somewhat in detail of a course to be pursued seemed very fitting and proper. Now, at the expiration of four years, during which public declarations have been constantly called forth on every point and phase of the great contest which still absorbs the attention and engrosses the energies of the nation, little that is new could be presented.

The progress of our arms, upon which all else chiefly depends is as well known to the public as to myself, and it is, I trust, reasonably satisfactory and encouraging to all. With high hope for the future, no prediction in regard to it is ventured.

On the occasion corresponding to this four years ago, all thoughts were anxiously directed to an impending civil war. All dreaded it; all sought to avoid it. While the inaugural address was being delivered from this place, devoted altogether to saving the Union without war, insurgent agents were in the city seeking to destroy it without war—seeking to dissolve the Union and divide the effects by negotiation.

Both parties deprecated war, but one of them would make war rather than let the nation survive, and the other would accept war rather than let it perish, and the war came.

One-eighth of the whole population were colored slaves, not distributed generally over the Union, but localized in the Southern part of it. These slaves constituted a peculiar and powerful interest. All knew that this interest was somehow the cause of the war. To strengthen, perpetuate and extend this interest, was the object for which the insurgents would rend the Union even by war, while the Government claimed no right to do more than to restrict the territorial enlargement of it.

Neither party expected for the war the magnitude or the duration which it has already attained. Neither anticipated that the cause of the conflict might cease with, or even before the conflict itself should cease. Each looked for an easier triumph, and a result less fundamental and astounding.

Both read the same Bible and prayed to the same God, and each invoke his aid against the other. It may seem strange that any men should dare to ask a just God's assistance in wringing their bread from the sweat of other men's faces, but let us judge not, that we be not judged. The prayers of both could not be answered. That of neither has been answered fully. The Almighty has his own purposes. 'Woe unto the world because of offences, for it must needs be that offences come: but woe to that man by whom the offence cometh.' If we shall suppose that American slavery is one of these offences, which in the providence of God must needs come, but which having continued through his appointed time, He now wills to remove, and that he gives to both North and South this terrible war as the woe due to those by whom the offence came, shall we discern therein any departure from those divine attributes which the believers in a living God always ascribe to Him? Fondly do we hope, fervently do we pray, that this mighty scourge of war may soon pass away. Yet, if God wills that it continue until all the wealth piled by the bondman's two hundred and fifty years of unrequited toil shall be sunk, and until every drop of blood drawn with the lash shall be paid with another drawn with the sword, as was said three thousand years ago; so, still it must be said, 'The judgments of the Lord are true and righteous altogether.'

With malice toward none, with charity for all, with firmness in the right, as God gives us to see the right, let us strive on to finish the work we are in, to bind up the nation's wounds, to care for him who shall have borne the battle and for his widow and orphans, to do all which may achieve and cherish a just and a lasting peace among ourselves and with all nations."

The words of Lincoln seemed to grow more clear and more remarkable as they approached the end. Perhaps in no language, ancient or modern, are any number of words found more touching and eloquent than his speech of November 19, 1863, at the Gettysburg celebration. He wrote it in a few moments, while on the way to the celebration, on being told that he would be expected to make some remarks, and after Mr. Everett's oration he rose and read it. It was as follows:

"Fourscore and seven years ago, our fathers brought forth on this continent a new nation, conceived in liberty, and dedicated to the proposition that all men are created equal. Now, we are engaged in a great civil war, testing whether that nation, or any nation, so conceived and dedicated, can long endure. We are met on a great battle-field of that war. We have come to dedicate a portion of that field as a final resting-place for those who here gave their lives that the nation might live. It is altogether fitting and proper that we should do this.

But in a larger sense, *we* cannot dedicate, *we* cannot consecrate, *we* cannot hallow, this ground. The brave men, living and dead, who struggled here, *have* consecrated it far above our poor power to add or detract. The world will little note, nor long remember what we *say* here, but it can never forget what they *did* here. It is for us, the living, rather to be dedicated here to the unfinished work which they who fought here have thus far so nobly advanced. It is rather for us to be here dedicated to the great task remaining before us, that from these honored dead, we take increased devotion to that cause for which they gave the last full measure of devotion; that we here highly resolve that these dead shall not have died in vain; that this nation, under God, shall have a new birth of freedom; and that government *of* the people, *by* the people, and *for* the people, shall not perish from the earth."

The audience had admired Mr. Everett's long address. At Mr. Lincoln's few words, they cheered and sobbed and wept. When Mr. Lincoln had ended, he turned and congratulated Mr. Everett on having succeeded so well. Mr. Everett replied, with a truthful and real compliment, "Ah, Mr. Lincoln, how gladly I would exchange all my hundred pages, to have been the author of your twenty lines!"

Probably no ruler ever made a more profoundly and peculiarly *Christian* impression on the mind of the world than Lincoln. In his religious faith two leading ideas were prominent from first to last—man's helplessness, both as to strength and wisdom, and God's helpfulness in both. When he left Springfield to assume the Presidency, he said to his townsmen:

"A duty devolves on me which is perhaps greater than that which has devolved on any other man since the days of Washington. He never would have succeeded but for the aid of divine Providence, on which he at all times relied, and I feel that I cannot succeed without the same Divine aid which sustained him. On the same Almighty Being I place my reliance for support, and I hope that you, my friends, will pray that I may receive that Divine assistance, without which I cannot succeed, but with which success is certain."

Abraham Lincoln's whole course showed that he possessed that faith without which, St. Paul says, it is impossible to please God, for "he that cometh to God *must believe that He* IS, and that He is a *rewarder of those who diligently seek him.*"

And now our Christian pilgrim having passed through the valley of the shadow of death, and slain and vanquished giants and dragons, at last had a little taste, a few days sojourn, in the land of Beulah.

Cheer after cheer rose up and shook the land as by one great stroke after another the awful convulsions of the conflict terminated in full, perfect, final victory.

Never did mortal man on this earth have a triumph more dramatic and astounding than Lincoln's victorious entry into Richmond. Years before, when a humble lawyer in Illinois, a man without prestige of person or manners or education, he had espoused what the world called the losing side, and been content to take the up-hill, laborious road. He had seen his rival, adorned with every external advantage of person, manners, eloquence and oratory, sweeping all prizes away from him, and far distancing him in the race of political ambition.

In those days, while confessing that he had felt the promptings of ambition, and the disappointment of ill success, there was one manly and noble sentiment that ought to be printed in letters of gold, as the motto of every rising young man. Speaking of the distinction at which Douglas was aiming, he said:

"SO REACHED AS THAT THE OPPRESSED OF MY SPECIES MIGHT HAVE EQUAL REASON TO REJOICE WITH ME, I SHOULD VALUE IT MORE THAN THE PROUDEST CROWN THAT COULD DECK THE BROW OF A MONARCH."

At this moment of his life he could look back and see far behind him the grave of the once brilliant Douglas, who died worn out and worn down with disappointed ambition, while he, twice elected to the Presidency, was now standing the observed of all the world, in a triumph that has no like in history. And it was a triumph made memorable and peculiar by the ecstacies and hallelujahs of those very oppressed with whose care years before he had weighted and burdened his progress. It was one of those earthly scenes which grandly foreshadow that great final triumph predicted in prophecy, when the Lord God shall wipe away all tears from all faces, and the rebuke of his people shall he utterly take away. A cotemporary witness has described Lincoln, calm and simple, leading his little boy by the hand, while the liberated blacks hailed him with hymns and prayers, mingling his name at each moment with ascriptions of praise and glory to Jesus the Great Liberator, whose day at last had come. Who can say of what ages of mournful praying and beseeching, what uplifting of poor, dumb hands that hour was the outcome? Years before, a clergyman of Virginia visiting the black insurrectionist, Nat Turner, in his cell before execution, gives the following wonderful picture of him: "In rags, in chains, covered with blood and bruises, he yet is inspired by such a force of enthusiasm, as he lifts his chained hands to heaven, as really filled my soul with awe. It is impossible to make him feel that he is guilty. He evidently believes that he was called of God to do the work he did. When I pointed out to him that it could not be, because he was taken, condemned, and about to be executed, he answered with enthusiasm, 'Was not Jesus Christ crucified? My cause *will* succeed yet!'"

Years passed, and the prophetic visions of Nat Turner were fulfilled on the soil of Virginia. It did indeed rain blood; the very leaves of the trees dripped blood; but the work was *done*, the yoke was broken, and the oppressed went free. An old negress who stood and saw the confederate prisoners being carried for safe keeping into the former slave pens, said grimly, "Well, de Lord am slow, but He am *sure!*"

As the final scenes of his life drew on, it seemed as if a heavenly influence overshadowed the great martyr, and wrought in him exactly the spirit that a man would wish to be found in when he is called to the eternal world. His last expressions and recorded political actions looked towards peace and forgiveness. On the day before his death he joyfully ordered the discontinuance of the draft. His very last official act was to give orders that two of the chief leaders of the rebellion, then expected in disguise at a sea port, on their flight to Europe, should not be arrested, but permitted to embark; so that he was thinking only of saving the lives of rebels, when they were thinking of taking his. If he had tried of set purpose to clear his soul for God's presence, and to put the rebels and their assassin champion in the wrong before that final tribunal, he could not have done better.

Mr. Lincoln seems to have had during his course a marked presentiment of the fate which had from the first been threatening him, and which the increasing pile of letters marked "Assassination," gave him constant reason to remember. In more than one instance he had in his public speeches professed a solemn willingness to die for his principles. The great tax which his labors and responsibilities made on his vitality, was perhaps one reason for his frequently saying that he felt that he should not live to go through with it. He observed to Mr. Lovejoy, during that gentleman's last illness, in February, 1864, "This war is eating my life out; I have a strong impression that I shall not live to see the end." In July following, he said to a correspondent of the Boston Journal, "I feel a presentiment that I shall not outlast the rebellion. When it is over, my work will be done."

Concerning the last painful history, there have been a thousand conflicting stories. From the mass of evidence the following brief account has been prepared, which sufficiently outlines the circumstances:

Who were the persons concerned in the assassination of President Lincoln, has never been judicially proved. Perhaps it never will be. The indictment against the conspirators named the following parties. David E. Herold, George A. Atzerodt, Lewis Payne, Michael O'Laughlin, Edward Spangler, Samuel Arnold, Mary E. Surratt, Samuel A. Mudd, John H. Surratt, John Wilkes Booth, Jefferson Davis, George N. Sanders, Beverly Tucker, Jacob Thompson, William C. Cleary, Clement C. Clay, George Harper, and George Young; and it added, "and others unknown." The assassin was John Wilkes Booth. And whether or no Jefferson Davis and his fellows in the rebel government were actually aiding and abetting in this particular crime, it has not been unjust nor unnatural to suspect them of it. For Mr. Davis certainly accredited Thompson, Sanders, Clay, and Tucker, as his official agents in Canada. These men in their turn, and acting in harmony with their instructions and the purposes of their government, gave a commission to that John A. Kennedy who was detected in attempting to kindle an extensive fire in the city of New

York, and consulted with him about his proposed plans. This was the substance of Kennedy's own confession, and he and his accomplices did kindle fires in four of the New York hotels. It is completely proved, again, that Davis paid sundry sums, in all $35,000 in gold, to incendiaries hired by his government to burn hospitals and steamboats at the West, and that Thompson paid money to a person engaged in Dr. Blackburn's attempt to spread yellow fever in our cities.

But more: when one Alston wrote to Davis, offering his services to try to "rid my country of some of her deadliest enemies, by striking at the very heart's blood of those who seek to enchain her in slavery"—adding the very significant remark, "I consider nothing dishonorable having such a tendency," Mr. Davis caused this proposition not to be refused, nor passed over in silence, nor indignantly exposed; but to be "respectfully referred, by direction of the President, to the honorable Secretary of War." Still more: it has been proved that in 1863, John Wilkes Booth declared that "Abraham Lincoln must be killed." The rebel agents in Canada, six months before the assassination, specifically made the same declaration. In the summer of 1864, Thompson said that he could at any time have the "tyrant Lincoln," or any of his advisers that he chose, "put out of the way," and that Thompson's agents would not consider doing this a crime, if done for the rebel cause; and Clay, when he heard of this, corroborated the sentiment, saying, "That is so; we are all devoted to our cause, and ready to go any length—to do anything under the sun." Many other such utterances by rebel leaders are proved and have become uncontradicted matter of history. Besides; when Mr. Davis, at Charlotte, North Carolina, while fleeing from Richmond, received the telegram announcing the fate of Mr. Lincoln, he calmly read it aloud to the people present, and without a word of disapproval, uttered a cold comment: "If it were to be done, it were better it were well done." And when Breckinridge said he regretted it, (not because it was wicked or dishonorable, but because it was unfortunate for the South just then,) Mr Davis replied in the same tone of cold indifference or of concealed satisfaction, and using the same words: "Well, General, I don't know; if it were to be done at all, it were better that it were well done; and if the same had been done to Andy Johnson, the Beast (i. e. Gen. Butler), and to Secretary Stanton, the job would then be complete." Those are not the words of an honorable man, nor of a disapprover. But they are exactly natural to an accessory before the fact, who does not confess his part in it, and prefers to dissemble his joy. It is not at all unreasonable to suspect that the men who are proved to have done thus and spoken thus, before and after the deed, and who have openly hired and approved the perpetration of such other deeds, were concerned in the planning and execution of this deed too.

Booth was an actor, and the son of a well known actor; and the son had inherited, apparently, much of the reckless and occasionally furious temper of his father. He was also a very violent and bitter rebel. During the fall of 1864, he had been in Canada, consulting with the rebel agents there, and mixed up with a number of other subordinate agents in the business of assassinating President Lincoln; and he was the most prominent candidate, so to speak, for the place of actual murderer. On November 11th, 1864, he was in New York, where, while riding with a companion in a street car, he dropped a letter which came into the possession of the government; it was a vigorous appeal to him to assassinate Mr. Lincoln. It said: "Abe must die, and now. You can choose your weapons, the cup, the knife, the bullet;" and again: "Strike for your home, strike for your country; bide your time, but strike sure." During the winter, Booth was engaging the assistance required for his scheme; and he had already fixed upon the scene of the murder; for, not later than January, he was urging one Chester to enter into the plan, and assuring him that all his part of it would be to stand at the back door of Ford's Theatre and open it. This was a safe calculation, for the President's enjoyment of dramatic performances was great, and enhanced by the difficulty of finding agreeable relaxations, and also by the awful pressure of his official duties and of the war, which intensified the need of relaxation.

The scheme as finally arranged, provided for the assassination of Mr. Lincoln, by Booth; of Mr. Johnson, by Atzerodt; of Mr. Seward, by Payne, (alias Powell); and of Gen. Grant, by O'Laughlin. For the President, an elaborate death trap was constructed in Ford's Theatre. The catches of the locks to all three doors of the President's box (one outer and two inner ones), were loosened by loosening their screws, and left so that a slight push would enable the assassin to enter even though the doors should be locked. A small hole was made through one of the two inner ones, to enable him to see before entering exactly how his victim sat, so that the final moves within the box could be laid out before entering it; and a wooden brace was prepared to set against the outer door (which opened inward) with one end, and with the other to fit a mortice cut in the wall behind, so that after entering, the assassin could fasten the door behind him sufficiently to prevent any interruption until his work was done. Arrangements were made for securing horses for the murderers to flee with. The stage carpenter or assistant, Spangler, was employed to be on hand and open and shut the back door of the theatre when wanted. Some scenes and miscellaneous matter that frequently impeded more or less the passage from the front of the stage to this back door, were piled up or otherwise put out of the way. A supply of weapons for the conspirators was provided. And a route for flight from Washington within the rebel lines was determined on. This route led southward from the city, over Anacostia Bridge, ten miles to Mrs. Surratt's house at Surrattsville, then some fifteen miles more to Dr. Mudd's house, then about twenty miles to a point where arrangements were made for crossing the Potomac and proceeding towards Richmond.

All being ready, Booth, about 9 P. M., on the 14th of April, 1865, went to the theatre. He first went to the back door, entered it and saw that all was prepared; left Spangler in charge, and left his horse to be held by another subordinate of the theatre. Then he went round to the front of the building, where three of the conspirators were waiting. It was now about half past nine. One act of the play, "Our American Cousin,"—was nearly through. "I think he will come out now," remarked Booth. It is very usual for the spectators to leave the theatre between the acts, often to return; and if Mr. Lincoln had happened to feel too busy to remain longer and had left then, probably Booth would have attacked him there, trusting to be able to escape into the theatre in the bustle and so through his guarded door. But the President did not come. Booth went into a saloon close by and drank some whisky. The spectators had returned for the next act. Booth entered the vestibule of the theatre, and from it the passage that leads from the street to the stage and also to the outer door of the President's box. As he did so, one of his companions followed him into the vestibule, looked up to the clock and called out the hour. It was approaching ten. Three successive times, at intervals of several minutes, the companion thus called out the hour. The third time he called, in a louder tone, "Ten minutes past ten o'clock!" At this Booth disappeared in the theatre, and the three others walked rapidly away. Booth went straight to the outer door of the President's box, paused and showed a visiting card to the President's messenger, who was in waiting; placed his hand and his knee against the door, and pushing it open, entered. He then quietly fastened the door with the brace that stood ready; looked through the hole in the inner door, and saw the President. Silently opening the door, he entered. Mr. Lincoln sat at the left hand front corner of the box, his wife at his right hand, a Miss Harris at the right hand front corner, and a Major Rathbone behind her. Mr. Lincoln was leaning forward and looking down into the orchestra. Booth stepped quickly up, and fired a pistol bullet into the President's head, behind and on the left side. The murdered man raised his head once; it fell back upon his chair, and his eyes closed. Major Rathbone, a cool, bold and prompt soldier, who had been absorbed in the play, now hearing the pistol-shot, turned, saw Booth through the smoke, and instantly sprang upon him. Booth, a nervous and strong man, expert in all athletic exercises, and a skillful fencer, wrenched himself free with a desperate effort, as he well needed to do. He had already dropped his pistol and drawn a heavy bowie knife, with which he made a furious thrust at his captor's heart. Rathbone parried it, but was wounded deeply in the arm and his hold loosed. Booth sprang for the front of the box; Rathbone followed, but only caught his clothes as he sprang over. Rathbone shouted "Stop that man!" and then turned to assist the President.

Booth leaped over the front of the box, down upon the stage, shouting as he went, "Revenge for the South!" His spur caught in the national flag as he descended; the entanglement caused him to fall almost flat on the stage as he came down; and either the wrench of tearing loose from the flag, or the fall, snapped one of the bones of his leg between knee and ankle. This fracture, though not preventing him at once from moving about, so far disabled him as probably to have been the occasion of his being overtaken and captured; so that it is scarcely extravagant to imagine the flag as having, in a sense, avenged the guilt of the crime perpetrated upon its chief official defender, by waylaying and entrapping the criminal in his turn, as he had done his victim. Booth instantly sprang up, turned towards the audience, and raising his bloody knife in a stage attitude, with a theatrical manner, vociferated the motto of the State of Virginia, "*Sic semper tyrannis!*"—a motto already turned into a discreditable satire by its contrast with the characteristic traffic of the great slavebreeding state, and even more effectually disgraced by the use now made of it, to justify assassination. It will be strange if some less dishonored words are not one day chosen for the device of Free Virginia.

Booth, thus vaporing for a moment, then rushed headlong across the stage, and darted by the side passage to the rear door. One man sprang from an orchestra seat upon the stage and shouted to stop him. One of the employes of the theatre, standing in the passage, was too much startled to stand aside, and the desperate fugitive struck him on the leg, cut at him twice, knocked him one side and darted on. The door was ready. He sprang out, and it shut behind him. Seizing the horse which was held in waiting for him, Booth, as if in a frenzy like that of the Malays when "running *amok*," struck the poor fellow who held it, with the butt of his knife, knocking him down; and then kicking him, sprang to the saddle, and after a few moments lost in consequence of some nervousness or fright of the animal, rode swiftly off. This was on the evening of Friday, the 14th; it was on Wednesday, the 26th, that Booth, after having been delayed by having his leg set, and crippled by it afterwards, was discovered in Garrett's barn, south of the Rappahannock, not far from twenty miles from the Potomac, and was surrounded, shot and taken.

The murdered President was quickly carried from the theatre to a house across the street and placed upon a bed. Surgical aid was at once obtained, but an examination at once showed that there was no hope of life. Mr. Lincoln's eyes had not opened, nor had consciousness returned at all, and they never did. The ball was a heavy one, from what is called a Derringer pistol, a short single-barreled weapon with a large bore. It had passed clear through the brain, and lodged against the bone of the orbit of the left eye, breaking that bone. It is almost certain that Mr. Lincoln suffered no pain after being shot, as the injury was of a nature to destroy conscious life. His exceedingly strong constitution and tenacity of life maintained respiration and circulation for a remarkably long time, but he died the next morning at about half past seven.

Of the particulars of that great national mourning which bowed the whole land, it is not needful to speak. Like many parts of that great history of which it formed a portion, there were often points in it of a peculiar and symbolic power, which rose to the sublime. Such was the motto—"Be still, and know that I am God"—which spoke from the walls of the New York depot when amid the hush of weeping thousands, the solemn death car entered. The contrast between the peaceful expression on the face of the weary man, and the surging waves of mourning and lamentation around him was touching and awful.

Not the least touching among these expressions of national mourning was the dismay and anguish of that poor oppressed race for whose rights he died.

A southern correspondent of the New York Tribune, the week following the assassination, wrote: "I never saw such sad faces, or heard such heavy heart-beatings, as here in Charleston the day the news came. The colored people were like children bereaved of a parent. I saw one old woman going up the streets, wringing her hands, and saying aloud as she walked, looking straight before her, so absorbed in her grief that she noticed no one;

'O Lord! Oh Lord! O Lord! Massa Sam's dead! Massa Sam's dead!'

'Who's dead, Aunty?' 'Massa Sam's dead!' she said, not looking at me, and renewing her lamentations.

'Who's Massa Sam?' said I.

'Uncle Sam,' she said, 'O Lord! O Lord!'

Not quite sure that she meant the President, I spoke again:

'Who's Massa Sam, Aunty?'

'Mr. Lincum!' she said, and resumed wringing her hands, mourning in utter hopelessness of sorrow."

The poor negroes on the distant plantations had formed a conception of Lincoln, much akin to that of a Divine Being. Their masters fled on the approach of our soldiers, and this gave the slaves the conception of a great Invisible Power which they called Massa Lincum. An old negro exhorter once, rising in an assembly of them, was heard solemnly instructing his fellows in the nature of this great unknown: "Bredren," he said solemnly, "Massa Lincum, he be ebery-where. He knows ebery ting;" and looking up solemnly, "He walk de earf like de Lord."

To them the stroke was almost as if we could possibly conceive death as happening to the God we worship; a mingled shock of grief, surprise and terror.

No death of a public man ever entered so deep into the life of individual families, so as to seem like a personal domestic sorrow. The assumption of mourning badges and garments, the hanging out of mourning tokens, was immediate in thousands of families, each obeying the same spontaneous impulse without stopping to consult the other. It seemed almost as if the funeral bells tolled of themselves and without hands. Wherever the news travelled, so immediately and without waiting for public consultation, were these tributes of mourning given.

One fact alone, proves the depth and strength of these feelings more than volumes of description. It is, the vast extent of the publications in which the history of Mr. Lincoln's life and times, his individual biography and real or written utterances, or his personal appearance, were in one way or another commemorated. A gentleman who has begun a collection of such materials had some time ago gathered two hundred different books on Mr. Lincoln, a hundred and twenty-five portraits, besides badges, mourning cards, autographs and manuscripts, as he reports, "almost without number." And in the list of publications about the rebellion compiled by Mr. Bartlett, are enumerated three hundred and eighty books, sermons, eulogies or addresses upon his life or death.

There is an astonishing contrast between the perfect sweetness and kindness of Mr. Lincoln's sentiments and utterances, whether private or public, individual or official, in reference to the rebels and the rebellion, and theirs about him. Doubtless no loyal citizen of the United States was so uniformly kind in feeling and decorous and even courteous in expression, about the rebels; and doubtless no such citizen was so odiously bespattered with the most hateful and vulgar and ferocious insult and abuse, both public and private. To give the quotations to prove the point would be simply disgusting. They were sprinkled through the newspapers and the public documents of the rebellion from beginning to end of it. A compend and a proof at once of the whole of them was that private bundle of letters threatening death, marked in Mr. Lincoln's own handwriting "Assassination," and kept in his private cabinet. And the assassination itself and the circumstances connected with it, constituted another proof and specimen, still more overwhelming. Never since the times of the Christian martyrs has history recorded a contrast more humiliating to humanity, between his kind words and kind intentions on the one hand, and infamous abusiveness and deliberate bloodthirsty ferocity in those who thus slew the best and kindest friend they had in the world.

Scarcely less striking was the contrast between the habitual tone of the foreign utterances about President Lincoln before his death and that of those after it; a change, moreover, whose promptness and evident manly good faith may in some measure atone for the unreasonable and even indecent character of many things said and printed in Europe. It is unnecessary to reproduce the offences: it is a more grateful task to quote a few specimens of the feelings and expressions with which the news of his death and of the manner of it was received abroad.

It may be premised, that some few persons of foreign birth and good position, had already discerned the truth of the character of Mr. Lincoln. A correspondent of the N. Y. Times wrote that paper from Washington, on one occasion, the following narrative:

"One day, as President Lincoln drove past a Washington hotel, sitting alone in his carriage, three gentlemen stood talking in front of the hotel. One of them, a foreigner of high cultivation and great distinction, with a gesture quite involuntary, raised his hat and remained uncovered until Mr. Lincoln had passed by. One of his companions, surprised at so much ceremony, observed, "You forget that you are in republican America and not in Russia." "Not at all, sir—not at all," was the reply, given with a certain indignation; "that is the only living ruler whom I sincerely reverence. I could not avoid showing the feeling, if I would. He is a patriot, a statesman, a great-hearted honest man. You Americans reverence nothing in the present." And after a few more sentences to the like effect, he ended by saying: "Not only your posterity, but the posterity of all the peoples which love honesty and revere patriotism, will declare that the part which President Lincoln was called to perform, required the exercise of as noble qualities as the 'Father of his Country' ever possessed. It is any thing but a credit to you that you do not better appreciate the man whom God has sent in these perilous times to rule the people of this republic."

The rebuke was received in silence. But such cases were very few. The general tone of foreign opinion about him was thoroughly unjust. Not so the obituary testimonials from across the sea.

On the first of May, 1865, Sir George Grey, in the English House of Commons, moved an address to the Crown, to express the feelings of the House upon the assassination of Mr. Lincoln. In this address he said that he was convinced that Mr. Lincoln "in the hour of victory, and in the triumph of victory, would have shown that wise forbearance, and that generous consideration, which would have added tenfold lustre to the fame that he had already acquired, amidst the varying fortunes of the war."

In seconding the same address, at the same time and place, Mr. Benjamin Disraeli said: "But in the character of the victim, and in the very accessories of his almost latest moments, there is something so homely and so innocent that it takes the subject, as it were, out of the pomp of history, and out of the ceremonial of diplomacy. It touches the heart of nations, and appeals to the domestic sentiments of mankind."

In the House of Lords, Lord John Russell, in moving a similar address, observed: "President Lincoln was a man who, although he had not been distinguished before his election, had from that time displayed a character of so much integrity, sincerity and straightforwardness, and at the same time of so much kindness, that if any one could have been able to alleviate the pain and animosity which have prevailed during the civil war, I believe President Lincoln was the man to have done so." And again, in speaking of the question of amending the constitution so as to prohibit slavery, he said: "We must all feel that there again the death of President Lincoln deprives the United States of the man who was the leader on this subject."

Mr. John Stuart Mill, the distinguished philosopher, in a letter to an American friend, used far stronger expressions than these guarded phrases of high officials. He termed Mr. Lincoln "the great citizen who had afforded so noble an example of the qualities befitting the first magistrate of a free people, and who, in the most trying circumstances, had gradually won not only the admiration, but almost the personal affection of all who love freedom or appreciate simplicity or uprightness."

Professor Goldwin Smith, writing to the London Daily News, began by saying, "It is difficult to measure the calamity which the United States and the world have sustained by the murder of President Lincoln. The assassin has done his best to strike down mercy and moderation, of both of which this good and noble life was the main stay."

Senhor Rebello da Silva, a member of the Portuguese Chamber of Peers, in moving a resolution on the death of Mr. Lincoln, thus outlined his character: "He is truly great who rises to the loftiest heights from profound obscurity, relying solely on his own merits as did Napoleon, Washington, Lincoln. For these arose to power and greatness, not through any favor or grace, by a chance cradle, or genealogy, but through the prestige of their own deeds, through the nobility which begins and ends with themselves—the sole offspring of their own works. * * * Lincoln was of this privileged class; he belonged to this aristocracy. In infancy, his energetic soul was nourished by poverty. In youth, he learned through toil the love of liberty, and respect for the rights of man. Even to the age of twenty-two, educated in adversity, his hands made callous by honorable labor, he rested from the fatigues of the field, spelling out, in the pages of the Bible, in the lessons of the gospel, in the fugitive leaves of the daily journal—which the aurora opens, and the night disperses—the first rudiments of instruction, which his solitary meditations ripened. The chrysalis felt one day the ray of the sun, which called it to life, broke its involucrum, and it launched forth fearlessly from the darkness of its humble cloister into the luminous spaces of its destiny. The farmer, day-laborer, shepherd, like Cincinnatus, left the plough-share in the half-broken furrow, and, legislator of his own State, and afterwards of the Great Republic, saw himself proclaimed in the tribunal the popular chief of several millions of people, the maintainer of the holy principle inaugurated by Wilberforce."

There are some vague and some only partially correct statements in this diffuse passage; but it shows plainly enough how enthusiastically the Portugese nobleman had admired the antique simplicity and strength of Mr. Lincoln's character.

Dr. Merle d' Aubigne, the historian of the Reformation, writing to Mr. Fogg, U. S. Minister to Switzerland, said: "While not venturing to compare him to the great sacrifice of Golgotha, which gave liberty to the captives, is it not just, in this hour, to recall the word of an apostle (1 John, iii: 16): 'Hereby perceive we the love of God, because he laid down his life for us: and we ought to lay down our lives for the brethren'? Who can say that the President did not lay down his life by the firmness of his devotion to a great duty? The name of Lincoln will remain one of the greatest that history has to inscribe on its annals. * * * Among the legacies which Lincoln leaves to us, we shall all regard as the most precious, his spirit of equity, of moderation, and of peace, according to which he will still preside, if I may so speak, over the restoration of your great nation."

The "Democratic Association" of Florence, addressed "to the Free People of the United States," a letter, in which they term Mr. Lincoln "the honest, the magnanimous citizen, the most worthy chief magistrate of your glorious Federation."

The eminent French liberal, M. Edouard Laboulaye, in a speech showing a remarkably just understanding and extremely broad views with respect to the affairs and the men of the United States, said: "Mr. Lincoln was one of those heroes who are ignorant of themselves; his thoughts will reign after him. The name of Washington has already been pronounced, and I think with reason. Doubtless Mr. Lincoln resembled Franklin more than Washington. By his origin, his arch good nature, his ironical good sense, and his love of anecdotes and jesting, he was of the same blood as the printer of Philadelphia. But it is nevertheless true that in less than a century, America has passed through two crises in which its liberty might have been lost, if it had not had honest men at its head; and that each time it has had the happiness to meet the man best fitted to serve it. If Washington founded the Union, Lincoln has saved it. History will draw together and unite those two names. A single word explains Mr. Lincoln's whole life: it was Duty. Never did he put himself forward; never did he think of himself; never did he seek one of those ingenious combinations which puts the head of a state in bold relief, and enhances his importance at the expense of the country; his only ambition, his only thought was faithfully to fulfil the mission which his fellow-citizens had entrusted to him. * * * His inaugural address, March 4, 1865, shows us what progress had been made in his soul. This piece of familiar eloquence is a master-piece; it is the testament of a patriot. I do not believe that any eulogy of the President would equal this page on which he has depicted himself in all his greatness and all his simplicity. * * * History is too often only a school of immorality. It shows us the victory of force or stratagem much more than the success of justice, moderation, and probity. It is too often only the apotheosis of triumphant selfishness. There are noble and great exceptions; happy those who can increase the number, and thus bequeath a noble and beneficent example to posterity! Mr. Lincoln is among these. He would willingly have repeated, after Franklin, that 'falsehood and artifice are the practice of fools who have not wit enough to be honest.' All his private life, and all his political life, were inspired and directed by this profound faith in the omnipotence of virtue. It is through this, again, that he deserves to be compared with Washington; it is through this that he will remain in history with the most glorious name that can be merited by the head of a free people—a name given him by his cotemporaries, and which will be preserved to him by posterity—that of Honest Abraham Lincoln."

A letter from the well known French historian, Henri Martin, to the Paris Siècle, contained the following passages: "Lincoln will remain the austere and sacred personification of a great epoch, the most faithful expression of democracy. This simple and upright man, prudent and strong, elevated step by step from the artizan's bench to the command of a great nation, and always without parade and without effort, at the height of his position; executing without precipitation, without flourish, and with invincible good sense, the most colossal acts; giving to the world this decisive example of the civil power in a republic; directing a gigantic war, without free institutions being for an instant compromised or threatened by military usurpation; dying, finally, at the moment when, after conquering, he was intent on pacification, * * * this man will stand out, in the traditions of his country and the world, as an incarnation of the people, and of modern democracy itself. The great work of emancipation had to be sealed, therefore, with the blood of the just, even as it was inaugurated with the blood of the just. The tragic history of the abolition of slavery, which opened with the gibbet of John Brown, will close with the assassination of Lincoln.

And now let him rest by the side of Washington, as the second founder of the great Republic. European democracy is present in spirit at his funeral, as it voted in its heart for his re-election, and applauded the victory in the midst of which he passed away. It will wish with one accord to associate itself with the monument that America will raise to him upon the capitol of prostrate slavery."

The London Globe, in commenting on Mr. Lincoln's assassination, said that he "had come nobly through a great ordeal. He had extorted the admiration even of his opponents, at least on this side of the water. They had come to admire, reluctantly, his firmness, honesty, fairness and sagacity. He tried to do, and had done, what he considered his duty, with magnanimity."

The London Express said, "He had tried to show the world how great, how moderate, and how true he could be, in the moment of his great triumph."

The Liverpool Post said, "If ever there was a man who in trying times avoided offenses, it was Mr. Lincoln. If there ever was a leader in a civil contest who shunned acrimony and eschewed passion, it was he. In a time of much cant and affectation he was simple, unaffected, true, transparent. In a season of many mistakes he was never known to be wrong. * * * By a happy tact, not often so felicitously blended with pure evidence of soul, Abraham Lincoln knew when to speak, and never spoke too early or too late. * * * The memory of his statesmanship, translucent in the highest degree, and above the average, and openly faithful, more than almost any of this age has witnessed, to fact and right, will live in the hearts and minds of the whole Anglo-Saxon race, as one of the noblest examples of that race's highest qualities. Add to all this that Abraham Lincoln was the humblest and pleasantest of men, that he had raised himself from nothing, and that to the last no grain of conceit or ostentation was found in him, and there stands before the world a man whose like we shall not soon look upon again."

In the remarks of M. Rouher, the French Minister, in the Legislative Assembly, on submitting to that Assembly the official despatch of the French Foreign Minister to the Chargé at Washington, M. Rouher remarked, of Mr. Lincoln's personal character, that he had exhibited "that calm firmness and indomitable energy which belong to strong minds, and are the necessary conditions of the accomplishment of great duties. In the hour of victory he exhibited generosity, moderation and conciliation."

And in the despatch, which was signed by M. Drouyn de L' Huys, were the following expressions: "Abraham Lincoln exhibited, in the exercise of the power placed in his hands, the most substantial qualities. In him, firmness of character was allied to elevation of principle. * * * In reviewing these last testimonies to his exalted wisdom, as well as the examples of good sense, of courage, and of patriotism, which he has given, history will not hesitate to place him in the rank of citizens who have the most honored their country."

In the Prussian Lower House, Herr Loewes, in speaking of the news of the assassination, said that Mr. Lincoln "performed his duties without pomp or ceremony, and relied on that dignity of his inner self alone, which is far above rank, orders and titles. He was a faithful servant, not less of his own commonwealth than of civilization, freedom and humanity."

By far the most beautiful of all these foreign tributes, was the very generous memorial of the London Punch. That paper had joined all the fashionable world in making merry at Lincoln's expense while he struggled, weary and miry, through the "valley of humiliation,"—but it is not every one who does a wrong who is capable of so full and generous a reparation. We give it entire, because, apart from its noble spirit, it is one of the most truthful summaries of Lincoln's character:

You lay a wreath on murdered Lincoln's bier!
  You, who with mocking pencil wont to trace,
Broad for the self-complacent British sneer,
  His length of shambling limb, his furrowed face,

His gaunt, gnarled hands, his unkempt, bristling hair,
  His garb uncouth, his bearing ill at ease,
His lack of all we prize as debonair,
  Of power or will to shine, of art to please!

You, whose smart pen backed up the pencil's laugh,
  Judging each step, as though the way were plain;
Reckless, so it could point its paragraph,
  Of chief's perplexity, or people's pain!

Beside this corpse, that bears for winding-sheet
  The stars and stripes he lived to rear anew,
Between the mourners at his head and feet,
  Say, scurril-jester, is there room for *you*?

Yes, he had lived to shame me from my sneer—
  To lame my pencil, and confute my pen—

To make me own this hind of princes peer,
  This rail-splitter a true-born king of men.

My shallow judgment I had learned to rue,
  Noting how to occasion's height he rose;
How his quaint wit made home-truth seem more true;
  How, iron-like, his temper grew by blows;

How humble, yet how hopeful he could be;
  How in good fortune and in ill the same;
Nor bitter in success, nor boastful he,
  Thirsty for gold, nor feverish for fame.

He went about his work—such work as few
  Ever had laid on head, and heart, and hand—
As one who knows where there's a task to do;
  Man's honest will must Heaven's good grace command,

Who trusts the strength will with the burden grow,
  That God makes instruments to work his will,
If but that will we can arrive to know,
  Nor tamper with the weights of good and ill.

So he went forth to battle, on the side
  That he felt clear was Liberty's and Right's,
As in his peasant boyhood he had plied
  His warfare with rude nature's thwarting mights;—

The uncleared forest, the unbroken soil,
  The iron bark that turn's the lumberer's axe,
The rapid, that o'erbears the boatman's toil,
  The prairie, hiding the mazed wanderer's tracks,

The ambushed Indian, and the prowling bear—
  Such were the needs that helped his youth to train:
Rough culture—but such trees large fruit may bear,
  If but their stocks be of right girth and grain.

So he grew up, a destined work to do,
  And lived to do it: four long suffering years'
Ill-fate, ill-feeling, ill-report, lived through,
  And then he heard the hisses change to cheers,

The taunts to tribute, the abuse to praise,
  And took both with the same unwavering mood;
  Till, as he came on light, from darkling days,
And seemed to touch the goal from where he stood,

  A felon hand, between the goal and him,
Reached from behind his back, a trigger prest—
And those perplexed and patient eyes were dim,
  Those gaunt, long-laboring limbs were laid to rest!

The words of mercy were upon his lips,
  Forgiveness in his heart and on his pen,
When this vile murderer brought swift eclipse
  To thoughts of peace on earth, good-will to men.

The old world and the new, from sea to sea,
  Utter one voice of sympathy and shame!
Sore heart, so stopped when it at last beat high!
  Sad life, cut short just as its triumph came.

Lincoln must be looked upon in the final review of his character, as one of those men elect of God, whom he calls and chooses to effect great purposes of his own, and fashions and educates with especial reference to that purpose. As is usual in such cases, the man whom God chooses for a work is not at all the man whom the world beforehand would choose, and often for a time the world has difficulty in receiving him. There was great questioning about him in the diplomatic circles of Europe, when the war began, and there was great searching of heart concerning him at home. There have been times when there were impatient murmurs that another sort of man was wanted in his chair—a man with more dash, more brilliancy, more Napoleonic efficiency. Yet in the contest such a man might have been our ruin. A brilliant military genius might have wrecked the republic on the rock of military despotism, where so many good ships have gone down; whereas, slow, cautious, honest old Abe only took our rights of habeas corpus, and other civil privileges, as he did the specie of old, to make the legal tender, and brought it all back safe and sound.

Lincoln was a strong man, but his strength was of a peculiar kind; it was not aggressive so much as passive, and among passive things it was like the strength not so much of a stone buttress as of a wire cable. It was strength swaying to every influence, yielding on this side and on that to popular needs, yet tenaciously and inflexibly bound to carry its great end. Probably by no other kind of strength could our national ship have been drawn safely through so dreadful a channel. Surrounded by all sorts of conflicting claims, by traitors, by half-hearted, timid men, by border State men and free State men, by radical abolitionists and conservatives, he listened to all, heard all, weighed all, and in his own time acted by his own honest convictions in the fear of God, and thus simply and purely he did the greatest work that has been done in modern times.

U. S. Grant

CHAPTER II.

ULYSSES SIMPSON GRANT.

A General Wanted—A Short War Expected—The Young Napoleon—God's Revenge Against Slavery—The Silent Man in Galena—"Tanning Leather" —Gen. Grant's Puritan Descent—How he Loaded the Logs—His West Point Career—Service in Mexico—Marries and Leaves the Army—Wood-Cutting, Dunning and Leather-Selling—Enlists against the Rebellion—Missouri Campaign—Paducah Campaign—Fort Donelson Campaign—Battle of Shiloh—How Grant Lost his Temper—Vicksburg Campaign—Lincoln on Grant's "Drinking" —Chattanooga—Grant's Method of Making a Speech—Appointed Lieutenant-General—The Richmond Campaign—"Mr. Grant is a Very Obstinate Man"—Grant's Qualifications as a Ruler—Honesty—Generosity to Subordinates—Sound Judgment of Men—Power of Holding his Tongue—Grant's Sidewalk Platform—Talks Horse to Senator Wade—"Wants Nothing Said"—The Best Man for Next President.

WHEN the perception of our late great military crisis first came upon us, and we found ourselves engaged in an actual and real war, our first inquiry was for our General.

For years and years there had been only peace talk and peace valuations in our market. There had, to be sure, been some frontier skirmishing—a campaign in Mexico, which drew off our more restless adventurers, and gave our politicians a little of a smart, martial air, in rounding their periods, and pointing their allusions. We had played war in Mexico as we read romances, and the principal interest of it was, after all, confined to our very small regular army of some twenty-five thousand men, where some got promotions in consequence of the vacancies made in this or that battle.

Gen. Scott won European renown and some laurels in this country. We created an office of Lieutenant General on purpose to do him honor; but the people, after all, laughed in their sleeves, and irreverently called our national hero "Old Fuss and Feathers;" a nickname which went far to show that whatever his talents in the field might be, he had not succeeded in establishing over the body of his countrymen the ascendency which strong minds hold over weak ones.

But when the hour of our trial came we had to look to him as our leader, and Gen. Scott accepted cheerfully the situation, whose reality and magnitude neither he nor we, nor any mortal living at that time, perceived, or could estimate. Seward smiled in his cabinet chair, and spoke of the affair as a little skirmish that would be over in ninety days. A battle or two, might occur, then an armistice, and then "We, Us and Company" would walk in with our red tape and circumlocution office, and tie up everything better than before. So Scott spread his maps and talked cheerfully, and the Washington cabinet congratulated one another. "This is to be my last campaign," said Scott, "and I mean it to be my best."

The country listened with earnest ears now to what our chief military man said. When the father of a family is lying between life and death, there is no more laughing at the doctor—and in the solemn hush that preceded *real* war, there was no more sneering at old Fuss and Feathers. People wanted to believe in him. They searched out his old exploits, talked of his old successes, that they might hope and believe that they had a deliverer and a leader in their midst.

Slowly, surely, it began to appear through many a defeat, many a disaster; through days and nights when men's hearts failed them for fear, and for looking for the things that were coming on the earth; through all such signs and wonders as usher in great convulsions of society—it began to be manifested that this nation was in a contest for which there were no precedents, which was to be as wide as from ocean to ocean, which was to number its forces by millions, and for which all former rules and ordinances of war, all records of campaigns and battles, were as mere obsolete ballads and old songs. The inquiry began to grow more urgent: Who is to be our General?

General Scott professed that the work was too great for him, but he called to his right hand and presented to the nation one whom he delighted to honor, and who was announced with songs and cheerings as the young Napoleon of America.

The nation received him with acclamation. They wanted a young Napoleon. A young Napoleon was just what they needed, and a young Napoleon therefore they were determined to believe that they had; and for a while nothing was heard but his praises. Every loyal paper was on its knees in humble expectancy, to admire and to defend, but not to criticise. Mothers were ready to send their sons to his banner; millionaires offered the keys of their treasure chests for his commissariat; the administration bowed to his lightest suggestion, gave him all he asked, hung on his lightest word. Everywhere he moved amid victorious plaudits, the palms and honors of victory everywhere credited to him in advance by the fond faith of the whole nation.

We waited for victories. Our men were burning with enthusiasm—begging, praying to be led to the field, and yet nothing was done. "It takes time to create an army," was the first announcement of our chief. We gave him time, and he spent it in reviews, in preparations, in fortifications and entrenchments. The time he took gave the enemy just what they stood in perishing need of—time to organize, concentrate, drill, arrange with Europe, and get ready for a four years' conflict.

It was God's will that we should have a four years' war, and therefore when we looked for a leader he sent us Gen. McClellan.

It was God's will that this nation—the North as well as the South—should deeply and terribly suffer for the sin of consenting to and encouraging the great oppressions of the South; that the ill-gotten wealth which had arisen from striking hands with oppression and robbery, should be paid back in the taxes of war; that the blood of the poor slave, that had cried so many years from the ground in vain, should be answered by the blood of the sons from the best hearth stones through all the free States; that the slave mothers, whose tears nobody regarded, should have with them a great company of weepers, North and South—Rachels weeping for their children and refusing to be comforted; that the free States, who refused to listen when they were told of lingering starvation, cold, privation and barbarous cruelty, as perpetrated on the slave, should have lingering starvation, cold, hunger and cruelty doing its work among their own sons, at the hands of these slave masters, with whose sins our nation had connived.

General McClellan was like those kings and leaders we read of in the Old Testament, whom God sent to a people with a purpose of wrath and punishment.

Slowly, through those dark days of rebuke and disaster, did the people come at last to a consciousness that they had trusted in vain—that such a continued series of disasters were not exceptions and accidents, but evidences of imbecility and incompetence in the governing power.

Meanwhile the magnitude of this colossal war had fully revealed itself—a war requiring combinations and forces before unheard of, as different from those of European battles as the prairies of the West differ from Salisbury Plain, or the Mississippi from the Thames—and we again feverishly asked, Where is our leader?

We had faith that some man was to arise; but where was he? Now one General, and now another took the place of power, and we hoped and confided, till disaster and reverses came and threw us on our unanswered inquiry.

Now it is very remarkable that in all great crises and convulsions of society, the man of the hour generally comes from some obscure quarter—silently, quietly, unannounced, unheralded, without prestige, and makes his way alone and single-handed.

John the Baptist said to the awakened crowd, thrilling with vague expectation of a coming Messiah, "There standeth one among you whom ye know not," and the same declaration might amount to a general principle, which would hold good in most cases when the wants of a new era in society call for a new leader.

When France lay convulsed after the terrible upheavings of the French revolution, there was one man strong enough to govern her, to bring back settled society, law and order—but he was doing duty in an obscure place as corporal of artillery; and in like manner when the American war broke out, the General who was to be strong enough, and wise enough, and energetic enough to lead our whole army to victory, was an obscure, silent, sensible man, who was keeping a leather and saddle store in Galena, Ill.

He was a man principally to be noted for saying little, and doing with certainty and completeness the duty he happened to have in hand. If he failed in any of the points required in a successful store-keeper in a Western town, it was in the gift of talking. He had no opinions on politics, no theories about the government of the country, to put at the service of customers. The petty squabbles of local politics he despised. When one endeavored to engage him in a discussion of some such matter, he is said to have answered:

"I don't know any thing of party politics, and I don't want to. There is one subject on which I feel perfectly at home. Talk to me of that and I shall be happy to hear you."

"What is that?"

"*Tanning leather.*"

Yet this quiet man, who confined his professions of knowledge entirely to the business he took in hand, was an educated man, who had passed with credit through the military academy at West Point, graduated with honor, been promoted for meritorious service in the Mexican war to the rank of captain, and whose powers of conversation, when he chooses to converse on any subject befitting an educated man, are said by those who know him best, to be quite remarkable.

In these sketches of our distinguished men, we have, whenever possible, searched somewhat into their pedigree; for we have firm faith in the old maxim that blood will tell.

It is interesting to know that there are authentic documents existing, by which Gen. Grant's family may be traced through a line of Puritan patriots far back to England.

A gentleman in Hartford, justly celebrated for his research in these matters, has kindly offered us the following particulars:

"On the first page of a thick little memorandum book which is now before me, well preserved in its original sheepskin binding, are the following entries, the obsolete spelling of which sufficiently attests their antiquity:

May the 29 16. 45, Mathew Grant and Susanna ware maried.

Mathew Grant was then three and fortey yeares of age, seven moneths and eyghtene dayes; borne in the yeare, 1601. October 27 Tuesdaye.

Susannah Graunt was then three and fourtey yeares of age seuen weeks & 4 dayes; borne in the yeare 1602 April the 5 Mondaye."

This, as appears, was a second marriage, and Susannah was widow of one William Rockwell; and immediately after the record, follow the names of the children of her first marriage, five in number. Ruth Rockwell, the second daughter of Susannah Grant, married Christopher Huntington, of Norwich, and their great granddaughter, Martha Huntington, married Noah Grant, a great grandson of Mathew.

From this marriage came a second Noah Grant, who was a captain in the old French war, and afterwards settled in Coventry, Conn. The third son of this Captain Noah Grant, who also bore the name of Noah, resided in Coventry, and had a son named for the Hon. Jesse Root, Chief Justice of the Superior Court of Connecticut from 1796 to 1807, and this Jesse Root Grant is the father of Ulysses S. Grant, the man whom this war anointed to be our leader and captain.

The Mathew and Susanna Grant whose marriage record is here given, came first to America in the Mary and John, in the company which settled Dorchester, Mass., in 1630. They sailed from Plymouth, in Devonshire, March 20th, and arrived at Nantasket, May 30th.

The style and spirit of these colonists may be inferred from the following words of Roger Clap, who was one of the passengers:

"These godly people resolved to live together; and therefore they made choice of these two reverend servants of God, Mr. John Wareham, and Mr. John Maverick, to be their ministers; so they kept a solemn day of fasting in the New Hospital in Plymouth, England, spending it in preaching and praying; where that worthy man of God, Mr. John White, of Dorchester, in Dorset, was present and preached unto us the Word of God, in the fore part of the day, and in the latter part of the day. As the people did solemnly make choice of and call those godly ministers to their office, so also the Rev. Mr. Wareham and Mr. Maverick did accept thereof, and expressed the same. So we came by the good hand of the Lord through the deeps comfortably."

Thus Mathew Grant and his brethren, even before leaving the old country, were gathered into church estate for the new, and the planters of Dorchester came thither as a Puritan church, duly organized, with their chosen and ordained pastor and teacher. In 1635–6, Mr. Wareham and a great part of his flock removed to Connecticut, and settled a new Dorchester, afterwards named Windsor. Mathew Grant was one of these earlier settlers, and was from the first a prominent man in the church and town. For many years he was the principal surveyor of lands in Windsor, town clerk and deacon, and the church records speak highly of his blameless life. He died in 1681, at the age of eighty.

Thus from the little body of men who assembled with fasting and prayer in Plymouth, to form themselves into a New England colony, descended in the course of time, a leader and commander that was to stay up the hands of our great nation in the time of its severest trial.

The genealogist who has traced the pedigree of Grant back to England, remarks, that in the veins of his family was, by successive marriages, intermingled the blood of many of the best old New England families.

Gen. Grant is a genuine son of New England, therefore to be looked on as a vigorous offshoot of the old Puritan stock. His father removed from Coventry, first to Pennsylvania, afterwards to Ohio, and finally to Illinois, where the Ulysses of these many wanderings received his classic name. He appears to be a man of no ordinary class for shrewdness and good sense. Gen. Grant's mother is one of those sedate, sensible, serious women, whose households are fit nurseries for heroes. Industry, economy, patience, temperance and religion, were the lessons of his early days. The writer of the "Tanner Boy" has embodied, probably on good authority, some anecdotes of the childhood of the boy, which show that there was in him good stuff to make a man of. One of these is worth telling:

"I want you to drive the team to such a spot in the woods," said the father, "where you will find the men ready to load it with logs, and you will then drive it home."

The boy drove to the spot, found the logs, but no men.

Instead of sitting down to crack nuts and wait, as most boys would, Ulysses said to himself, "I was sent to bring these logs, and bring them I must, men or no men," and so by some ingenious mechanical arrangements, he succeeded in getting them on to the cart alone, and drove home with them quietly, as if it were a matter of course.

"Why, my son," exclaimed his father, "where are the men?"

"I don't know, and I don't care," said the boy. "I got the load without them."

This boy was surely father to the man who took Vicksburg.

There are other anecdotes given of his fighting a schoolboy who traduced Washington; of his steady perseverance in his school studies; and of a school saying of his, that *can't* was never a word in his dictionary. His industry and energy caused his appointment to West Point, where the young tanner boy took rank with the scions of the so-styled Southern aristocracy. It is recorded in his new position that certain sneers on his industrial calling were promptly resisted, and that he insisted upon the proper deference to himself and his order, as a boy of the working classes, and maintained it by a stalwart good right arm, which nobody cared to bring down in anger.

Grant graduated with respectable credit from West Point, in 1843. He is said to have been the best rider in his class, but not remarkable otherwise. In the same class were Gen. W. B. Franklin, Gen. I. T. Quimby, Gen. J. J. Reynolds, Gen. C. C. Augur, Gen. C. S. Hamilton, Gen. F. Steele, Gen. R. Ingalls, and Gen. H. M. Judah, all useful and a number of them eminent officers in the Union Army during the Rebellion. There were also in the same class several members who adhered to the rebel cause; R. S. Ripley, S. G. French, F. Gardner, who surrendered Port Hudson to Gen. Banks, E. B. Holloway, and one or two others. At his graduation, no second lieutenancy was vacant in the United States Army, and Grant therefore received a brevet commission as second lieutenant in the Fourth United States Infantry. With his regiment or detachments of it, he now served for a time on the western frontier, near St. Louis, up the Red River, and elsewhere. When in 1845, Gen. Taylor was ordered into Texas, the Fourth Regiment and Grant with it formed part of his force, and they continued in active service throughout the Mexican War. In this war, Lieutenant Grant showed great readiness, sense, and courage. He was in every one of its important battles except Buena Vista; to us the words of one of his eulogists, "in all the battles in which any one man could be." He was repeatedly mentioned in the reports of his commanding officers for meritorious conduct. He was appointed first Lieutenant on the field of battle, at Molino del Rey, for gallantry; and was breveted Captain for meritorious conduct in the battle of Chapultepec.

In 1848, after the end of the war, Capt. Grant married a Miss Dent, from near St. Louis, and for some years lived in the monotonous routine of the peace establishment; at Detroit, at Sackett's Harbor, and in Oregon. To this period of his life belongs a story that being a good chess player, and very fond of the game, he found while at Sackett's Harbor an opponent of superior force. With this champion our stubborn infantry captain used to play, and as regularly to get beaten. But he played on, and was accustomed to insist upon protracting the sitting until his opponent had actually become so tired that his mind would not work; when Grant would comfortably balance the account.

His full commission as captain reached him in August, 1853, but in 1854, having made up his mind that there was to be a long peace, he resigned his captaincy and set about establishing himself in civil life. His first attempt was, to manage a small farm to the southwest of St. Louis, where he used to cut wood and haul it to Carondelet, delivering it himself. He diversified his year during summer, with acting as a collector of debts in that region. But there is nothing to show that he enjoyed either wood cutting or dunning, and he certainly did not grow rich at them. In 1859, he tried in vain to get the appointment of county engineer; and he then went into the leather trade, in partnership with his father, at Galena. The firm quickly attained high standing for intelligence and integrity, and the business, at the breaking out of the war, was prosperous.

It is narrated that Grant's determination to enter the service against the rebellion was taken and stated along with the drawing on of his coat, instantly upon reading the telegram which announced the surrender of Sumter. He came into the store in the morning, read the dispatch, and as he took up his coat, which he had laid off, and put it on again, he observed in his quiet way, "The government educated me for the army, and although I have served through one war, I am still a little in debt to the government, and willing to discharge the obligation."

Grant, bringing with him a company of volunteers that he had enlisted, in a few days appeared in the council-chamber of governor Yates, of Illinois, and tendered his services to the country as volunteer. The governor immediately proposed to place him on his own staff, as mustering officer of volunteers. Grant expressed a wish for more active service, but was overruled for the time by the wishes of the governor, who represented that his military education and experience would be of great advantage in forming the raw material now to be made into an army.

In this comparatively humble sphere Grant began his second military career. He did with all his might whatever he did, and his exertions in obtaining volunteers were such that the quota of Illinois was more than full at the appointed time, and at once set in the field. In June, 1861, he entered actual service, with the rank of colonel of volunteers; and took hold of work with such purpose and efficiency that he was almost immediately elevated to be Brigadier General.

The patriotic and energetic Governor Yates, gives the following account of the first months of Grant's services during the Rebellion.

"In April, 1861, he tendered his personal services to me, saying, that he 'had been the recipient of a military education at West Point, and that now, when the country was involved in a war for its preservation and safety, he thought it his duty to offer his services in defense of the Union, and that he would esteem it a privilege to be assigned to any position where he could be useful.' The plain, straightforward demeanor of the man, and the modesty and earnestness which characterized his offer of assistance, at once awakened a lively interest in him, and impressed me with a desire to secure his counsel for the benefit of volunteer organization then forming for Government service. At first I assigned him a desk in the Executive office; and his familiarity with military organization and regulations made him an invaluable assistant in my own and the office of the Adjutant-General. Soon his admirable qualities as a military commander became apparent, and I assigned him to command of the camps of organization at 'Camp Yates,' Springfield, 'Camp Grant,' Mattoon, and 'Camp Douglas,' at Anna, Union County. * * * "The Twenty-first regiment of Illinois volunteers, * * * had become very much demoralized under the thirty days' experiment, and doubts arose in relation to their acceptance for a longer period. I was much perplexed to find an efficient and experienced officer to take command of the regiment, and take it into the three years' service. * * * I decided to offer the command to Captain Grant, at Covington, Kentucky, tendering him the colonelcy. He immediately reported, accepting the commission, taking rank as colonel of that regiment from the 15th of June, 1861. Thirty days previous to that time, the regiment numbered over one thousand men; but in consequence of laxity of discipline of the first commanding officer, and other discouraging obstacles connected with the acceptance of troops at that time, but six hundred and three men were found willing to enter the three years' service. In less than ten days Colonel Grant filled the regiment to the maximum standard, and brought it to a state of discipline seldom attained in the volunteer service in so short a time. His was the only regiment that left the camp of

9

organization on foot. * * * Colonel Grant was afterwards assigned to command for the protection of the Quincy and Palmyra, and Hannibal and St. Josephs Railroads. He soon distinguished himself as a regimental commander in the field, and his claims for increased rank were recognized by his friends in Springfield, and his promotion insisted upon, before his merits and services were fairly understood at Washington."

Grant's brigadier's commission reached him August 9th, 1861, and his first service under it was, a march to Ironton, in Missouri, for the purpose of preventing an attack from the rebel Jeff Thompson. Grant had already once declined a brigadiership when offered him by Gov. Yates, for the reason that he considered the appointment more properly due to another person; but though the youngest of the colonels in Missouri, he had been acting brigadier there.

Soon after this he was placed in command at the great central point of Cairo, which was the key of the West.

The country was full of confusion and disorder. Rebel sympathizers every where, openly and secretly, were embarrassing the Federal and assisting the rebel army. The professedly neutral State of Kentucky was used as the camping ground and retreat of these forces which thus annoyed our army. Grant quietly determined to command this dangerous territory. He took the town of Paducah, a strong post on the Ohio River, near the mouth of the Tennessee River, in Kentucky, by which he at once gained possession of interior navigable waters, which the traitors had been using for their own purposes. The strength and decision with which he took possession of the town intimidated all rebel sympathizers. He then issued the following address to the inhabitants, which is as good a specimen of condensed and effective military style as we have on record:

"I am come among you, not as an enemy, but as your fellow-American; not to maltreat and annoy you, but to respect and enforce the rights of all loyal citizens. I am here to defend you against the common enemy, who has planted his guns on your soil, and fired upon you; and to assist the authority and sovereignty of your government. I have nothing to do with opinions, and shall deal only with armed rebellion and its aiders and abetters. You can pursue your usual avocations without fear. The strong arm of the government is here to protect its friends, and punish its enemies. Whenever it is manifest that you are able to defend yourselves, maintain the authority of the government, and protect the rights of loyal citizens, I shall withdraw the forces under my command.

U. S. Grant,
Brig. Gen. Commanding.

While in command at Cairo, Grant used to dress rather carelessly, very much after Gen. Taylor's fashion; he went about wearing an old "stove-pipe hat," and always with a cigar. Some one, it is said, once jeered about the "stove-pipe general" and his cigars, and was silenced by the reply that "such a bright stove-pipe might be excused for smoking."

The remainder of General Grant's military career must be narrated with a brevity which by no means does justice to the subject. It may be said to consist of five campaigns; those of Fort Donelson, Corinth and Iuka, Vicksburg, Chattanooga, and Richmond. Of these, each pointed out its commander as the best man for the next, until by simple upward gravitation of natural fitness, he rose to his present great military post of general of all the armies of the United States.

Grant's operations in Northern Missouri, his dash on Belmont, and his seizure of Paducah, though all creditable military services, were thrown into the shade by the brilliant Fort Donelson campaign, which opened the career of Union successes in the West.

The Fort Donelson expedition was intended to break in two the rebel defensive line, which stretched the whole length of the State of Kentucky, from Columbus on the Mississippi, through Bowling Green, to Cumberland Gap. On this line, the rebels, under General A. S. Johnston, stood looking northward with threatening and defiant aspect. Grant saw that if he could seize Forts Henry and Donelson, which had been built to shut up the Tennessee and Cumberland rivers, the Union gunboats could range up and down through the heart of rebeldom, and the Union armies with them, and that thus the great rebel defensive line, cut through in the middle, would be broken as a chain is when a link is destroyed. He therefore asked leave of his immediate superior, Halleck, to take the forts; received it, concerted his plan of attack with Admiral Foote, and moved from Cairo, February 2d, 1862.

The success of this expedition is well known. It should be recorded, however, even in this short summary, that to Grant is due the credit of possessing the military tact and promptness that showed him when to make the decisive attack, and impelled him to do it. This time was after that considerable success of the rebel sally from Fort Donelson on Saturday, Feb. 15th, under Pillow, which drove away so large a portion of the Union army from its place, and indeed left room enough for the whole rebel force to walk out of the fort and escape, if they had so chosen. This was done while Grant had gone to consult with Admiral Foote. When he came back, and saw how his troops had been driven, to any common mind the case would have seemed a pretty bad one; but Grant really does not appear to have seen any bad side to any case he had charge of during the war. At Belmont, when he was told that he was surrounded, he simply answered, "Well, then, we must cut our way out." His own description, afterwards given to Gen. Sherman, at Shiloh, of the impression now made on his mind by seeing how his troops had been pounded and driven, was as follows: "On riding upon the field, I saw that either side was ready to give way if the other showed a bold front. I took the opportunity, and ordered an advance along the whole line." In both cases, the thing was done.

At daylight on Sunday, the 16th, Gen. Buckner, (whose two superior officers, Floyd and Pillow, had run away,) sent a flag of truce asking for commissioners to consider terms of capitulation. Grant replied by the bearer, in a letter, two of whose phrases have become permanent contributions to the proverbial part of the English language:

"Yours of this date, proposing an armistice, and appointment of commissioners to settle terms of capitulation, is just received. No terms other than unconditional and immediate surrender can be accepted. I propose to move immediately upon your works."

Buckner's reply was in a very disgusted tone, and it may be excused to him under the circumstances, that he used some very curious explanatory phrases, and that he called names. But he came down, though it was from an extremely high horse, rejoining:

"The distribution of the forces under my command, incident to an unexpected change of commanders, and the overwhelming force under your command, compel me, notwithstanding the brilliant success of the confederate arms yesterday, to accept the ungenerous and unchivalrous terms which you propose."

The correctness of Grant's estimate of this whole movement was well proved by its instantaneous result—the evacuation of Columbus at one end of the rebel line, and of Bowling Green in the middle, and the falling back of the whole rebellion down to the southern boundary of Tennessee. The first great victory since Bull Run, the first important campaign in the West, it encouraged and elevated the spirits of the whole North, and in equal measure it alarmed and enfeebled the South. It had flung back the rebellion two hundred miles, along the whole length of Kentucky, across that State and Tennessee. With soldierly promptitude and energy, Grant followed up his victory by pushing the enemy, according to the Napoleonic maxim, that "victory is, to march ten leagues, beat the enemy, and pursue him ten leagues more."

Immediately after Donelson, Grant was made major general of volunteers by commission dated on the day of the fall of the fort, and was placed in command of the "Military District of West Tennessee," consisting of a long triangle with its northern point at Cairo, its base at the south, on the Mississippi State line, and its sides the Tennessee and Mississippi rivers. Thus promoted, Grant had already pushed southward. Foote's gunboats ascended the Cumberland, the troops kept abreast of them; Clarksville, with twenty days' subsistence for Grant's whole army, was occupied on Feb. 20th, four days after the capture of Donelson; and on the 23d, the advance of Buell's army, operating in conjunction with Grant's, entered Nashville.

When the rebel military line already mentioned, running lengthwise of the State of Kentucky, was broken up by Grant's getting through and behind it at Fort Donelson, the rebel leaders sought to hold another east and west line, coinciding nearly with the southern line of Tennessee, along the important Memphis and Charleston Railroad, and their commander in the West, Albert Sydney Johnston, set about concentrating his forces at Corinth, on that road. Halleck, by this time commanding the whole Department of the Mississippi, now prepared to attack Corinth. It was with this design that Grant's army was sent up the Tennessee, and encamped at Shiloh. But the rebels did not wait to be attacked. They advanced themselves, with the bold and judicious design of beating the army at Shiloh, and then of marching northward, regaining all the ground they had lost, and retaliating by an invasion of the States north of the Ohio.

This hardy attempt was well nigh successful. The night before the battle of Shiloh, Beauregard, as the rebel council of war separated, had prophesied: "To-morrow night we sleep in the enemy's camp." The sudden and vehement assault of the morning, maintained with tremendous and pertinacious fury all day long, had steadily crushed the Union army backward towards the Tennessee river, until towards sunset it had been pounded into a heterogeneous, irregular line of desperate fighters, and behind them a great mass of terrified and disheartened runaways, hiding under the river bank. What the heathen called Fortune, what Christians recognize as an overruling Providence, caused a conjuncture of circumstances by which, between night and morning, the relative number and spirits of the troops on both sides, and the result of the fight, were totally reversed. These circumstances were, the powerful resistance offered, at the end of the Sunday's disastrous fight, to the final charges of the rebels, by the artillery massed at the left end or key of the Union position, close to the river; by the further obstacle of a ravine stretching back from the river before the Union lines just at that point; by the powerful effect of the monstrous shells sent up this ravine and into the rebel lines from the two Union gunboats, Tyler and Lexington; and finally, by the coming upon the field of the advance of Buell's army. Beauregard's men slept in the Union camp, as he had said, but during the night Buell's troops and Gen. Lewis

Wallace's division came upon the field. Monday morning, instead of last night's picture of 30,000 rebels, flushed with all day's victory, against at most 23,000 disorganized and all but overpowered Union troops, the daylight broke on a Union army of 50,000, being Grant's 23,000, somewhat refreshed and reorganized, and entirely inspirited; and 27,000 reinforcements, fresh and unbroken; while the rebel army, exhausted by its own efforts, had received no increase, had lost by stragglers, had rested ill in the cold rain, and had been all night long awakened every few minutes by the unwelcome reveillee of the great gunboat shells that were flung amongst them from the river. Weary and overweighted as they were, the rebels fought well, however, and it was not until four in the afternoon that they retreated, fighting still, and in good order, toward Corinth, whence they had set out.

When the rebels first attacked, Grant was at Savannah, seven miles down the river. Hastening back, he was on the field at the earliest possible moment, and did whatever could be done to withstand the tremendous force of the rebel advance. When Buell came upon the field toward night, the aspect of affairs so struck him that his first inquiry of Grant was, what preparations he had made for retreat.

"I have not despaired of whipping them yet," was the thoroughly characteristic reply. One account adds, that when Buell urged that a prudent general ought to provide for possibilities of defeat, and repeated his inquiry, Grant pointed to his transports and said, "Don't you see those boats?" "Yes," said Buell, "but they will not carry more than ten thousand, and we have more than thirty thousand." "Well," returned Grant, "ten thousand are more than I mean to retreat with."

One prominent, elaborate and ambitious account of this battle, by a writer who has been complimented as "the Napier of the War," is visibly framed with the intention of omitting Grant entirely from this battle; since no part of the narrative suggests that he gave a single order, or shows that he was on the field. But this slander by omission is utterly gratuitous. General Sherman's report tells how Grant "was early on the field, and visited his (Sherman's) division in person about ten A. M., when the battle was raging fiercely;" and again, how Grant, who had been on the field and frequently under fire, all day long, returned to him at 5 P. M., and explained the situation of the rest of the field. Sherman adds, "he agreed that the enemy had expended the *force* of his attack, and we estimated our loss and approximated our then strength. * * * He then ordered me to get all things ready, and at daylight the next day to assume the offensive. * * * I know I had orders from General Grant to assume the offensive before I knew General Buell was on the west side of the Tennessee." It was doubtless at this time that Grant made to Sherman the remark already quoted, as to the readiness of either side, at Donelson, to retreat.

Another witness, who, unlike our deceitful "Napier of the Rebellion," was on the field of Shiloh, describes how "throughout the battle, Grant rode to and fro on the front, smoking his inevitable cigar, with his usual stolidity and good fortune; horses and men were killed all around him, but he did not receive a scratch."

The consequence of Shiloh was, the withdrawal of the rebels from their second line of defence, by their evacuation of Corinth on the 30th of May, seven weeks afterwards, the disappointment both of their great plan of a northern invasion and of their secondary plan of holding the Memphis and Charleston Railroad line, and the opening of all Tennessee, and the North of Mississippi and Alabama, to the Union forces; the opening of the Mississippi River from Memphis down to Vicksburg; the subsequent movement which resulted in the battle of Murfreesboro and the securing of Chattanooga on the east; and the series of efforts which culminated in the capture of Vicksburg on the west. In short, this battle flung the Rebellion, in the Valley of the Mississippi, into a defensive posture, out of which it never escaped during the remainder of the war.

A few days after the proclamation which gave freedom to the slaves, General Grant expressed his concurrence in it after his sober fashion, by a dry phrase in a general order on the subject of organizing colored regiments. "It is expected," he says, "that all commanders will especially exert themselves in carrying out the policy of the administration, not only in organizing colored regiments, and rendering them effective, but also in removing prejudice against them."

The taking of Fort Donelson had given Grant a reputation as a prompt and vigorous fighter, and a sensible commander. The battle of Shiloh, when its extremely important results came to be understood, added to his reputation in a proportionate degree. While therefore one line of operations was decided upon, which pointed eastward and was to end in the occupation of Chattanooga, Rosecrans being placed in command, to the westward and southward, a second great enterprise was aimed, which was entrusted to Grant; which should end in the occupation of Vicksburg, and should thus complete the task which the men of the northwest had proposed to themselves at the beginning of the war, of "hewing their way to the sea."

Vicksburg and Port Hudson were now the only remaining two of that series of positions, most of them really impregnable from the river, by which the rebels had throttled the great artery of western commerce.

His previous career naturally enough pointed out Grant for the command of the Vicksburg campaign; and the event showed that his absolute inability to let go where he had once taken hold, his inevitable continuance in hammering at his object, were exactly the qualities needed.

For a little while, General Halleck himself came and commanded in person against Corinth, General Grant being second in command. It was during this period that both the two occasions occurred, which are said to have been the only ones when Grant was ever known to lose his temper. His steady nature and calm good humor had become proverbial among his fellows even while he was a student; for about the time of his leaving West Point, the cadets said of him, to use his father's words, that the only difficulty about him was, that "if he ever was engaged in war, he was too good natured to be kicked into a fight." The two occasions spoken of are said to have been; one, when he discovered a soldier defiling the water of a clear spring; and the other, when he wished to "move at once upon the works" of Beauregard at Corinth, ten days before General Halleck was ready; as he saw that by so doing the whole rebel army in the place could be taken. Of his urgency with Halleck, his father Mr. Jesse R. Grant, says, "He (Grant) is sure he used stronger language to General Halleck than he had ever used before to any person, and expected to be arrested and tried. But the General said to him, 'If I had let you take your own course, you would have taken the rebel army. Hereafter I will not dictate to you about the management of an army!'"

Halleck now left, being appointed General-in-Chief; and Grant remained in command of the Army of the Tennessee, and of the military districts of Cairo, West Tennessee and Mississippi. The rebels knew as well as he that his face was set steadfastly towards Vicksburg; and to begin with, they attacked his troops at Corinth and Iuka in great force and with tremendous fury, in order to break up his plans. At both places they were however defeated. In October, the rebel General Pemberton was placed in command in Northern Mississippi, and in the last two months of 1862, took place Grant's first attempt against Vicksburg. The place had already been attacked by the two powerful fleets of Farragut and Davis, during seventy days, from the preceding May 18th to July 27th; but though 25,000 shot and shell had been thrown into it, not one gun had been dismounted, and only seven men were killed and fifteen wounded; a result which showed plainly enough how the place was to be taken if at all.

Grant's movement was to be by land, southward from his post at Corinth, directly at Pemberton; while Sherman was to get footing if possible close to Vicksburg. The loss of Grant's main depot of supplies at Holly Springs, midway in his progress, broke down his part of the plan, and Pemberton then reinforcing Vicksburg, repulsed Sherman and broke down the rest of it.

Grant now established his head-quarters at Memphis, January 10th, 1863, and moved his army towards his goal by water. On the 2d of February, he reached Young's Point, a little above the city; his army was already there and at Milliken's Bend, just below.

His purpose was one; to get his army across to the Vicksburg side and thence to prosecute his attack. First he tried a canal across the neck of the river peninsula opposite Vicksburg. Through this, if he could get the water to accept it as a new bed, he could take his forces below the city, out of reach of its guns, and cross over. But a flood burst into the unfinished canal and drowned out the plan. Then he tried to clear out a longer water route to do the same thing, through a string of bayous and rivers back in the Louisiana swamps. A fall in the river broke up this plan, as a rise had done that before it. Then he tried a longer route of the same sort, beginning at Lake Providence, seventy-five miles north of Vicksburg, but it was found impracticable. Then resorting to the east side of the Mississippi, he sent a naval expedition to try to penetrate Yazoo Pass, and thence through the inconceivable tangle of the Yazoo swamps and their rivers, to get behind the outer rebel defences north of Vicksburg, and so make a lodgment. But this plan was checkmated by the hasty erection in the heart of the swamp region, at the junction of the Tallahatchie and Yazoo Rivers, of a powerful fort, which the fleet tried in vain to silence. Then he sent another fleet to try another part of the same monstrous tangle, by way of the Big Sunflower River, but that effort miscarried much as the preceding one did.

The obstinate commander had now tried six assaults upon his prey, and had been busily working at his failures for nearly four months. March 29th, 1863, he set his forces in motion for the seventh and successful effort. This was by what he had in fact recognized from the beginning as the best line of operation—by the south. It was however also the most difficult. As one of the historians of the war observes, a measure of the difficulties offered is given by the fact that General W. T. Sherman was not disposed to advise it. The same writer adds, "It can only be said that there was that in the composition of General Grant's mind that prompted him to undertake that which no one else would have adventured."

Colonel Grierson's cavalry force was now launched down from Tennessee to go tearing through the whole interior of Mississippi, and thoroughly frighten all its people, while he should break up, as he circuited far around Vicksburg, as many as possible of the railroads, bridges, and other means of communication, leading from the city back into the country, or from one part of the State to another. Grant's own troops moved down the river a total distance of seventy-five miles. The fleet and transports ran the batteries and ferried the army across at Bruinsburg; Grant moved at once three miles inland, and May 1st, beat Gen. Bowen at Port Gibson. Then he moved eastward, drove Johnston out of Jackson, an important center for railroad lines, and broke up all the communications in the neighborhood; then turning short about, he approached Vicksburg by forced marches; on May 10th met Pemberton at Champion Hills and defeated him; followed him sharply up, forced the passage of the Big Black, drove Pemberton into the city, and on May 16th had formed his lines of attack. After a vigorous siege, whose progress attracted the attention of the whole civilized world, the place surrendered with 27,000 men, on July 4th, 1863. The whole number of prisoners made since crossing the Mississippi was 37,000. This great achievement freed the Mississippi, cut the rebellion in two, and rendered it out of the question for the rebels to hold the Mississippi Valley.

The taking of Vicksburg was remarkable, not so much as a successful engineering attack against earthworks, as it was when considered as the culmination of a well planned campaign. The place was in fact taken a good ways away from it. Grierson's wide destruction of the railroads and bridges, and the far wider fright which he spread among the rebels, were part of the fatal preliminaries which were the most decisive parts of the attack. Such were also the series of battles which so relentlessly pounded Pemberton backwards into the trap where he was finally caged; particularly the expulsion of the rebel forces from Jackson, just before the siege. All these operations gradually fixed Pemberton where he could not get out, and where his friends could not help him out; and so he waited until he had no more provisions, and then gave up. There seems no reason for believing that the assault which Grant had arranged to give on the 6th, if the surrender had not been made on the 4th, would have been more successful than either of the previous assaults; the earthworks of Vicksburg were skillfully and strongly built, and were much the stronger because they stood on ground itself naturally very strong. The great feature of the transaction was therefore the broad and far-seeing wisdom of a general who can organize campaigns, rather than the mere ability of a colonel to make a furious assault at the head of his regiment, That this was the nature of the campaign, appears from the history of the preliminary part of it; and so it does, from Grant's own dispatch to Sherman, on hearing that Johnston was doing his best to get together an army to relieve the place. "They seem," wrote Grant, "to put a great deal of faith in the Lord and Joe Johnston, but *you* must whip Johnston at least fifteen miles from here." That battle never happened.

It is said that during the dreary days of the siege of Vicksburg, a knot of men collected in a druggist's shop in Cincinnati, were discussing the probabilities of his success in taking Vicksburg. An aged countryman, who had been a silent listener, was at last appealed to for his opinion.

"I rather think he'll do it," said the stranger, in a tone of certainty.

"What makes you think so?" said the company.

"Well, I don't know; but our Ulysses always did do whatever he said he would. You see Ulysses is my boy," added the old man; and the event justified his confidence.

Never was an enterprise hedged in with difficulties more gigantic; but against these Grant placed the silent, inflexible force of a will which no length of time could weary, no obstacles discourage, and the combinations of a brain which seemed equally capable of attending to the vastest plans and the most trivial minutiæ.

We can all remember that thrill of joy and thankfulness which vibrated through the country when the telegraph flashed through it the news of this victory. It was a double triumph for the nation. Not only was Vicksburg taken, but the General and commander that the nation had long been looking for was at last made manifest.

In vain did envy and jealousy at this point intrigue against him, and endeavor to fill the ear of the President with suspicions. "I assure you he is a hard drinker," said one of these detractors. The "slow, wise smile" that we so well remember, rose over that rugged face as Lincoln made answer:

"I wish you would tell me exactly *what* he drinks. I should like to send some of the same brand to all my other Generals."

No; there was no deceiving Lincoln. He knew a man when he saw him, and was ready to put all power in hands that he saw were strong enough to use it.

General Grant's commission as major-general in the regular army was dated July 4, 1863, the day of the occupation of Vicksburg. In the succeeding October he was placed in command of the great "Military Division of the Mississippi," consisting of the three "Departments" of the Ohio, the Cumberland, and the Tennessee, and including the command of four strong armies; his own, Hooker's, and those of the Cumberland and the Ohio.

Grant's next victory was that of Chattanooga, Nov. 25, 1863, which substantially repaired the ill effects of the defeat of Rosecrans at Chickamauga, and assured the possession of the mountain citadel from which in the next spring Sherman sallied on his way to Atlanta.

A very thorough effort to extract a speech from Grant was made at St. Louis, January 29, 1864, after the victory of Chattanooga. There was a public dinner in his honor. When the regular toast to "our distinguished guest" was offered and drank, and the band had capped the compliment with "Hail to the Chief," the guest would, on political principles have talked for at least half an hour. Grant got up and said: "Gentlemen—in response it will be impossible for me to do more than to thank you." In the evening there was a serenade, and a great crowd to hear it. When Grant came out on the balcony, everybody shouted "Speech, speech!" and then was the time for another able political manifesto, say of an hour long. The General took off his hat. Everybody was perfectly still. At last a speech from the Silent General! But that commander had now "found a can't in his dictionary." "Gentlemen," he said, "I thank you for this honor. I cannot make a speech. It is something I have never done, and never intend to do, and I beg you will excuse me." So he put on his hat, took out a cigar, lit it, smoked, and looked at the rockets. The crowd kept bawling out, "Speech, speech, speech!" A foolish local politician who had been let into the balcony, offered the General a piece of worn-out clap-trap to fling to the crowd. "Tell them," said he, "that you can fight for them, but can't talk to them." The General quietly intimated that he should leave such things for others to say. Still they bawled "Speech!" and once more the "very obstinate man," taking his cigar from his lips, leaned over the railing and puffed forth the smoke as if to speak. "Now, then," said the excited crowd, and they were all still. "Gentlemen," said Grant, "making speeches is not my business. I never did it in my life, and I never will. I thank you, however, for your attendance here."

On March 10th, 1864, Grant was appointed Lieutenant General, and placed in command of all the armies of the United States. The first law passed at that winter's session had been a joint resolution thanking Grant and the officers and men that had fought under him, and providing for an honorary medal to be presented to him by the United States, in testimony thereof.

The Union armies, as Grant himself had already remarked, in his dry way, had hitherto "acted independently, and without concert, like a baulky team, no two pulling together."

Henceforward, in his single strong hand, those armies worked together. The rebel leaders could no longer beat a Union army at one end of the line of hostilities by massing all their troops upon it, and then whirl them away to the other end and beat another. As Grant was engaged in crossing the Rapidan at the opening of the final Richmond campaign, he sat down on a log by the roadside and wrote a few words which were telegraphed from Washington. They let Sherman loose to co-operate in the South with the Army of the Potomac in the north—and the Rebellion was ground to dust between the two.

In this final movement, the first act was the battle of the Wilderness. There is a story that upon the next morning after the first day's struggling in those tangled and all but impassable woods, Lee and his officers came out as aforetime, to see the Union forces going back again over the river; and that when he saw, instead, signs of their resuming the attack, he remarked to his companions, "They have a general now. It is all up with us!" The story may not be true; but its facts were. It was after six days of battle that Grant sent to Washington the dispatch which ended with the grim remark, "I propose to fight it out on this line if it takes all summer." Spottsylvania followed, and Cold Harbor; the investment of Petersburg, and that long series of assaults, forays, entrenchments and battles which ended with the surrender of Lee and the explosion of the Rebellion.

In the early days of the campaign, Mrs. Grant gave an opinion about Richmond, which was as well founded as that of the General's father about Vicksburg.

Somebody was so good as to express to her a hope that her husband would take Richmond. Mrs. Grant observed, with a dry simplicity of phrase that sounded as if she had gone to school to her husband as well as married him; "Well, I don't know. I think he may. *Mr. Grant always was a very obstinate man!*"

From the time of Grant's first appointment, he has gone on steadily, firmly, and without bluster or parade, doing the impossible, and demonstrating his early saying, that there was no can't in his dictionary. In quiet reticence and persevering patience he resembles the Duke of Wellington more than any of the great military leaders. Like Wellington and George Washington, he seems possessed of a buoyancy of capacity which always and steadily rises to the height of any emergency.

How modestly and quietly he received promotion; how earnestly and wisely he set to work, when all the reins of power were in his hands, to organize that last splendid campaign that issued in the taking of Richmond and the surrender of Lee, the people do not need to be told. It will be had in everlasting remembrance.

Never had man more efficient Generals to second him. Grant's marshals were not inferior to Napoleon's, and the unenvying, patriotic ability with which he and they worked together is not the least noticeable feature in the campaign whose glory they share with him.

The war closed leaving General Grant, who entered it an obscure trader, in a position perhaps as noticeable and brilliant as any in the civilized world. He stands in the front rank among the leaders of human society, and in our American affairs, still critical, he shows a judgment, and a prudence, and a temperate wisdom which seem to point him out as no less fit to rule in peace than in war.

General Grant has many qualities which fit him to be a ruler of men, Among them are some plain and common-place virtues. Such is his unflinching adherence to what he thinks is right. Such is his unconditional public and private honesty. This was well exemplified in the solicitous care with which he kept the cotton business outside of his command in the West, as long as possible, from a well founded dislike of its immense corrupting power.

When at last he had to consent to allow the progress of trade into the territory taken from the rebels, he specified that, at least, it should be kept in the hands of honest and trusty and undoubted Unionists. He was then asked to name such men. He replied, "I will do no such thing. If I did, it would appear in less than a week that I was a partner of every one of the persons trading under my authority."

Such another virtue is, that scrupulous official economy by which General Grant has already saved our over-taxed country five million dollars a year, by cutting down expenses in the War Department.

He also possesses other very noticeable qualifications of a more special sort, and so much rarer among public men, that they must be named even in the shortest inventory of General Grant's character. Two of these are, the broadest and most generous justice in attributing the credit of doing well where it belongs, and remarkable wisdom in judging and selecting men. Of the former quality, his letter to Sherman at the time of his appointment as Lieutenant-General is a good instance. That letter, exceedingly honorable evidence of simplicity and justice in the writer, and of merit in the recipient, was as follows:

"DEAR SHERMAN:—The bill reviving the grade of Lieutenant-General in the army has become a law, and my name has been sent to the Senate for the place. I now receive orders to report to Washington immediately in person, which indicates a confirmation, or a likelihood of confirmation.

I start in the morning to comply with the order.

Whilst I have been eminently successful in this war, in at least gaining the confidence of the public, no one feels more than I how much of this success is due to the energy and skill, and the harmonious putting forth of that energy and skill, of those whom it has been my good fortune to have occupying subordinate positions under me.

There are many officers to whom these remarks are applicable to a greater or less degree, proportionate to their ability as soldiers; but what I want is to express my thanks to you and McPherson, as the men to whom, above all others, I feel indebted for whatever I have had of success.

How far your advice and assistance have been of help to me you know. How far your execution of whatever has been given you to do entitles you to the reward I am receiving, you cannot know as well as I.

I feel all the gratitude this letter would express, giving it the most flattering construction.

The word *you* I use in the plural, intending it for McPherson also. I should write to him, and will some day; but, starting in the morning, I do not know that I will find time just now.

Your friend,

U. S. GRANT, Major-General."

Of his wisdom in selecting and trusting assistants and subordinates, the list of their names is a very sufficient evidence. The proved possession of this one faculty goes very far to prove that its possessor is competent to govern; and when a strong will and stainless public and private morals are added, the presumption grows very much stronger.

A gigantic power of minding his own business and holding his tongue is even a greater wonder in General Grant than his being honest and just. An instance of his successful resistance to the most violent pumping of him for a speech, has been given; and other such brilliant "flashes of silence," as Sydney Smith would have called them, illuminate his whole career during and since the war. He has been recently subjected to a very similar and more vexatious series of similar endeavors by the politicians who have been buzzing about him as he has become more and more plainly needed as next President. These noxious creatures have tried every conceivable trick to make him say something to show him a member of their party—for mere patriotism and uprightness will not serve these bigoted sectarians.

Thus far the silent soldier has defied them all. In January, 1864, somebody said something to him about the Presidency. He put the subject by, saying, "Let us first settle the war, and it will be time enough then to talk upon that subject." A little while afterwards some one referred to a certain resolute effort to make him talked of as a candidate, and he then laid down his famous Side-walk Platform: "When this war is over," said he, "I intend to run for mayor of Galena, and if elected I intend to have the sidewalk fixed up between my house and the depot." Properly understood, this is a very quiet but very sarcastic valuation of office-seeking.

Not long ago, Senator Wade complained to a newspaper reporter who immediately printed the story, that he "had often tried to find out whether Grant was for Congress or Johnson, or what the devil he was for, but never could get anything out of him, for as quick as he'd talk politics Grant would talk horse, and he could talk horse by the hour." This was a horrible irritation to the old politician, who could not be content to judge the man by his acts. This was a great error. One would imagine that of all men a veteran politician would have been first to recognize the utter emptiness of words and professions. If Gen. Grant's views are not consistent with the unbroken record of his whole life of action, he is the most gigantic hypocrite the world ever saw, and in that event it is certainly useless to try to make him expose himself now. If his views are in harmony with his acts, it is assuredly useless to state them, and as a respectable citizen and a man of dignified self-respect, he may justly be offended at such superfluous attempts to coax him to make affidavits to his own character.

A Texas political editor, in November, 1867, while Gen. Grant was acting Secretary of War, pushed his way into the General's private office, and "had an interview" with him. He went right to work with his feelers, as is the method of this species of insect, and told Grant that "the people of his section wanted the General for President." Grant turned the subject. The editor, being one of that sort of "gentlemen" who see no connection between politics and politeness, turned the subject promptly back again, saying, "General, we want to run you for President, and I want to know what I can say when I return home." Grant answered with peremptory decision, "Say nothing, sir; I want nothing said."

No other but a man of his peculiar character and power could have borne the ordeal of forming a part of the President's suite in his late unpopular progress through the Northern States. The discretion, delicacy and wisdom with which he sustained himself, show a character capable of the most skillful adaptations. We are indebted to his wise presence and temperate advice in averting the threatened danger of civil war in Maryland: for, like all wise and great Generals, Grant is duly impressed with the horrors of war, and will be always for every possible means of averting such an evil.

In all these respects Grant has shown a wise statesmanship, which points him out to the country as the fittest one to replace to it what was lost in the sudden death of Lincoln. Should an appeal be made to the people, we think there is no name that would meet a more overwhelming and enthusiastic response.

CHAPTER III.

WILLIAM LLOYD GARRISON.

Mr. Garrison's Birth and Parents—His Mother—Her Conversion—His Boyhood—Apprenticed to a Printer—First Anti-Slavery Address—Advice to Dr. Beecher—Benjamin Lundy—Garrison goes to Baltimore—First Battle with Slavery—In Jail—First number of the Liberator—Threats and Rage from the South—The American Anti-Slavery Society—First Visit to England—The Era of Mob Violence—The Respectable Boston Mob—Mr. Garrison's account—Again in Jail—The Massachusetts Legislature Uncivil to the Abolitionists—Logical Vigor of the Slaveholders—Garrison's Disunionism—Denounces the Church—Liberality of the Liberator—The Southerners' own Testimony—Mr. Garrison's Bland Manners—His Steady Nerves—His use of Language—Things by their Right Names—Abolitionist "Hard Language;" Garrison's Argument on it—Protest for Woman's Rights—The triumph of his Cause—"The Liberator" Discontinued—Second Visit to England—Letter to Mrs. Stowe.

We have written the name of a man who has had a more marked influence on our late national history than any other person who could be mentioned. No man has been more positively active in bringing on that great moral and political agitation whose issues have been in those recent scenes and events which no American can ever forget.

When we remember that it was begun by one man, singlehanded, alone, unfriended, despised and poor, we must feel in advance that such a man came of no common stock, and possessed no common elements of character. We are interested to inquire after the parentage and the early forming causes which have produced such results. In Mr. Garrison's case he frankly ascribes all that he is, or has ever been or done, to the training, example and influence of a mother whose

Wm. Lloyd Garrison.

early history and life-long character were of uncommon interest.

She was born of English stock, in the province of New Brunswick, and grew up in that lethargic state of society which has received not an impulse or a new idea since the time of Queen Anne. Her parents attended the Established Church, drank the king's health on all proper occasions, and observed the gradual growing up of a beautiful and spirited daughter with tranquil satisfaction.

At the age of eighteen this young girl, with a party of gay companions, went from curiosity to attend the religious services of some itinerating Baptists, who were startling the dead echoes of that region by a style of preaching, praying and exhorting, such as never had been heard there before. They were commonly called Ranters, and the young people promised themselves no small amusement from the spectacle of their extravagances.

But the beautiful and gay girl carried unknown and dormant in her own nature, the elements of an earnest and lofty religious character, which no touch of the droning services of a dead church had ever yet stirred to consciousness—and the wild singing, the fervent exhortations, the vivid and real emotions which were exhibited in this meeting, fired the electric train and roused the fervor of her own nature. Life, death, eternity, all became vivid and real to her, and the command to come out from a vain world and be separate; to confess Christ openly before men, seemed to her to have a living and present power.

It is very commonly the case that minds for the first time awakened to the real power of religion, feel that the only true faith is to be found under the forms and ideas which have so moved them, and that to confess Christ means a visible union with any particular body of Christians who have made real to them the Christian idea. Such was the call felt by this young girl to join herself with this despised body of Christians.

Her parents were greatly shocked and annoyed when they found that instead of ridiculing the Ranters, she was going again and again to their services, with an undissembled earnestness: and when finally she announced to them her purpose to unite herself to them in the public ordinance of baptism, their indignation knew no bounds, and they threatened her that if she did she should never enter their doors again, or be to them more than a stranger.

Then was the crisis in which the woman stood between two worlds—two kinds of life—on one side, the most earnest and whole-hearted excitement of the higher moral feelings, on the other side, the material good things of this world.

The mother of Lloyd Garrison hesitated not a moment between the convictions of her conscience and a worldly good. Like the primitive Christians, she went down into the waters of baptism feeling that she was leaving father, mother, and home, and casting herself on God alone.

Her parents, with true John Bull obstinacy, made good their word, and shut their doors upon her; but an uncle, struck perhaps with her courage and constancy, opened to her an asylum where she remained till her marriage. In later years her parents became reconciled to her.

The religious life thus begun was carried on with a marked and triumphant fullness. She was a woman of enthusiastic convictions, of strong mind, and of great natural eloquence, and during the infancy and childhood of William Lloyd he was often with her in the prayer-meetings, which were vivified by the electric eloquence of her prayers and exhortations—for the Baptist as well as Methodist denominations, allowed to women as well as men, a Christian equality in the use of the gifts of instruction.

The father of Garrison, a man possessed of some genius and many fascinating and interesting traits, was one of the victims of intemperance in those days when so many families were saddened by its blight; and at quite an early age Mrs. Garrison was left with a family of helpless little ones, with no other heritage but her faith in God, and her own undaunted and courageous spirit. She was obliged to put her boys out at a very tender age, to struggle for themselves, while she followed the laborious profession of a sick nurse.

William Lloyd, her second son, was by temperament fitted to be impressed by a woman like his mother. He had listened to the burning recital of her experience, and his heart, even in early infancy, learned to thrill in sympathy with the solemn grandeur of religious devotion and absolute self-sacrifice. All his mother's religious ideas became his own; and even as a boy he was a strict and well versed Baptist, having at his tongue's end every argument which supported the peculiar faith which his mother's enthusiasm had taught him to regard as the only true one.

The necessities of life, however, early separated him from her society. When only nine years of age he was placed in the shop of a shoe-maker to learn the trade, but the confinement and employment were unfavorable to his health and uncongenial to his feelings. He was longing for educational advantages, and bent on a career in the world of ideas.

He was taken from this situation and sent to school at Newburyport, paying for his board and schooling by sawing wood, doing errands, and performing other labors out of school hours.

After some unsuccessful experiments at different situations, he found at last a congenial sphere in being apprenticed as a printer to Ephraim W. Allen, editor of the Newburyport *Gazette.*

His bent had always been for letters, and he engaged in this occupation with enthusiasm, and that minute and careful faithfulness and accuracy in regard to the smallest minutiæ which formed a very marked trait in his character. In all that relates to the expression of ideas by the written or printed signs of language, Garrison had a natural aptitude, and attained to a peculiar perfection.

His handwriting was, and is, even at this time of life, as perfect in point of legibility, neatness, and exact finish, as if he had been by profession a writing-master.

Even in the days when the *Liberator* was the most despised and rejected of all papers, the very lowest in the scale of genteel appreciation, its clear and elegant typography, and the grace and completeness of its mechanical disposition, won for it admiration. He understood to a nicety that art which solicits the eye of a reader, and makes a printed sheet look attractive.

It was not long before his fervid mind began to reach beyond the mechanical setting of his types, to the intellectual and moral purposes to be accomplished through them.

Garrison was one of the ordained priests of nature, one of the order of natural prophets who feel themselves to have a message to society, which they must and will deliver.

He began sending anonymous articles to the paper on which he was employed, which were well received, and which, consequently, he had more than once the pleasure of setting up in type.

Encouraged by their favorable reception, he gradually began to offer articles to other journals. A series of articles for the Salem *Gazette*, under the signature "Aristides," attracted particular attention, and were commended by Robert Walsh in the Philadelphia National *Gazette*, who attributed them to Timothy Pickering; a compliment of no small significance to a young mechanic.

In 1824, his employer, Mr. Allen, was obliged for a long time to be absent from the charge of his paper, when Mr. Garrison acted as editor of the Newburyport *Herald*, of which he had been previously printer.

In 1826 he became proprietor and editor of a paper called the *Free Press*, in his native town. He toiled at it with unceasing industry, and that patient cheerfulness of enthusiasm which made every labor light.

He printed his own editorials, *without previously writing them*, a fact which more than anything else shows how completely he had mastered the mechanical part of his profession. But with all this industry and talent, the work of keeping up a newspaper of so high a moral tone as that to which he was always aspiring, was simply beyond the ability of a poor man, and he was obliged to relinquish it. He went to Boston and engaged as a journeyman printer for a time, till in 1827 he became the editor of the *National Philanthropist*, the first journal that advocated total abstinence, and in 1828 he joined a friend at Bennington, Vt., in a journal devoted to peace, temperance, and anti-slavery.

On the 4th of July, 1829, he delivered an address in Park Street church, Boston, on the subject of slavery. At that time the subject had taken a deep and absorbing hold upon his mind. He then regarded the American Colonization Society's as the most practical and feasible issue in the case—an opinion which he afterwards most fully retracted. At this time he visited the leading orthodox ministers and editors in and about Boston. Being himself a child of the church, he desired to stir up in behalf of the slave that efficiency of church activity that was effecting so much in the cause of temperance. Burning with zeal, he sought the then active leader of the orthodox party, and begged him to become leader in the movement, and command the forces in a general anti-slavery crusade.

Dr. Beecher received him favorably, listened to him courteously, wished him success, but said in regard to himself he had so "many irons in the fire" that he could not think of putting in another. "Then," said Garrison, "*you had better let all others go, and attend to this one alone.*" The results of time have shown that the young printer saw further than the sages of his day.

It is worth remembering by those who criticized Garrison's generalship in leading the anti-slavery cause, that in the outset he was not in the least ambitious of being a general, and would willingly have become *aide-de-camp* to the ruling forces of the religious world. That the campaign was carried on out of the church of New England, and not in and by it, was because the church and the religious world at that hour were absorbed in old issues—old activities and schemes of benevolence—and had not grace given them to see that the great critical national question of the day had thus been passed out of their hands.

The articles in Garrison's paper, however, attracted the attention of a little obscure old man, a Quaker, who was laboring in the city of Baltimore, for the cause of the suffering slaves, with a devotion and self-sacrifice worthy of the primitive Christians.

Benjamin Lundy, a quiet, persistent, drab-clothed, meek old man, one of those valiant little mice who nibble undismayed on the nets which enchain the strongest lions, was keeping up, in the city of Baltimore, an anti-slavery paper which was read only by a few people who thought just as he did, and which was tolerated in southern society only because everybody was good-naturedly sure that it was no sort of matter what it said.

Benjamin, however, took his staff in hand, and journeyed on foot up to Bennington, Vt., to see the man who wrote as if he cared for the slave. The strict Baptist and the meek Quaker met on the common ground of the cross of Christ. Both were agreed in one thing; that here was Jesus Christ, in the person of a persecuted race, hungry, thirsty, sick and in prison, with none to visit and relieve; and the only question was, would they arise and go to His help?

So Mr. Garrison went down to the city of Baltimore, to join his forces with Benjamin Lundy. "But," as he humorously observed, "I wasn't much help to him, for he had been all for gradual emancipation, and as soon as I began to look into the matter, I became convinced that immediate abolition was the doctrine to be preached, and I scattered his subscribers like pigeons."

Good little Benjamin took the ruinous zeal of his new partner with the tolerance which his sect extends to every brother who "follows his light;" but a final assault of Garrison on one of the most villainous aspects of slavery, quite upset the enterprise, and landed him in prison. The story is in this wise: A certain ship, the Francis Todd, from Newburyport, came to Baltimore and took in a load of slaves for the New Orleans market. All the harrowing cruelties and separations which attend the rending asunder of families, and the sale of slaves, were enacted under the eyes of the youthful philanthropist, and in a burning article he denounced the inter-state slave trade as piracy, and piracy of an aggravated and cruel kind, inasmuch as those born and educated in civilized and Christianized society, have more sensibility to feel the evils thus inflicted, than imbruted savages. He denounced the owners of the ship, and all the parties in no measured terms, and expressed his determination to "cover with thick infamy all who were engaged in the transaction." Then, to be sure, the sleeping tiger was roused, for there was a vigor and power in the young editor's eloquence that quite dissipated the good-natured contempt which had hitherto hung round the paper. He was indicted for libel, found guilty, of course, condemned, imprisoned in the cell of a man who had been hanged for murder. His mother at this time was not living, but her heroic, undaunted spirit still survived in her son, who took the baptism of persecution and obloquy not merely with patience, but with the joy which strong spirits feel in endurance. He wrote sonnets on the walls of his prison, and by his cheerful and engaging manners made friends of his jailor and family, who did everything to render his situation as comfortable as possible. Some considerable effort was made for his release, and much interest was excited in various quarters for him

He was finally liberated by Arthur Tappan, who paid the exorbitant fine for want of which he was imprisoned. He went out of jail, as people generally do who are imprisoned for conscience's sake, more devoted than ever to the cause for which he suffered. The river of his life, which hitherto had had many branches, all flowing in the direction of general benevolence, now narrowed and concentrated itself into one intense volume, to beat day and night against the prison walls of slavery, till its foundations should be washed away, and it should tumble to dust.

He issued a prospectus of an anti-slavery journal at Washington, and lectured through the northern cities, and was surprised to find the many and vital cords by which the Northern States were held from the expression of the natural feelings of humanity on a subject whose claims were so obvious. In Boston he in vain tried to get the use of a hall to lecture in; but a mob was threatened, and of all the public edifices in the city, not one could be found whose owner would risk it until a club of professed infidels came forward, and offered their hall as a tribute to free speech.

On Jan. 1, 1831, Mr. Garrison issued the first number of the *Liberator.* He had no money. The rank, respectability and religion of Boston alike disowned him. At first, he and his partner, Isaac Knapp, were too poor even to hire an office of their own, but the foreman in the office of the *Christian Examiner* generously employed them as journeymen, taking their labor as compensation for the use of his type. Mr. Garrison, after working as journeyman printer all day, spent the greater part of the night in writing and printing his paper; and under such auspices the first number came out.

Nothing more remarkable in human literature has ever appeared than those few memorable paragraphs in which this obscure, unfriended young mechanic thus issued his declaration of war against an evil embodied in the Constitution and protected by the laws of one of the most powerful nations of the earth. David meeting Goliath with a sling and stone was nothing to it. The words have a prophetic assurance that sounds solemn in the remembrance of recent events. He speaks as one having authority:

"During my recent tour for the purpose of exciting the minds of the people by a series of discourses on the subject of slavery, every place that I visited gave fresh evidence of the fact that a greater revolution in public sentiment was to be effected in the free States—and particularly in New England—than at the South. I found contempt more bitter, opposition more active, detraction more relentless, prejudice more stubborn, and apathy more frozen than among slaveholders themselves. Of course there were individual exceptions to the contrary. This state of things afflicted, but did not dishearten me. I determined, at every hazard, to lift up the standard of emancipation in the eyes of the nation, within sight of Bunker Hill, and in the birth-place of liberty. That standard is now unfurled; and long may it float, unhurt by the spoliations of time or the missiles of a desperate foe; yea, till every chain be broken, and every bondman set free! Let Southern oppressors tremble; let their secret abettors tremble; let all the enemies of the persecuted black tremble. Assenting to the self-evident truths maintained in the American Declaration of Independence, 'that all men are created equal, and endowed by their Creator with certain inalienable rights, among which are life, liberty, and the pursuit of happiness,' I shall strenuously contend for the immediate enfranchisement of our slave population.

* * * * * *

"I am aware that many object to the severity of my language; but is there not cause for severity? I will be as harsh as truth, and as uncompromising as justice. On this subject I do not wish to think, or speak, or write with moderation. No! No! Tell a man whose house is on fire to give a moderate alarm; tell him to moderately rescue his wife from the hands of the ravisher; tell the mother to gradually extricate her babe from the fire into which it has fallen; but urge me not to use moderation in a cause like the present! I am in earnest. I will not equivocate—I will not excuse—I will not retreat a single inch. AND I WILL BE HEARD. The apathy of the people is enough to make every statue leap from its pedestal, and to hasten the resurrection of the dead.

It is pretended that I am retarding the cause of emancipation by the coarseness of my invective, and the precipitancy of my measures. The charge is not true. On this question, my influence, humble as it is, is felt at this moment to a considerable extent; and it shall be felt in coming years—not perniciously, but beneficially—not as a curse, but as a blessing; and POSTERITY WILL BEAR TESTIMONY THAT I WAS RIGHT. I desire to thank God that He enables me to disregard 'the fear of man which bringeth a snare,' and to speak truth in its simplicity and power; and I here close with this dedication:

* * * * * *

"Oppression! I have seen thee, face to face,
And met thy cruel eye and cloudy brow;
But thy soul-withering glance I fear not now—
For dread to prouder feelings doth give place,
Of deep abhorrence! Scorning the disgrace

Of slavish knees that at thy footstool bow,
I also kneel—but with far other vow
Do hail thee and thy herd of hirelings base;
I swear, while life-blood warms my throbbing veins,
Still to oppose and thwart, with heart and hand,
Thy brutalizing sway—till Afric's chains
Are burst, and Freedom rules the rescued land,
Trampling Opression and his iron rod;
Such is the vow I take—so help me God!"

Just thirty-five years after, on the first of January, 1866, Garrison had the happiness of announcing that the glorious work to which he had devoted himself was finally finished; and with humble ascriptions of all the praise and glory to God, he proclaimed the cessation of the *Liberator*. His own son had been a leader in that conquering army which entered Charleston amid the shouts of liberated slaves, and the fetters and hand-cuffs of the slave-mart were sent as peaceful trophies to the *Liberator* office in Boston. Never was it given to any mortal in one generation to witness a more perfect triumph of a moral enterprise!

But before this triumph came were years of sharp conflict. Tones so ringing and so resolute, coming from the poorest den in Boston, could not but find listeners! The vital instincts of all forms of oppression are surprisingly acute, and prompt to discriminate afar what is really a true and what a false alarm. A storm of agitation began, which swelled, and eddied, and howled, and shook, and convulsed the nation from year to year, till the end came.

The first number of the *Liberator* brought fifty dollars from James Forten, a colored man of Philadelphia, and the names of twenty-five subscribers; and before long an obscure room was rented as an office, where Garrison and his partner made their bed on the floor, boarded themselves, and printed their paper.

A Southern magistrate, trembling for the institutions of his country, wrote a somewhat dictatorial appeal to the mayor of Boston, Harrison Gray Otis, to suppress that paper. Mr. Otis wrote in reply, that having ferreted out the paper and the editor, he found that his office was an obscure hole, his only visible auxiliary a negro boy, his supporters a few insignificant persons of all colors—from which he argued that there was no occasion for alarm, even though the obscure paper should prove irrepressible. Very differently, however, thought the South. Every mail brought to Garrison threats of assassination, and letters whose mingled profanity and obscenity can only be described as John Bunyan describes the discourse of Apollyon, "He spake as a dragon." The Governors of one or two States set a price upon his head. The Governor of Georgia, in terms somewhat more decent, offered five thousand dollars to any one who should arrest and bring to trial under the laws of that State, the editor or publisher of the *Liberator*. Many of Mr. Garrison's friends, deeming his life in danger, besought him to wear arms. He was, however, from religious conviction, a non-resistant of evil, interpreting with literal strictness the Saviour's directions on that subject; and so committed his life simply to the good providence of God.

On January 1, 1832, he secured the co-operation of eleven others, who, with himself, organized the American Anti-Slavery Society upon the principle of immediate emancipation. Affiliated associations sprang up all over the country—books, tracts, lectures, all the machinery of moral agitation, began active movement. He went to England as agent for the Emancipation Society, to hold counsel with the men who had pioneered the same work successfully in England. He was warmly received by Wilberforce, Brougham, Clarkson, and their associates, and succeeded in opening their eyes to the entire inefficiency of the Colonization Society as a substitute for the great duty of immediate emancipation, so that Wilberforce, with eleven of his coadjutors, issued a protest against it, not as in itself considered, but as it had been made a shield to the consciences of those who deferred their immediate duty to the slave on the ground of this distant and precarious remedy.

While in England this time, Mr. Garrison was invited to Stafford House, and treated with marked attention by the Duchess of Sutherland, then in the zenith of that magnificent beauty which, in union with a generous nature and winning manners, made her one of the most distinguished leaders among the nobility of the times. With a heart to feel every grand and heroic impulse, she had entered with enthusiasm into the anti-slavery movement of her own country, and was prepared to welcome the obscure, unknown apostle of the same faith from American shores. At her request, Garrison sat for his portrait to one of the most distinguished artists of the time, and the copy was retained among the memorabilia of Stafford House. Garrison humorously remarked that many had desired to have his head before now, but the solicitation had never come in so flattering a form. The noble woman has lived to enjoy the triumph of that cause in which her large heart gave her that right of personal possession which belongs to the very highest natures.

On his return from England he assisted in organizing the American Anti-Slavery Society in Philadelphia, the declaration of whose principles was prepared by him. From this time the anti-slavery agitation was intensified, and the era of mob violence swept over the country. The holding of an anti-slavery society in any place was the appointed signal for scenes of riotous violence. In Philadelphia, Pennsylvania Hall was burned, the negroes abused and maltreated. In Cincinnati, Birney's printing-press and types were thrown into the Ohio, and the negroes for days were hunted like beasts. In Alton, Lovejoy was shot while defending his printing-press, and Boston, notwithstanding the sepulchres of the fathers, and the shadow of Bunker Hill spire, had her hour of the powers of darkness. Leading presses abused the abolitionists in terms which aroused every vindictive passion of the mob, and in October, 1835, a meeting of the *Female* Anti-Slavery Society of Boston was riotously broken up by a collection of persons, described in the journals of the day as "gentlemen of property and standing."

The heroines of that memorable day and time, were ladies from the very first Massachusetts families; sprung from the old heroic stock of her historic fame. For vigor of mind, for education, for beauty, accomplishments and genius, some of them might be cited who would scarce find superiors in any land. Their meeting was in every way feminine and proper, and in strict accordance with the spirit and customs of New England, which recognize female organizations for various benevolent purposes, as one of the most approved means for carrying on society.

There was no more reason why a female Anti-Slavery Society should not meet quietly, transact its own business and listen to speeches of its own chosen orators, than the Female Foreign Missionary Society or the Female Home Missionary Society, or the Female Temperance Union.

But certain newspapers of Boston called attention to the fact that this meeting was so to be held, in articles written in that well known style which stirs up and invites that very mobocratic spirit which it pretends to deprecate.

These papers proceeded to say that those ladies were about to hold a dangerous kind of meeting, which would be sure to end in a mob, that they were about to be addressed by George Thompson, who was declared to be nothing more nor less than a British agitator, sent over to make dissension and trouble in America, and kept here for that purpose by British funds.

It was now stated in the public prints that several store keepers in the immediate vicinity of the Hall, had petitioned the Mayor to suppress the meeting, as in case of a riot in the neighborhood their property might be in danger. A placard was posted and circulated through the city to the following purport, that

'The infamous foreign scoundrel, Thompson, would hold forth in Anti-Slavery Hall in the afternoon, and that the present was a fair opportunity for the friends of the Union 'to snake him out;' that a purse of $100 has been subscribed by a number of patriotic citizens to reward the individual who would lay violent hands on him, so that he might be brought to the tar kettle before dark."

In consequence, the Mayor sent a deputy to Mr. Garrison to know if Mr. Thompson did intend to address the meeting, for if he did not he wished to apprise the people of it in order to tranquilize the excitement, and if he did, it would be necessary to double the constabulary forces.

Mr. Garrison sent him word that Mr. Thompson was out of town, and would not be present at the meeting. The remainder of this scene is best given in Mr. Garrison's own words:

"As the meeting was to commence at 3 o'clock, P. M., I went to the hall about twenty minutes before that time. Perhaps a hundred individuals had already gathered around the street door and opposite to the building, and their number was rapidly augmenting. On ascending into the hall, I found about fifteen or twenty ladies assembled, sitting with serene countenances, and a crowd of noisy intruders (mostly young men) gazing upon them, through whom I urged my way with considerable difficulty. 'That's Garrison,' was the exclamation of some of their number, as I quietly took my seat. Perceiving that they had no intention of retiring, I went to them and calmly said—'Gentlemen, perhaps you are not aware that this is a meeting of the Boston *Female* Anti-Slavery Society, called and intended exclusively for *ladies*, and those only who have been invited to address them. Understanding this fact, you will not be so rude or indecorous as to thrust your presence upon this meeting. If, *gentlemen*,' I pleasantly continued, 'any of you are *ladies*—in disguise—why, only apprise me of the fact, give me your names, and I will introduce you to the rest of your sex, and you can take seats among them accordingly.' I then sat down, and, for a few moments, their conduct was more orderly. However, the stair-way and upper door of the hall were soon densely filled with a brazen-faced crew, whose behavior grew more and more indecent and outrageous. Perceiving that it would be impracticable for me, or any other person, to address the ladies; and believing, as I was the only male abolitionist in the hall, that my presence would serve as a pretext for the mob to annoy the meeting, I held a short colloquy with the excellent President of the Society, telling her that I would withdraw, unless she particularly desired me to stay. It was her earnest wish that I would retire, as well for my own safety as for the peace of the meeting. She assured me that the Society would resolutely but calmly proceed to the transaction of its business, and leave the issue with God. I left the hall accordingly, and would have left the building, if the stair-case had not been crowded to excess. This being impracticable, I retired into the Anti-Slavery Office, (which is separated from the hall by a board partition,) accompanied by my friend, Mr. Charles C. Burleigh. It was deemed prudent to lock the door, to prevent the mob from rushing in and destroying our publications.

In the mean time, the crowd in the street had augmented from a hundred to thousands. The cry was for 'Thompson! Thompson!'—but the Mayor had now arrived, and, addressing the rioters, he assured them that Mr. Thompson was not in the city, and besought them to disperse. As well might he have attempted to propitiate a troop of ravenous wolves. None went away—but the tumult continued momentarily to increase. It was apparent, therefore, that the hostility of the throng was not concentrated upon Mr. Thompson but that it was as deadly against the Society and the Anti-Slavery cause. The fact is worthy of special note—for it incontestably proves that the object of these 'respectable and influential' rioters was to put down the cause of Emancipation, and that the prejudice against Mr. Thompson was only a mere pretext.

Notwithstanding the presence and frantic behavior of rioters in the hall, the meeting of the Society was regularly called to order by the President. She read a select and exceedingly appropriate portion of scripture, and offered a fervent prayer to God for direction and succour and the forgiveness of enemies and rioters. It was an awful, sublime and soul-thrilling scene * * * The clear, untremulous tone of that Christian heroine in prayer, occasionally awed the ruffians into silence, and was heard distinctly even in the midst of their hisses, yells and curses—for they could not long silently endure the agony of conviction, and their conduct became furious. They now attempted to break down the partition, and partially succeeded; but that little band of women still maintained their ground unshrinkingly, and endeavored to transact their business.

An assault was now made upon the door of the office, the lower panel of which was instantly dashed to pieces. Stooping down, and glaring upon me as I sat at the desk, writing an account of the riot to a distant friend, the ruffians cried out—'There he is! That's Garrison! Out with the scoundrel!' &c., &c. Turning to Mr. Burleigh I said—'You may as well open the door, and let them come in and do their worst.' But he, with great presence of mind, went out, locked the door, put the key into his pocket, and by his admirable firmness succeeded in keeping the office safe.

Two or three constables having cleared the hall and staircase of the mob, the Mayor came in and *ordered* the ladies to desist, assuring them that he could not any longer guarantee protection, if they did not take immediate advantage of the opportunity to retire from the building. Accordingly, they adjourned, to meet at the house of one of their number, for the completion of their business; but as they passed through the crowd, they were greeted with 'taunts, hisses, and cheers of mobocratic triumph, from gentlemen of property and standing from all parts of the city.' Even their absence did not diminish the throng. Thompson was not there—the ladies were not there—but '*Garrison* is there!' was the cry. 'Garrison! Garrison! We must have Garrison! Out with him! Lynch him!' These and numberless other exclamations arose from the multitude. For a moment their attention was diverted from me to the Anti-Slavery sign, and they vociferously demanded its possession.

It is painful to state, that the Mayor promptly complied with their demand! So agitated and alarmed had he become that in very weakness of spirit he ordered the sign to be hurled to the ground, and it was instantly broken in a thousand fragments by the infuriated populace. The sign being demolished the cry for Garrison was resumed more loudly than ever. It was now apparent that the multitude would not disperse till I left the building, and as egress out of the front door was impossible, the Mayor and some of his assistants as well as some of my friends earnestly besought me to escape in the rear of the building. At this moment an abolition brother, whose mind had been previously settled on the peace question, in his anguish and alarm for my safety, and in the view of the helplessness of the civil authority, said, 'I must henceforth repudiate the principle of non-resistance. When the civil arm is powerless, my own rights are trodden in the dust, and the lives of my friends are put in imminent peril by ruffians, I will hereafter stand ready to defend myself and them at all hazards.' Putting my hand upon his shoulder, I said, 'Hold, my dear brother! You know not what spirit you are of. Of what value or utility are the principles of peace and forgivness, if we may repudiate them in the hour of peril and suffering? Do you wish to become like one of those violent and blood-thirsty men who are seeking my life? Shall we give blow for blow, and array sword against sword? God forbid! I will perish sooner than raise my hand against any man, even in self-defence, and let none of my friends resort to violence for my protection. If my life be taken, the cause of emancipation will not suffer. God reigns—his throne is undisturbed by this storm—he will make the wrath of man to praise him, and the remainder he will restrain—his omnipotence will at length be victorious.'

Preceded by my faithful and beloved friend Mr. J—— R—— C——, I dropped from a back window on to a shed, and narrowly escaped falling headlong to the ground. We entered into a carpenter's shop, through which we attempted to get into Wilson's Lane, but found our retreat cut off by the mob. They raised a shout as soon as we came in sight, but the proprietor promptly closed the door of his shop, kept them at bay for a time, and thus kindly afforded me an opportunity to find some other passage. I told Mr. C. it would be futile to attempt to escape—I would go out to the mob, and let them deal with me as they might elect; but he thought it was my duty to avoid them as long as possible. We then went up stairs, and finding a vacancy in one corner of the room, I got into it, and he and a young lad piled up some boards in front of me, to shield me from observation. In a few minutes several ruffians broke into the chamber, who seized Mr. C. in a rough manner, and led him out to the view of the mob, saying, 'This is not Garrison, but Garrison's and Thompson's friend, and he says he knows where Garrison is, but won't tell.' Then a shout of exultation was raised by the mob, and what became of him I do not know; though, as I was immediately discovered, I presume he escaped without material injury. On seeing me, three or four of the rioters, uttering a yell, furiously dragged me to the window, with the intention of hurling me from that height to the ground; but one of them relented, and said, 'Don't let us kill him outright.' So they drew me back, and coiled a rope about my body—probably to drag me through the streets. I bowed to the mob, and requesting them to wait patiently until I could descend, went down upon a ladder that was raised for that purpose. I fortunately extricated myself from the rope, and was seized by two or three of the leading rioters, powerful and athletic men, by whom I was dragged along bareheaded, (for my hat had been knocked off and cut in pieces on the spot,) a friendly voice in the crowd shouting, 'He shan't be hurt! He is an American!' This seemed to excite sympathy in the breasts of some others, and they reiterated the same cry. Blows, however, were aimed at my head by such as were of a cruel spirit, and at last they succeeded in tearing nearly all my clothes from my body. Thus was I dragged through Wilson's Lane into State street, in the rear of the City Hall, over the ground that was stained with the blood of the first martyrs in the cause of LIBERTY and INDEPENDENCE, in the memorable massacre of 1770; and upon which was proudly unfurled, only a few years since, with joyous acclamations, the beautiful banner presented to the gallant Poles by the young men of Boston! What a scandalous and revolting contrast! My offence was in pleading for LIBERTY—liberty for my enslaved countrymen, colored though they be—liberty of speech and of the press for ALL! And upon that 'consecrated spot' I was made an object of derision and scorn.

They proceeded with me in the direction of the City Hall, the cry being raised, 'To the Common!'

whether to give me a coat of tar and feathers, or to throw me into the pond, was problematical. As we approached the south door, the Mayor attempted to protect me by his presence; but as he was unassisted by any show of authority or force, he was quickly thrust aside; and now came a tremendous rush on the part of the mob to prevent my entering the hall. For a time the conflict was desperate; but at length a rescue was effected by a posse that came to the help of the Mayor, by whom I was carried up to the Mayor's room.

In view of my denuded condition, one individual in the Post office below stairs kindly lent me a pair of pantaloons, another a coat, a third a stock, a fourth a cap, &c. After a brief consultation, the mob densely surrounding and threatening the City Hall and Post Office, the Mayor and his advisers said that my life depended on committing me to jail, ostensibly as a disturber of the peace. Accordingly a hack was got ready at the door and I was put into it, supported by Sheriff Parkman and Ebenezer Bailey, the Mayor leading the way. And now ensued a scene which baffles all description. As the ocean lashed to fury by a storm, seeks to whelm a bark beneath the waves, so did the mob, enraged at their disappointment, rush like a whirlwind upon the frail vehicle in which I sat, and endeavored to drag me out of it. Escape seemed a physical impossibility. They clung to the wheels—dashed open the doors—seized hold of the horses—and tried to upset the carriage. They were, however, vigorously repulsed by the police, a constable sprang in by my side, the doors were closed, and the driver, using his whip on the bodies of the horses and the heads of the rioters, happily made an opening through the crowd, and drove with all speed to Leverett street.

In a few moments I was locked up in a cell, safe from my persecutors, accompanied by two delightful associates, a good conscience and a cheerful mind. In the course of the evening several of my friends came to my grated window to sympathise and confer with me, with whom I held strengthening conversation, till the hour of retirement, when I threw myself on my prison bed, and slept tranquilly. In the morning, I inscribed upon the walls of my cell, with a pencil, the following lines:

'Wm. Lloyd Garrison was put into this cell on Wednesday afternoon, Oct. 21, 1835, to save him from the violence of a "respectable and influential" mob, who sought to destroy him for preaching the abominable and dangerous doctrine that "all men are created equal," and that all oppression is odious in the sight of God. "Hail, Columbia!" Cheers for the Autocrat of Russia, and the Sultan of Turkey!

Reader, let this inscription remain till the last slave in this despotic land be loosed from his fetters.'

'When peace within the bosom reigns,
And conscience gives th' approving voice,
Though bound the human form in chains,
Yet can the soul aloud rejoice.

'Tis true, my footsteps are confined—
I cannot range beyond this cell;
But what can circumscribe my mind?
To chain the winds attempt as well!'

'Confine me as a prisoner—but bind me not as a slave.
Punish me as a criminal—but hold me not as a chattel.
Torture me as a man—but drive me not like a beast.
Doubt my sanity—but acknowledge my immortality.'

In the course of the forenoon, after passing through the mockery of an examination, for form's sake, before Judge Whitman, I was released from prison; but, at the *earnest solicitation of the city authorities*, in order to tranquilize the public mind, I deemed it proper to leave the city for a few days, accompanied by my wife, whose situation was such as to awaken the strongest solicitude for her life."

At this distance of time it is difficult to conceive of such scenes as occurring in Boston. They are to be accounted for by two things. First, the intense keenness of the instincts of the Slave-holding power in the United States, in discriminating from afar what the results of the Anti-Slavery discussion would be, and the real power which was arising in the apparently feeble body of the Abolitionists; and second, the thousand ties of politics, trade, blood relationship, friendship and religion that interlaced the South with the North, and made the North for many years a tool of southern dictators and a mere reflection of southern sympathies. There was scarcely a thing in northern society that was not interwoven and intertwisted with southern society. Northern schools and colleges were full of southern scholars—northern teachers were all the while seeking places on southern plantations. The great political bodies had each its southern wing, every religious denomination had its southern members and southern interests. Every kind of trade and industrial calling had its southern outlet. The ship builders of Maine went to Charleston for their cargoes. Plantations were fitted out at the North, by every kind of trade. Our mercantile world was truly and in fact one firm with the South and felt any disturbance to them as virtually as the South itself.

Hence Garrison's instinctive feeling that the battle was to be fought *in the North*, where as yet there was a free press and the right of free speech.

It was not long before the South perceived that if free inquiry and free discussion were going to be allowed in Massachusetts, it would be all over with them, and like men who were brought up always to have their own way and had but to command to be obeyed, several southern states sent immediate and earnest communications to the Massachusetts Legislature, requesting the General Court to enact laws making it penal for the citizens of Massachusetts to form abolition societies or print and publish abolition sentiments.

The Governor of Massachusetts, in his message to the Legislature at this time, expressed his belief that the abolitioinsts were guilty of an offence punishable by common law.

This part of the Governor's message, together with the resolutions from the Legislatures of slave-holding states, was referred to a committee of five.

The Massachusetts Anti-Slavery Society addressed a memorial to this committee, praying to be permitted to appear before them and show that they had done nothing but what they had a perfect constitutional right to do by the laws of Massachusetts.

On the Fourth and Eighth of March, 1836, these memorable interviews took place at the state house, in the chamber of the representatives.

A committee of some of the leading abolitionists attended—Mr. I. May, Mr. E. Gray Loring, Mr. Sewell, Dr. Follen, of Harvard College, and Mr. Garrison. Dr. Channing also met with them as an expression of sympathy and to mark his sense of the vitally important nature of the transactions to the rights of personal liberty in Massachusetts.

The meeting was attended by many spectators, and the abolitionists had opportunity to defend their course and conduct.

Mr. Garrison's speech at this time is one of the most energetic and characteristic of his utterances. After alluding to the duty of all men to plead for the rights of the dumb and the oppressed, he then went on to say:

"Mr. Chairman, there is one aspect of this great question which has not yet been presented to the committee. The liberties of the people of the free States are identified with those of the slave population. If it were not so, there would be no hope, in my breast, of the peaceful deliverance of the latter class from their bondage. Our liberties are bound together by a ligament as vital as that which unites the Siamese twins. The blow which cuts them asunder, will inevitably destroy them both. Let the freedom of speech and of the press be abridged or destroyed, and the nation itself will be in bondage; let it remain untrammelled, and southern slavery must speedily come to an end." The chairman of the committee however insulted the abolitionists, refused them a fair hearing, and substantially turned them out of the Legislature, to protest at their leisure. The Legislature however did not pass the laws demanded by the South.

Miss Martineau, who visited Boston in those days, described feelingly what she justly called the martyr age in America.

The abolitionists in Boston at this time, were ostracized from genteel society. Rank and fashion cut them in the street, and crossed out their names from visiting lists. Whoever joined them must expect as a matter of course to give up what was called in Boston, good society.

Their houses were constantly threatened by anonymous letters, nor was the threat a vain one.

One of the most accomplished women of Boston, whose genius and beauty and fine manners won her a distinguished position afterwards in European society, lives to remember now, how her house was fired while she was still an invalid in her chamber with an infant daughter only three weeks old, and how she was obliged to sit by an open window to get air for herself and infant, from the smoke that filled the house after the fire had been discovered and brought under.

Now there were in the whole North, thousands of people who thought slavery a wrong, an inhumanity, and who wished with a greater or less degree of ardor that it might cease from the earth. But all these people were associated for some purpose social, moral or religious, with people at the South, who were in a state of feverish combativeness on this subject, who were accustomed to command from their cradles, impatient of contradiction, and violent in their passions; and in every way and form, and every branch of life in state and church, the demand was stringent and imperative: You shall not say that slavery is wrong—you shall not agitate that question or discuss it at all, and you shall join with us to discountenance and put down all who endeavor to agitate the public mind. If you don't *we* won't have any thing to do with you or your purposes or schemes."

This was the language which kept the whole North boiling like a pot for years. On the one hand, the force of conscience and humanity, and on the other, the passionate determined resistance of the South operating through northern men, who, though disliking slavery yet had their various purposes to carry, for which they needed the help of the South.

So even the religious societies felt that their great moral and religious work was so important that they must yield a little, in order to gain the help of southern Christians. The Tract Society struck out from English reprints every line and sentence which might be supposed to reprove slavery; the Sunday School Union followed suit. The various religious bodies, embarrassed by their southern wings, spent their time in every annual meeting in ingenious skirmishing, in which the main body sought to keep the peace between the active minority of abolitionists, and the irritated, determined, dictatorial southern brethren, whose sentiments were exactly expressed by Dr. Plummer, of Virginia:

"If abolitionists will set the world in a blaze, it is but fair that they should receive the first warming at the fire. Let them understand that they will be caught if they come among us, and they will take good heed to keep out of our way; there is not one among them that has any idea of shedding his blood for his cause."

The ministers of the slaveholding region were driven on by the unsparing, uncompromising slave-owners, and were the most high-handed defenders of the system. Northern religious bodies, in order to carry on their purposes in union with the South, were obliged to make constant concessions at which their conscience revolted. The Methodist church, in 1840, passed a law forbidding their colored members to give testimony in church trials in slave States. The debates on this question are worth looking back to now, as they give a dramatic reality to the great driving, pushing process which was then going on in favor of slavery.

A trembling brother, after voting for this astounding prohibition, which took away the last hope of even a hearing in Christ's church for the poor hunted slave—rose the day after he had helped pass it, and humbly and plaintively tried to get it taken back.

He said that the resolution "was introduced under peculiar circumstances, during considerable excitement, and he went for it as a *peace offering to the South*, without sufficiently reflecting upon the precise import of its phraseology, but after a little deliberation he was sorry! He was convinced that if the resolution remained on the journal, it would be disastrous to the whole Northern church."

Dr. A. J. Few, of Georgia, arose, and it is instructive to see how resolute men, who have made up their minds, and know exactly what they mean to do, despise timid men, who are divided between policy and conscience. Dr. Few said:

"Look at it! What do you declare to us, in taking this course! Why, simply, as much as to say, 'We cannot sustain you in the condition which you cannot avoid! We cannot sustain you in the *necessary conditions* of slaveholding; one of its *necessary conditions* being the rejection of negro testimony!' If it is not sinful to hold slaves, under all circumstances, *it is not sinful to hold them in the only condition, and under the only circumstances in which they can be held.* The rejection of negro testimony is one of the necessary circumstances under which slaveholding can exist; indeed, it is utterly impossible for it to exist without it; therefore it is not sinful to hold slaves *in the condition and under the circumstances in which they are held at the South, inasmuch as they can be held under no other circumstances.* * * * If you believe that slaveholding is necessarily sinful, come out with the abolitionists, and honestly say so. If you believe that slaveholding is necessarily sinful, you believe we are necessarily sinners; and if so, come out and honestly declare it, *and let us leave you.* * * * We want to know distinctly, precisely and honestly the position which you take. We cannot be tampered with by you any longer. We have had enough of it. We are tired of your sickly sympathies. * * * If you are not opposed to the principles which it involves, unite with us, like *honest men*, and go home, and boldly meet the consequences."

From this it appears that the Southern slaveocracy was not only a very united, determined body, but also remarkably logical as to the necessary ways and means which were essential to the support of their system, and that not only they were prepared to go the whole length themselves, but they meant to have nothing to do with any one who would not go the whole length with them.

The result of this one victory was to split the Methodist church in two. Mr. Peck was right in supposing that there was yet enough conscience in the Northern Methodists to feel the impossibility of holding a book of discipline which called slavery "the sum of all villainies," and yet keeping union with those who were making it the first object of life to uphold it. Some such crisis of conscience, always brought on by the slave-driving, dictatorial, determined and logical South, in time rent asunder all the principal denominations into a northern and southern wing. For however they might have been disposed towards the policy of non-intervention, the South never allowed them to stand long on that ground. They must not only cease to remonstrate against slavery, but help them by consenting to positive laws and measures in its defence. So great was the power of this dictatorial spirit, that when the New School Presbyterian church had broken off from the great body of southern churches, who went with the Old School, yet the one or two synods who were left among them extorted from the whole body the decree that "masters ought not to be disciplined for selling slaves without their consent, even when fellow members of the same churches with themselves."

Now this history of what went on in the church of America—for the church, meaning by it all the religious denominations, did embody as a general fact, the whole religious and moral force of the country, shows more strongly than anything else what was likely to be going on in bodies that did not profess any moral character or considerations. If this was the state to which the dictation of the southern slavepower had driven the church, what was to be hoped of the political world and the world of trade?

Mr. Garrison looked over this dark field, and saw the battle—for there *was* a battle all over the land—a battle in which the truth and the right were being steadily, daily and everywhere beaten. The church and the world seemed to be vieing with each other who could retreat fastest before their victorious masters, and every day some new right of humanity was thrown down for the pursuing army to worry and tear—just as retreating fugitives throw back a lamb or a dog to stop a pack of hungry wolves.

Garrison saw at once that the root of all this defeat and disaster was the desire of UNION with slaveholders, and forthwith he unfurled his banner and sounded his trumpet to the watchword, NO UNION WITH SLAVEHOLDERS.

Immediately the Constitution of the United States was brought up before him. Does not the constitution form a union with slaveholders? Has it not express compromises designed to protect slave property? Is not the basis of representation throughout all the southern states made on three-fifths of a slave population? Now Mr. Garrison, what do you say to that?

"What I say," said Garrison, "is, that slavery is a sin against God and man, and if the constitution of the United States does agree to defend and protect it, it is a sinful league, and it is a covenant with death, and an agreement with hell," and out came the *Liberator* with the solemn curses of the old prophets at its head, and the Garrisonian abolitionists organized themselves on the principle that they would hold no union with slaveholders in church or in state, they would belong to no religious or secular body which did not treat slavery as a sin against God, and they would lift up their testimony against every person, party or denomination in church or in state that made any concession to the slaveholding power, for the sake of accomplishing *any* purpose whatsoever.

Here we see the whole scope of subject-matter for the *Liberator*, and for all the lectures and speeches from the platforms of the Garrisonian abolition societies for years and years. For as there was scarcely a thing in society in those days that was not the joint work of the North and the South, and as the South *never* made a concession, of course there was through all the various ramifications of political, social and religious life, a continued series of concessions on the part of the North. These concessions were always, everywhere unsparingly discussed, reproved and denounced by the Garrisonians, and so there was controversy constantly and everywhere.

The ministry of New England, from the days of President Edwards, had adopted a peculiar and pungent style of preaching immediate repentance of sin. They repudiated all half efforts, insensible approaches, dream-like floatings toward right, and narrowed the question of individual responsibility down to the present moment, and urged repentance on the spot as the duty of all. Garrison had received his early education in this school, and he drove his preaching of immediate repentance for the sin of slavery, his requirements for an instant clearing of the soul from all complicity with it, with the solemnity of an old Puritan. He had the whole language of the Old Testament at his tongue's end, and a text from the old prophets ready like an arrow on a bow-string, to shoot into every loop-hole of the concessions and compromises that were constantly going on. He reproved without fear or favor, ministers, elders, Christians, statesmen, governors, authors, and denounced the whole church as contaminated by the sanction and support it gave to the accursed thing.

He was denounced in turn by the church as an infidel and an opposer of religion, but he persisted in hurling right and left the stern denunciations of the Old Testament: "When thou sawest a thief, thou *consentedst* with him—thou hast been partaker with adulterers," and he declared that the visible union of church and state with an organization which practiced systematic robbery on four millions of human beings, and made legal marriage among them an impossibility, was in the very highest sense consenting with thieves, and being made partakers with adultery.

There is not the least doubt that the course of *entire* separation from slaveholders in church and state, would have been a perfect and efficient stop to the evil, could it have been compassed. Could we once imagine a state of things in which every man and woman in the United States who admitted that slavery was an injustice, should come to the point of refusing all fellowship or connection with it, either in church or state, or in any of the traffic or intercourse of life, we should imagine a state in which there would have been immediately a majority which could have revised the constitution of the United States, and cast out the offensive clauses, as has since been done.

But measures so stringent and thorough, supposed an education of the public conscience which had not yet taken place, and the Garrisonian Abolitionists therefore were always a small minority, extremely unfashionable and every where spoken against. Small as they were, they were the indispensables of the great conflict—its very heart. Garrison and his band of coadjutors formed a *steady force* which acted night and day with unvarying consistency. While everybody else in the United States had something else to conserve, some side issues to make, some other point to carry, Garrison and his band had but one thing to say—that American slavery is a sin ; but one thing to do—to preach immediate repentance and forsaking of sin. They withdrew from every organization which could in any way be supposed to tolerate or hold communion with it, and walked alone, a small, but always active and powerful body. They represented the pure, abstract form of every principle as near as it is possible for it to be represented by human frailty. Free speech, free inquiry and freedom of conscience found perfect expression in their meetings, and the *Liberator* was the one paper in which any honest, well-meaning person might print *any* conscientious opinion, however contrary to those generally received in society. Of course it became the channel for much crude thought, for much startling and strange expression; and its circulation was confined almost entirely to the small party whose opinions it expressed. A large portion of the Liberator was every week devoted to extracts cut from southern papers, giving a vivid picture of the barbaric state of society, produced by slavery. Here, without note or comment, came the accounts clipped from different southern papers, of the assaults, frays and murders daily perpetrated by white men on each other in a land where violence was ever above law. There were, too, the advertisements of slave auctions and runaway negroes; of blood-hounds kept for human hunting; while in a weekly corner called the "Refuge of Oppression," all the violent doctrines of the most rabid slave holders found every week a faithful reproduction in their own language. For an exact picture of the image and body of the most extreme form of southern slave holding and its results on society, the *Liberator* was as perfect a moral daguerreotype as could be produced.

A solemn instance of the terrible sequence of Divine retribution has been presented to this generation which will not soon be forgotten. All this disgusting, harrowing, dreadful record of cruelty, crime and oppression which the *Liberator* went on, year after year, in vain holding up to the inspection of the North, as being perpetrated within the bounds of slaveholding society, was shrunk from as too dreadful and disgusting to be contemplated.

"We do not wish to have our feelings harrowed; we do not wish to be appalled and disgusted with records of cruelty and crime," was the almost universal voice of good society at the North, as they went steadily on, compromising with and yielding to the exactions of a barbarous oligarchy. God so ordered it in return, that the cup of trembling which had so long been drunk by the slave alone, should be put into the hands of thousands of the sons and daughters of the free North. Thousands of them were starved, tortured, insulted, hunted by dogs, separated from home and friends, and left to linger out a cruel death in life, through the barbarity of those very slaveholders, with whose sins we had connived, with whose cruelties practiced on the helpless negroes we had refused to interfere. So awful a lesson of the justice of a living God we trust will never be forgotten. If every northern man and woman had from the very first been as careful in regarding the rights of the slave, as determined to hold no fellowship with evil as Garrison, the solution of our great national question might have been a far more peaceful one.

In the days of the great conflict, Mr. Garrison was accused of being in a bad spirit, of the utterance of violent, angry and abusive language. A very mistaken idea of his personal character, in fact, went abroad in the world.

In his personal intercourse he is peculiarly bland and urbane, one of the few men capable of conducting an argument on the most interesting subject without the slightest apparent excitement of voice or manner, allowing his adversary every polite advantage and admitting all his just statements with perfect fairness. It is said that a fiery young southerner once fell into a discussion on slavery with him when he was travelling incog., on board a steamboat. Garrison quite won his heart by the fairness and courtesy with which he discussed the subject, and brought him to admissions which the frank southerner in a good humor was quite willing to make. On parting he said to him, "If that Garrison there in Boston were only like you, we should be more ready to listen to him."

A great deal of this amiability doubtless is owing to the singular steadiness and healthiness of Garrison's nervous system. In this he was one of the most peculiarly constituted men, in whom nature ever combined traits expressly for a great work. All his personal habits are those of a methodical unexcitable man, and not in the least like the hurry and enthusiasm of a fanatic. He is methodical, systematic and precise in all his arrangements, neat and careful in respect to the minutest trifle.

His handwriting is always of the finished completeness of a writing master, and in the most vehement denunciations, not a letter was ever misplaced or a comma or exclamation point, omitted. Every thing he ever wrote was perfected for the press as it left his pen. Such habits as these speak a composed and equable nervous system. In fact, Garrison's nerves never knew what it was to shiver and vibrate either with irritation or with fear. He is gifted with the most perfect imperturbable cheerfulness, which no outward discomposure seems to have any power to shake.

His politely bowing to the furious Boston mob before descending to put himself in their hands, is a very characteristic thing, and during all the tossings and tumults of the hour that followed, Garrison was probably the serenest person that ever had his clothes torn off his back for expressing his opinions.

That language in the Liberator which looked to the world as if it must have been uttered in a passion, because it was so far above the usual earnestness of expression on such subjects, was in his case the result of a deliberate system.

Garrison said that the world blinded conscience and made false issues with itself by the habitual calling of things by the wrong names; that there was no kind of vice which might not be disguised under a polite phrase. Theft might be spoken of as an ingenious transfer of property—adultery as a form of the elective affinity, and so on, but that all such phraseology had an immoral tendency.

In like manner the stealing of men and women from Africa—the systematic appropriation of all the fruits of their industry and labor—was robbery. Whoever did this was a thief.

Garrison called slaveholders, no matter of what rank in society, of what personal amiabilities and virtues, man-thieves. Whoever formed union with slaveholders, united with man-thieves, and as the partaker in law is judged as being a thief, those who united with man-thieves became themselves thieves.

Having reasoned this out logically, Garrison steadily and systematically applied these terms wherever he thought they applied. The Garrisonian tract, "The church a den of thieves," is a specimen of this kind of logic, and this unsparing use of terms. Whatever may be thought of the justice of such reasoning or the propriety of such logical application of terms, we still wish the fact to stand out clear, that these denunciations were not boiled up by heated passions, but reasoned out by logic, and that it was a part of a systematic plan to bring back the moral sense of society by a habit of calling things by discriminating names. Thus in the Liberator every agent of the United States who helped to catch and return a slave was always spoken of as a kidnapper—all defences of the fugitive slave law were familiarly denominated defences of kidnapping. Theodore Parker, in his sermons about the time of the fugitive slave law, makes very effective use of these terms, and it is not to be denied that the habit of thus constantly using language which in a word makes a moral discrimination is a very powerful influence in forming popular opinion.

People will boggle a great while about fulfilling constitutional obligation when catching a slave is put in those terms, but when it is put as "kidnapping," the question becomes far more direct and simple. The Garrisonians doubtless were philosophical in the precision of the moral nomenclature they adopted; and their success in stimulating drugged and paralyzed moral sentiment was largely owing to it.

To be sure, in the application of wholesale moral syllogism to particular individual cases, there was often something that appeared extremely hard and unjust to the individual. When an amiable northern Doctor of Divinity, who never owned a slave in his life and never expected to, found himself cited in the Liberator by the familiar designation of a man-thief, because he had been in the General Assembly, good naturedly uniting with a large body of southern slaveholders in suppressing all inquiry into their great systematic robbery, the northern Doctor was naturally indignant and so were all his friends and adherents.

To be sure it was only a skillful turning of that syllogistic crank by which New England theology demonstrated that every individual not conscious of a certain moral change of heart, was a malignant enemy of God, and had not a spark of moral excellence of any kind, no matter what sort of a man he might be, or what moral virtues he might practice.

Garrison simply reversed the crank and turned this unsparing kind of logic back on the church and clergy, who felt some of the surprise and pain of the eagle in the fable who found himself shot through by an arrow feathered from his own wing; and in both cases it may be doubted whether great moral syllogisms do not involve many instances of individual and personal injustice.

But it is best to let Garrison state his own case as he did in the Liberator:

"I am accused of using hard language. I admit the charge. I have not been able to find a soft word to describe villainy, or to identify the perpetrator of it. The man who makes a chattel of his brother—what is he? The man who keeps back the hire of his laborers by fraud—what is he? They who prohibit the circulation of the Bible—what are they? They who compel three millions of men and women to herd together, like brute beasts—what are they? They who sell mothers by the pound, and children in lots to suit purchasers—what are they? I care not what terms are applied to them, provided they do apply. If they are not thieves, if they are not tyrants, if they are not men-stealers, I should like to know what is their true character, and by what names they may be called. It is as mild an epithet to say that a thief is a thief, as it is to say that a spade is a spade.

"The anti-slavery cause is beset with many dangers; but there is one which we have special reason to apprehend. It is that this hollow cant about hard language will insensibly check the free utterance of thought and close application of truth which have characterized abolitionists from the beginning. As that cause is becoming popular, and many may be induced to espouse it from motives of policy rather than from reverence for principle, let us beware how we soften our just severity of speech, or emasculate a single epithet. The whole scope of the English language is inadequate to describe the horrors and impurities of slavery. Instead therefore, of repudiating any of its strong terms, we rather need a new and stronger dialect.

* * * * * *

"The cry of hard language has become stale in my ears. The faithful utterance of that language has, by the blessing of God, made the anti-slavery cause what it is, ample in resources, strong in numbers, victorious in conflict. * * * Soft phrases and honeyed accents were tried in vain for many a year;—they had no adaptation to the subject. 'Canst thou draw out the leviathan, SLAVERY, with a hook? or his tongue with a cord which thou lettest down? Canst thou put a hook into his nose? or bore his jaw through with a thorn? Will he make many supplications unto thee? wilt thou take him for a servant forever? Shall not one be cast down at the sight of him? Out of his nostrils goeth smoke, as out of a seething pot or caldron. His breath kindleth coals, and a flame goeth out of his mouth. His heart is as firm as a stone; yea, as hard as a piece of the nether mill-stone. When he raiseth up himself, even the mighty are afraid. He esteemeth iron as straw, and brass as rotten wood.' O, the surpassing folly of those 'wise and prudent' men, who think he may be coaxed into a willingness to be destroyed, and who regard him as the gentlest of all fish—provided he be let alone! They say it will irritate him to charge him with being a leviathan; he will cause the deep to boil like a pot. Call him a dolphin, and he will not get angry! If I should call these sage advisers by their proper names, no doubt they would be irritated too."

The era of mob violence, which swept over the country in consequence of the anti-slavery agitation, led to a discussion of the peace question, in which Garrison took an earnest part as a champion of the principles of non-resistance, and in 1838 he led the way in organizing the New England Non-Resistance Society, whose declaration of sentiments was prepared by him. The active part taken by the women of the country in these moral changes, led to a discussion of the rights of women. Mr. Garrison was at once an advocate for the principle that women should be allowed liberty to do whatever God and nature qualified them to do—to vote, to serve on committees, and to take part in discussions on equal terms with the other sex. Upon this principle there was a division in the Anti-Slavery Society in 1840; and in the World's Anti-Slavery Convention, held that year in London, Mr. Garrison, being delegate from that society, refused to take his seat because the female delegates from the United States were excluded. Probably no act of Mr. Garrison's eventful life was a more difficult and triumphant exercise of consistent principle than this.

He had come over to England for sympathy, for at home he was despised, and rejected, and hated, and Exeter Hall was filled with an applauding, tumultuous crowd, ready to make him the lion of the hour, but not ready to receive his female coadjutors.

As usual, Mr. Garrison conferred not with flesh and blood for a moment, but rose, bade farewell to the society, and leaving his protest, walked out serenely through the crowd, and thus sealed his protest in favor of the equal rights of woman.

The consideration that he thus renounced an overwhelming public sympathy, and cut himself loose from the patronage of all good society in England, could not weigh a moment with him in comparison with a principle, and the doctrine of the moral, social and political equality of woman may be said to have found in Garrison its first public champion.

The question now arises: If Garrison and his little band were indeed morally right in their position—*No union with slave-holders*, on what ground did the whole valiant anti-slavery corps proceed who did not come out from the church or the state, but saw their way clear to remain in existing organizations, and fight in and by them.

The free soil party of the political abolitionists generally were headed by men of pure and vital moral sense, who believed just as sincerely as Mr. Garrison that slavery was a wrong and an injustice. How then could they avoid the inference that they could have no union with slave-holders? The statement of this ground properly belongs to the biographical sketches of Charles Sumner and Henry Wilson, which will immediately follow this.

The Garrisonians, and Mr. Garrison at their head, had so perfect an instinct in their cause that they always could feel when a party was at heart morally sincere and in earnest. So, though they always most freely and most profusely criticised the works and ways of the political abolitionists, they were on the whole on excellent terms with them.

They had gotten up such a name for speaking just their minds of every body and thing, that their privilege of criticism came to be allowed freely, and on the whole the little band was thought by the larger one to do good political work by their more strictly and purely moral appeals to the conscience of the community. Where there had been pretty active Garrisonian labor in lecturing, came in the largest political vote.

It is but justice to say that Mr. Garrison's conduct throughout his course demonstrated that it was not a constitutional love of opposition, or a delight in fault-finding which inspired his denunciations of slavery and of the Union as the defence of slavery. For from the time of the Emancipation Proclamation, Garrison became a warm, enthusiastic Unionist. When the United States flag, cleansed of all stain of slavery, was once more erected on Fort Sumter, Garrison made the voyage down to testify by his presence at the scene his devotion and loyalty to the flag of his country.

Garrison's non-resistant principles did not allow him to take any active part in the war. But in the same manner they caused him to allow perfect and free toleration to such of his sons as desired to enter the army. The right of individual judgment in every human being was always sacred with him, and the military command which took possession of Charleston had among its officers a son of William Lloyd Garrison.

The scene in the Boston Music Hall, on the 1st of January, 1864, when the telegraphic dispatch of the Emancipation Proclamation was received by an enthusiastic concourse of citizens, and welcomed by the first literary talent of Boston, was one of those occurrences of the visible triumph of good men in their day and generation, of which the slavery conflict gives many instances.

This scene was in all respects a remarkable one, as marking the moral progress of Boston, but in order to feel its full power we must again run our eye over the events of the past few years, of which it was the outcome.

It was only thirty-four years since the Legislature of Georgia had passed an act signed by Gov. Lumpkin, offering the sum of five thousand dollars for whoever would bring into the State of Georgia the person of William Lloyd Garrison, there to answer to the laws of Georgia for the publication of the *Liberator*—an "incendiary sheet." Everybody knew that this proclamation meant a short shrift and a long rope to Garrison, but there was at that time no counter movement on the part of his own State for his protection, no official declaration on the part of the Massachusetts Legislature to certify that she considered offering rewards for the kidnapping of her citizens to be a violation of State rights. In fact, so completely was Garrison, thus threatened by the South, unprotected by law and public sentiment at the North, that five years later, when the outcry from slaveholding legislatures became stronger, a Massachusetts Governor actually recommended imposing pains and penalties on the abolitionists for the discussion of the subject, and the Legislature actually took into discussion the propriety of doing so.

Was ever thirty years productive of a greater moral change than this 1st of January, 1864, witnessed?

An assemblage of all that Boston had to show of intellect, scholarship, art, rank and fashion, all came together of one accord to one place to celebrate the triumph of those great principles for which Garrison had once been dragged with a rope ignominiously through the streets of Boston.

Now that serene head, with its benevolent calmness, rising in one of the most conspicuous and honored seats in the house, was the observed of all observers. The hisses of mob violence, the scoffs and sneers, had changed to whispered tributes all over the house,

"There he is, look!" and mothers pointed him to their children. "There is the good man who had the courage to begin this glorious work, years ago!"

Of Garrison's appearance at this time, it is sufficient to say that it was no more nor less serene and untroubled than when he stood amid the hisses of the mob in Faneuil Hall. He had always believed in this victory as steadfastly in the beginning as in the end, for God, who makes all his instruments for his own purposes, had given him in the outset that "faith which is the substance of things hoped for, and the evidence of things not seen," and to God alone, without a thought of self, did he ascribe the glory.

On the 1st of January, 1865, Mr. Garrison having finished the work for which the Liberator was established in Boston, came out with his last editorial announcing the discontinuing of that paper. He says:

"The object for which the *Liberator* was commenced—the extermination of chattel slavery—having been gloriously consummated, it seems to me specially appropriate to let its existence cover the historic period of the great struggle; leaving what remains to be done to complete the work of emancipation to other instrumentalities, (of which I hope to avail myself,) under new auspices, with more abundant means and with millions instead of hundreds for allies.

"Most happy am I to be no longer in conflict with the mass of my fellow-countrymen on the subject of slavery. For no man of any refinement or sensibility can be indifferent to the approbation of his fellow-men, if it be rightly earned. But to obtain it by going with the multitude to do evil, is self-degradation and personal dishonor. Better to be always in a minority of one with God—branded as a madman, incendiary, fanatic, heretic, infidel—frowned upon by the powers that be, and mobbed by the populace—or consigned ignominiously to the gallows, like him whose 'soul is marching on,' though his 'body lies mouldering in the grave,' or burnt to ashes at the stake, like Wickliffe, or nailed to the cross, like Him who 'gave himself for the world,' in defence of the RIGHT, than like Herod, having the shouts of the multitude crying, 'It is the voice of a god, and not of a man!'

"Commencing my editorial career when only twenty years of age, I have followed it continuously till I have attained my sixtieth year—first in connection with *The Free Press*, in Newburyport, in the spring of 1826; next, with *The National Philanthropist*, in Boston, in 1827; next, with *The Journal of the Times*, in Bennington, Vt., in 1828-9; next, with *The Genius of Universal Emancipation*, in Baltimore, in 1829-30; and finally, with the *Liberator*, in Boston, from the 1st of January, 1831, to the 1st of January, 1866,—at the start, probably the youngest member of the editorial fraternity in the land, now, perhaps, the oldest, not in years, but in continuous service,—unless Mr. Bryant, of the New York *Evening Post*, be an exception.

"Whether I shall again be connected with the press, in a similar capacity, is quite problematical; but at my period of life, I feel no prompting to start a new journal at my own risk, and with the certainty of struggling against wind and tide, as I have done in the past.

"I began the publication of the *Liberator* without a subscriber, and I end it—it gives me unalloyed satisfaction to say—without a farthing as the pecuniary result of the patronage extended to it during thirty-five years of unremitted labors.

"From the immense change wrought in the national feeling and sentiment on the subject of slavery, the *Liberator* derived no advantage at any time in regard to its circulation.

* * * * * * *

"Farewell, tried and faithful patrons! Farewell, generous benefactors, without whose voluntary but essential pecuniary contributions the *Liberator* must have long since been discontinued! Farewell, noble men and women who have wrought so long and so successfully, under God, to break every yoke! Hail, ye ransomed millions! Hail, year of jubilee! With a grateful heart and a fresh baptism of the soul, my last invocation shall be—

'Spirit of Freedom! on—
Oh! pause not in thy flight
Till every clime is won,
To worship in thy light:
Speed on thy glorious way,
And wake the sleeping lands!
Millions are watching for the ray,
And lift to thee their hands.
Still 'Onward!' be thy cry—
Thy banner on the blast;
And as thou rushest by,
Despots shall shrink aghast.
On! till thy name is known
Throughout the peopled earth;

14

On! till thou reign'st alone,
Man's heritage by birth;
On! till from every vale, and where the mountains rise,
The beacon lights of Liberty shall kindle to the skies!'

WM. LLOYD GARRISON."

There were those in the party of the Garrisonian Abolitionists whose course at this time seemed to justify the popular impression that faultfinding had so long been their occupation, that they were not willing to accept even their own victory at the price of giving up their liberty of denunciation. It is doubtless very dangerous to the finer tissues of one's moral nature to live only to deny and contend and rebuke.

But Mr. Garrison showed conclusively that it was love of right and not love of contention, that animated him by this prompt, whole hearted acknowledgment of the good when it came. No American citizen ever came more joyfully and lovingly into the great American Union, than he who so many years had stood outside of it, for conscience' sake; and he showed just as much steadiness and independence in disregarding the criticisms of some of his former coadjutors, as he formerly had in disregarding those of pro-slavery enemies. He would not say that a work was *not* done which *was* done—he was honest and fair in acknowledging honest and fair work, and he very wisely distinguished between emancipation, as a fixed and final fact, and reconstruction, as belonging to the new era founded on emancipation. In his last editorial he very quietly and sensibly states his views on this subject, and repels the charge which had been made that he was deserting the battle before the victory was won. He ends by saying:

"I shall sound no trumpet and make no parade as to what I shall do for the future. After having gone through with such a struggle as has never been paralleled in duration in the life of any reformer, and for nearly forty years been the target at which all poisonous and deadly missiles have been hurled, and having seen our great national iniquity blotted out, and freedom 'proclaimed throughout all the land to all the inhabitants thereof,' and a thousand presses and pulpits supporting the claims of the colored population to fair treatment where not one could be found to do this in the early days of the anti-slavery conflict, I might, it seems to me—be permitted to take a little repose in my advanced years, if I desired to do so. But, as yet, I have neither asked nor wished to be relieved of any burdens or labors connected with the good old cause. I see a mighty work of enlightenment and regeneration yet to be accomplished at the South, and many cruel wrongs done to the freedmen which are yet to be redressed; and I neither counsel others to turn away from the field of conflict, under the delusion that no more remains to be done, nor contemplate such a course in my own case."

Mr. Garrison's health, which had suffered severely from his long labors, required the relief of foreign travel.

He once more revisited England, where his course was one unbroken triumph. A great breakfast was given in his honor at St. James' Hall, London, at which John Bright presided. The Duke of Argyle presented a complimentary address to Mr. Garrison, congratulating him on the successful termination of the Anti-Slavery struggle. Lord John Russell seconded this address, and at this time magnanimously retracted certain hasty sayings in regard to the recent conflict in America, at its commencement. In the city of Edinburgh he was received in a crowded public meeting with tumultuous cheering, and the freedom of the city was solemnly presented to him by the Lord Provost and magistracy. In a private letter he says:

"I need not tell you that I went to England with no purpose or thought of being lionized, but only quietly to see old friends, to seek recreation, hoping to renovate my failing health by the voyage. But I shall ever gratefully remember those friendly manifestations towards me and my native land."

In conclusion, it is but justice to human nature in general and to New England in particular, to say that the poets of New England, true to a divine inspiration always honored Garrison, even in his days of deepest darkness and rebuke. Longfellow, Russell, Lowell, Whittier and Emerson, came out boldly with Anti-Slavery poems. They were the wise men, star-led, who brought to the stable and the manger of the infant cause, the gold, frankincense and myrrh. It was a great opportunity, and they had grace given them to use it, and not all the fame they had won otherwise, honors them so much as those tributes to humanity and liberty which they bestowed in the hour of her utmost need.

We will conclude this sketch by a letter from Mr. Garrison, which best shows the spirit in which he regards the result of the great conflict.

"DEAR MRS. STOWE:

For your very appreciative and congratulatory letter on the "marvellous work of the Lord," which the Liberator marks as finished, I proffer you my heartfelt thanks, and join with you in a song of thanksgiving to Him, who, by a mighty hand and an outstretched arm has set free the captive millions in our land.

"The instrumentalities which the God of the oppressed has used for the overthrow of the slave system, have been as multifarious and extraordinary as that system has been brutal and iniquitous. Every thing that has been done, whether to break the yoke or to rivet it more strongly, has been needed to bring about the great result. The very madness of the South has worked as effectively anti-slavery-wise as the most strenuous efforts of the abolitionists.

"The outlawry of all Northern men of known hostility to slavery—the numberless pro-slavery mobs and lynchings, her defiant and awful defence of the traffic in human flesh, her increasing rigor and cruelties towards the slaves, and finally her horrible treason and rebellion to secure her independence as a vast slaveholding empire, through all time, all mightily helped to defeat her impious purpose and to hasten the year of jubilee. Thus it is that

God moves in a mysterious way,
His wonders to perform;
He plants his footsteps in the sea,
And rides upon the storm.

And who but God is to be glorified?

CHAPTER IV.

CHARLES SUMNER.

Mr. Sumner an Instance of Free State High Culture—The "Brahmin Caste" of New England—The Sumner Ancestry; a Kentish Family—Governor Increase Sumner; His Revolutionary Patriotism—His Stately Presence; "a Governor that can Walk"—Charles Sumner's Father—Mr. Sumner's Education, Legal and Literary Studies—Tendency to Ideal Perfection—Sumner and the Whigs—Abolitionism Social Death—Sumner's Opposition to the Mexican War—His Peace Principles—Sumner opposes Slavery Within the Constitution, as Garrison Outside of it—Anti-Slavery and the Whigs—The Political Abolitionist Platform—Webster asked in vain to Oppose Slavery—Sumner's Rebuke of Winthrop—Joins the Free Soil Party—Succeeds Webster in the Senate—Great Speech against the Fugitive Slave Law—The Constitution a Charter of Liberty—Slavery not in the Constitution—First Speech after the Brooks Assault—Consistency as to Reconstruction.

In the example of Abraham Lincoln we have shown the working-man, self-educated, rising to greatness and station, under influences purely American. It is our pride to say that in no other country of the world could a man of the working classes have had a career like that of Lincoln.

We choose now another name made famous by the great struggle for principle and right which has ended in our recent war. As Lincoln is a specimen of the facilities, means of self-education and advance in life which America gives to the working man, so Charles Sumner is a specimen of that finish, breadth, and extent of culture which could be produced by the best blood and the best educational institutions of the oldest among the *free* States of America.

Charles Sumner

We may speak properly of the blood of the Sumner family, for they belong to what Dr. Oliver Wendell Holmes so happily characterizes as the "Brahmin caste of New England," that "harmless, inoffensive, untitled aristocracy," in whom elevated notions of life, and aptitudes for learning, seem, in his own words, to be "hereditary and congenital." "Families whose names are always on college catalogues; and who break out every generation or two in some learned labor which calls them up after they seem to have died out." A glance at the Cambridge catalogue will show a long line of Sumners, from 1723 down to the graduation of our present Senator.

Like many other American families distinguished for energy and intellectual vigor, the Sumner family can trace back their lineage to the hardy physical stock of the English yeomanry. The race, afterwards emigrating to Oxfordshire, had its first origin in Kent, and it is curious to see how to this day it preserves physical traits of its origin. The Kentish men were tall, strong, long-limbed, and hardy, much relied on for archery and holding generally the front of the battle. The Sumners in America have been marked men in these same physical points; men of commanding stature and fine vital temperament, strong, athletic, and with the steady cheerfulness of good health and good digestion.

One of the early ancestors of this family, who lived in Roxbury, is thus characterized in the Antiquarian Register: "Never was there a man better calculated for the sturdy labors of a yeoman. He was of colossal size and equal strength of muscle, which was kept in tone by regularity and good habits. He shrunk from no labor, however arduous and fatiguing it might seem to others. Instances of the wonderful feats of strength performed by him were related after his death by his contemporaries in his native place and the vicinity."

The son of this man was the venerated Increase Sumner, the cousin of Charles Sumner's father, one of the most distinguished Judges and Governors of Massachusetts. He was indeed one of the nursing fathers of the State of Massachusetts during the critical period when, just emerging from the tutelage of England, she was trying the experiment of a State constitutional government.

Some of the sayings of Increase Sumner are important, as showing of what stock it was that our present Massachusetts Senator came, and what were the family traditions in which he was educated. In a letter just in the beginning of the revolutionary war, he says:

"The man who, regardless of public happiness, is ready to fall in with base measures, and sacrifice conscience, honor and his country, merely for his own advancement, must (if not wretchedly hardened,) feel a torture, the intenseness of which nothing in this world can equal."

Again, in one of his judicial charges, he says:

"America furnishes one of the few instances of countries where the blessings of civil liberty and the rights of mankind have been the primary objects of their political institutions; in which the rich and poor are equally protected; where the rights of conscience are fully enjoyed, and where merit and ability can be the only claim to the favor of the public. May we not then pronounce that man destitute of the true principles of liberty and unworthy the blessing of society, who does not at all times lend his aid to support and maintain a government on the preservation of which depends his own political as well as private happiness?"

Never was a Governor of Massachusetts carried to the chair with more popular enthusiasm than Increase Sumner, to which, doubtless, his stately person and appearance of high physical vigor added greatly. Hancock had been crippled with gout, and Adams had been bent with infirmity, and the populace, ever prone to walk by sight, were cheered by the stately steppings of their new leader. "Thank God, we have got a Governor *that can walk*, at last," said an old apple woman, as he passed in state at the head of the legislative body, from hearing the election sermon in the Old South.

The father of Charles Sumner was no less distinguished for the personal and mental gifts of the family. He was an able lawyer, and for many years filled the office of high sheriff of Suffolk county, and is still spoken of with enthusiasm by those who remember him, as a magnificent specimen of a man of the noblest type; noble in person, in manners and in mind, and of most immaculate integrity. He was the last high sheriff who retained the antique dress derived from English usage, and the custom well became his lordly person and graceful dignity of manner.

Charles Sumner, therefore, succeeded to physical vigor, to patriotic sentiment and noble ideas as his birthright. His education was pursued in the Boston

Latin school and in Phillips Academy, which is still proud of the tradition of his sojourn, and lastly in Harvard College, where he graduated in 1830.

In the same place he pursued his law studies, under Judge Story, and was admitted to the bar in 1834. No young man could rise more rapidly. He soon gained a large practice, and was appointed reporter of the Circuit Court of the United States, in which capacity he published three volumes, known as Sumner's Reports, containing the decisions of Judge Story. He also edited the *American Jurist*, a quarterly law journal. The first three winters after his admission to the bar he lectured in the Cambridge Law School with such approval that in 1836, he was offered a professorship in the Law School, which he declined.

In 1837 he visited Europe for purposes of travel and general improvement, and remained there for three years, returning in 1840. As the result of this sojourn, he added to his previous classical and legal knowledge an extensive and accurate acquaintance with the leading languages and literature of modern Europe. Possessed of a memory remarkable for its extent and accuracy, all these varied treasures were arranged in his mind where they could be found at a moment's notice. We have heard of his being present once at a dinner, among the Cambridge *élite*, when Longfellow repeated some French verses, which he said had struck him by their euphony and elegance, but to which he could not at the moment assign the name of the author. Sumner immediately rose from the table, took down a volume of Voltaire, and without a moment's hesitation turned to the passage. He has sometimes been accused of a sort of pedantry in the frequent use of classical and historical illustration in his speeches, but the occurrence of these has been the result of a familiarity which made their use to him the most natural and involuntary thing in the world.

In the outset of Sumner's career it was sometimes said of him that he was a brilliant theorizer, but that he would never be a practical politician. His mind, indeed, belongs to that class whose enthusiasms are more for ideas and principles than for men. He had the capacity of loving the absolute right, abstracted from its practical uses. There was a tendency in his mind to seek ideal perfection and completeness. In study, his standard was that of the most finished scholarship; in politics and the general conduct of life it was that of the severest models of the antique, elevated and refined by Christianity.

He returned to his native city at a time when the intention in good faith to be an ideal patriot and Christian, was in the general estimation of good society, a mark of a want of the practical faculties. The Whig party, in whose ranks, by birth and tradition, he belonged, looked upon him as the son of their right hand; though they shook their heads gently at what seemed to them the very young and innocent zeal with which he began applying the weights and measures of celestial regions to affairs where, it was generally conceded, it would be fatal to use them.

Just at this season, the great Babylon, which now is cast down with execration, sat as a queen at Washington, and gave laws, and bewitched northern politicians with her sorceries. Church and State were entangled in her nets, and followed, half willingly, half unwilling, at her chariot wheels. The first, loudest, most importunate demand of this sorceress was, that the rule "Do unto others as ye would that others should do unto you" should be repealed. There was no objection to its forming a part of the church service, and being admired in general terms, as an ideal fragment of the apostolic age, but the attempt to apply it to the regulation of national affairs was ridiculed as an absurdity, and denounced as a dangerous heresy.

What then was the dismay of Beacon Street, the consternation of State Street, when this young laurelled son of Cambridge, fresh from his foreign tour, with all his career of honor before him, showed symptoms of declining towards the abolitionists. The abolitionists, of all men! Had not Garrison been dragged by a halter round his neck through the streets of Boston? And did not the most respectable citizens cry, Well done? Was it not absolute social and political death to any young man to fall into those ranks?

Had not the Legislature of the sovereign state of Georgia in an official proclamation signed by their governor, set a price on Garrison's head as an incendiary, and had not a Governor of Massachusetts in his message to a Massachusetts Legislature, so far sympathized with his southern brethren as to introduce into his inaugural a severe censure of the abolitionists, and to intimate his belief that in their proceedings they were guilty of an offence punishable by common law? Had not Massachusetts legislatures taken into respectful consideration resolutions from slaveholding legislatures, dictating to them in that high style for which such documents are famous, that they should pass laws making it penal to utter abolitionist sentiments?

All this had been going on during the three years while Sumner was in Europe, and now, when he was coming home to take his place as by right in the political ranks, did it not become him to be very careful how he suffered indiscreet moral enthusiasm to betray him into expressions which might identify him with these despised abolitionists? Was not that socially to forfeit his birthright, to close upon him every parlor and boudoir of Beacon Street, to make State Street his enemy, to shut up from him every office of advancement or profit, and make him for every purpose of the Whig party a useless impracticable instrument?

And so the rising young man was warned to let such things alone; not to strive for the impossible ambrosia of the higher morals, and to content himself like his neighbors, with the tangible cabbage of compromise, as fitted to our mortal state.

He was warned with fatherly unction, by comfortable old Whigs, who to-day are shouting, even louder than he, "Down with Babylon, raze it, raze it to the foundations!"

But in spite of such warnings and cautions, Sumner became an ardent and thoroughgoing anti-slavery man, and did not hesitate to avow himself an abolitionist and to give public utterance to his moral feelings, contrary to the stringent discipline of the Whig party.

On the 4th of July, 1844, Sumner pronounced in Boston, in view of the threatening Mexican war, an oration on "The True Grandeur of Nations."

This discussed the general questions of war from the Christian stand point, and deprecated the threatened one on Christian principles. It might have passed as a harmless peace tract in ordinary times, but just at this period, it was too evidently the raising a standard against Babylon to be considered acceptable doctrine, for had not Babylon issued a decree that Gospel or no Gospel, a war with Mexico must take place, so that she might gain more slave territory? Let the young man look to himself, applying such impossible, impracticable tests to such delicate political questions! The speech, however, was widely circulated, both here and in England, and was said by Cobden to be one of the noblest contributions ever made to the cause of peace.

November 4, 1845, Sumner spoke more decidedly against the Mexican war, in a public meeting at Faneuil Hall, and the next year came out boldly in the Whig convention with an address, on "The Anti-Slavery Duties of the Whig Party."

In this speech, Sumner, as openly as Garrison, declared himself the eternal opponent of slavery, and defined his position and marked out his work *within* the constitution of the United States, and *by* the constitution, just as Garrison had marked out his work outside of the constitution, and against it.

Sumner took the ground that the constitution of the United States was not a covenant with death, or an agreement with hell, but an instrument designed to secure liberty and equal rights, and that the present sanction and encouragement it was giving to slavery was owing to a perversion of its original design. He maintained that the constitution nowhere recognises slavery as an institution, that the slave is nowhere spoken of in it as a chattel but as a person, and that those provisions in the constitution which confer certain privileges on slaveholders were supposed to be temporary compromises with what the founders of the constitution imagined would prove only a temporary institution—soon to pass entirely away from the country. He asserts in this speech:

"There is in the constitution no compromise on the subject of slavery of a character not to be reached legally and constitutionally, which is the only way in which I propose to reach it. Wherever power and jurisdiction are secured to Congress, they may unquestionably be exercised in conformity with the constitution. And even in matters beyond existing powers and jurisdiction there is a constitutional mode of action. The constitution contains an article pointing out how at any time amendments may be made thereto. This is an important article, giving to the constitution a progressive character, and allowing it to be moulded to suit new exigences and new conditions of feeling. The wise framers of this instrument did not treat the country as a Chinese foot, never to grow after its infancy, but anticipated the changes incident to its growth."

Accordingly, Sumner proposed to the Whig party, as a rallying watch-word, the

REPEAL OF SLAVERY UNDER THE CONSTITUTION AND LAWS OF THE FEDERAL GOVERNMENT.

Of this course he said: "The time has passed when this can be opposed on constitutional grounds. It will not be questioned by any competent authority, that Congress may by express legislation abolish slavery, 1st, in the District of Columbia; 2d, in the Territories, if there should be any; 3d, that it may abolish the slave-trade on the high seas between the states; 4th, that it may refuse to admit any new state with a constitution sanctioning slavery. Nor can it be doubted that the people of the free States may in the manner pointed out by the constitution, proceed to its amendment."

Here we have, in a few words, the platform of the Political Abolitionists, every step of which has actually been accomplished.

But at that time it was altogether too exalted doctrine to be received by the Whig party, and Sumner tried his eloquence upon them in vain. In vain he called upon Daniel Webster to carry out this glorious programme in his place in the Senate.

"Assume," he says, "these unperformed duties. The aged shall bear witness of you; the young shall kindle with rapture as they repeat the name of Webster; and the large company of the ransomed shall teach their children and their children's children to the latest generation, to call you blessed; while all shall award you another title, not to be forgotten in earth or heaven—*Defender of Humanity*."

But Webster had other aspirations. He wanted to be president of the United States, to be that he must please the South, and so instead of Defender of Humanity he turned to be a defender of kidnapping and of the fugitive slave law.

In 1846, Sumner, in a public letter, rebuked Robert C. Winthrop, then a Massachusetts representative, for voting for the Mexican war. In this letter he characterizes the Mexican war as an unjust attack on a sister republic, having its origin in a system of measures to extend slavery; as being dishonorable and cowardly, as being the attack of a rich and powerful country on a weak and defenceless neighbor; and having thus characterized it, he adds:

"Such, sir, is the act of Congress to which, by your affirmative vote, the people of Boston have been made parties. Through you they have been made to declare an unjust and cowardly war, with falsehood, in the cause of slavery. Through you they have been made partakers in the blockade of Vera Cruz, in the seizure of California, in the capture of Santa Fe, and in the bloodshed of Monterey. It were idle to suppose that the poor soldier or officer alone is stained by this guilt—it reaches back and incarnadines the halls of Congress; nay, more, through you it reddens the hands of your constituents in Boston.

* * * * * *

"Let me ask you, sir, to remember in your public course the rules of right which you obey in your private capacity. The principles of morals are the same for nations as for individuals. Pardon me if I suggest that you do not appear to have acted invariably in accordance with this truth.

* * * * * *

"It has been said in apology by your defenders that the majority of the Whig party joined with you. * * * In the question of right and wrong it can be of little importance that a few fallible men, constituting what is called a majority, were all of one mind. But these majorities do not make us withhold our condemnation from the partakers in those acts. Aloft on the throne of God, and not below in the footsteps of the trampling multitude of men, are to be found the sacred rules of right which no majorities can displace or overturn. And the question returns, WAS IT RIGHT *to vote for an unjust and cowardly war, with falsehood, for slavery?*"

These extracts will give a tolerable certainty that the old Whig party of Massachusetts, which was thoroughly dead in the trespasses and sins of pro-slavery compromise, found Charles Sumner, with all his learning, and vigor and talent, a rather uncomfortable member, and that he soon found that the Whig party was no place for him.

In 1848 he left them to unite in forming the Free Soil party, in which the platform of principles he had already announced, was to form the distinctive basis.

And now came the great battle of the Fugitive Slave Law. The sorceress slavery meditated a grand *coup d' etat* that should found a Southern slave empire, and shake off the troublesome North, and to that intent her agents concocted a statute so insulting to Northern honor, so needlessly offensive in its provisions, so derisive of what were understood to be its religious convictions and humane sentiments, that it was thought verily, "The North never will submit to this, and we shall make here the breaking point." Then arose Daniel Webster, that lost Archangel of New England—he who had won her confidence by his knowledge of and reverence for all that was most sacred in her, and moved over to the side of evil! It was as if a great constellation had changed sides in the heavens, drawing after it a third part of the stars. The North, perplexed, silenced, troubled, yielded for a moment. For a brief space all seemed to go down before that mighty influence, and all listened, as if spell bound, to the serpent voice with which he scoffed at the idea that there was a law of God higher than any law or constitution of the United States.

But that moment of degradation was the last. Back came the healthy blood, the re-awakened pulse of moral feeling in New England, and there were found voices on all sides to speak for the right, and hearts to respond, and on this tide of re-awakened moral feeling, Sumner was carried into the United States Senate, to take the seat vacated by Webster. The right was not yet victorious, but the battle had turned so far that its champion had a place to stand on in the midst of the fray.

And what a battle was that! What an ordeal! What a gauntlet to run was that of the man in Washington who in those days set himself against the will of the great sorceress! Plied with temptation on the right hand and on the left, studied, mapped out like a fortress to be attacked and taken, was every Northern man who entered the arena. Could he be bought, bribed, cajoled, flattered, terrified? Which, or all? So planned the conspirators in their secret conclaves.

The gigantic Giddings—he who brought to the strife nerves toughened by backwoods toil, and frontier fights with Indians—once said of this warfare:

"I've seen hard fighting with clubs and bullets; I've seen men falling all around me; but I tell you it takes more courage to stand up in one's seat in Congress and say the right thing, than to walk up to the cannon's mouth. There's no such courage as that of the anti-slavery men there."

Now, Sumner's superb vitality, that hardy yeoman blood which his ancestors brought from England, stood him in excellent stead. His strong and active brain was based on a body muscular, vigorous, and healthy, incapable of nervous tremor, bearing him with a steady *a-plomb* through much that would be confusing and weakening to men of less physical force. Sumner had not the character of a ready debater; not a light-armed skirmisher was he; he resembled rather one of the mailed warriors of ancient tourney. When he had deliberately put on his armor, all polished and finished down to buckle and shoe-latchet, and engraved with what-not of classic, or Venetian, or Genoese device; when he put down his visor, steadied his lance, took sure aim, and went man and horse against his antagonist, all went down before him, as went down all before the lance of Cœur-de-Lion.

Such a charge into the enemy was his first great speech, "Freedom National, Slavery Sectional," which he directed against the Fugitive Slave Law. It was a perfect land-slide of history and argument; an avalanche under which the opposing party were logically buried, and it has been a magazine from which catapults have been taken to beat down their fortresses ever since.

If Daniel Webster merited the title of the great expounder of the constitution, Sumner at this crisis merited that of the great defender of the constitution. In this speech we see clearly the principle on which Charles Sumner, while holding the same conscientious ground with Mr. Garrison in regard to the wickedness of slavery, could yet see his way clear to take the oath to support and defend the constitution of the United States.

It was because he believed *ex animo*, that that constitution was an agreement made TO PROMOTE AND DEFEND LIBERTY, and though including in itself certain defective compromises, which never ought to have been there, had yet within itself the constitutional power of revoking even those compromises, and coming over entirely on to the ground of liberty.

The fugitive slave law, as it was called, he opposed on the ground that it was unconstitutional, that it was contrary to the spirit and intention of the constitution, and to the well known spirit and intention of the men who made that constitution. In this part, Mr. Sumner, going back to the history of the debates at the formation of the constitution, gave a masterly *resumé* of the subject, showed that the leading men of those days were all strong anti-slavery men, that they all looked forward to the gradual dying out of slavery as certain, and that with great care they avoided in the constitution any legal recognition of such an unlawful, unnatural relation. That the word slave did not exist in the document, and that when the slaves of the South were spoken of in relation to apportioning the suffrage, they were spoken of as "persons," and not as chattels; that even the very clause of the constitution which has been perverted into a foundation for the fugitive slave law, had been purposely so framed that it did not really describe the position of slaves under southern law, but only that of such laborers as were by law denominated and recognized as *persons*. By slave law the slaves were not regarded as "persons held to service and labor," but as chattels personal, and it was only apprentices and free *persons* to whom the terms could literally be made to apply.

He showed by abundant quotations from the debates of the times that this use of language was not accidental, but expressly designed to avoid corrupting the constitution of the United States with any recognition of the principle that man could hold *man* as *property*. He admitted that the makers of it knew and admitted that under it slaveholders could recover their slaves, but considering slaveholding as a temporary thing, they had arranged so that the language of their great national document should remain intact and uncorrupt. From this masterly speech we extract the concluding summary:

"At the risk of repetition, but for the sake of clearness, review now this argument, and gather it together. Considering that slavery is of such an offensive character that it can find sanction only in positive law and that it has no such 'positive' sanction in the constitution; that the constitution, according to its Preamble, was ordained to 'establish justice,' and 'secure the blessings of liberty;' that in the convention which framed it, and also elsewhere at the time, it was declared not to 'sanction slavery;' that according to the

Declaration of Independence, and the address of the Continental Congress, the nation was dedicated to 'liberty' and the 'rights of human nature;' that according to the principles of common law, the constitution must be interpreted openly, actively, and perpetually for Freedom; that according to the decision of the Supreme Court, it acts upon slaves, *not as property*, but as *persons;* that, at the first organization of the national government, under Washington, slavery had no national favor, existed nowhere on the national territory, beneath the national flag, but was openly condemned by the nation, the church, the colleges and literature of the time; and finally, that according to an amendment of the constitution, the national government can only exercise powers delegated to it, among which there is none to support slavery; considering these things, sir, it is impossible to avoid the single conclusion that slavery is in no respect a national institution, and that the constitution nowhere upholds property in man.

"But there is one other special provision of the constitution, which I have reserved to this stage, not so much from its superior importance, but because it may fitly stand by itself. This alone, if practically applied, would carry freedom to all within its influence. It is an amendment proposed by the first Congress, as follows: 'No *person* shall be deprived of life, *liberty*, or property, *without due process of law*.' Under this ægis the liberty of every person within the national jurisdiction is unequivocally placed. I say every person. Of this there can be no question. The word 'person,' in the constitution, embraces every human being within its sphere, whether Caucasian, Indian, or African, from the President to the slave."

The moral influence of these doctrines on the political abolitionists was very great. Garrison's sharp, clear preaching of the Bible doctrine of sin and repentance, had awakened a great deal of moral feeling in the land, and it became a real case of conscience to a great many, how they could in any way take the oath to support a constitution which they thought supported slavery. On this subject, in all pure and noble minds, there began to be great searchings of heart, but the clearness, the fulness, the triumphant power with which Sumner and others brought out the true intention of the constitution, and the spirit of its makers, gave a feeling of clean and healthy vigor through the whole party. Even the Garrisonians could perceive at any rate, that here was a ground where honest Christians might plant their feet, and get a place in the government to fight on, until by the constitutional power of *amendment* they might some day cast out wholly the usurping devil of slavery, which had lived and thriven so much beyond the expectations of our fathers.

Sumner's mind is particularly remarkable for a nice sense of moral honor. He had truly that which Burke calls "that chastity of honor which felt a stain like a wound," and he felt keenly the disgrace and shame of such an enactment as the fugitive slave law. He never spoke of it as a law. He was careful to call it only an *enactment*, an attempt at law, which being contrary to the constitution of the country, never could have the binding force of a law.

Next in the political world came the defeat, disgrace, fall and broken hearted death of Webster, who, having bid for the Presidency, at the price of all his former convictions, and in the face of his former most solemnly expressed opinions, was treated by the haughty Southern oligarchy with contemptuous neglect. "The South never pay their slaves," said a northern farmer when he heard that Webster had lost the nomination. Webster felt with keen pangs, that for that slippery ungrateful South, he had lost the true and noble heart of the North. In the grave with Webster died the old Whig party.

But still, though this and that man died, and parties changed, the unflinching Southern power pushed on its charge. Webster being done with, it took up Douglas as its next tool, and by him brought on the repeal of the Missouri compromise and the Kansas and Nebraska battle. The war raged fiercer and hotter and in the fray, Sumner's voice was often heard crying the war cry of liberty.

And now the war raged deadlier, as came on the struggle for the repeal of the Missouri compromise, when the strokes of Sumner's battle axe, long and heavy, were heard above the din, and always with crushing execution. The speech on "The Crime against Kansas," wrought the furnace of wrath to a white heat. What was to be done with this man? Call him out and fight him? He was known to be on principle a non-resistant. Answer him? Indeed! who ever heard of such a proceeding? How could they? Had he not spoken the truth? What shall we do then? Plantation manners suggested an answer. "Come behind him at an unguarded moment, take him at a disadvantage, three to one, knock him down and kill him."

So said—and but for his strong frame, wonderful in its recuperative power, and but for the unseen protection of a higher power,—it would have been so done.

Everybody knows the brutal history of that coarse and cowardly assault, and how the poor bully who accomplished it was *fêted* and caressed by Southern men and women in high places, who hastened by presents of canes, and snuff boxes, and plate, to show forth how well he had expressed the Southern idea of chivalry.

Three or four years spent abroad, under medical treatment, were necessary to enable even Sumner's vigorous vitality to recover from an assault so deadly; but at last he came back to take his seat in the Senate.

The poor cowardly bully who had assailed him, was dead—gone to a higher judgment seat; Butler was dead—and other accomplices of the foul deed were gone also. Under all these circumstances there is something thrilling in the idea of Sumner rising in the very seat where he had been stricken down, and pronouncing that searching speech to which his very presence there gave such force, "The Barbarism of Slavery."

If he had wished revenge he might have had it, in the fact that he had the solemn right, as one raised from the dead, to stand there and give in his awful testimony. How solemn and dignified, in view of all these circumstances, seem the introductory words of his speech:

"Mr. President, undertaking now, after a silence of more than four years, to address the Senate on this important subject, I should suppress the emotions natural to such an occasion, if I did not declare on the threshold my gratitude to that Supreme Being, through whose benign care I am enabled, after much suffering and many changes, once again to resume my duties here, and to speak for the cause which is so near my heart, to the honored commonwealth whose representative I am, and also to my immediate associates in this body, with whom I enjoy the fellowship which is found *in thinking alike concerning the Republic.* I owe thanks which I seize this moment to express for the indulgence shown me throughout the protracted seclusion enjoined by medical skill; and I trust that it will not be thought unbecoming in me to put on record here, as an apology for leaving my seat so long vacant, without making way, by resignation for a successor, that I acted under the illusion of an invalid, whose hopes for restoration to his natural health constantly triumphed over his disappointments.

"When last I entered into this debate it became my duty to expose the crime against Kansas, and to insist upon the immediate admission of that Territory as a State of this Union, with a constitution forbidding slavery. Time has passed, but the question remains. Resuming the discussion precisely where I left it, I am happy to avow that rule of moderation which, it is said, may venture even to fix the boundaries of wisdom itself. I have no personal griefs to utter; only a barbarous egotism could intrude these into this chamber. I have no personal wrongs to avenge; only a barbarous nature could attempt to wield that vengeance which belongs to the Lord. The years that have intervened, and the tombs that have been opened since I spoke, have their voices too, which I cannot fail to hear: Besides, what am I—what is any man among the living or among the dead, compared with the Question before us? It is this alone which I shall discuss, and I open the argument with that easy victory which is found in charity."

Though Sumner was thus moderate in allusion to himself or others, it was still the constant suggestion to the minds of all, of the perfect reason *he*, of all men, had, to know the truth of what he spoke, that gave a vehement force to his words. That was a speech unanswerable, unanswered. The South had tried the argument of force, and it had failed! There he was again!—their accuser at the bar of the civilized world!

In the present administration, as Chairman of the Committee on Foreign Relations, Sumner has with his usual learning and power defended American honor against the causeless defamations and sneers of those who should have known better. None of our public men, perhaps, is more favorably known in the Old World. His talents and accomplishments, as well as his heroic stand for principle, have given him the familiar *entrée* to all that is best worth knowing in England; and it is for that reason more admirable that he should, with such wealth of learning and elegance of diction, have remonstrated with that great nation on her injustice to us. His pamphlet on "Our Foreign Relations" carries a weight of metal in it that is overpowering; it is as thoroughly exhaustive of the subject as any of his greatest speeches,—grave, grand, and severely true. It is the strong blood of England herself speaking back to the parent land as sorrowfully as Hamlet to his mother.

In the recent debates on Reconstruction, Sumner has remained true to that "chastity of honor" in relation to the United States Constitution, which has been characteristic of him, in opposing that short sighted republican policy which proposed to secure the political privileges of the blacks by introducing the constitutional amendment, providing that any state disfranchising negroes should be deprived of a corresponding portion of its representation in Congress.

Sumner indignantly repelled the suggestion of introducing any such amendments into the constitution, as working dishonor to that instrument by admitting into it, in any form, or under whatsoever pretext, the doctrine of the political inequality of races of men. In this we recognize a faultless consistency of principle.

Sumner was cheered in the choice which he made in the darkest hour, by that elastic hope in the success of the right, which is the best inheritance of a strong, and healthy physical and moral organization. During the time of the Fugitive Slave Law battle, while the conflict of his election was yet uncertain, he was speaking incidentally to a friend of the tremendous influences which the then regnant genius of Daniel Webster could bring to crush any young man who opposed him. He spoke with feeling of what had to be sacrificed by a Boston young man who set himself to oppose such influences. The friend, in reply, expressed some admiration of his courage and self-sacrificing. He stopped, as he was walking up and down the room, and said, with simplicity, "Courage! No, it doesn't require so very much courage, because I know that in a few years we shall have all this thing down under our feet. We shall set our heel upon it," and he emphasized the sentence by bringing his heel heavily down upon the carpet.

"Do you really think so?"

"I know so; of course we shall."

Those words, spoken in the darkest hour of the anti-slavery conflict, have often seemed like a prophecy, in view of all the fast rushing events of the years that followed. Now they are verified. Where is the man who counselled the North to conquer their prejudices? Where is the man who raised a laugh in popular assemblies at the expense of those who believed the law of God to be higher than the law of men? There is a most striking lesson to young men in these histories.

The grave of the brilliant and accomplished Douglas lay far back on the road by which Lincoln rose to fame and honor, and the grave of Webster on that of Charles Sumner, and on both of those graves might be inscribed "Lo, this is the man that made not God his trust." Both scoffed at God's law, and proclaimed the doctrine of expediency as above right, and both died broken down and disappointed; while living and honored at this day, in this land and all lands, are the names of those, who in its darkest and weakest hour, espoused the cause of Liberty and Justice.

S. P. Chase

CHAPTER V.

SALMON P. CHASE.

England and our Finances in the War—President Wheelock and Mr. Chase's seven Uncles—His Uncle the Bishop—His sense of Justice at College—His Uncle the Senator—Admitted to the Bar for Cincinnati—His First Argument before a U. S. Court—Society in Cincinnati—The Ohio Abolitionists—Cincinnati on Slavery—The Church admits Slavery to be "an Evil"—Mr. Chase and the Birney Mob—The Case of the Slave Girl Matilda—How Mr. Chase "Ruined Himself"—He Affirms the Sectionality of Slavery.—The Van Zandt Case—Extracts from Mr. Chase's Argument—Mr. Chase in Anti-Slavery Politics—His Qualifications as a Financier.

WHEN a future generation shall be building the tombs of our present prophets, and adorning the halls of the Capitol with the busts of men now too hard at work to be sitting to the sculptor, then there will be among the marble throng one head not inferior to any now there in outside marks of greatness—a head to which our children shall point and say, "There is the financier who carried our country through the great slavery war!"

Not a small thing that to say of any man; for this war has been on a scale of magnitude before unheard of in the history of wars. It has been, so to speak, a fabulous war, a war of a tropical growth, a war to other wars, like the great Californian pine to the bramble of the forest. A thousand miles of frontier to be guarded, fleets to be created, an army to be organized and constantly renewed on a scale of numbers beyond all European experience—an army, too, for the most part, of volunteer citizens accustomed to generous diet, whose camp fare has been kept at a mark not inferior to the average of living among citizens at home. And all this was to be effected in no common times. It was to be done amid the revolutions of business, the disturbances of trade and manufacture, then turning into new courses; and above all, the breaking up of the whole system of cotton agriculture, by which the greatest staple of the world was produced. These changes convulsed and disarranged financial relations in all other countries, and shook the civilized world like an earthquake.

It is not to be wondered at that a merely insular paper, like the London *Times*, ignorant of all beyond the routine of British and continental probabilities, should have declared us madmen, and announced our speedy bankruptcy. We all know that paper to be conducted by the best of old world ability, and are ready to concede that the grave writers therein used their best light, and certainly they did their best to instruct us. How paternally did it warn us that we must not look to John Bull for funds to carry out such extravagances! How ostentatiously did the old banking houses stand buttoning their pockets, saying, "Don't come to *us* to borrow money!" and how did the wonder grow when the sun rose and set, and still new levies, new fleets, new armies!—when hundreds of thousands grew to millions, and still there was no call for foreign money, and government stocks stood in the market above all others in stability.

One thing, at least, became plain; that whatever might be the case with the army, *financially* the American people had a leader who united them to a man, and under whose guidance the vast material resources of the country moved in solid phalanx to support its needs.

When a blade does good service, nothing is more natural than to turn and read upon it the stamp that tells where and by whom it was fashioned; and so when we see the quiet and serenity in which our country moved on under its burdens, we ask, Whence comes this man who has carried us so smoothly in such a storm?

America is before all other things an agricultural country, and her aristocracy, whether of talent or wealth, generally trace back their origin to a farm. The case of Secretary Chase is no exception.

It is one of the traditions of Dartmouth College that old President Wheelock, in one of his peregrinations, once stopped in the town of Cornish, N. H.; a place where the Connecticut river flows out from the embrace of the White Mountains. Here he passed a night at a farm-house, the dwelling of Samuel Chase, a patriarchal farmer, surrounded by seven sons, as fine, strong and intelligent as those of Jesse of Old Testament renown. The President used his visit to plead the cause of a college education for these fine youths to such good purpose, that five of the boys, to wit: Salmon, Baruch, Heber, Dudley and Philander became graduates of Dartmouth College. Two remained to share the labors of the farm, one of whom was the father of Secretary Chase.

All the boys thus educated attained more than the average mark in society, and some to the highest distinction. Dudley Chase was one of the most distinguished lawyers and politicians of New England—a member of the United States Senate, and for many years Chief Justice of Vermont. It is said that he was so enthusiastic a classical scholar that he carried a Greek Homer and Demosthenes always in his pocket, for his recreation in intervals of public business. He lived to a patriarchal age, an object of universal veneration.

Salmon Chase, another brother, was a lawyer in Portland, the acknowledged leader of that distinguished bar. He died suddenly, while pleading in court, in 1806, and in memorial of him our Secretary received the name of Salmon Portland, at his birth, which occurred in 1808. The youngest of the graduates, Philander Chase, was the well-known Episcopal Bishop of Ohio and Illinois. He was the guardian under whose auspices the education of Salmon P. Chase was conducted.

In regard to Chase's early education, we have not many traditions. His parents were of the best class of New Hampshire farmers; Bible-reading, thoughtful, shrewd, closely and wisely economical. It is said that in that region literary material was so scarce that the boy's first writing lessons were taken on strips of birch bark.

When his father died, there was found to be little property for the support of the family, and only the small separate estate of his mother was left. She was of Scotch blood—that blood which is at once shrewd, pious, courageous and energetic, and was competent to make a little serve the uses of a great deal.

But an education, and a college education, is the goal towards which such mothers in New England set their faces as a flint—and by infinite savings and unknown economies they compass it.

When Chase was fourteen years old, his uncle, the Bishop, offered to take and educate him, and he went to Ohio along with an elder brother who was attached to Gen. Cass's expedition to the upper waters of the Mississippi.

While at Buffalo the seniors of the party made an excursion to Niagara, but had no room in their vehicle for the boy. Young Chase, upon this, with characteristic energy, picked up another boy who wanted to see the falls, and the two enterprising young gentlemen footed it through the snow for twenty miles, and saw the falls in company with their elders.

He remained two years with the Bishop, who was a peremptory man, and used his nephew as he did himself and everybody else about him, that is, made him *work* just as hard as he could.

The great missionary Bishop had so much to do, and so little to do it with, that he had to make up for lack of money by incessant and severe labor, and with such help as he could get. His nephew being his own flesh and blood, he felt perhaps at liberty to drive a little more sharply than the rest, as that is the form in which the family instinct shows itself in people of his character.

The Bishop supplemented his own scanty salary by teaching school and working a farm, and so Salmon's preparatory studies were seasoned with an abundance of severe labor.

The youth was near sighted, and troubled with an obstinate lisp. The former disability was incurable, but the latter he overcame by means of a long and persevering course of reading aloud.

On the whole, the Bishop seems to have thought well of his nephew, for one day in refusing him leave to go in swimming, he did so with the complimentary exclamation, "Why, Salmon, the country might lose its future President, were I to let you get drowned."

After being fitted under his uncle, Chase entered Dartmouth College.

One anecdote of Chase's college life is characteristic, as showing that courageous and steady sense of justice which formed a leading feature of his after life. One of his classmates was sentenced by the faculty to be expelled from college on a charge of which Chase knew him to be wholly innocent. Chase, after in vain arguing the case with the president, finally told him that he would go too, as he would not stay in an institution where his friends were treated with such injustice. The two youths packed up their goods and drove off. But the faculty sent word after them almost before they had got out of the village, that the sentence was rescinded and they might come back. They said, however, that they must take time to consider whether they would do so, and they took a week, having a pleasant vacation, after which they returned.

After graduating, Mr. Chase found himself dependent on his own exertions to procure his support in his law studies. He went to Washington intending to open a private school. He waited in vain for scholars till his money was gone, and then, feeling discouraged, asked his uncle the Senator to get him an office under government.

The old gentleman, who seems to have been about as stern in his manner of expressing family affection as his brother the Bishop, promptly refused:

"I'll give you half a dollar to buy you a spade to begin with," he said, "for then you might come to something at last, but once settle a young man down in a government office, he never does any thing more—it's the last you hear of him. I've ruined one or two young men in that way, and I'm not going to ruin you."

Thus with stern kindness was Chase turned off from what might have made a contented common-place man of him, and pricked up to the career which gave us a Secretary of the Treasury and a Chief Justice of the United States. He succeeded at last in obtaining the ownership of a select classical school already established, while he pursued his legal studies under the auspices of Wirt.

In 1830 he was examined for admission to the bar. At the close of the examination he was told that he had better read for another year. He replied that he could not do that, as he was all ready to commence practice in Cincinnati.

"Oh, at Cincinnati!" replied the Judge, as if any law or no law was enough for such a backwoods settlement—"well then, Mr. Clerk, swear in Mr. Chase."

His early days of legal practice, like those of most young lawyers, were days of waiting and poverty. The only professional work he did for a considerable time was to draw an agreement for a man, who paid him half a dollar, and a week afterwards came and borrowed it back. In one of his early cases he had occasion to prove the bad character of a witness who was on the other side, on which the fellow, who was a well known rough, threatened to "have his blood," and undertook to assault him. But as the rowdy came up at the close of the court, he met so quiet and stern a look from Mr. Chase's eyes that he turned and sneaked off without opening his mouth or raising his hand.

Mr. Chase's first argument before a United States Court was at Columbus, O., in 1834. The case was to him a very important one, and when he arose to make his argument he found himself so agitated that he could not utter a word. He had therefore to sit down, and after waiting a few moments, tried again, and made his plea. After he was through, one of the Judges came to him and shook hands with him, saying, "I congratulate you most sincerely." Chase, who was feeling very disagreeably, inquired with surprise what he was congratulated for?

"On your failure," answered the judge, who added, "A person of ordinary temperament and abilities would have gone through his part without any such symptoms of nervousness. But when I see a young man break down once or twice in that way, I conceive the highest hopes of him."

This may have been interpreted as a good natured attempt on the part of the Judge to reassure the young lawyer, but there is a deep and just philosophy in it. The class of men who have what Carlye calls "a composed stupidity, or a cheerful infinitude of ignorance," are not liable ever to break down through a high sense of the magnitude of their task, and the importance of a crisis. Such as their work is, they are always in a prepared frame of mind to do it.

Although the Washington judge who passed Mr. Chase into the legal profession had so small an opinion of Cincinnati, yet no place could have afforded a finer and more agreeable position to a rising young man, than that city in those days. A newly settled place, having yet lingering about it some of the wholesome neighborly spirit of a recent colony—with an eclectic society drawn from the finest and best cultivated classes of each of the older States, there was in the general tone of life a breadth of ideas, a liberality and freedom, which came from the consorting together of persons of different habits of living.

In no city was real intellectual or moral worth in a young candidate likely to meet a quicker and a more appreciative patronage.

Gradually Mr. Chase gained the familiar *entrée* of all that was worth knowing, and was received with hospitable openness in the best society. His fine person, his vigorous, energetic appearance, and the record of talent and scholarship he brought with him, secured him, in time the patronage of the best families, and a valuable and extensive practice. His industry was incessant, and his capability of sustained labor uncommon, as may be gathered from the fact that besides the labors of his office, he found time to prepare an edition of the Statutes of Ohio, with notes, and a history of the State, which is now a standard authority in the Ohio courts.

In the outset of Chase's career, he, like Charles Sumner, and every rising young American of his time, met the great test question of the age. To Chase it came in the form of an application to plead the cause of a poor black woman, claimed as a fugitive slave. For a rising young lawyer to take in hand the cause of a poor black, *now*, would be only a road to popularity and fame. But then the case was far otherwise.

If the abolition excitement had stirred up Boston it had convulsed Cincinnati. A city separated from slave territory only by a fordable river, was likely to be no quiet theatre for such discussions. All the horrors, all the mean frauds and shocking cruelties of the interstate slave-trade, were enacting daily on the steamboats which passed before the city on the Ohio River, and the chained gangs of broken-hearted human beings, torn from home and family, to be shipped to Southern plantations, were often to be seen on steamboats lying at the levee.

The chapter in Uncle Tom's Cabin called "Select Incidents of Lawful Trade" was no fancy painting. It was an almost literal daguerreotype of scenes which the author of that book had witnessed in those floating palaces which plied between Cincinnati and New Orleans, and where too, above in the cabin, were happy mothers, wives, husbands, brothers and sisters, rejoicing in secure family affection, and on the deck below, miserable shattered fragments of black families, wives torn from husbands, children without mothers and mothers without children, with poor dumb anxious faces going they knew not whither, to that awful "down river"—whence could come back letter or tidings never more—for slavery took care that slaves should write no letters.

Such scenes as these, almost daily witnessed, gave the discussion of the great question of slavery a startling and tangible reality which it never could have had in Boston. For the credit of human nature we are happy to state that the Ohio was lined all along its shores, where it ran between free and slave territory, with a chain of abolitionist forts, in the shape of societies prosecuting their object with heroic vigor; and what made the controversy most peculiarly intense was the assistance which these abolitionists stood always ready to give to the escaping fugitive. For a belt of as much as fifty miles all along the river, the exertions of the abolitionists made slave property the most insecure of all kinds of possessions.

The slave power, as we have seen, was no meek non-resistant, and between it and the abolitionists there was a hand-to-hand grapple, with a short knife, and deadly home thrusts. The western man is in all things outspoken and ardent; and Garrison's logical deductions as to the true nature of slavery came molten and red hot, as fired from the guns of western abolitionists. To do them justice, they were sublimely and awfully imprudent, heroically regardless of any considerations but those of abstract truth and justice; they made no more effort to palliate slavery or conciliate the slaveholders than the slaveholders made efforts to palliate their doings, or conciliate them. War, war to the knife, was the word on both sides, the only difference being that the knife of the abolitionist was a spiritual one, and the knife of the slaveholders a literal one.

The Lane Theological Seminary was taken possession of as an anti-slavery fortification by a class of about twenty vigorous, radical young men, headed by that brilliant, eccentric genius, Theodore D. Weld; who came and stationed themselves there ostensibly as theological students under Dr. Beecher and Professor Stowe, *really* that they might make of the Seminary an anti-slavery fort.

Now at this time, "good society," so called, as constituted in Cincinnati, had all that easy, comfortable indifference to the fortunes and sufferings of people not so well off as itself, which is characteristic of good society all the world over. It is so much easier to refine upon one's own ideal of life, to carpet one's floors, and list one's doors and windows and keep out the cold, stormy wind of debate and discussion, than it is to go out into the highways and hedges and keep company with the never-ending sins and miseries and misfortunes and mistakes of poor, heavy-laden humanity, that good society always has sat as a dead weight on any rising attempt at reform.

Then again, Cincinnati was herself to a large extent a slaveholding city. Her property was in slaveholding states. Negroes were negotiable currency; they were collateral security on half the contracts that were at the time being made between the thriving men of Cincinnati and the planters of the adjoining slave states. If the bold doctrine of the abolitionists was true—if slavery was *stealing*, then were the church members in the fairest Cincinnati churches *thieves*—for in one way or another, they were to a large extent often the holders of slaves.

The whole secret instinct of Cincinnati, therefore, was to wish that slavery might in some way be defended, because Cincinnati stood so connected with it in the way of trade, that conscientious scruples on this point were infinitely and intolerably disagreeable. The whirlwind zeal of the abolitionists, the utter, reckless abandon and carelessness of forms and fashions with which they threw themselves into the fight, therefore furnished to good society a cloak large and long, for all their own sins of neglect. They did not defend slavery, of course, these good people—in fact, they regarded it as an evil. They were properly and decorously religious—good society always is, and so willing in presbytery and synod to have judiciously worded resolutions from time to time introduced, regretting slavery as an evil. The meetings of ecclesiastical bodies afforded at this time examples of most dexterous theological hair-splitting on this subject. Invariably in every one of them, were the abolitionists forward and fiery, calling slavery by that ugly old Saxon word, "a sin." Then there were the larger class of brethren, longing for peace, and hating iniquity, who had sympathy for the inevitable difficulties which beset well-meaning Christian slaveholders under slave laws. Now if these consented to call slavery a sin, they imposed on themselves the necessity of either enforcing immediate repentance and change of life on the sinner, or excluding him from the communion. So they obstinately intrenched themselves in the declaration that slavery is—an EVIL.

When a synod had spent all its spare time in discussing whether slavery ought to be described in a resolution as an evil or as a moral evil, they thought they had about done their share of duty on the subject; meanwhile, between the two, the consciences of those elders and church members who were holding slaves on bond and mortgage, or sending down orders to sell up the hands of plantations as securities for their debts, had a certain troublous peace.

How lucky it was for these poor tempest-tossed souls that the abolitionists were so imprudent and hot headed, that they wore garments of camel's hair, and were girt about the loins with a leathern girdle, and did eat locusts and wild honey, being altogether an unpresentable, shaggy, unkempt, impracticable set of John the Baptist reformers. Their unchristian spirit shocked the nerves of good pious people far more than the tearing up of slave families, or the wholesale injustice of slavery. "The abolitionists do things in such bad taste," said good society, "that it really makes it impossible for us to touch the subject at all, lest we should become mixed up with them, and responsible for their proceedings." To become mixed up with and responsible for the proceedings of slaveholders, slave-traders, and slave-drivers, who certainly exhibited no more evidences of good taste in their manner of handling subjects, did not somehow strike good society at this time as equally objectionable.

It had got to be a settled and received doctrine that the impudent abolitionists had created such a state of irritation in the delicate nerves of the slaveholding power, that all good Christian people were bound to unite in a general effort to calm irritation by suppressing all discussion of the subject.

When, therefore, James G. Birney, a southern abolitionist, who had earned a right to be heard, by first setting free his own slaves, came to Cincinnati and set up an abolition paper, there was a boiling over of the slaveholding fury. For more than a week Cincinnati lay helpless in a state of semi-sack and siege, trod under the heels of a mob led by Kentucky bullies and slave-traders. They sacked Birney's anti-slavery office, broke up his printing press and threw the types into the river, and then proceeded to burn negro houses, and to beat and maltreat defenceless women and children, after the manner of such evil beasts generally.

At the time the mob were busy destroying the printing press, Mr. Chase threw himself in among them with a view to observe, and if possible to obstruct their proceedings.

He gathered from their threats while the process of sacking the office was going on, that their next attack would be on the life of Mr. Birney. On hearing this, he hastened before them to Mr. Birney's hotel, and stood in the door-way to meet them when they came up.

No test of personal courage or manliness is greater than thus daring to stand and oppose a mob in the full flush of lawless triumph. Mr. Chase had a fine commanding person, and perfect courage and coolness, and he succeeded in keeping back the mob, by arguing with them against lawless acts of violence to persons or property, until Birney had had time to escape.

The upper ten of Cincinnati, when tranquility was once more restored to that community, were of course very much shocked and scandalized by the proceedings of the mob, but continued to assert that all these doings were the fault of the abolitionists. What could be expected if they *would* continue discussions which made our brethren across the river so uncomfortable? If nobody would defend the rights of negroes there would be no more negro mobs, and good society became increasingly set in the belief that speaking for the slave in any way whatever was actually to join the abolitionists, and to become in fact a radical, a disorganizer, a maker of riots and disturbances.

No young lawyer who acted merely from humane sentiment, or common good natured sympathy, would have dared at that time to plead a slave's cause against a master's claim. Then and always there were a plenty of people to feel instinctive compassion, and in fact slily to give a hunted fugitive a lift, if sure not to lose by it—but to take up and plead professionally a slave's cause against a master was a thing which no young man could do without making up his mind to be counted as one of the abolitionists, and to take upon his shoulders the whole responsibility of being identified with them.

Mr. Chase was a man particularly alive to the value of all the things which he put in peril by such a step. He had a remarkable share of what is called the "Yankee" nature, which values and appreciates material good. He had begun poor, and he knew exactly what a hard thing poverty was. He had begun at the bottom of the social ladder, and he knew exactly how hard it was to climb to a good position. He had just got such a position, and he truly appreciated it. His best patrons and warmest friends now, with earnestness warned him not to listen to the voice of his feelings, and take that course which would identify him with the fanatical abolitionists. They told him that it would be social and political death to him to take a step in that direction.

For all that, when the case of the slave girl Matilda was brought to his door he defended it deliberately, earnestly and with all his might. Of course it was decided against him, as in those days, such cases were sure to be.

As Chase left the court room after making his plea in this case, a man looked after him and said, "There goes a fine young fellow who has just ruined himself." Listening, however, to this very speech was a public man of great ability whose efforts afterwards went a long way towards making Chase United States Senator; and to-day we see that same young lawyer on the bench, Chief Justice of the United States.

The decision of Chase in this matter was not merely from the temporary impulse of kindly feelings, but from a deep political insight into the tendencies and workings of the great slave power. His large, sound, logical brain saw in the future history of that power all that it has since brought to light. He saw that the exorbitant spirit of its exactions was directed against the liberties of the free States and the principles on which free government is founded.

The plea of Chase, in this case, was the first legal break-water in Ohio to the flood of usurpation and dictation which has characterized the slaveocracy from its commencement. In this plea he took a ground then unheard of, to wit: That the phrase in the Constitution which demanded the giving up of fugitives to service on demand of masters, did not impose on the magistrates of the free States the responsibility of catching and returning slaves. He denied that Congress had any right to impose any such duties on State magistrates, or to employ State resources in any way for this purpose. This principle was afterwards recognized by the United States in the slave law of 1850, by appointing special United States Commissioners for the conducting of such cases.

From the time of this plea many of the former patrons and friends of the rising young lawyer walked no more with him; but he had taken his ground like a strong man armed, and felt well able to keep his fortress single handed till recruits should gather around him.

He was soon called on to defend James G. Birney for the crime of sheltering a fugitive slave. In this plea he asserted the great principle afterwards affirmed by Charles Sumner in Congress, that slavery is sectional and freedom national. As slavery was but a local institution, he claimed that it ceased when the slave was brought by his master to a free State. This assertion caused great excitement in a community separated from a slave State only by the Ohio, where slave masters were constantly finding it convenient to cross with their slaves, or to send them across, to the neighboring city. Of course the decision went against him. What judge who had any hopes of the presidency, or the Supreme Bench, would dare offend his southern masters by any other?

In 1846 came on the great Van Zandt case. Van Zandt was originally a thriving Kentucky farmer and slave owner. He figured in Uncle Tom's Cabin under the name of Van Tromp. He was a man who, under a shaggy exterior, had a great, kind, honest heart, and in that day, when ministers and elders were studying the Bible to find apologies for slavery, Van Zandt needed no other light than that of this same heart to teach him that it was vile and devilish, and so, setting his slaves free, he came over and bought a farm in the neighborhood of Cincinnati; and it was well known that no hungry, wandering fugitive was ever turned from Van Zandt's door. The writer has still memory of the wild night ride of husband and brother through woods, and over swelled creeks dangerous enough to cross, which carried a poor, hunted slave girl to this safe retreat. But Van Zandt was at last found out, and the slaveocrats brought suit against him. Chase and Seward defended him, and made noble pleas—pleas as much for the rights of the whites as of the blacks. Of course, like all cases of the kind at that date, the judgment had been pre-ordained before the court sat. Chase's elaborate and unanswerable argument before the United States Court, was afterward printed in a pamphlet of some three hundred and fifty octavo pages.

The opening of this great plea and its close we shall quote as best showing the solemn and earnest spirit in which this young lawyer entered upon his work.

"MR. CHIEF JUSTICE AND JUDGES:

I beg leave to submit to your consideration an argument in behalf of an old man, who is charged, under the act of Congress of February 12, 1793, with having concealed and harbored a fugitive slave.

Oppressed, and well nigh borne down by the painful consciousness, that the principles and positions which it will be my duty to maintain, can derive no credit whatever from the reputation of the advocate, I have spared no pains in gathering around them whatever of authority and argument the most careful research and the most deliberate reflection could supply. I have sought instruction wherever I could find it; I have looked into the reported decisions of almost all the state courts, and of this court; I have examined and compared state legislation and federal; above all, I have consulted the constitution of the Union, and the history of its formation and adoption. I have done this, because I am well assured, that the issues, now presented to this court for solemn adjudication, reach to whatever is dear in constitutional liberty, and what is precious in political union. Not John Van Zandt alone—not numerous individuals only—but the States also, and the Nation itself, must be deeply affected by the decision to be pronounced in this case."

Then followed the technical and legal plea which is a most close and unanswerable legal argument, showing conclusively that under the words of the statute the defendant could not be held guilty.

After this, follows a clear and masterly argument on the unconstitutionality of the then existing fugitive slave law, of 1793. In this, Chase took with great skill, boldness, ingenuity and learning, the same course afterwards taken by Sumner in his great speech before Congress, on the Fugitive Slave Law of 1850.

The conclusion is solemn and weighty—and in the light of recent events has even a prophetic power:

"Upon questions,—such as are some of those involved in this case,—which partake largely of a moral and political nature, the judgment, even of this Court, cannot be regarded as altogether final. The decision, to be made here, must, necessarily, be rejudged at the tribunal of public opinion—the opinion, not of the American People only, but of the Civilized World. At home, as is well known, a growing disaffection to the Constitution prevails, founded upon its supposed allowance and support of Human Slavery; abroad, the national character suffers under the same reproach. I most earnestly hope, and,—I trust it may not be deemed too serious to add,—I most earnestly pray, that the judgment of your honors in this case, may commend itself to the reason and conscience of Mankind; that it may rescue the Constitution from the undeserved opprobrium of lending its sanction to the idea that there may be property in men; that it may gather around that venerable charter of Republican Government the renewed affection and confidence of a generous People; and that it may win for American Institutions the warm admiration and profound homage of all, who, everywhere, love Liberty and revere Justice."

The question was decided as all such cases in those times invariably were decided.

The Judge never undertook even the form of answering the argument; never even adverted to it, but decided directly over it, with a composure worthy of a despotism. It was a decision only equalled by that of the most corrupt judges of the corrupt age of Charles II.

Honest Van Zandt was ruined, "scot and lot," by a fine so heavy that all he had in the world would not pay it, and he died broken-hearted; a solemn warning to all in his day, how they allowed themselves to practise Christian charity in a way disagreeable to the plantation despots.

As for Chase, he was undiscouraged by ill success, and shortly reaffirmed his argument and principles in the case of Driskull vs. Parish. He was at least educating the community; he was laying foundations of resistance on which walls and towers should by-and-by arise. Humanity and religion had already made the abolitionists numerically a large and active body in Ohio. They needed only a leader like Chase, of large organizing brain and solid force of combination, to shape them into a political party of great efficiency. To this end his efforts were henceforth directed. In 1841, he united in a call for an Anti-Slavery Convention in Columbus, and in this convention was organized the Liberty party of Ohio. In 1845 he projected a Southwestern Anti-Slavery Convention.

The ground taken was substantially that to which a bloody, weary experience has brought the whole nation now, to wit: "That whatever is worth preserving in republicanism can be maintained only by uncompromising war against an usurping slave-power, and that all who wish to save the nation must unite in using all constitutional measures for the extinction of slavery in their own States, and the reduction of it to constitutional limits in the United States.

This convention met in Cincinnati, in 1845, and Chase prepared the address, giving the history of slavery thus far, and showing the condition of the Whig and Democratic parties respecting it; and urging the importance of a political combination unequivocally committed to the denationalizing of slavery and the slave power. So vigorous were the tactics of this party, so strongly moving with the great central currents of God's forward providences, that in 1847 Chase was made Governor of Ohio, by the triumph of those very principles which in the outset threatened utter loss to their advocate. In 1847 he attended a second Liberty Convention; and afterwards took part in the Buffalo Convention, the celebrated Buffalo Platform being mainly his work.

In 1849, he was chosen United States Senator from Ohio, and his presence was hailed as a tower of strength to the hard fighting anti-slavery party at Washington. When, directly after the passage of the Fugitive Slave Law, the Democratic party in Ohio voted for Pierce, knowing him directly committed to its enforcement, Chase withdrew from it, and addressed a letter to B. F. Butler, of New York, recommending the formation of an Independent Democratic party. He prepared a platform for this purpose, which was substantially adopted by the convention of the Independent Democracy of 1852.

And now came on the battle of Kansas and Nebraska. Chase was one of the first to awaken the people to this new danger. He, in conference with the anti-slavery men of Congress, drafted an address to the people to arouse them as to this sudden and appalling conspiracy, which was intended to seize for slavery all the unoccupied land of the United States, and turn the balance of power and numbers forever into the slaveholders' hands. It was a critical moment; there was but little time to spare; but the whole united clergy of New England, of all denominations, Catholic and Protestant, found leisure to send in their solemn protest. When that nefarious bill passed, Chase protested against it on the night of its passage, as, with threats, and oaths, and curses, it was driven through. It seems in the retrospect but a brief passage from that hour of apparent defeat to the hour which beheld Lincoln in the presidential chair and Chase, Secretary of the Treasury. His history in that position has verified the sagacity that placed him there. It has been the success of a large, sound, organizing brain, apt and skillful in any direction in which it should turn its powers. It was the well-known thrift and shrewdness of the Yankee farmer, thrift and shrewdness cultivated in years of stern wrestling with life, coming out at the head of the United States treasury in a most critical hour. No men are better to steer through exigencies than these same Yankee farmers, and it seems the savor of this faculty goes to the second and third generations.

We have said before, that if Chase made sacrifices of tangible and material present values for abstract principles, in his early days, it was not because, as is sometimes the case, he was a man merely of ideas, and destitute of practical faculties. On the contrary, the shrewd, cautious, managing, self-preserving faculties were possessed by him to a degree which caused him to be often spoken of by the familiar proverb, "a man who can make every edge cut." By nature, by descent, by hard and severe training, he was a rigid economist, and a man who might always safely be trusted to make the very most and best of a given amount of property.

It is praise enough to any financier who could take a nation in the sudden and unprepared state ours was, and could carry it along for three or four years through a war of such gigantic expenditure, to say that the country was neither ruined, beggared, nor hopelessly embarrassed, but standing even stronger when he resigned the treasury than when he took it.

His financial management was at first to raise the money needed for the war by loans, until the expenses became so great as to be beyond the capacity of the specie in the country. Then, still adhering to the principle of raising the means for the war within the United States, he introduced the legal tender paper currency, and by providing that it should be a necessary basis for banking operations, he shrewdly placed the whole banking capital of the United States in a position where it must live or die with the country. This not only provided funds, but made every dollar of money act as a direct stimulus to the patriotism of those who supplied it.

On June 30, 1864, Chase resigned his position in the treasury. That Providence which has ordained so many striking and peculiar instances of victory and reward for men who espoused the cause of humanity in its dark hours, had also one for Chase.

Oct. 12, 1864, by the death of Taney, the Chief Justiceship of the United States Supreme Court became vacant, and Lincoln expressed the sense of the whole American people in calling Chase to fill that venerable office.

The young lawyer, who without name or prestige, dared to put in pleas for the poorest of his brethren, when the slave power was highest and haughtiest, and whose pleas were overruled with the most chilling contempt, now by God's providence holds that supreme position on the national bench from which, let us trust, the oppressor and the tyrant have faded away forever!

H. Wilson

CHAPTER VI.

HENRY WILSON.

Lincoln, Chase and Wilson as Illustrations of Democracy—Wilson's Birth and Boyhood—Reads over One Thousand Books in Ten Years—Learns Shoemaking—Earns an Education Twice Over—Forms a Debating Society—Makes Sixty Speeches for Harrison—Enters into Political Life on the Working-Men's Side—Helps to form the Free Soil Party—Chosen United States Senator over Edward Everett—Aristocratic Politics in those Days—Wilson and the Slave-holding Senators—The Character of his Speaking—Full of Facts and Practical Sense—His Usefulness as Chairman of the Military Committee—His "History of the Anti-Slavery Measures in Congress"—The 37th and 38th Congresses—The Summary of Anti-Slavery Legislation from that Book—Other Abolitionist Forces—Contrast of Sentiments of Slavery and of Freedom—Recognition of Hayti and Liberia; Specimen of the Debate—Slave and Free Doctrine on Education—Equality in Washington Street Cars—Pro-Slavery Good Taste—Solon's Ideal of Democracy Reached in America.

It is interesting to notice how, in the recent struggle that has convulsed our country and tried our republican institutions, so many of the men who have held the working oar have been representative men of the people. To a great extent they have been men who have grown up with no other early worldly advantages than those which a democratic republic offers to every citizen born upon her soil. Lincoln from the slave states, and Chase and Henry Wilson in the free, may be called the peculiar sons of Democracy. That hard Spartan mother trained them early on her black broth to her fatigues, and wrestlings, and watchings, and gave them their shields on entering the battle of life with only the Spartan mother's brief —"With this, or upon this."

Native force and Democratic institutions raised Lincoln to the highest seat in the nation, and to no mean seat among the nations of the earth; and the same forces in Massachusetts caused that State, in an hour of critical battle for the great principles of democratic liberty, to choose Henry Wilson, the self-taught, fearless shoemaker's apprentice of Natick, over the head of the gifted and graceful Everett, the darling of foreign courts, the representative of all the sentiments and training which transmitted aristocratic ideas have yet left in Boston and Cambridge. All this was part and parcel of the magnificent drama which has been acting on the stage of this country for the hope and consolation of all who are born to labor and poverty in all nations of the world.

Henry Wilson, our present United States Senator, was born at Farmington, N. H., Feb. 12, 1818, of very poor parents. At the age of ten he was bound to a farmer till he was twenty-one. Here he had the usual lot of a farm boy—plain, abundant food, coarse clothing, incessant work, and a few weeks' schooling at the district school in winter.

In these ten years of toil, the boy, by twilight, firelight, and on Sundays, had read over one thousand volumes of history, geography, biography and general literature, borrowed from the school libraries and from those of generous individuals.

At twenty-one he was his own master, to begin the world; and in looking over his inventory for starting in life, found only a sound and healthy body, and a mind trained to reflection by solitary thought. He went to Natick, Mass., to learn the trade of a shoemaker, and in working at it two years, he saved enough money to attend the academy at Concord and Wolfsborough, N. H. But the man with whom he had deposited his hard earnings became insolvent; the money he had toiled so long for, vanished; and he was obliged to leave his studies, go back to Natick and make more. Undiscouraged, he resolved still to pursue his object, uniting it with his daily toil. He formed a debating society among the young mechanics of the place; investigated subjects, read, wrote and spoke on all the themes of the day, as the spirit within him gave him utterance. Among his fellow-mechanics, some others were enkindled by his influence, and are now holding high places in the literary and diplomatic world.

In 1840, young Wilson came forward as a public speaker. He engaged in the Harrison election campaign, made sixty speeches in about four months, and was well repaid by his share in the triumph of the party. He was then elected to the Massachusetts Legislature as representative from Natick.

Having entered life on the working man's side, and known by his own experience the working man's trials, temptations and hard struggles, he felt the sacredness of a poor man's labor, and entered public life with a heart to take the part of the toiling and the oppressed.

Of course he was quick to feel that the great question of our time was the question of labor and its rights and rewards. He was quick to feel the "irrepressible conflict," which Seward so happily designated, between the two modes of society existing in America, and to know that they must fight and struggle till one of them throttled and killed the other; and prompt to understand this, he made his early election to live or die on the side of the laboring poor, whose most oppressed type was the African slave.

In the Legislature, he introduced a motion against the extension of slave territory; and in 1845, went with Whittier to Washington with the remonstrance of Massachusetts against the admission of Texas as a slave State.

When the Whig party became inefficient in the cause of liberty through too much deference to the slave power, Henry Wilson, like Charles Sumner, left it, and became one of the most energetic and efficient organizers in forming the Free Soil party of Massachusetts. In its interests, he bought a daily paper in Boston, which for some time he edited with great ability.

Meanwhile, he rose to one step of honor after another, in his adopted State; he became President of the Massachusetts Senate; and at length after a well contested election, was sent to take the place of the accomplished Everett in the United States Senate.

His election was a sturdy triumph of principle. His antagonist had every advantage of birth and breeding, every grace which early leisure, constant culture, and the most persevering, conscientious self-education could afford. He was, in graces of person, manners and mind, the ideal of Massachusetts aristocracy, but he wanted that clear insight into actual events, which early poverty and labor had given to his antagonist. His sympathies in the great labor question of the land were with the graceful and cultivated aristocrats rather than the clumsy, ungainly laborer; and he but professed the feeling of all aristocrats in saying at the outset of his political life, while Wilson was yet a child, that in the event of a servile insurrection, he would be among the first to shoulder a musket to defend the masters.

But the great day of the Lord was at hand. The events which since have unrolled in fire and blood, had begun their inevitable course; and the plain working-man was taken by the hand of Providence towards the high places where he, with other working men, should shape the destiny of the labor question for this age and for all ages.

Wilson went to Washington in the very heat and fervor of that conflict which the gigantic Giddings, with his great body and unflinching courage, said to a friend, was to him a severer trial of human nerve than the facing of cannon and bullets. The slave aristocracy had come down in great wrath, as if knowing that its time was short. The Senate chamber rang with their oaths and curses as they tore and raged like wild beasts against those whom neither their blandishments nor their threats could subdue. Wilson brought there his face of serene good nature, his vigorous, stocky frame, which had never seen ill-health, and in which the nerves were yet an undiscovered region. It was entirely useless to bully, or to threaten, or to cajole that honest, good-humored, immovable man, who stood like a rock in their way, and took all their fury as unconsciously as a rock takes the foam of breaking waves. In every anti-slavery movement he was always foremost, perfectly awake, perfectly well informed, and with that hardy, practical business knowledge of men and things which came from his early education, prepared to work out into actual forms what Sumner gave out as splendid theories.

Wilson's impression on the Senate was not mainly that of an orator. His speeches were as free from the artifices of rhetoric as those of Lincoln, but they were distinguished for the weight and abundance of the practical information and good sense which they contained. He never spoke on a subject till he had made himself minutely acquainted with it in all its parts, and was accurately familiar with all that belonged to it. Not even John Quincy Adams or Charles Sumner could show a more perfect knowledge of what they were talking about than Henry Wilson. Whatever extraneous stores of knowledge and belles lettres may have been possessed by any of his associates, no man on the floor of the Senate could know more of the *United States of America* than he; and what was wanting in the graces of the orator, or the refinements of the rhetorician was more than made amends for in the steady, irresistible, strong tread of the honest man, determined to accomplish a worthy purpose.

Wilson succeeded Benton as chairman of the Military Committee of the Senate, and it was fortunate for the country that when the sudden storm of the war broke upon us, so strong a hand held this helm. Gen. Scott said that he did more work in the first three months of the war than had been done in his position before for twenty years; and Secretary Cameron attributed the salvation of Washington in those early days, mainly to Henry Wilson's power of doing the apparently impossible in getting the Northern armies into the field in time to meet the danger.

His recently published account of what Congress has done to destroy slavery, is a history which no man living was better fitted to write. No man could be more minutely acquainted with the facts, more capable of tracing effects to causes, and thus competent to erect this imperishable monument to the honor of his country.

It is meet that the poor, farm-bound apprentice, the shoemaker of Natick, should thus chronicle the great history of the deliverance of labor from disgrace in this democratic nation.

There is something sublime in the history of the movements of the 37th and 38th Congresses of the United States. Perhaps never in any country did an equal number of wise and just men meet together under a more religious sense of their responsibility to God and to mankind. Never had there been a deeper and more religious awe presiding over popular elections than those which sent those men to Congress to man our national ship in the terrors of the most critical passage our stormy world has ever seen. They were the old picked, tried seamen, stout of heart, giants in conscience and moral sense. They were the scarred veterans of long years of battling for the great principles of the Declaration of Independence, men who in old times had come through great battles with the beasts of the slavery Ephesus, and still wore the scars of their teeth. They had seen their president stricken down at their head, and though bleeding inwardly, had closed up their ranks shoulder to shoulder, to go steadily on with the great work for which he died.

These men it was who while the din of arms was resounding through the country, while Washington was one great camp and hospital, and the confusing rumors of wars were coming to it from the east and from the west, from the north and from the south—took up and carried to the end the grandest national moral reform ever accomplished in a given time. Many men of the common sort would have said, "This is no time to be driving at moral reforms. We must drive this war through first, and when we have done this, we will begin to wipe up, and adjust, and put away." So gigantic a war was apology enough to satisfy the consciences of men who looked only to precedents and the rules of ordinary statesmanship, but our Congress was largely made up of men who walked by a higher light, and judged by a higher standard than ever has been given to mere statesmanship before. The spirit of the old Puritans, their unworldly, God-fearing spirit, their steadfast flint-facedness in principle, came to a final and culminating development in these Congresses.

Henry Wilson has written a "History of the Anti-Slavery Measures in Congress," in a brief, clear, compact summary, and made of it a volume which ought to be in every true American library. It is a volume of which every American has just and honest reason to be proud, and to which every Republican the whole world over, should look with hope and trust, as exhibiting the magnificent morality, the dauntless courage, the unwearied faith, hope and charity that are the crown jewels of republics. We should be glad to see this book of Henry Wilson's in every farm house of New England, lying by the family Bible, under the old flag of the Union. The men who carried through these magnificent reforms—THEY ARE OUR JEWELS.

Mr. Wilson gives in his book a condensed summary of the debates in the House relative to each step of the reform. For the most part it is a record of noble, Christian, unworldly patriotic sentiment—a sort of ideal statesmanship becoming real in tangible good deeds.

Every day some new den in the Augean stable was exposed and opened up to daylight, and the cleansing baptism of liberty applied. There was some fluttering and screaming of owls and bats, and now and then the poor old dilapidated dragon of slavery gave a bootless hiss, but nobody minded it. It was a whole-hearted, clean, pure, noble time in Congress, when those walls, so long defiled with the brawls, the mingled profanity and obscenity of slaveholders and slavebreeders, now rang only to manly sentiments and cleanly, noble, Christian resolves, such as make the heart strong to hear. We quote from the close of Mr. Wilson's book the summary of what was done by these Congresses in the way of reform legislation.

"As the Union armies advanced into the rebel States, slaves, inspired by the hope of personal freedom, flocked to their encampments, claiming protection against rebel masters, and offering to work and fight for the flag whose stars for the first time gleamed upon their vision with the radiance of liberty. Rebel masters and rebel-sympathizing masters sought the encampments of the loyal forces, demanding the surrender of the escaped fugitives; and they were often delivered up by officers of the armies. To weaken the power of the insurgents, to strengthen the loyal forces, and assert the claims of humanity, the 37th Congress enacted an article of war, dismissing from the service officers guilty of surrendering these fugitives.

Three thousand persons were held as slaves in the District of Columbia, over which the nation exercised exclusive jurisdiction; the 37th Congress made these three thousand bondmen freemen, and made slaveholding in the capital of the nation for evermore impossible.

"Laws and ordinances existed in the national capital that pressed with merciless rigor upon the colored people: the 37th Congress enacted that colored persons should be tried for the same offences, in the same manner, and be subject to the same punishments, as white persons; thus abrogating the 'black code.'

"Colored persons in the capital of this Christian nation were denied the right to testify in the judicial tribunals; thus placing their property, their liberties, and their lives, in the power of unjust and wicked men; the 37th Congress enacted that persons should not be excluded as witnesses in the courts of the District on account of color.

"In the capital of the nation, colored persons were taxed to support schools from which their own children were excluded; and no public schools were provided for the instruction of more than four thousand youth; the 38th Congress provided by law that public schools should be established for colored children, and that the same rate of appropriations for colored schools should be made as are made for schools for the education of white children.

"The railways chartered by Congress, excluded from their cars colored persons, without the authority of law; Congress enacted that there should be no exclusion from any car on account of color.

"Into the territories of the United States,— one-third of the surface of the country,—the slaveholding class claimed the right to take and hold their slaves under the protection of law; the 37th Congress prohibited slavery for ever in all the existing territory, and in all territory which may hereafter be acquired; thus stamping freedom for all, for ever, upon the public domain.

"As the war progressed, it became more clearly apparent that the rebels hoped to win the Border slave States; that rebel sympathizers in those States hoped to join the rebel States; and that emancipation in loyal States would bring repose to them, and weaken the power of the Rebellion; the 37th Congress, on the recommendation of the President, by the passage of a joint resolution, pledged the faith of the nation to aid loyal States to emancipate the slaves therein.

"The hoe and spade of the rebel slave were hardly less potent for the Rebellion than the rifle and bayonet of the rebel soldier. Slaves sowed and reaped for the rebels, enabling the rebel leaders to fill the wasting ranks of their armies, and feed them. To weaken the military forces and the power of the Rebellion, the 37th Congress decreed that all slaves of persons giving aid and comfort to the Rebellion, escaping from such persons, and taking refuge within the lines of the army; all slaves captured from such persons, or deserted by them; all slaves of such persons, being within any place occupied by rebel forces, and afterwards occupied by the forces of the United States,—shall be captives of war, and shall be for ever free of their servitude, and not again held as slaves.

"The provisions of the Fugitive-slave Act permitted disloyal masters to claim, and they did claim, the return of their fugitive bondmen; the 37th Congress enacted that no fugitive should be surrendered until the claimant made oath that he had not given aid and comfort to the Rebellion.

"The progress of the Rebellion demonstrated its power, and the needs of the imperilled nation. To strengthen the physical forces of the United States, the 37th Congress authorized the President to receive into the military service persons of African descent; and every such person mustered into the service, his mother, his wife and children, owing service or labor to any person who should give aid and comfort to the Rebellion, was made for ever free.

"The African slave-trade had been carried on by slave pirates under the protection of the flag of the United States. To extirpate from the seas that inhuman traffic, and to vindicate the sullied honor of the nation, the Administration early entered into treaty stipulations with the British Government for the mutual right of search within certain limits; and the 37th Congress hastened to enact the appropriate legislation to carry the treaty into effect.

"The slaveholding class, in the pride of power, persistently refused to recognize the independence of

Hayti and Liberia; thus dealing unjustly towards those nations, to the detriment of the commercial interests of the country; the 37th Congress recognized the independence of those republics by authorizing the President to establish diplomatic relations with them.

"By the provisions of law, white male citizens alone were enrolled in the militia. In the amendment to the acts for calling out the militia, the 37th Congress provided for the enrollment and drafting of citizens, without regard to color; and, by the Enrollment Act, colored persons, free or slave, are enrolled and drafted the same as white men. The 38th Congress enacted that colored soldiers shall have the same pay, clothing, and rations, and be placed in all respects upon the same footing, as white soldiers. To encourage enlistments, and to aid emancipation, the 38th Congress decreed that every slave mustered into the military service shall be free for ever; thus enabling every slave fit for military service to secure personal freedom.

"By the provisions of the fugitive-slave acts, slave-masters could hunt their absconding bondmen, require the people to aid in their recapture, and have them returned at the expense of the nation. The 38th Congress erased all fugitive-slave acts from the statutes of the Republic.

"The law of 1807 legalized the coastwise slave-trade; the 38th Congress repealed that act, and made the trade illegal.

"The courts of the United States receive such testimony as is permitted in the States where the courts are holden. Several of the States exclude the testimony of colored persons. The 38th Congress made it legal for colored persons to testify in all the courts of the United States.

"Different views are entertained by public men relative to the reconstruction of the governments of the seceded States, and the validity of the President's proclamation of emancipation. The 38th Congress passed a bill providing for the reconstruction of the governments of the rebel States, and for the emancipation of the slaves in those States; but it did not receive the approval of the President.

"Colored persons were not permitted to carry the United States mails; the 38th Congress repealed the prohibitory legislation, and made it lawful for persons of color to carry the mails.

"Wives and children of colored persons in the military and naval service of the United States were often held as slaves; and, while husbands and fathers were absent fighting the battles of the country, these wives and children were sometimes removed and sold, and often treated with cruelty; the 38th Congress made free the wives and children of all persons engaged in the military or naval service of the country.

"The disorganization of the slave system, and the exigencies of civil war, have thrown thousands of freedmen upon the charity of the nation; to relieve their immediate needs, and to aid them through the transition period, the 38th Congress established a Bureau of Freedmen.

"The prohibition of slavery in the Territories, its abolition in the District of Columbia, the freedom of colored soldiers, their wives and children, emancipation in Maryland, West Virginia, and Missouri, and by the re-organized State authorities of Virginia, Tennessee, and Louisiana, and the President's Emancipation Proclamation, disorganized the slave system, and practically left few persons in bondage; but slavery still continued in Delaware and Kentucky, and the slave codes remain, unrepealed in the rebel States. To annihilate the slave system, its codes and usages; to make slavery impossible, and freedom universal,—the 38th Congress submitted to the people an anti-slavery amendment to the Constitution of the United States. The adoption of that crowning measure assures freedom to all.

"Such are the "ANTI-SLAVERY MEASURES" of the Thirty-seventh and Thirty-eighth Congresses during the past four crowded years. Seldom in the history of nations is it given to any body of legislators or lawgivers to enact or institute a series of measures so vast in their scope, so comprehensive in their character, so patriotic, just, and humane.

"But, while the 37th and 38th Congresses were enacting this anti-slavery legislation, other agencies were working to the consummation of the same end,—the complete and final abolition of slavery. The President proclaims three and a half millions of bondmen in the rebel States henceforward and for ever free. Maryland, Virginia, and Missouri adopt immediate and unconditional emancipation. The partially re-organized rebel States of Virginia and Tennessee, Arkansas and Louisiana, accept and adopt the unrestricted abolition of slavery. Illinois and other States hasten to blot from their statute-books their dishonoring black codes.

The Attorney-General officially pronounces the negro a citizen of the United States. The negro, who had no status in the Supreme Court, is admitted by the Chief Justice to practice as an attorney before that august tribunal. Christian men and women follow the loyal armies with the agencies of mental and moral instruction to fit and prepare the enfranchised freedmen for the duties of the higher condition of life now opening before them."

We cannot quit this subject without remarking on the striking character of the debates Mr. Wilson's book records on these subjects. The great majority of Congress utters aloud and with one consent, just, manly, noble, humane, large-hearted sentiments and resolves, while a poor wailing minority is picking up and retailing the old worn out jokes and sneers and incivilities and obscenities of the dying dragon of slavery.

As a specimen of the utter naiveté and ignorance of comity and good manners induced by slavery, in contrast with the courtesy and refinement of true republicanism, we give this fragment of a debate on the recognition of Hayti and Liberia.

Mr. Davis, of Kentucky, after plaintively stating that he is weary, sick, disgusted, despondent with the introduction of slaves and slavery into this chamber, proceeds to state his terror lest should these measures take effect, these black representatives would have to be received on terms of equality with those of other nations. Mr. Davis goes on to say: "A big negro fellow, dressed out in his silver and gold lace, presented himself in the court of Louis Napoleon, I admit, and was received. Now, sir, *I* want no such exhibition as that in our country. The American minister, Mr. Mason, was present on that occasion; and he was sleeved by some Englishman—I have forgotten his name—who was present, who pointed out to him the ambassador of Soulouque, and said, 'What do you think of him?' Mr. Mason turned round and said, 'I think, clothes and all, he is worth a thousand dollars.'"

Mr. Davis evidently considered this witticism of Mr. Mason's as both a specimen of high bred taste and a settling argument.

In reply, Mr. Sumner drily says: "The Senator alludes to some possible difficulties, I hardly know how to characterize them, which may occur here in social life, should the Congress of these United States undertake at this late day, simply in harmony with the law of nations, and following the policy of civilized communities, to pass the bill under discussion. I shall not follow the senator on those sensitive topics. I content myself with a single remark. I have more than once had the opportunity of meeting citizens of these republics; and I say nothing more than truth when I add, that I have found them so refined, and so full of self-respect, that I am led to believe no one of them charged with a mission from his government, will seek any society where he will not be entirely welcome. Sir, the senator from Kentucky may banish all anxiety on that account. No representative from Hayti or Liberia will trouble him."

Mr. Crittenden of Kentucky said: "I will only say, sir, that I have an innate sort of confidence and pride that the race to which we belong is a superior race among the races of the earth, and I want to see that pride maintained. The Romans thought that no people on the face of the earth were equal to the citizens of Rome, and it made them the greatest people in the world. * * * The spectacle of such a diplomatic dignitary in our country, would, I apprehend, be offensive to the people for many reasons, and wound their habitual sense of superiority to the African race."

Mr. Thomas of Maine, on the other hand, presents the true basis of Christian chivalry: "I have no desire to enter into the question of the relative capacity of races; but if the inferiority of the African race were established, the inference as to our duty would be very plain. If this colony has been built up by an inferior race of men, they have upon us a yet stronger claim for our countenance, recognition, and, if need be, protection. The instincts of the human mind and heart concur with the policy of men and governments to help and protect the weak. I understand that to a child or to a woman I am to show a degree of forbearance, kindness, and of gentleness even, which I am not necessarily to extend to my equal."

In like manner contrast a passage of sentiment between two senators on the education bill.

Mr. Carlile of Virginia, "did not see any good reason why the Congress of the United States should itself enter upon a scheme for educating negroes." He understood "the reason assigned for the government of a State undertaking the education of the citizens of the State is that the citizens in this country are the governors;" but he presumed "we have not yet reached the point when it is proposed to elevate to the condition of voters the negroes of the land."

Mr. Grimes in reply said, "It may be true, that, in that section of the country where the senator is most acquainted, the whole idea of education proceeds from the fact, that the person who is to be educated is merely to be educated because he is to exercise the elective franchise; but I thank God that I was raised in a section of the country where there are nobler and loftier sentiments entertained in regard to education. We entertain the opinion that all human beings are accountable beings. We believe that every man should be taught so that he may be able to read the law by which he is to be governed, and under which he may be punished. We believe that every accountable being should be able to read the word of God, by which he should guide his steps in this life, and shall be judged in the life to come. We believe that education is necessary in order to elevate the human race. We believe that it is necessary in order to keep our jails and our penitentiaries and our alms-houses free from inmates. In my section of the country, we do not educate any race upon any such low and grovelling ideas as those that seem to be entertained by the senator from Virginia."

But the warmest battle was on the question of the right of colored persons to ride in the cars. The chivalry maintained their side by such kind of language as this: "Has any *gentleman* who was born a gentleman, or any man who has the instincts of a gentleman, felt himself degraded by the fact that he was not honored by a seat beside some free negro? Has any lady in the United States felt herself aggrieved that she was not honored with the company of Miss Dinah or Miss Chloe, on board these cars?"

Again, in the course of the debate, another senator says of Mr. Sumner, "*He* may ride with negroes, if he thinks proper, so may I; but if I see proper not to do so, I shall follow my natural instincts, as he follows his."

"I shall vote for this amendment," says Henry Wilson; "and my own observation convinces me that justice, not to say decency, requires that I should do so. Some weeks ago, I rode to the capitol in one of these cars. On the front part of the car, standing with the driver, were, I think, five colored clergymen of the Methodist Episcopal church, dressed like gentlemen, and behaving like gentlemen. These clergymen were riding with the driver on the front platform, and inside the car were two drunken loafers, conducting and behaving themselves so badly that the conductor threatened to turn them out."

"The senator from Illinois tells us," said Mr. Wilson, "that the colored people have a legal right to ride in these cars now. We know it; nobody doubts it; but this company into which we breathed the breath of life, outrages the rights of twenty-five thousand colored people in this District, in our presence, in defiance of our opinions. * * * I tell the senator from Illinois that I care far more for the rights of the humblest black child that treads the soil of the District of Columbia than I do for the prejudices of this corporation, and its friends and patrons. The rights of the humblest colored man in the capital of this Christian nation are dearer to me than the commendations or the thanks of all persons in the city of Washington who sanction this violation of the rights of a race. I give this vote, not to offend this corporation, not to offend anybody in the District of Columbia, but to protect the rights of the poor and the lowly, trodden under the heel of power. I trust we shall protect rights, if we do it over prejudices and over interests, until every man in this country is fully protected in all the rights that belong to beings made in the image of God. Let the free man of this race be permitted to run the career of life; to make of himself all that God intended he should make, when he breathed into him the breath of life."

So there they had it, at the mouth of an educated northern working-man, who knew what man as man was worth, and the retiring senators, giving up the battle, wailed forth as follows:

"Poor, helpless, despised, inferior race of white men, you have very little interest in this government, you are not worth consideration in the legislation of this country; but let your superior Sambo's interest come in question, and you will find the most tender interest on *his* behalf. What a pity there is not somebody to lamp-black white men, so that their rights could be secured."

Mr. Powell thought that the Senator from Massachusetts, the next time one of his Ethiopian friends comes to complain to him on the subject, should bring an action for him in court, and adds, with the usual good taste of his party: * * "The Senator has indicated to his fanatical brethren those people who meet in free love societies, the old ladies and the sensation preachers, and those who live on fanaticism, that he has offered it, and I see no reason why we should take up the time of the Senate in squabbling over the Senator's amendments, introducing the negro into every wood-pile that comes along."

Mr. Saulsbury closes a discussion on negro testimony with the following pious ejaculation: "He did not wish to say any more about the *nigger* aspect of the case. It is here every day; and I suppose it *will* be here every day for years to come, till the Democratic party comes in power and wipes all legislation of this character out of the statute-book, which I trust in God they will do."

All this sort of talk, shaken in the face of the joyous band of brothers who were going on their way rejoicing, reminds us forcibly of John Bunyan's description of the poor old toothless giant, who in his palmy days used to lunch upon pilgrims, tearing their flesh and cracking their bones in the most comfortable way possible, but who now having sustained many a severe brush, was so crippled with rheumatism that he could only sit in the mouth of his cave, mumbling, "You will never mend till more of you are burned."

Thank God for the day we live in, and for such men as Henry Wilson and his compeers of the 37th and 38th Congresses. They have at last put our American Union in that condition which old Solon gave as his ideal of true Democracy, namely:

A STATE WHERE AN INJURY TO THE MEANEST MEMBER IS FELT AS AN INJURY TO THE WHOLE.

Horace Greeley

CHAPTER VII.

HORACE GREELEY.

The Scotch-Irish Race in the United States—Mr. Greeley a Partly Reversed Specimen of it—His Birth and Boyhood—Learns to Read Books Upside Down—His Apprenticeship on a Newspaper—The Town Encyclopaedia—His Industry at his Trade—His First Experience of a Fugitive Slave Chase—His First Appearance in New York. The Work on the Polyglot Testament—Mr. Greeley as "the Ghost"—The First Cheap Daily Paper—The Firm of Greeley & Story—The New Yorker, the Jeffersonian and the Log Cabin—Mr. Greeley as Editor of the New Yorker—Beginning of The Tribune—Mr. Greeley's Theory of a Political Newspaper—His Love for The Tribune—The First Week of that Paper—The Attack of the Sun and its Result—Mr. McElrath's Partnership—Mr. Greeley's Fourierism—"The Bloody Sixth"—The Cooper Libel Suits—Mr. Greeley in Congress—He goes to Europe—His course in the Rebellion—His Ambition and Qualifications for Office—The Key-Note of his Character.

No race has stronger characteristics, bodily or mental, than that powerful, obstinate, fiery, pious, humorous, honest, industrious, hard-headed, intelligent, thoughtful and reasoning people, the Scotch-Irish. The vigorous qualities of the Scotch-Irish have left broad and deep traces upon the history of the United States. As if with some hereditary instinct, they settled along the great Allegheny ridge, principally from Pennsylvania to Georgia, in the fertile valleys and broader expanses of level land on either side, especially to the westward. In the healthy and genial air of these regions, renowned for the handsomest breed of men and women in the world, the Scotch-Irish acted out with thorough freedom, all the vigorous and often violent impulses of their nature. They were pioneers, Indian-fighters, politicians, theologians;

and they were as polemic in everything else as in theology. Jackson and Calhoun were of this blood. An observant traveller in Tennessee described to the writer the interest with which he found in that state literally hundreds of forms and faces with traits so like the lean erect figure, high narrow head, stiff black hair, and stern features of the fighting old President, that they might have been his brothers. Many of our eminent Presbyterian theologians like the late Dr. Wilson, of Cincinnati, have been Scotch-Irish too, and with their spiritual weapons they have waged many a controversy as unyielding, as stern and as unsparing as the battle in which Jackson beat down Calhoun by showing him a halter, or as that brutal knife fight in which he and Thomas H. Benton nearly cut each other's lives out.

Horace Greeley is of this Scotch-Irish race, and after a rule which physiologists well know to be not very uncommon, he presents a direct reverse of many of its traits, more especially its physical ones. Instead of a lean, erect person, dry hard muscles, a high narrow head, coarse stiff black hair, and a stern look, he tends to be fat, is shambling and bowed over in carrying himself, thinskinned and smooth and fair as a baby, with a wide, long, yet rounded head, silky-fine almost white hair, and a habitually meek sort of smile, which however must not be trusted to as an index of the mind within. Meek as he looks, no man living is readier with a strong sharp answer. Non-resistant as he is physically, there is not a more uncompromising an opponent and intense combatant in these United States. Mentally, he shows a predominance of Scotch-

Irish blood modified by certain traits which reveal themselves in his readiness to receive new theories of life.

Mr. Greeley was born Feb. 3d, 1811, at his father's farm, in Amherst, New Hampshire. The town was part of a district first settled by a small company of sixteen families of Scotch-Irish from Londonderry. These were part of a considerable emigration in 1718 from that city, whose members at first endeavored to settle in Massachusetts; but they were so ill received by the Massachusetts settlers that they found it necessary to scatter away into distant parts of the country before they could find rest for the soles of their feet.

The ancestors of Mr. Greeley were farmers, those of the name of Greeley being often also blacksmiths. The boy was fully occupied with hard farm work, and he attended the American farmers' college, the District School. He had an intense natural love for acquiring knowledge, and learned to read of himself. He could read any child's book when he was three, and any ordinary book at four; and having, as his biographer, Mr. Parton, suggests, still an overplus of mental activity, he learned to read as readily with the book sideways or upside down, as right side up.

Mr. Greeley, like a number of men who have grown up to become capable of a vast quantity of hard work and usefulness, was extremely feeble at birth, and was even thought scarcely likely to live when he first entered the world. During his first year he was feeble and sickly. His mother, who had lost her two children born next before him, seemed to be doubly fond of her weak little one, both for the sake of those that were gone, and of his very weakness, and she kept him by her side much more closely than if he had been strong and well; and day after day, she sung and repeated to him an endless store of songs and ballads, stories and traditions. This vivid oral literature doubtless had great influence in stimulating the child's natural aptitude for mental activity.

Mr. Greeley's father was not a much better financier than his son. In 1820, in spite of all the honest hard-work that he could do, he became bankrupt, and in 1821 moved to a new residence in Vermont.

Mr. Greeley seems to have had such an inborn instinct after newspapers and newspaper work, as Mozart had for music and musical composition. He himself says on this point, in his own "Recollections" in The New York Ledger, "Having loved and devoured newspapers—indeed every form of periodical—from childhood, I early resolved to be a printer if I could." When only eleven years old he applied to be received as an apprentice in a newspaper office at Whitehall, Vt., and was greatly cast down by being refused for his youth. Four years afterwards, in the spring of 1826, he obtained employment in the office of the Northern Spectator, at East Poultney, Vt., and thus began his professional career.

As a young man, Mr. Greeley was not only poorly but most extremely carelessly dressed; absent minded yet observant; awkward and indeed clownish in his manners; extremely fond of the game of checkers, at which he seldom found an equal; and of fishing and bee-hunting. Fonder still he was of reading and acquiring general knowledge, for which a public library in the town offered valuable advantages; and he very soon became, as a biographer says, a "town encyclopedia," appealed to as a court of last resort, by every one who was at a loss for information. In the local debating society of the place he was assiduous and prominent, and was noticeable both for the remarkable body of detailed facts which he could bring to bear upon the questions discussed, and for his thorough devotion to his argument. Whatever his opinion was, he stuck to it against either reasoning or authority.

In his calling as a printer, he was most laborious, and quickly became the most valuable hand in the office. He also began here his experience as a writer—if that may be called written which was never set down with a pen. For he used to compose condensations of news paragraphs, and even original paragraphs of his own, framing his sentences in his mind as he stood at the case, and setting them up in type entirely without the intermediate process of setting them down in manuscript. This practice was exactly the way to cultivate economy, clearness, and directness of style; as it was necessary to know accurately what was to be said, or else the letters in the composing stick would have to be distributed and set up again; and it was natural to use the fewest and plainest possible words.

While Horace was thus at work, his father had again removed beyond the Alleghanies, where he was doing his best to bring some new land under cultivation. The son, meanwhile, and for some time after his apprenticeship too, used to send to his father all the money that he could save from his scanty wages. He continued to assist his father, indeed, until the latter was made permanently comfortable upon a valuable and well stocked farm; and even paid up some of his father's old debts in New Hampshire thirty years after they were contracted.

Mr. Greeley has recorded that while in Poultney he witnessed a fugitive slave chase. New York had then yet a remainder of slavery in her, in the persons of a few colored people who had been under age when the state abolished slavery, and had been left by law to wait for their freedom until they should be twenty-eight years old. Mr. Greeley tells the story in the N. Y. Ledger, in sarcastic and graphic words, as follows:

"A young negro who must have been uninstructed in the sacredness of constitutional guaranties, the rights of property, &c., &c., &c., feloniously abstracted himself from his master in a neighboring New York town, and conveyed the chattel personal to our village; where he was at work when said master, with due process and following, came over to reclaim and recover the goods. I never saw so large a number of men and boys so suddenly on our village-green, as his advent incited; and the result was a speedy disappearance of the chattel, and the return of his master, disconsolate and niggerless, to the place whence he came. Everything on our side was impromptu and instinctive, and nobody suggested that envy or hate of the South, or of New York, or of the master, had impelled the rescue. Our people hated injustice and oppression, and acted as if they couldn't help it."

In June 1830, the Northern Spectator was discontinued, and our encyclopedic apprentice was turned loose on the world. Hereupon he traveled, partly on foot and partly by canal, to his father's place in Western Pennsylvania. Here he remained a while, and then after one or two unsuccessful attempts to find work, succeeded at Erie, Pa., where he was employed for seven months. During this time his board with his employer having been part of his pay, he used for other personal expenses six dollars in cash. The wages remaining due him amounted to just ninety-nine dollars. Of this he now gave his father eighty-five, put the rest in his pocket and went to New York.

He reached the city on Friday morning at sunrise, August 18th, 1831, with ten dollars, his bundle, and his trade. He engaged board and lodging at $2.50 a week, and hunted the printing offices for employment during that day and Saturday in vain; fell in with a fellow Vermonter early Monday morning, a journeyman printer like himself, and was by him presented to his foreman. Now there was in the office a very difficult piece of composition, a polyglot testament, on which various printers had refused to work. The applicant was, as he always had been, and will be, very queer looking; insomuch that while waiting for the foreman's arrival, the other printers had been impelled to make many personal remarks about him. But though equally entertained with his appearance, the foreman, rather to oblige the introducer than from any admiration of the new hand, permitted him a trial, and he was set at work on the terrible Polyglot. We transcribe Mr. Parton's lively account of the sequel:

"After Horace had been at work an hour or two, Mr. West, the 'boss,' came into the office. What his feelings were when he saw the new man may be inferred from a little conversation on the subject which took place between him and the foreman:

"'Did you hire that d—— fool?' asked West, with no small irritation.

"'Yes; we must have hands, and he's the best I could get,' said the foreman, justifying his conduct, though he was really ashamed of it.

"'Well,' said the master, 'for Heaven's sake pay him off to-night, and let him go about his business.'

"Horace worked through the day with his usual intensity, and in perfect silence. At night he presented to the foreman, as the custom then was, the 'proof' of his day's work. What astonishment was depicted in the good-looking countenance of that gentleman, when he discovered that the proof before him was greater in quantity and more correct than that of any other day's work on the Polyglot! There was no thought of sending the new journeyman about his business now. He was an established man at once. Thenceforward, for several months, Horace worked regularly and hard on the Testament, earning about six dollars a week."

While a journeyman here, he worked very hard indeed, as he was paid by the piece, and the work was necessarily slow. At the same time, according to his habit, he was accustomed to talk very fluently, his first day's silent labor having been an exception; and his voluble and earnest utterance, singular, high voice, fullness, accuracy, and readiness with facts, and positive though good-natured tenacious disputatiousness, together with his very marked personal traits, made him the phenomenon of the office. His complexion was so fair, and his hair so flaxen white, that the men nicknamed him "the Ghost." The mischievous juniors played him many tricks, some of them rough enough, but he only begged to be let alone, so that he might work, and they soon got tired of teasing from which there was no reaction. Besides, he was forever lending them money, for like very many of the profession, the other men in the office were profuse with whatever funds were in hand, and often needy before pay-day; while his own unconscious parsimony in personal expenditures was to him a sort of Fortunatus' purse—an unfailing fountain.

For about a year and a half Mr. Greeley worked as a journeyman printer. During 1832 he had become acquainted with a Mr. Story, an enterprising young printer, and also with Horatio D. Sheppard, the originator of the idea of a Cheap Daily Paper. The three consulted and co-operated; in December the printing firm of Greeley & Story was formed, and on the first of January, 1833, the first number of the first cheap New York Daily, "The Morning Post," was issued, "price two cents," Dr. Sheppard being editor. Various disadvantages stopped the paper before the end of the third week, but the idea was a correct one. The New York Sun, issued in accordance with it nine months later, is still a prosperous newspaper; and the great morning dailies of New York, including the Tribune, are radically upon the same model.

Though this paper stopped, the job printing firm of Greeley & Story went on and made money. At

Mr. Story's death, July 9, 1833, his brother-in-law, Mr. Winchester, took his place in the office. In 1834 the firm resolved to establish a weekly; and on March 22d, 1834, appeared the first number of the Weekly New Yorker, owned by the firm, and with Mr. Greeley as editor. He had now found his proper work, and he has pursued it ever since with remarkable force, industry and success.

This success, however, was only editorial, not financial, so far as the New Yorker was concerned. The paper began with twelve subscribers, and without any flourishes or promises. By its own literary, political and statistical value, its circulation rose in a year to 4,500, and afterwards to 9,000. But when it stopped, Sept. 20, 1841, it left its editor laboring under troublesome debts, both receivable and payable. The difficulty was manifold; its chief sources were, Mr. Greeley's own deficiencies as a financier, supplying too many subscribers on credit, and the great business crash of 1837.

During the existence of the New Yorker, Mr. Greeley also edited two short-lived but influential campaign political sheets. One of these, the Jeffersonian, was publishedweekly, at Albany. This was a Whig paper, which appeared during a year from March, 1838, and kept its editor over-busy, with the necessary weekly journey to Albany, and the double work. The other was the Log Cabin, the well-known Harrison campaign paper, issued weekly during the exciting days of "Tippecanoe and Tyler too," in 1840, and which was continued as a family paper for a year afterwards. Of the very first number of this famous little sheet,

48,000 were sold, and the edition rapidly increased to nearly 90,000. Neither of these two papers, however, made much money for their editor. But during his labors on the three, the New Yorker, Jeffersonian, and Log Cabin, he had gained a standing as a political and statistical editor of force, information and ability.

Mr. Greeley's editorial work on the New Yorker was a sort of literary spring-time to him. The paper itself was much more largely literary than the Tribune now is. In his editorial writing in those days, moreover, there is a certain rhetorical plentifulness of expression which the seriousness and the pressures of an overcrowded life have long ago cut sharply and closely off; and he even frequently indulged in poetical compositions. This ornamental material, however, was certainly not his happiest kind of effort. Mr. Greeley does his best only by being wholly utilitarian. Poetry and rhetoric appear as well from his mind as a great long red feather would, sticking out of his very oldest white hat.

The great work of Mr. Greeley's life, however—The New York Tribune—had not begun yet, though he was thirty years old. Its commencement was announced in one of the last numbers of the Log Cabin, for April 10, 1841, and its first number appeared on the very day of the funeral solemnities with which New York honored the memory of President Harrison. Mr. Greeley's own account, in one of his articles in the New York Ledger, is an interesting statement of his Theory of a Political Newspaper. He says:

"My leading idea was the establishment of a journal removed alike from servile partizanship on the one hand, and from gagged, mincing neutrality on the other. Party spirit is so fierce and intolerant in this country, that the editor of a non-partizan sheet is restrained from saying what he thinks and feels on the most vital, imminent topics; while, on the other hand, a Democratic, Whig, or Republican journal is generally expected to praise or blame, like or dislike, eulogize or condemn, in precise accordance with the views and interest of its party. I believed there was a happy medium between these extremes—a position from which a journalist might openly and heartily advocate the principles and commend the measures of that party to which his convictions allied him, yet dissent frankly from its course on a particular question, and even denounce its candidates if they were shown to be deficient in capacity, or (far worse) in integrity. I felt that a journal thus loyal to its own convictions, yet ready to expose and condemn unworthy conduct or incidental error on the part of men attached to its party, must be far more effective, even partywise, than though it might always be counted on to applaud or reprobate, bless or curse, as the party prejudices or immediate interest might seem to prescribe."

Mr. Greeley has now been the chief editor of the Tribune for twenty-six years, and the persistent love with which he still regards his gigantic child strikingly appears in the final paragraph of the same article:

"Fame is a vapor; popularity an accident; riches take wings; the only earthly certainty is oblivion—no man can foresee what a day may bring forth; and those who cheer to-day will often curse to-morrow; and yet

I cherish the hope that the Journal I projected and established will live and flourish long after I shall have moldered into forgotten dust, being guided by a larger wisdom, a more unerring sagacity to discover the right, though not by a more unfaltering readiness to embrace and defend it at whatever personal cost; and that the stone which covers my ashes may bear to future eyes the still intelligible inscription, 'Founder of THE NEW YORK TRIBUNE.' "

The Tribune began with some 600 subscribers. Of its first number 5,000 copies were printed, and, as Mr. Greeley himself once said, he "found some difficulty in giving them away." At the end of the first week the cash account stood, receipts, $92; expenditures, $525. Now the proprietor's whole money capital was $1,000, borrowed money. But—as has more than once been the case with others—an unjust attack on the Tribune strengthened it. An unprincipled attempt was made by the publisher of the Sun, to bribe and bully the newsmen and then to flog the newsboys out of selling the Tribune. The Tribune was prompt in telling the story to the public, and the public showed that sense of justice so natural to all communities, by subscribing to it at the rate of three hundred a day for three weeks at a time. In four weeks it sold an edition of six thousand, and in seven it sold eleven thousand, which was then all that it could print. Its advertising patronage grew equally fast. And what was infinitely more than this rush of subscribers, a steady and judicious business man became a partner with Mr. Greeley in the paper, at the end of July, not four months from its first issue. This was Mr.

Thomas McElrath, whose sound business management undoubtedly supplied to the concern an element more indispensable to its continued prosperity, than any editorial ability whatever.

The Tribune, as we have seen, like the infant Hercules in the old fable, successfully resisted an attempt to strangle it in its cradle. From that time to this, the paper and its editor have lived in a healthy and invigorating atmosphere of violent attacks of all sorts, on grounds political, social, moral and religious. The paper has not been found fault with, however, for being flat or feeble or empty. The first noticeable disturbance after the Sun attack was the Fourierite controversy. Perhaps Mr. Greeley's Fourierism—or Socialism, as it might be better called—was the principal if not the sole basis of all the notorious uproars that have been made for a quarter of a century about his "isms," and his being a "philosopher." During 1841 and several following years, the Tribune was the principal organ in the United States of the efforts then made to exemplify and prove in actual life the doctrines of Charles Fourier. The paper was violently assaulted with the charge that these doctrines necessarily implied immorality and irreligion. The Tribune never was particularly "orthodox," and while it vigorously defended itself, it could not honestly in doing so say what would satisfy the stricter doctrinalists of the different orthodox religious denominations. Moreover, the practical experiments made to organize Fourierite "phalanxes" and the like, all failed; so that in one sense, both the Fourierite movement was a failure, and The Tribune was vanquished in the discussion.

But the controversy was a great benefit to the cause of associated human effort; and there can be no doubt that the various endeavors at the present day in progress to apply the principle of association to the easing and improving of the various concerns of life, present a much more hopeful prospect than would have been the case without the ardent and energetic advocacy of The Tribune.

The next quarrel was with "the Bloody Sixth," as it was called, i. e. the low and rowdy politicians of the Sixth Ward, then the most corrupt part of the city. These politicians and their followers, enraged at certain exposures of their misdeeds in the spring of 1842, demanded a retraction, and only getting a hotter denunciation than before, promised to come down and "smash the office." The whole establishment was promptly armed with muskets; arrangements were made for flinging bricks from the roof above and spurting steam from the engine boiler below; but the "Bloody Sixth" never came.

The Cooper libel suits were in consequence of alleged libelous matter about J. Fenimore Cooper, who was a bitter tempered and quarrelsome man, and to the full as pertinacious as Mr. Greeley himself. This matter was printed November 17, 1841. The first suit in consequence was tried December 9, 1842. The damages were laid at $3,000. Cooper and Greeley each argued on his own side to the Court, and Cooper got a verdict for $200. Mr. Greeley went home and wrote a long and sharp narrative of the whole, for which Cooper instantly brought another suit; but he found that his prospect this time did not justify his perseverance, and the suit never came to trial.

In 1844 Mr. Greeley worked with tremendous intensity for the election of Henry Clay, but to no purpose. In February, 1845, the Tribune office was thoroughly burnt out, but fortunately with no serious loss. The paper was throughout completely opposed to the Mexican War. In 1848, and subsequently, the paper at first with hopeful enthusiasm and at last with sorrow chronicled the outbreak, progress and fate of the great Republican uprising in Europe. During the same year Mr. Greeley served a three months' term in Congress, signalizing himself by a persistent series of attacks both in the House and in his paper, on the existing practice in computing and paying mileage—a comparatively petty swindle, mean enough doubtless, in itself, but very far from being the national evil most prominently requiring a remedy. This proceeding made Mr. Greeley a number of enemies, gained him some inefficient approbations, and did not cure the evil. In 1857 he went to Europe, to see the "Crystal Palace" or World's Fair at London, in that year. He was a member of one of the "juries" which distributed premiums on that occasion; investigated industrial life in England with some care; and gave some significant and influential information about newspaper matters, in testifying before a parliamentary committee on the repeal of certain oppressive taxes on newspapers. He made a short trip to France and Italy; and on his return home, reaching the dock at New York about 6 A. M., he had already made up the matter for an "extra," while on board the steamer.

He rushed at once to the office, seizing the opportunity to "beat" the other morning papers, by an "exclusive" extra, sent off for the compositors, who had all gone to bed at their homes; began setting up the matter himself; worked away along with the rest until his exclusive extra was all ready, and then departed contentedly to his own home.

Mr. Greeley had always been a natural abolitionist; but, with most of the Whig party, he had been willing to allow the question of slavery to remain in a secondary position for a long time. He was however a willing, early, vigorous and useful member of the Republican party, when that party became an unavoidable national necessity, as the exponent of Freedom. With that party he labored hard during the Fremont campaign, through the times of the Kansas wars, and for the election of Mr. Lincoln. When the Rebellion broke out he stood by the nation to the best of his ability, and if he gave mistaken counsels at any time, his mistakes were the unavoidable results of his mental organization, and not in the least due to any conscious swerving from principle, either in ethics or in politics.

Mr. Greeley has at various times been spoken of as a candidate for State offices, and he undoubtedly has a certain share of ambition for high political position—an ambition which is assuredly entitled to be excused if not respected by American citizens. Yet any sound mind, it is believed, must be forced to the belief that his highest and fittest place is the Chief Editor's chair in the office of The Tribune. There he wields a great, a laboriously and honestly acquired influence, an influence of the greatest importance to Society. His friends would be sorry to see him leave that station for any other.

Mr. Greeley's character and career as an editor and politician can be understood and appreciated by remembering his key note:—*Benevolent ends, by utilitarian means.*

He desires the amelioration of all human conditions and the instrumentalities which he would propose are generally practical, common sense ones. Of magnificence, of formalities, of all the conventional part of life, whether in public or private, he is by nature as utterly neglectful as he is of the dandy element in costume, but he has a solid and real appreciation of many appreciable things, which go to make up the sum total of human advancement and happiness.

Eng^d by A H Ritchie

D. G. Farragut

CHAPTER VIII.

DAVID GLASCOE FARRAGUT.

The Lesson of the Rebellion to Monarchs—The Strength of the United States—The U. S. Naval Service—The Last War—State of the Navy in 1861—Admiral Farragut Represents the Old Navy and the New—Charlemagne's Physician, Farraguth—The Admiral's Letter about his Family—His Birth—His Cruise with Porter when a Boy of Nine—The Destruction of the Essex—Farragut in Peace Times—Expected to go with the South—Refuses, is Threatened, and goes North—The Opening of the Mississippi—The Bay Fight at Mobile—The Admiral's Health—Farragut and the Tobacco Bishop.

THE course and character and result of the Rebellion taught many a great new lesson; in political morals and in political economy; in international law; in the theory of governing; in the significance of just principles on this earth. Perhaps all those lessons, taught so tremendously to the civilized world, might be summed in one expression; the Astounding Strength of a Christian Republic. For, whichever phase of the Rebellion we examine in considering it as a chapter of novelties in the world's history, we still come back to that one splendid, heart-filling remembrance;—How unexpected, how unbelieved, how inexhaustible, how magnificent beyond all history, the strength of the United States!

"There goes your Model Republic," sneered all the Upper Classes of Europe, "knocked into splinters in the course of one man's life! A good riddance!" And reactionary Europe set instantly to work to league itself with our own traitors, now that the United States was dead, to bury it effectively. But the Imperial Republic, even more utterly unconscious than its enemies, of what it could suffer and could do, stunned at first and reeling under a blow the most tremendous ever aimed at any government, clung close to Right and Justice, and rising in its own blood, went down wounded as it was, into the thunder and the mingled blinding lightning and darkness of the great conflict, unknowing and unfearing whether life or death was close before. As its day, so was its strength. As the nation's need grew deeper and more desperate, in like measure the nation's courage, the conscious calmness, the unmoved resolution, the knowledge of strength and wealth and power, grew more high and strong, and whereas the world knew that no nation had ever survived such an assault, and knew, it said, that ours would not, lo and behold, the United States achieved things beyond all comparison more unheard of, more wonderful, than even the treasonable explosion for whose deadly catastrophe all the monarchists stood joyfully waiting. They were disappointed. And ever since, they know that if the Rebellion was not the death-toll of Republics, it was the death-toll of many other things, and ever since, all the kings are setting their houses in order.

There were three great national material instrumentalities which the Free Christian People of the United States created in their peril, being the sole means which could have won in the war, and being moreover exactly the means which England and Europe asserted that we were peculiarly unable to create or to use;

they were: the Supply of Money; the Army on the land, and the Fleet on the sea.

Of these three, the story of the fleet has a peculiar interest of its own. The United States Navy was always a popular service in the country, for the adventurous genius and inventive faculties of our people, developed and stimulated by its successful prosecution of commerce, had easily dealt with the naval problems of fifty years ago. In the war of 1812, the superior skill of our shipbuilders and sailors launched and navigated a small but swift and powerful and well managed navy, and the single common-sense application of sights for aiming, to our ship-guns, in like manner as to muskets, gave our sailors a murderous superiority in sea fights which won us many a victory.

But in times of peace, a free nation almost necessarily falls behind a standing army nation in respect of military and naval mechanism and stored material and readiness of organization; and accordingly, after forty years of little but disuse, our navy, as the muscles of an arm shrink away if it is left unmoved, showed little of the latest improvements in construction and armament, and indeed there was very little navy to show at all. At Mr. Lincoln's inauguration, the whole navy of the United States consisted of seventy-six vessels, carrying 1,783 guns; and of these, only twelve were within reach, so effectively had Mr. Buchanan's Secretary of the Navy, Toucey, dispersed them in readiness for the secession schemes of his fellows in the cabinet. And even of those twelve, but a few were in Northern ports. The navy conspirators had no mind to have a southern blockade brought down on them, and so took good care to send our best ships on long fancy voyages to Japan or otherwhere—and to clap on board of them certain officers whose loyalty and ability they wished to put out of the way. Thus General Ripley found himself, to his indignation, over in Asia when the explosion took place.

It was from this beginning—practically nothing—that the energy and skill of American inventors and seamen created a navy beyond comparison the strongest on the face of the earth, reaching a strength of 600 ships, and 51,000 men; which effectively maintained the most immense and difficult blockade of history; which performed with brilliant and glorious success, enterprises whose importance and danger are equal to any chronicled in the wonderful annals of the sea; which fully completed its own indispensable share in the work of subduing the rebellion; and which revolutionized the theory and practice of naval warfare.

In this chapter of the history of the navy the most famous name is that of Admiral Farragut, not so much in consequence of any identification with the mechanical inventions of the day, as because his past professional career and his recent brilliant and daring victories, have linked together the elder with the younger fame of our navy, and have done it by the exercise of professional and personal courage and skill, rather than by the ingenious use of newly discovered scientific auxiliaries. The hardy courage of unmailed breasts always appeals more strongly to admiration and sympathy, than that more thoughtful and doubtless wiser proceeding which would win fights from behind invulnerable protections.

A friend of the writer was, during the Rebellion, investigating some subject connected with the history of medicine. In one of the books he examined he found mention made of Charlemagne's physician, a wonderfully skilful and learned man, named *Farraguth.* Our famous Admiral was then in the Gulf of Mexico, engaged in the preparations for the attack on Mobile which took place during August of that year. So odd was this coincidence, that its discoverer wrote to the Admiral to ask whether he knew anything of this mediæval doctor, and received in reply a very friendly and agreeably written letter, from which some extracts may here be given without any violation of confidence, as giving the most authentic information about his ancestry.

"My own name is probably Castilian. My grandfather came from Ciudadela, in the island of Minorca. I know nothing of the history of my family before they came to this country and settled in Florida. You may remember that in the 17th century, a colony settled there, and among them, I believe, was my grandfather. My father served through the war of Independence, and was at the battle of the Cowpens. Judge Anderson, formerly Comptroller of the Treasurer, has frequently told me that my father received his majority from George Washington on the same day with himself; and his children have always supposed that this promotion was for his good conduct in that fight. Notwithstanding this statement * * * * I have never been able to find my father's name in any list of the officers of the Revolution.

"With two men, Ogden and McKee, he was afterwards one of the early settlers of Tennessee. Mr. McKee was a member of Congress from Alabama, and once stopped in Norfolk, where I was then residing, on purpose, as he said, to see me, as the son of his early friend. He said he had heard that I was "a chip of the old block"—what sort of a block it was I know not. This was thirty years ago. My father settled twelve miles from Knoxville, at a place called Campbell's Station, on the river, where Burnside had his fight. Thence we moved to the South, about the time of the Wilkinson and Blennerhassett trouble. My father was then appointed a master in the Navy, and sent to New Orleans in command of one of the gunboats. Hence the impression that I am a native of New Orleans. But all my father's children were born in Tennessee, and as I have said in answer to enquiries on this subject, we only moved South to crush out a couple of rebellions.

"My mother died of yellow fever the first summer in New Orleans, and my father setttled at Pascagoula, in Mississippi. He continued to serve throughout the 'last war,' and was at the battle of New Orleans, under Commodore Paterson, though very infirm at that time. He died the following year, and my brothers and sisters married in and about New Orleans, where their descendants still remain. * * * *

"As to the name, Gen. Goicouria, a Spanish hidalgo from Cuba, tells me it is Castilian, and is spelled in the same way as the old physician's—Farraguth."

Admiral David Glascoe Farragut was born at Campbell's Station, in East Tennessee, in 1801. While only a little boy, at nine years of age, his father, who had been a friend and shipmate of the hardy sea-king, Commodore Porter, procured him a midshipman's berth under that commander, and the boy, accompanying Porter in the romantic cruise of the Essex, served a right desperate apprenticeship to his hazardous profession. His first sea-fight was the short fierce combat of Porter in the Essex, on April 13th, 1812, with the English sloop-of-war, Alert. No sooner did the Alert spy the Essex, than she ran confidently close upon her weather quarter, and with three cheers opened her broadside. Porter, not a whit abashed, replied with such swift fury that the Englishman, smashed into drowning helplessness, and with seven feet of water in his hold, struck his colors in eight minutes, escaping out of the fight by surrender even more hastily than he had gone into it.

In that desperate and bloody fight in Valparaiso harbor, when the British captain Hillyar, with double the force of the Essex, and by means of a most discreditable breach of the law of neutrality, made an end of the Essex, Midshipman Farragut, twelve years of age, stood by his commander to the very last. When those who could swim ashore had been ordered overboard, Porter himself, having helped work the few remaining guns that could be fired, hauled down his flag, and surrendered the bloody wreck that was all he had left under him, for the sake of the helpless wounded men who must have sunk along with him. Farragut was wounded, and was sent home with the other officers of the ship, on parole; and Porter, in his report to the Secretary of the Navy, made special and honorable mention of the lad, and mentioned with the appropriate regret of a just and brave man, that the boy was "too young for promotion." Probably not another living man on the face of the earth had so early and so thorough a baptism of blood and fire, and bore himself through it so manlike.

Commodore Porter had been so much interested in the youth that he gave him the means of pursuing an education in general studies and military tactics. But Farragut's vocation was the sea, and as soon as the war was over he got another ship. Peace is the winter of soldiers and sailors; when they sit still and wait for the deadly harvest that brings them prosperity. The times were as dull for Farragut as for the rest, and for forty-five years he was sailing about the world or quietly commanding at one or another station, and at long intervals rising by seniority from one grade to another. In 1825 he became lieutenant, in 1841 commander, in 1851 captain. When the rebellion came he was sixty years old, had been in the service forty-eight years, and to the country at large was utterly unknown. This is not strange; for throughout all his youth and manhood he had had no opportunity to show the heroic qualities which when a boy of twelve he had proved himself to possess even then in such manly measure.

He was living at Norfolk; was a native of the South; and his second wife, with whom he was now living, was from a Norfolk family. It was therefore taken for granted that Farragut would go with the South, and when he frankly avowed his patriotism, he was met with astonishment and then with threats.

They told him it would probably be unsafe for him to remain in the South, with such sentiments. "Very well," he replied, "I will go where I *can* live with such sentiments." Accordingly, he left Norfolk for the North on the night of April 18, 1861, the very night before the rebels there fired the navy-yard. He established himself for a time near Tarrytown, on the Hudson river. The very air was full of suspicion in those days, and Captain Farragut being unknown to the people in the vicinity, and walking about in the fields alone a good deal, a report got out at one time among the neighbors that he was one of a gang that had arranged to cut the Croton Aqueduct and burn down New York.

Farragut's very first appointment was that to the command of the naval part of the New Orleans expedition, for which his orders reached him January 20, 1862, and on Feb. 3d, in his famous flag-ship, the Hartford, he sailed from Hampton Roads for Ship Island.

The opening of the Mississippi river has passed into history. Of all the series of strange and novel and desperate combats which accomplished the task, the passage of the forts and the capture of New Orleans was beyond comparison the most dangerous and difficult, and its success was the most brilliant. The services which succeeded this were less showy, but included much that was excessively laborious, and that was dangerous enough for any ordinary ambition; and from beginning to end the whole task required not only high courage, indefatigable activity, incessant labor, and the ordinary professional knowledge of a sailor, but an invention always ready to contrive new means for new ends, prompt judgment to adopt them if suggested by others, wisdom and tact in dealing with the rebel authorities, and patience in waiting for the co-operation of the military forces or the development of the plans of the government. In carrying his fleet past Port Hudson and Vicksburg, in helping Grant to cross the river and take the latter place, in all his operations, whether alone or with the land commanders, Admiral Farragut gave proof of the possession of all these qualities.

The "Bay Fight" at Mobile, and the resulting capture of Forts Powell and Gaines, was another scene as terrible as New Orleans, and still more splendidly illuminated by the perfect personal courage of the Admiral, who has already gone into history, song and painting, as he stood lashed in the rigging of the old Hartford, clear above the smoke of the battle, and, even when he saw the monitor Tecumseh sunk—the very ship he had been waiting for for months—yet ordered his wooden fleet straight forward despite forts, gunboats, ram and torpedoes, and won a second victory of that most glorious sort only possible to the high, clear and intelligent courage of a leader who is both truly heroic and truly wise.

The fame which the Admiral earned in the war has been in some measure paid him, in the testimonials of admiration and respect which he has received both at home and abroad. It would require a book to give account of the greetings and the thanks he has received from his own countrymen; and on the official voyage which he has made since the war to the principal ports of Europe, as the representative of the naval power of the United States. The civilities and attentions conferred upon himself and his officers, were not solely that formal politeness which one nation observes to another, but were in large measure the more enthusiastic acknowledgment which men pay to lofty personal qualities.

Admiral Farragut is a man of remarkably pure and vigorous health, and though no longer young, is more elastic, vigorous and enduring than most young men. His health and strength are the just recompense for a cleanly and temperate life. He seems to have that sort of innate or constitutional abhorrence for every unclean thing, which has characterized some great reformers. There is a pleasant story of a rebuke once administered by him in a most neat and decorous, but very effective manner, to a tobacco-smoking bishop, which conveys a good lesson. At dinner with Farragut, and after the meal was over, the Bishop, about to select a cigar, offered the bunch to the sailor. "Have a cigar, Admiral?" said he. "No, Bishop," said the Admiral, with a quizzical glance, "I don't smoke—*I swear a little, sometimes.*"

We regret that the limits of our sketches do not allow us to do justice to those wonderful, inspiring, romantic scenes by which our navy gained possession of New Orleans and Mobile. But if one wants to read them in poetry, terse and vivid, with all the fire of poetry and all the explicitness of prose, we beg them to read the "River Fight," and "Bay Fight," of Henry Brownell, who was in both scenes as a volunteer officer. There he will find Homeric military ardor baptized by Christian sentiment.

Full red the furnace fires must glow,
  That melts the ore of mortal kind;
The mills of God are grinding slow,
  But ah, how close they grind!
To-day the Dahlgren and the drum
  Are dread Apostles of his name,
His kingdom here can only come
  In chrism of blood and flame.

John A. Anderson

CHAPTER IX.

JOHN ALBION ANDREW.

Governor Andrew's Death Caused by the War—The Governors Dr. Beecher Prayed for—Governor Andrew a Christian Governor—Gov. Andrew's Birth—He goes to Boston to Study Law—Not Averse to Unfashionable and Unpopular Causes—His Cheerfulness and Social Accomplishments—His Sunday School Work—Lives Plainly—His Clear Foresight of the War—Sends a Thousand Men to Washington in One Day—Story of the Blue Overcoats—The Telegram for the Bodies of the Dead of Baltimore—Gov. Andrew's Tender Care for the Poor—The British Minister and the Colored Women—The Governor's Kindness to the Soldier's Wife—His Biblical Proclamations—The Thanksgiving Proclamation of 1861—The Proclamation of 1862—His Interest in the Schools for the Richmond Poor—Cotton Mather's Eulogy on Governor Winthrop—Gov. Andrew's Farewell Address to the Massachusetts Legislature—State Gratitude to Governor Andrew's Family.

Among the many heroic men who have sacrificed their lives in the great battle of liberty in our country, there is no one who deserves a more honored memory than John A. Andrew, Governor of Massachusetts.

We speak of him as dying in battle, for it is our conviction that Governor Andrew was as really a victim of the war as if, like Lincoln, he had been shot down by a bullet. His death was caused by an over tax of the brain in the critical and incessant labors of the five years' war. He had been previously warned by a physician that any such strain would expose him to such a result, so that in meeting the duties and exigencies of his office at the time he did, he just as certainly knew that he was exposing himself to sudden death as the man who goes into battle. He did not fail till the battle was over and the victory won, then with a smile of peace on his lips, he went to rest by the side of Lincoln.

It was a customary form in the prayers of the Rev. Dr. Beecher, to offer the petition that God would make our "Governors as at the first, and our counsellors as at the beginning." These words, spoken with a yearning memory of the old days of the pilgrim fathers, when religion was the law of the land, and the laws and ordinances of Christ were the standard of the government, found certainly a fulfillment in the exaltation of John A. Andrew to be the Governor of Massachusetts.

It has been said of Lincoln by a French statesman that he presents to the world a new type of pure, Christian statesmanship. In the same manner it may be said of John A. Andrew, that he presents a type of a consistently Christian State Governor.

The noble men of America who have just consummated in the 37th and 38th Congresses the sublimest national and moral reform the world ever saw, are the spiritual children of the pilgrim fathers. So are Garrison, Phillips, John Brown, and other external helpers in bringing on the great day of moral victory. They were men either tracing their descent in lineal blood to Puritan parentage, or like Garrison, spiritually born of the eternal influences which they left in the air of the society they moulded.

These sons of the Puritans do not, it is true, in all points hold the technical creed of their ancestors, any more than the Puritans held the creed of the generation just before them. Progress was the root idea with the Puritans, and as they stood far in advance in matters of opinion, so their sons in many respects stand at a different line from them; in this, quite as much as in anything else, proving their sonship. The parting charge of the old pastor Robinson to the little band of pilgrims was of necessity a seed of changes of opinion as time should develop fit causes of change.

"If God reveal anything unto you by any other instrument of his, be ready to receive it as ever you were to receive any truth by my ministry; for I am verily persuaded and confident that the Lord hath much truth yet to break forth from his holy word. For my part, I cannot sufficiently bewail the condition of the reformed churches who are come to a period in their religion, and will go at present no further than the instruments of their first reformation. The Lutherans cannot be drawn to go beyond what Luther said; and whatsoever part of his will our good God has imparted unto Calvin they will rather die than embrace it. And the Calvinists you see stick fast where they were left by that great man of God, who yet saw not all things."

But that part of the Puritan idea which consisted in unhesitating loyalty to Jesus Christ as master in practical affairs, and an unflinching determination to apply his principles and precepts to the conduct of society, and to form and reform all things in the state by them, was that incorruptible seed which has descended from generation to generation in Massachusetts, and shown itself in the course of those noble men who have brought on and carried through the late great revolution. This recent conflict has been in fact *a great revival of religion*, by which the precepts of the

Sermon on the Mount have been established in political forms.

John Albion Andrew was born in the little town of Windham, Cumberland county, Maine. It was like the most of the nests where New England greatness is hatched—a little, cold, poor, barren mountain town, where the winter rages for six months of the year. We hear of him in these days as a sunny-faced, curly-headed boy, full of fun and frolic and kind-heartedness, and we can venture to say how he pattered barefooted after the cows in the dim grey of summer mornings, how he was forward to put on the tea-kettle for mother, and always inexhaustible in obligingness, how in winter he drew the girls to school on his sled, and was doughty and valiant in defending snow forts, and how his arm and prowess were always for the weak against the strong and for the right against the wrong. All these inherent probabilities might be wrought into myths and narratives, which would truly represent the boy who was father to the man, John A. Andrew.

He graduated from Bowdoin College in the class of 1837, and came to Boston to study law in the office of Henry H. Fuller, whence in 1840, he was admitted to the bar.

During the earlier portions of his educational career, both in college and at the bar, he had no very brilliant successes. He had little ambition to dazzle or shine, or seek for immediate effect; he was indifferent to academic honors, his heart and mind being set upon higher things. He read and studied broadly and carefully, in reference to his whole manhood rather than to the exigencies of a passing occasion. Besides his legal studies, he was a widely read belles-lettres student, and his memory was most retentive of all sorts of literature, grave and gay, tragic and comic. He was one that took the journey of life in a leisurely way, stopping to admire prospects and to gather the flowers as he went on.

From the very earliest of his associations in Boston, he allied himself not only with popular and acceptable forms of philanthropy, but also with those which were under the ban of polite society. One who knew him well says: "Few men were connected with so many unpopular and unfashionable causes. Indeed, it was only sufficient to know that an alliance with any cause was considered to involve some loss of social caste, or business patronage, to be pretty sure that John A. Andrew was allied with it."

His cheerful, jovial spirit, and the joyousness with which he accepted the reproach of a cause, took from it the air of martyrdom. His exquisite flow of natural humor oiled and lubricated the play of his moral faculties, so that a gay laugh instead of an indignant denunciation would be the weapon with which he would meet injurious language or treatment heaped on him for conscience sake. Like Lincoln, he had the happy faculty of being able to laugh where crying did no good, and the laughter of some good men, we doubt not, is just as sacred in heavenly eyes as the tears of others. They who tried to put men under society's ban for their conscientious opinions, got loss on their own side in excluding Andrew, since no man had in a higher degree all the arts and faculties of agreeable-ness in society. No man had a wider or more varied flow of conversation. No man could tell a better story or sing a gayer song. No man was more gifted with that electrical power of animal cheerfulness, which excites others to gayety and mirth. In the intervals of the gravest cases, when pressed down, overwhelmed, and almost bewildered, he would still find spare hours when at the bedside of some desponding invalid, or in the cheerless chamber of old age, he would make all ring again with a flow of mimicry and wit and fun, as jolly as a bob-o-link on a clover head.

Some of the most affecting testimonials to his worth come from these obscure and secluded sources. One aged friend of seventy or more, tells how daily, amid all the cares of the state house and the war, he found some interval to come in and shed a light and cheerfulness in her shaded chamber.

His pastor speaks of him as performing the duties of a Sunday school superintendent during the labors of his arduous station. He was a lover of children and young people, and love made labor light. While he did not hesitate, when necessary, to carry forward the great public cause on the Sabbath day, yet his heart and inclinations ever inclined him to the more purely devotional uses of those sacred hours. The flame of devotion in his heart was ever burning beneath the crust of earthly cares, but ready to flame up brightly in those hours consecrated by the traditions of his Puritan education.

In one respect Governor Andrew was not patterned on the old first magistrates of Massachusetts. Massachusetts was at first decidedly an aristocratic community. A certain of idea rank and stateliness hedged in the office of the governor. He stood above the people at an awful distance and moved among them as a sort of superior being.

Nothing could be more opposed to the frank, companionable nature of Governor Andrew than any such idea. He was a true democrat to the tips of his finger nails, and considered a Governor only as the servant of the people. In this respect, more truly than even the first Puritan governors, did he express the idea given by Christ of rank and dignity, "Whosoever will be chief among you let him be your servant."

Governor Andrew from the first rejected and disclaimed everything which seemed to mark him out from the people by outward superiority. He chose to live in a small, plain house, in a retired and by no means fashionable part of the city, and to conduct all his family arrangements on a scale of the utmost simplicity. When the idea was suggested to him that the Governor of Massachusetts ought to have some extra provision to enable him to appear with more worldly pomp and stateliness, he repelled it with energy, "Never, while the country was struggling under such burdens, and her brave men bearing such privations in the field, would he accept of anything more than the plain average comforts of a citizen." The usual traditional formulas and ceremonials of his position were only irksome and embarrassing to him. One of his aids relates that being induced by urgent solicitation to have the accustomed military coat of the Governor of Massachusetts, with all its gold lace and buttons, he wore it twice, and then returning with his aids to his private cabinet, he pulled it off and threw it impatiently into a corner, saying, "Lie there, old coat—you won't find me wearing you again, soon." The ceremonies on public occasions were always irksome and fatiguing to him, and he would recreate himself by singing "Johnny Schmauker" with his aids in his private apartments afterwards. We think good Governor Winthrop would have rolled up his eyes in horror at such carelessness of etiquette and station.

As a public man, Governor Andrew was distinguished for quickness, perspicasity, and energy. The electric, social element of his being made him an apt reader of human nature, and gave him that prophetic insight into what would arise from the doings of men, which enabled him to see afar off and provide for possible emergencies. Thus at the time he was appointed Governor, nothing was farther from the thoughts of the body of Northern men than that there could ever be really and in fact a war in America. All the war talk and war threats that had come from the South had been pleasantly laughed at, as mere political catch words and nursery tales meant to frighten children.

But Andrew felt the atmosphere chilling with the coming storm, and from the moment of his election, he began making active preparations for war, which were at the time as much laughed at as Noah's for the flood.

But the time came which the laughers and skeptics said would not come, and behold on the 15th of April, the President's requisition for troops! Thanks to the previous steps taken by Governor Andrew, the Massachusetts sixth regiment started from Boston in the afternoon of the 17th, leaving the 4th all but ready to follow. *Only one day* was necessary to get a thousand men started—and this company was the first that entered Washington *in uniform* and with all the moral effect of uniformed soldiers. This leads us to the celebrated story of the blue overcoats, which is this: Shortly after Lincoln's election, Benjamin F. Butler took tea with Jefferson Davis in Washington, and there satisfied himself in personal conversation that a war must be the result of the machinations that were going on. He posted to Boston and communicated what he knew to Governor Andrew, who immediately called a secret session of the legislature in which he told the crisis and asked for an appropriation to get troops in readiness. They voted twenty-five thousand dollars which Governor Andrew put into arms, ammunition and stores for an immediate equipment for the field. Among other things, he had two or three thousand army overcoats made and stored in the State house.

When the call came, the sixth regiment had not half a quota, but was immediately made up by the fiery zeal of enlisting citizens, who contended for places and even paid large bounties to buy the chance to go. They came into Boston an army of zealous new recruits. The Governor uniformed them at one stroke with his overcoats, and had each man's outfit ready for him so that in one day they were marching from Boston to the capital; and in six days, on Sunday, he was able to announce to the government that the whole quota of men required of Massachusetts were already either in Washington or in Fortress Monroe, on their way thither.

When news came back of the fight in Baltimore, and the murder of some of his brave men, Andrew sent a telegram which showed that if he did not care to wear the uniform of a Massachusetts Governor, he knew how to assert the honor of Massachusetts, and to make other States feel that she had a Chief Magistrate in whose sight the blood of every Massachusetts man was sacred.

He telegraphed to the Mayor of Baltimore:

"I pray you let the bodies of our Massachusetts soldiers, dead in Baltimore, be laid out, preserved in ice, and tenderly sent forward by express to me. All expenses will be paid by the commonwealth."

The tender and fatherly feeling expressed in this telegram is the key note to all Governor Andrew's conduct of the war. Though he would not waste one cent on the trappings of rank, or his own personal dignity or convenience, he gave unlimited orders for marks of tender and delicate devotion to even the remains of the brave who had fallen for their country.

In the same manner he gave himself no rest, in his labors for the families of the brave men who were in the field. This interest was the deeper, the humbler the walk in life of its objects.

The British minister, Sir Frederick Bruce, once called upon him at the State House, and found the room nearly filled with colored women who had come to hear news of fathers, brothers and sons enlisted in the black regiments of Massachusetts. He waited patiently while the Governor inquired into the sorrows and grievances, and listened to the perplexities of these poor anxious souls, and tried in his hopeful cheery way to smooth away difficulties and inspire hope. It was not till the humblest and poorest had had their say, that the turn of the British Minister came, who, as he shook the Governor's hand, said that the scene before him had given him a new idea of the paternal character of a Republican Government.

Of a like nature is another anecdote, one of many which since the Governor's death, have risen like flowers upon his grave.

A poor woman, the wife of a soldier, came to his room to have some business done in relation to the pension of a poorer sister. The Governor told her that her application must be made at another bureau in another part of the State house. Observing something of delicacy and timidity in her air, he asked her where she lived and finding it out of Boston, enquired if she had any friends or relations in the city with whom she could rest during the hours before the opening of the office. Finding that she was utterly a stranger in Boston, and evidently in delicate health, the Governor provided her a sofa in a private nook and told her to rest herself, and offered her from his own frugal stores a glass of wine and a cracker for refreshment. The fatherly kindness and consideration of his manner was more even, than the favors he gave.

His sympathy with the soldiers in the field was a sort of personal identification. He put himself into the Massachusetts army and could say as Paul said of the churches: "who is weak, and I am not weak? who is offended, and I burn not?" One incident illustrative of this is thus related by Edwin Whipple in his eulogy:

Receiving, in the depth of winter, an urgent request from the War Office that a regiment, not yet properly equipped, should be sent immediately to Washington, he despatched it on the assurance that all its wants should be supplied on its arrival. Hearing that it had been stopped on the way, and that it was undergoing cruel privations, he started instantly for the camp, determined at least to share the misery he might not be able to relieve; and he would not budge an inch until the regiment was sent on to its destination. Indeed he would have blushed to enter heaven, carrying thither the thought that he had regarded his own comfort rather than the least duty he owed to the poorest soldier-citizen.

The proclamations of Governors, Presidents and public men have generally been mere stately generalities and formalities. But with the great stirring of the deeper religious feelings of the community, these papers on the part of our public men have become individual and human—animated by a deeply religious spirit.

The proclamations of Governor Andrew for the usual State Thanksgivings and fasts, customary in Massachusetts were peculiar and unusual documents, and show more than any thing else how strongly the spirit and traditions of his old Puritan ancestry wrought in him, and how completely his mind was permeated with the Hebraistic imagery of the Old Testament.

His first thanksgiving proclamation after the commencement of the war, is a document worth preserving entire.

"By His Excellency JOHN A. ANDREW, Governor: A proclamation for a day of Public Thanksgiving and Praise.

"The example of the Fathers, and the dictates of piety and gratitude, summon the people of Massachusetts, at this, the harvest season, crowning the year with the rich proofs of the Wisdom and Love of God, to join in a solemn and joyful act of united Praise and Thanksgiving to the Bountiful Giver of every good and perfect gift.

"I do, therefore, with the advice and consent of the Council, appoint Thursday, the twenty-first day of November next—the same being the anniversary of that day, in the year of our Lord sixteen hundred and twenty, on which the Pilgrims of Massachusetts, on board the May Flower, united themselves in a solemn and written compact of government—to be observed by the people of Massachusetts as a day of Public Thanksgiving and Praise. And I invoke its observance by all people with devout and religious joy.

"Sing aloud unto God, our strength; make a joyful noise unto the God of Jacob.

"Take a Psalm and bring hither the timbrel, the pleasant harp with psaltery.

"Blow up the trumpet in the new moon, in the time appointed, on our solemn feast day.

"For this was a statute for Israel, and a law of the God of Jacob. Psalms 81, v. 1 to 4.

"O bless our God, ye people, and make the voice of his praise to be heard:

"Which holdeth our soul in life, and suffereth not our feet to be moved.

"For thou, O God, hath proved us; thou hast tried us, as silver is tried. Psalms 66, v. 8 and 9.

"Let us rejoice in God and be thankful for the fulness with which he has blessed us in our basket and in our store, giving large rewards to the toil of the husbandman, so that 'our paths drop fatness.'

"For the many and gentle alleviations of the hardships which in the present time of public disorder have afflicted the various pursuits of industry.

"For the early evidence of the reviving energies of the business of the people:

"For the measure of success which has attended the enterprise of those who go down to the sea in ships, of those who search the depths of the ocean to add to the food of man, and of those whose busy skill and handicraft combine to prepare for various use the crops of the earth and sea:

"For the advantages of sound learning, placed within the reach of all children of the people, and the freedom and alacrity with which these advantages are embraced and improved:

"For the opportunities of religious instruction and worship, universally enjoyed by consciences untrammelled by any human authority:

"For the redemption of the world by Jesus Christ, for the means of grace and the hope of glory:

"And with one accord let us bless and praise God for the oneness of heart, mind and purpose in which he has united the people of this ancient Commonwealth for the defence of the rights, liberties, and honor, of our beloved country.

"May we stand forever in the same mind, remembering the devoted lives of our fathers, the precious inheritance of freedom received at their hands, the weight of glory which awaits the faithful, and the infinity of blessing which it is our privilege, if we will, to transmit to the countless generations of the future.

"And while our tears flow, in a stream of cordial sympathy, with the daughters of our people, just now bereft, by the violence of the wicked and rebellious, of the fathers and husbands and brothers and sons, whose heroic blood has made verily sacred the soil of Virginia, and mingling with the waters of the Potomac, has made the river now and forever ours; let our souls arise to God on the wings of Praise, in thanksgiving that He has again granted to us the privilege of living unselfishly, and of dying nobly, in a grand and righteous cause:

"For the precious and rare possession of so much devoted valor and heroism:

"For the sentiment of pious duty which distinguished our fathers in the camp and in the field:

"And for the sweet and blessed consolations which accompany the memories of these dear sons of Massachusetts on to immortality:

"And in our praise let us also be penitent. Let us 'seek the truth and ensue it,' and prepare our minds for whatever duty shall be manifested hereafter.

"May the controversy in which we stand be found worthy in its consummation of the heroic sacrifices of the people and the precious blood of their sons, of the doctrine and faith of the fathers, and consistent with the honor of God and with justice to all men.

"And,

"'Let God arise, let his enemies be scattered; let them also that hate him, flee before him.'

"'As smoke is driven away, so drive those away.' Psalms, 68, v. 1 and 2.

"'Scatter them by thy power, and bring them down, O Lord, our shield.' Psalms, 59, v. 11.

Given at the Council Chamber, this thirty-first day of October, in the year of our Lord one thousand eight hundred and sixty-one, and the eighty-sixth of the Independence of the United States of America.

JOHN A. ANDREW.

"By His Excellency the Governor, with the advice and consent of the Council.

OLIVER WARNER, Secretary.

"God save the Commonwealth of Massachusetts."

The next year, 1862, the annual thanksgiving proclamation has the following characteristic close:

"Rising to the height of our great occasion, re-enforced by courage, conviction and faith, it has been the privilege of our country to perceive, in the workings of Providence, the opening ways of a sublime Duty. And to Him who hath never deserted the faithful, unto Him 'who gathereth together the outcasts of Israel, who healeth the broken in heart,' we owe a new song of thanksgiving. 'He sheweth his word unto Jacob, his statutes and his judgments unto Israel. He has not dealt so with any nation.'

"Putting aside all fear of man, which bringeth a snare, may this people put on the strength which is the divine promise and gift to the faithful and obedient; 'Let the high praises of God be in their mouth, and a two edged sword in their hand.' Not with malice and wickedness, but with sincerity and truth, let us keep this feast; and while we 'eat the fat and drink the sweet, forget not to send a portion to him for whom nothing is prepared.' Let us remember on that day the claims of all who are poor, or desolate, or oppressed, and pledge the devotion of our lives to the rescue of our country from the evils of rebellion, oppression and wrong; and may we all so order our conduct hereafter, that we may neither be ashamed to live, nor afraid to die."

When the war was over, and the victory won, the generous and brotherly spirit of Governor Andrew showed itself in the instant outflowing of charity towards our misguided and suffering brethren, and he was one of the first and warmest to respond to the cry for aid to the starving thousands at the South. "I was for a vigorous prosecution of the war while there was a war," he said, "but now the war is over, I am for a vigorous prosecution of the peace."

It is not generally known that the moment the national flag made Richmond a safe place to be visited by northern men, teachers were at once sent from Boston to found a series of common schools for the poor white children of Richmond. The building formerly employed as a laboratory for the preparing of torpedos and other implements of war, was converted into a school room for these poor vagrants, who had suffered from cold, hunger and neglect during the chances of the war. The teachers carried with them not only school books for the children, but gifts of clothing and supplies of food, whereby they carried comfort to many a poor family. In this most peculiarly Christian work, Governor Andrew sympathized deeply. His was a nature that, while it could be surpassed by none in energetic resistance to wrong, was ever longing the rather to express itself in deeds of kindness.

Governor Andrew's farewell address to the Legislature of Massachusetts was a state paper worthy of the State and worthy of him. We shall make a few extracts:

"At the end of five years of executive administration, I appear before a convention of the two Houses of her General Court, in the execution of a final duty. For nearly all that period, the Commonwealth, as a loyal State of the American Union, has been occupied within her sphere of co-operation, in helping to maintain, by arms, the power of the nation, the liberties of the people, and the rights of human nature.

"Having contributed to the army and the navy—including regulars, volunteers, seamen and marines, men of all arms, and officers of all grades, and of the various terms of service—an aggregate of one hundred and fifty-nine thousand one hundred and sixty-five men; and having expended for the war, out of her own treasury, twenty-seven million seven hundred and five thousand one hundred and nine dollars,—besides the expenditures of her cities and towns, she has maintained, by the unfailing energy and economy of her sons and daughters, her industry and thrift even in the waste of war. She has paid promptly, and *in gold*, all interest on her bonds—including the old and the new—guarding her faith and honor with every public creditor, while still fighting the public enemy; and now, at last, in retiring from her service, I confess the satisfaction of having first seen all of her regiments and batteries (save two battalions) returned and mustered out of the army; and of leaving her treasury provided for, by the fortunate and profitable negotiation of all the permanent loan needed or foreseen—with her financial credit maintained at home and abroad, her public securities unsurpassed, if even equalled, in value in the money market of the world by those of any State or of the Nation.

* * * * * *

"But, perhaps, before descending for the last time from this venerable seat, I may be indulged in some allusion to the broad field of thought and statesmanship, to which the war itself has conducted us. As I leave the Temple where, humbled by my unworthiness, I have stood so long, like a priest of Israel sprinkling the blood of the holy sacrifice on the altar—I would fain contemplate the solemn and manly duties which remain to us who survive the slain, in honor of their memory and in obedience to God."

The Governor then goes on to state his views of reconstruction, and we will say no state paper ever more truly expressed the Christian idea of statesmanship as applied to the most profound problem of modern times.

In conclusion, it seems to us that Governor Andrew so fully lived in the spirit of the old Christian Governors of Massachusetts, that the words of Cotton Mather, in his mourning for Governor Winthrop, fully apply to him: "We are now," he says, "to mourn for a governor who has been to us as a friend in his counsel for all things, help for our bodies by physic, for our estate by law, and of whom there was no fear of his becoming an enemy, like the friends of David; a governor who hath been unto us as a brother; not usurping authority over the church; often speaking his advice, and often contradicted, even by young men, and some of low degree; yet not replying, but offering satisfaction when any supposed offences have arisen; a governor who has been to us as a mother, parent-like distributing his goods to brethren and neighbors at his first coming, and gently bearing our infirmities without taking notice of them."

It is pleasant to record for the honor of republics, that while the disinterestedness of Governor Andrew had left him in honorable poverty, the contributions of Boston and Massachusetts immediately flowed in to supply to his family that estate which their father's patriotism and devotion did not allow him to seek for them. There must have been thousands of grateful hearts in Massachusetts, in homes of comparative indigence whence have come joyful contributions to that testimonial of Massachusetts to her beloved and faithful citizen Governor.

Schuyler Colfax

CHAPTER X.

SCHUYLER COLFAX.

General William Colfax, Washington's Friend—Mr. Colfax his Grandson—Mr. Colfax's Birth and Boyhood—Removes to Indiana—Becomes Deputy County Auditor—Begins to Deal with Politics—Becomes an Editor—The Period of Maximum Debt—Mr. Colfax's First Year—He is Burnt Out—His Subsequent Success as an Editor—His Political Career as a Whig—Joins the Republican Party—Popularity in his own District—The Nebraska Bill—Mr. Colfax goes into Congress—The Famous Contest for Speakership—Mr. Colfax Saves his Party from Defeat—Banks Chosen Speaker—Mr. Colfax's Great Speech on the Bogus Laws of Kansas—The Ball and Chain for Free Speech—Mr. Colfax Shows the Ball, and A. H. Stephens Holds it for him—Mr. Colfax Renominated Unanimously—His Remarkable Success in his own District—Useful Labors in Post Office Committee—Early for Lincoln for President—Mr. Colfax urged for Post Master General—His Usefulness as Speaker—The Qualifications for that Post—Mr. Colfax's Public Virtues.

General William Colfax, the grandfather of Hon. Schuyler Colfax, was a citizen of New Jersey, and was the commanding officer of Gen. Washington's life guards throughout the Revolutionary War. His holding that very confidential and responsible post is sufficient evidence of his steadiness, sense, courage and discretion. It is a further testimonial to the same effect, that Gen. Colfax latterly became one of the most intimate personal friends of the great revolutionary chieftain. Gen. Colfax's wife was Hester Schuyler, a cousin of Gen. Philip Schuyler.

General Colfax's son, Schuyler Colfax, the father of the Speaker, was an officer of one of the New York city banks, and died four months before his son was born.

Schuyler Colfax was born in New York city, March 23, 1823, and was the only son of his widowed mother. He was taught in the common schools of the city—finished his education at the high school then standing in Crosby St., and at ten years had received all the school training he ever had. He now became a clerk in a store, and after three years removed to Indiana with his mother and her second husband, a Mr. Matthews. They settled in St. Joseph County. Here the youth for four years again served as clerk in the village of New Carlisle. When 17 years old he was appointed deputy county auditor, and for the better fulfilment of his official duties, he now removed to the county town, South Bend, where he has lived ever since.

Like almost every western citizen of any activity of body and mind, young Colfax took practical hold of political matters about as soon as he could vote. He talked and thought, and began to print his views from time to time in the local newspaper of the place. His peculiar faculty of dealing fairly and at the same time pleasantly, with men of all sorts, his natural sobriety and sensibleness of opinion, and his power of stating things plainly and correctly, made him what may be called a natural newspaper man. He was employed during several sessions to report the proceedings of the State Senate for the Indianapolis Journal, and in this position made many friends, and gained a good reputation for political information and ability as a writer.

In 1845, he became proprietor and editor of the "St. Joseph Valley Register," the local paper of his town, South Bend. This was the beginning of his independent career, and if hope had been absent, the prospect would have looked meagre enough. He was a youth of just over twenty-one, and he had two hundred and fifty subscribers. But the youthful editor had hope, and what was far more important, remarkable tact and capacity for his laborious profession. By good fortune and perseverance, he was able to tide over the first dangerous crisis for a poor man who undertakes a large literary enterprise—the period of maximum debt, so fatal to new periodicals. This is a point like the darkest hour just before day, when the newspaper or magazine is very likely steadily gaining in reputation and even in circulation, but when the circulation has not quite reached the paying point, and the paper bills have been postponed to the latest possible moment, while the constant outgoes for paying the journeymen, and for the other weekly office expenses, have kept up their monotonous drain. With Mr. Colfax this period was at the end of the first year of his paper, when he owed $1,375. The concern gradually became productive, however. A few years afterwards the office was burned down, and the uninsured editor was left to begin his business over again. He did so, and has earned a very comfortable living by it, though he is by no means a rich man.

Besides paying well, the "Register," as conducted by Mr. Colfax, is entitled to the much higher praise of having been a useful, interesting and a morally pure paper, always on the side of what is good and right in morals and in society. It has been, for instance, constantly in favor of temperance reform; and it has always avoided the masses of vile detail which so many papers of respectable position manage to distribute in families under pretence that they must give full news of police reports and criminal trials.

Mr. Colfax was a Whig as long as there was a Whig party, and at its death, like all its members of clear heads, progressive tendencies, and decided character, he joined the Republican party. Before the rise of this great new organization, however, he had already risen to considerable influence in the Whig party, and had held several positions of political trust. In 1848 he was a delegate to the convention which nominated Gen. Taylor, and was one of its secretaries. In 1849 he was a member of the convention which revised the constitution of the State of Indiana, having been chosen in a manner especially honorable to him personally, as his district was politically opposed to him. Mr. Colfax, in this convention, was considered a judicious legislator, a ready debater and a fine speaker. A little after this time he declined a nomination to the Indiana Senate, for the sufficient reason that he could not afford at that time to be absent from his business.

Mr. Colfax's first nomination for Congress was in 1851, and he was beaten, though only by 200 majority, in a district strongly opposed to him in politics. His competitor was that Dr. Graham N. Fitch who was afterwards the congenial yokefellow of Mr. Bright in the U. S. Senate, on the side of the South, during Mr. Buchanan's presidency. Mr. Colfax's friends were of opinion, however, that the fatal 200 against him were illegal votes, imported by means of a certain railroad then constructing in those parts, and from among the laborers employed upon it. In 1852 he was a delegate to the Whig National Convention that nominated Gen. Scott, and as at the convention of 1848, was a secretary. He declined a second congressional nomination, and his district, which he had lost by only 200, was now lost by 1,000.

The Thirty-Third Congress, whose legal existence covered the period from Dec. 5, 1853, to March 3, 1855, Franklin Pierce being President, passed the Nebraska Bill. Upon this, the North, driven at last to the wall, turned short about in its career of surrender, and set itself to put a limit to the spread of slavery. The old established professional politicians of those days did not understand this crisis, and very many of them did not know anything about the change of public opinion—or rather of public intention—that was going on, until to their immense surprise and disgust, an anti-slavery-extension constituency that they knew not of, suddenly voted them out of their offices. Such a bat-eyed politician was Mr. Colfax's own representative in Congress at this time. Even after having been elected as a Free Soil Democrat, and after undergoing a special season of argument and entreaty by his friends and neighbors during a visit home while the Nebraska Bill was pending, the short-sighted legislator went back and voted for it. He very quickly reaped his reward, however. Had he known enough to take the opportunity of doing right, he would have found out that for once it was the way to temporal success, for unquestionably he would have been re-elected, and assuredly Mr. Colfax would have done his best to re-elect him. As it was, the energetic editor was at once selected by the anti-Nebraska men of that region to take the lead in punishing the delinquent. He was unanimously chosen candidate for Congress, and after the candid and jolly western fashion, the two nominees went round the district, yoked together for combat, like those duellists who are tied together by their left wrists and wield their knives with their right hands. The result was, Mr. Colfax's election by 2,000 majority, the previous majority of his competitor having been 1,000 the other way.

When the Thirty-Fourth Congress met, Dec. 3d, 1855, there was a majority opposed to the administration, but this opposition was of materials inharmonious among themselves. The anti-Nebraska members, properly so called, numbered about 108, the administration men, or Democrats, about 75, the third party, or "Know Nothing" men about 40; and there were a few who could not be classified. Now, the anti-Nebraska men alone had twenty less than the necessary majority (128) out of the 234 members of the House; and if the Know Nothings and Democrats should effect a complete union, they could choose a Speaker. Whether they would do so was the principal question of the famous contest for the Speakership which now ensued, which lasted from Dec. 3, 1855, to Feb. 2, 1856, two full months, and which resulted in the election of Mr. Banks—the first formal national triumph of the national anti-slavery sentiment. Its importance might be overlooked, but it was great, and lay in this: that the Speaker has power to constitute the committees of the House—who prepare and in very great measure decide, all its business—just as he pleases.

Accordingly, if he were a pro-slavery man, past experience gave full guarantee that those committees would be so formed as to effectually silence the voice of the anti-slavery sentiment of the House, and to bejuggle the whole of its legislation into an apparent and deceitful endorsement of the administration. To resist this dangerous and humiliating result, required, under the circumstances, a good deal of courage, both moral and physical, and powers of endurance almost equal to the extremities of a siege; but the resolute phalanx of the anti-slavery men, cheered daily by their consciences within, and the earnest and increasing applause of every friend of man without, fought the battle bravely through.

During the contest, Mr. Colfax, who was a steady and unflinching soldier on the right side, served his cause at one very critical moment. It was the end of the first month of the struggle. There had been sixty or seventy ballots, and for the last thirty or forty of them the votes had been just about the same; for Banks, anti-Nebraska, 103 to 106; Richardson, Democratic, 74 or 75; Fuller, Know Nothing, 37 to 41; and Pennington, a second anti-Nebraska candidate, 5 to 8. Various experiments had been tried to relieve the dead-lock. It had been suggested that the lowest candidate should be dropped at each vote, until one of the last two must be chosen; that after three ballots, the candidate having most votes should be elected; and other plans were submitted, but all to no effect. About the end of December, Mr. Campbell, of Ohio, elected as an anti-Nebraska man, but of a sufficiently singular sort, either very unwise or very unsound, offered a resolution that Mr. Orr of South Carolina, "be invited to preside temporarily until a Speaker be elected." This extremely sly contrivance came within a hair-breadth of succeeding; for it looked like a mere amicable expedient to facilitate business, while it was in fact almost certain that once in, the subtle and energetic Orr, aided by the whole South, the Democrats, most of the Know Nothings, and perhaps some weak brethren of the anti-slavery opposition, would stay in. A motion to lay Campbell's resolution on the table failed by a majority of twenty; it looked as if Orr would be really Speaker in five minutes. Mr. Colfax now rose in the very nick of time, and made a motion which irresistibly reminds us of the device with which Hushai confounded the wisdom of Ahithophel. It was an amendment proposing to put the three contending parties on a fair equality during the contest, by allowing each to elect a temporary chairman, and these three to preside alternately in the order they might themselves agree upon. On this motion debate arose; there was a recess before any vote was reached; and the dangerous plan for making Orr Speaker was staved off. By next morning, Campbell's friends succeeded in inducing him to withdraw his resolution, and the contest settled back to its monotonous course of roll-calls and adjournments, until the final adoption of a plurality rule by the administration men, who, when they did it, thought it would help them, and the consequent election of Banks, at the 134th ballot, February 2d, 1856, by 103 to 100 for Aiken. The Know Nothings nearly all went to the Democratic side when the real pinch came.

It was during this session—June 21, 1856,—that Mr. Colfax delivered his well known and powerful speech on the bogus "Laws" of Kansas, imposed on that State by the fraud and violence of the pro-slavery ruffians of those days. This speech, a word-for-word quotation of clause after clause of this infamous code, accompanied with a plain, sober and calmly toned explanation of the same, produced a very great effect, and was considered so able a summary of the case involved, that during the Presidential campaign of that year, a half million of copies of it were distributed among the voters of the United States. By way of driving quite home the truths of the case, Mr. Colfax, where he quoted the clause which inflicted imprisonment at hard labor *with ball and chain*, upon any one who should ever *say* "that persons have not the right to hold slaves in this Territory," lifted from his desk and showed to the House an iron ball of the statutory dimensions (viz., 6 inches diameter, weighing about 30 lbs., apologizing for not also exhibiting the six-foot chain prescribed along with it. Alexander H. Stephens, afterwards Vice President of the Rebels, who sat close by, asked to take this specimen of pro-slavery jewelry for freemen, and having tested its weight, would have returned it. But Mr. Colfax smilingly asked him to hold it for him until he was through speaking, and while the pro-slavery leader dandled the decoration proposed by his friends for men guilty of free speech, Mr. Colfax, in a few telling sentences, showed that Washington and Jefferson and Webster and Clay had said the words which would have harnessed them, a quaternion of convicts, into the chain-gang of the border ruffians.

The close of this weighty speech is here quoted, not merely for the noble tone of its assertion of lofty principles, but also for the sake of showing the opportune manner in which, by citing one of the departed great men of our land, he at once added to his argument the strength of a mighty name, did justice to a man much spoken against but of many noble traits, and also illustrated a striking peculiarity of Mr. Colfax himself—the warmth, strength and unending persistency of his friendship. He closed as follows:

"As I look, sir, to the smiling valleys and fertile plains of Kansas, and witness there the sorrowful scenes of civil war, in which, when forbearance at last ceased to be a virtue, the Free State men of the Territory felt it necessary, deserted as they were by their Government, to defend their lives, their families, their property, and their hearthstones, the language of one of the noblest statesmen of the age, uttered six years ago at the other end of this Capitol, rises before my mind. I allude to the great statesman of Kentucky, Henry Clay. And while the party which, while he lived, lit the torch of slander at every avenue of his private life, and libelled him before the American people by every epithet that renders man infamous, as a gambler, debauchee, traitor, and enemy of his country, are now engaged in shedding fictitious tears over his grave, and appealing to his old supporters to aid by their votes in shielding them from the indignation of an uprisen people, I ask them to read this language of his, which comes to us as from his tomb to-day. With the change of but a single geographical word in the place of "Mexico," how prophetically does it apply to the very scenes and issues of this year! And who can doubt with what party he would stand in the coming campaign, if he were restored to us from the damps of the grave, when they read the following, which fell from his lips in 1850, and with which, thanking the House for its attention, I conclude my remarks.

"But if, unhappily, we should be involved in war, in civil war, between the two parties of this Confederacy, in which the effort upon the one side should be to restrain the introduction of slavery into the new Territories, and upon the other side to force its introduction there, what a spectacle should we present to the astonishment of mankind, in an effort not to propagate rights, but—I must say it, though I trust it will be understood to be said with no design to excite feeling—a war to propagate wrongs in the Territories thus acquired from Mexico! It would be a war in which we should have no sympathies, no good wishes—in which all mankind would be against us; for, from the commencement of the Revolution down to the present time, we have constantly reproached our British ancestors for the introduction of slavery into this country.'"

Mr. Colfax's constituents, extremely satisfied with his course and abilities, renominated him by acclamation while he was in Washington this year, and he was re-elected after the usual joint canvass, although the presidential election of that fall went against his party. That such would be the result, Mr. Colfax had confidently predicted, as a consequence of the third-party nomination of Mr. Fillmore. But he worked with none the less zeal for his principles and his party. He had breadth and soundness and clearness of view enough to sight along the rising plane of the successive anti-slavery votes of 1844, 1848, 1852, and 1856, and to see that the Party of Freedom and Right was the Party of the Future; and while doubtless he would have been just as steadfast in doing right if he had no hope of a right-doing government, yet the very best of men works with a more cheery strength when, to use the words of the story, he can "see the chips fly." It was with sentiments of lofty resolution that he wrote, some months before the Republican nomination was made, and just after that of Mr. Fillmore; "Whether the Republican ticket shall be successful or defeated this year, the duty to support it, to proclaim and defend its principles, to arm the conscience of the nation, is none the less incumbent. The Republican movement is based on Justice and Right, consecrated to Freedom, commended by the teachings of our Revolutionary Fathers, and demanded by the extraordinary events of our recent history, and though its triumphs may be delayed, nothing is more certain."

In 1858 Mr. Colfax was again nominated by acclamation, and re-elected by a triumphant majority, and so he has been in every election since, carrying his district against untiring and desperate and enormous efforts directed against him specially as a representative man, not merely by his local opponents, but by the whole forces of every kind which the party opposed to his could concentrate within his district.

Such a series of political successes shows not only the power of the public speaker, and the discretion of the politician, but shows also a hearty and vigorous unity of noble thoughts between the constituency and the representative, and also a magnetic personal attractiveness which holds fast forever any friend once made. Mr. Colfax hath friends, because he hath showed himself friendly.

During the 36th Congress, (December, 1859, to March, 1861,) Mr. Colfax was chairman of the Committee on Post Offices and Post Roads, and did much and useful work in keeping alive and healthy the somewhat unwieldy machinery of that important institution. He was in particular, successful in promoting the extension of mail facilities among the new mining communities in the Rocky Mountain gold fields, and in procuring the passage of the very important bills for the Daily Overland Mail, and for the Overland Telegraph to San Francisco, by way of Pike's Peak and Utah.

It was a matter of course that Mr. Colfax should go with all his heart into the great struggle of 1860. He felt and understood with unusual earnestness and clearness the importance of the principles involved, and the hazards of the political campaign. Into a paragraph or two written some time before the Chicago nomination, he condensed a whole code of political wisdom, and can now be seen to have pointed out Abraham Lincoln as the best candidate, by describing the political availability and ethical soundness of the position Mr. Lincoln then occupied. He wrote:

"We differ somewhat from those ardent cotemporaries who demand the nomination of their favorite representative man, whether popular or unpopular, and who insist that this must be done, even if we are defeated. We do agree with them in declaring that we shall go for no man who does not prefer free labor and its extension, to slave labor and its extension,—who though mindful of the impartiality which should characterize the Executive of the whole Union, will not fail to rebuke all new plots for making the government the propagandist of slavery, and compel promptly and efficiently the suppression of that horrible slave-trade which the whole civilized world has banned as infamous, piratical and accursed. But in a Republican National Convention, if any man could be found, North, South, East or West, whose integrity, whose life, and whose avowals rendered him unquestionably safe on these questions, and yet who could yet poll one, two or three hundred thousand votes more than any one else, we believe it would be both wisdom and duty, patriotism and policy, to nominate him by acclamation and thus render the contest an assured success from its very opening. We hope to see 1866 realize the famed motto of Augustine—"In essentials unity, in non-essentials liberty, in all things charity."

That is very broad and sound sense. It was in exact accordance with this doctrine and with these intimations as to who was the right man, that Mr. Lincoln was nominated, according to the desire of Mr. Colfax's heart; and in the coming campaign in his own very important state of Indiana, he did most valuable service in assuring the victory.

Upon Mr. Lincoln's election, a very powerful influence, made up of public sentiment, the efforts of newspapers, the urgent recommendations of governors and legislatures, and in particular of the Republican presidential electors, members of legislature, congressmen, and whole body of voters of Indiana, united to press upon the new President the appointment of Mr. Colfax to the office of Post Master General. Mr. Lincoln however had resolved to make Hon. C. B. Smith, of Indiana, Secretary of the Interior, and could give no other Cabinet place to that State. But as long as he lived, he loved and respected and trusted Mr. Colfax; and it is on record that "he rarely took any steps affecting the interests of the nation without making his intentions known to Mr. Colfax, in whose judgment he placed the utmost confidence."

Continuing in Congress, Mr. Colfax served with efficient and patriotic fervor in his place, and in December, 1863, was chosen, and has since remained speaker. In this extremely responsible, important and laborious place, his official career has been openly visible to all men, while only those among whom he presides can competently appreciate the rare personal and acquired qualifications which he has so ably exercised—the even good temper, the exhaustless patience, the calm prompt presence of mind, the immense range of honest questions and sly quirks of parliamentary law which he must have at his tongue's end; even the vigorous health and enduring physical frame which enable him to sit through session after session, day after day, without losing his readiness or decisiveness of thought and action.

He has, however, maintained and even increased his reputation as a wise and just legislator, a most useful public servant, a shrewd and kindly chairman, and a skillful parliamentarian. His duties have not been in their nature so brilliant as the deeds of our great commanders by land or by sea; nor so prominent even as the labors of some civilian officials; but they have been such as to require the greatest and most solid and useful of the civic virtues, courage, integrity, forethought, justice, and steady inexhaustible industry.

Edwin M. Stanton

CHAPTER XI.

EDWIN M. STANTON.

Rebel Advantages at Opening of War—They knew all about the Army Officers—Early Contrast of Rebel Enthusiasm and Union Indifference—Importance of Mr. Stanton's Post—His Birth and Ancestry—His Education and Law Studies—County Attorney—State Reporter—Defends Mr. McNulty—Removes to Pittsburg—His Line of Business—The Wheeling Case—He Removes to Washington—His Qualifications as a Lawyer—He Enters Buchanan's Cabinet—His Unexpected Patriotism—His Own Account of the Cabinet at News of Anderson's Move to Sumter—The Lion before the Old Red Dragon—Appointed Secretary of War—"Bricks in his Pockets"—Stanton's Habitual Reserve—His Wrath—"The Angel Gabriel as Paymaster"—Anecdotes of Lincoln's Confidence in Stanton—Lincoln's Affection for him—The Burdens of his Office—His Kindness of Heart within a Rough Outside—The Country his Debtor.

MR. GREELEY, in his History of the American Conflict, gives a survey of the advantages possessed by the rebels at the commencement of the war, in the martial character of their leaders. Jefferson Davis was a regularly educated graduate of West Point, who had been five years at the head of the War Department of the United States, and while in that situation had matured his future plans. He and his successor, Floyd, up to the year 1861, had arranged the United States military service to suit themselves, and left it in precisely the best condition for their designs. "They knew every officer in the United States service, knew the military value of each, whom to call away and organize to lead their own forces, and who, even if loyal, would serve their purposes better being left in our armies than taken into theirs."

"On the other hand, President Lincoln, without military education or experience, found himself suddenly plunged into a gigantic and to him unexpected war, with no single member of his cabinet even pretending to military genius or experience, and with the offices of his army filled to his hand by the chiefs of the rebellion. Whereas the whole rebel officers were enthusiasts who had forsaken all old connections to join the new army, the officers remaining were some of them old and feeble, like Scott, and others of that moderate kind of nature which inclines to remain stationary with the old institutions, rather than to make a fiery forward movement. Some two hundred of the very bravest and most skilful of our army officers went over to the new cause, to which they carried all the enthusiasm of youth and hope. Lincoln, in fact, was in the condition of a man who should be put to a naval race in an old ship from which his competitors had taken their pick of all the best sails, spars and hands.

"It is notorious that during the first year or two of the war, while with every Confederate officer the rebellion was an enthusiasm and a religion, for which he was willing at any moment to die, there were on the Union side many officers, and those of quite high rank, who seemed to take matters with extreme coolness, and to have no very particular enthusiasm for fighting at all. These officers seemed to consider secession as a great and unlucky mistake—a mistake, too, for which they seemed to think the intemperate zeal of the Black Republicans was particularly in fault, and their great object seemed to be to conduct the war with as little fighting as possible, using most conciliatory language, and always being sure to return fugitive slaves whenever they could get a good opportunity, thus apparently expecting in some favorable hour to terminate hostilities with another of those grand compromises which had been tried with such signal success in years past."

The advancement of Stanton to the post of Secretary of War, was a movement made after it became somewhat more a settled point than at first appeared, that war should mean war.

His position during the whole war was, next to that of the President, the most important, responsible and influential civil post in the United States, and his services as an organizer, an administrative and executive officer, and as a fearless, energetic, resolute, powerful, and patriotic citizen, were perhaps as nearly indispensable to the success of the nation in the war as those of any other one man. Yet the recorded materials for preparing an account of him are excessively scanty; far more so than for any of his companions in the chief offices of Mr. Lincoln's cabinet. This fact is in a certain sense a very creditable one to him; since it is the result of his life-long practice not to talk about himself, and not to talk about his work, but only to do it.

Edwin M. Stanton was born at Steubenville, in Ohio, in the year 1815. His ancestors were of the Quaker persuasion, as were those of Mr. Lincoln and Attorney General Bates. His parents removed to Ohio from Culpepper county, in the mountain region of Virginia. Stanton received the usual school training of a country boy, became a student of Kenyon College, in 1833, but only remained a year and left. This was the end of his scholastic education. It is easy, to those who know the decisive, impetuous, self-reliant nature of the man, and who remember the rough, plain, independent atmosphere of the backwoods country where he grew up, to imagine how easily any supposed indignity from his instructors would drive him out of their precincts, or how readily he would give up the idea of further studies as unnecessary, if his supply of money failed. However this was, he took up an employment which allowed him to continue some kind of mental training, for he became a bookseller's clerk at Columbus. He also studied law, and in 1836 was admitted to the bar. He first opened an office at Cadiz, Harrison county, Ohio, and his robust force and direct sense quickly gave him the best of whatever practice the country afforded. He became the county prosecuting attorney in about a year; in another he had removed to the larger business center of his native place, Steubenville. His practice rapidly increased, and during three years from 1839 he was Reporter of the Ohio Supreme Court decisions. During his career at Steubenville, he was the counsel of Caleb J. McNulty, clerk of the House of Representatives, on his trial for embezzling public money, and cleared him. This case made a good deal of noise in its day.

In 1848, his business still increasing, Mr. Stanton removed again, this time to Pittsburg, where he remained until 1857, becoming without question the first lawyer at that bar, and beginning to be employed in many of that important and vigorously contested class of cases which are carried up to the United States Supreme

Court at Washington. One of these, the Wheeling Bridge case, is perhaps that in which Mr. Stanton gained his greatest reputation as a lawyer. It is a curious illustration of his carelessness about his reputation, that not long ago, when an intimate personal friend of Mr. Stanton wanted a copy of his argument in this case to use in a biographical sketch, the Secretary was unable to furnish it.

In 1857 he removed once more, to Washington, still following his business. This now began to consist largely of heavy patent cases, a peculiar and difficult but very gainful department of legal practice. It is observable that the class of cases in which Mr. Stanton has been prominent, are those in which the executive mental faculties have most to do with the subject-matter—patent cases, land cases, vigorous controversies between great corporations about travelled routes or conflicting rights. Such cases arise among executive men, and Mr. Stanton's immense endowment of executive energy qualified him to succeed easily in dealing with them.

Mr. Stanton was naturally a Democrat; the vigorous traits of his character harmonizing spontaneously with the rough, aggressive energy of the Jacksonians. Probably his politics may have had some influence in causing Attorney-General Black to employ him, in 1858, to go to California and argue for the United States some very important land claim cases there. At any rate, if he had not been a Democrat, and a thorough-going one, he would not have been selected by Mr. Buchanan in December, 1860, to succeed Mr. Black as

Attorney-General, when on Mr. Cass' resignation Mr. Black became Secretary of State.

The gang of treasonable schemers who were in those days using their high positions to bind the country hand and foot, as securely as they could, in preparation for secession, undoubtedly had reckoned that in the new Attorney-General, if they did not find an ally, they would not encounter an obstacle. But his patriotism was of a very different kind from that of too many of his party. When the question before him, instead of being one of high or low tariff, or of one or another sort of currency, became a question whether he should go with his party in permitting his country to be ruined, or should join with all true patriots irrespective of party considerations, to preserve his country, he did not hesitate at all. He neither made allowances for the disreputable fright of old Mr. Buchanan, nor the far more disreputable schemes of the traitors who were bullying the feeble and helpless Old Public Functionary; but stood firmly amongst them all, a fearless and determined defender of the rights of the national government.

Mr. Stanton once gave a curious and striking sketch of the manners of Mr. Buchanan's cabinet in those days. While speaking of the results of Anderson's move to Sumter, he remarked:

"This little incident was the crisis of our history—the pivot upon which everything turned. Had he remained in Fort Moultrie, a very different combination of circumstances would have arisen. The attack on Sumter, commenced by the South, united the North, and made the success of the Confederacy impossible. I shall never forget our coming together by special summons that night. Buchanan sat in his arm chair in a corner of the room, white as a sheet, with the stump of a cigar in his mouth. The dispatches were laid before us; and so much violence ensued that he had to turn us all out of doors."

What sort of a scene, and what sort of language and goings on are covered under that phrase of Mr. Stanton's, those who are familiar with the manners of the old Red Dragon of slavery, under moments of excitement, may imagine. Oaths and curses, threats of cutting out hearts and tearing out bowels, were usual amenities, forms of argumentation and statement quite familiar, on such occasions. Mr. Stanton, as any one may see by a glance at his head, is one of those men built on the *lion* pattern, a man who never knew what fear was—a man, also, awful and tremendous in powers of wrath and combativeness, and we may be sure at this moment the lion stood at bay, and that his roar in answer to the dragon's hiss, was something to shake the cabinet and frighten poor Mr. Buchanan quite out of his proprieties. We may be sure the traitors did not go without a full piece of Stanton's mind, stormed after them with shot and shell, worthy a future Secretary of the War Department.

Mr. Stanton's appointment as Secretary of War was January 20, 1862; his predecessor, Mr. Cameron, having resigned a week before. This appointment was probably in a great measure due to the fresh recollection of the fearless vigor with which Mr. Stanton, along with Messrs. Dix and Holt, had asserted the rights of the nation under Buchanan. Mr. Lincoln, in making his selection, had the double good fortune of appointing a man of first-class merit for the position, and one whose "section" was in the right part of the country. It is on record that "in answering some questions on the subject, he observed that his first wish had been to choose a man from a border state, but that he knew New England would object; that on the other hand he would have also been glad to choose a New Englander, but he knew the Border States would object. So on the whole he concluded to select from some intervening territory, 'and to tell you the truth, gentlemen,' he added, 'I don't believe Stanton knows where he belongs himself!' Some of the company now said something about Mr. Stanton's impulsiveness, to which Mr. Lincoln replied with one of those queer stories with which he used to answer friends and enemies alike; 'Well,' said he, 'we may have to treat him as they are sometimes obliged to treat a Methodist minister I know of out West. He gets wrought up so high in his prayers and exhortations that they are obliged to put bricks in his pockets to keep him down. We may be obliged to serve Stanton the same way, but I guess we'll let him jump a while first!'"

The existence of the country was bound up in the war, and it was a matter of course that the War Department should attract the greatest part of Mr. Lincoln's solicitude and attention, and that he should be more frequently and confidentially in intercourse with its Secretary, than with the other Departments of the Government. Mr. Lincoln and Mr. Stanton had never met, it is said, until when the Secretary received his commission from the President; nor had Mr. Stanton any knowledge of the intention to appoint him until the day before the nomination.

Mr. Stanton's Secretaryship is a noble record of vast energy, untiring labor, thorough patriotism, and fervent and unfailing courage. Mr. Lincoln, a shrewd and wise judge of men, knew him familiarly, and loved and valued him more and more the longer and closer was their intercourse. Indeed, Mr. Stanton is probably a man closely shut up and inexpressive of his good and loveable traits and sentiments, beyond almost any one living; and it must have required the whole tremendous pressure and heat of the war, to soften his iron crust sufficiently to let even the keen eyed President find out how human and noble a heart was silently beating inside. The most interesting of the scanty anecdotes which are in existence about the Secretary are such as show the unlimited trust which Mr. Lincoln came to bestow upon him, or the rough and vigorous utterances by which he customarily revealed when he revealed at all, anything in the nature of feelings on his official duties or in reference to the war. Like many other men of real goodness hidden beneath a rugged outside, Mr. Stanton's most utterable sentiment was wrath, and he often, as it were, shot out a sentiment of goodness inside of a bullet of anger, as a gruff benefactor might fling a gift at his intended beneficiary. Such was the "jumping" which Mr. Lincoln proposed to allow, before keeping down his energetic Secretary with bricks in his pockets. Such was the strong figure in which one day he conveyed to a brother Secretary his views on the fitness of appointees. Mr. Usher, when Secretary of the Interior, once asked

Mr. Stanton to appoint a "young friend," paymaster in the army. "How old is he?" asked Stanton, in his curt manner. "About twenty-one, I believe," said Mr. Usher; "he is of good family and of excellent character." "Usher," exclaimed Mr. Stanton, in peremptory reply, "I would not appoint the Angel Gabriel a paymaster if he was only twenty-one!"

There was just as much unceremoniousness, and even very much more peremptory force and earnestness in the vigorous rebuke which Mr. Stanton administered to Mr. Lincoln on the night of March 30, 1865, for the unseasonable favors which he was inclined to offer to the rebels, to the detriment of justice and of the paramount rights of the nation. On this occasion, while the last bills of the session were under examination for signing, and while the President and all with him were enjoying the expectation of to-morrow's inauguration, a dispatch came in from Grant, which stated his confidence that a few days must now end the business with Lee and Richmond, and spoke of an application made by Lee for an interview to negotiate about peace. Mr. Lincoln intimated pretty clearly an intention to permit extremely favorable terms, and to let his General-in-Chief negotiate them; even to an extent that overpowered the reticent habits of his Secretary of War, who, after holding his tongue as long as he could, broke out sternly:

"Mr. President, to-morrow is inauguration day. If you are not to be the President of an obedient and united people, *you had better not be inaugurated.* Your work is already done, if any other authority than yours is for one moment to be recognized, or any terms made that do not signify that you are the supreme head of the nation. If generals in the field are to negotiate peace, or any other chief magistrate is to be acknowledged on this continent, *then you are not needed and you had better not take the oath of office.*"

"Stanton, you are right," said the President, his whole tone changing. "Let me have a pen."

Mr. Lincoln sat down at the table, and wrote as follows:

"The President directs me to say to you that he wishes you to have no conference with General Lee, unless it be for the capitulation of Lee's army, or on some minor or purely military matter. He instructs me to say that you are not to decide, discuss, or confer upon any political question; such questions the President holds in his own hands, and will submit them to no military conference or conventions. In the mean time you are to press to the utmost your military advantages."

The President then read over what he had written, and then said:

"Now Stanton, date and sign this paper, and send it to Grant. We'll see about this peace business."

An account which appeared in a Cincinnati paper during the war, of a curious transaction at Washington, shows that Mr. Lincoln was as steady in trusting to Mr. Stanton's own wisdom in action, as he was ready to acknowledge the justice of the Secretary's reproofs on a question of constitutional propriety. This account is as follows:

"While the President was on his way back from Richmond, and at a point where no telegraph could reach the steamer upon which he was, a dispatch of the utmost importance reached Washington, demanding the immediate decision of the President himself. The dispatch was received by a confidential staff officer, who at once ascertained that Mr. Lincoln could not be reached. Delay was out of the question, as important army movements were involved. The officer having the dispatch went with it directly to Mr. Stanton's office, but the Secretary could not be found. Messengers were hastily dispatched for him in all directions. Their search was useless, and a positive answer had been already too much delayed by the time it had occupied. With great reluctance the staff officer sent a reply in the President's name. Soon after, Mr. Stanton entered himself, having learned of the efforts made to find him. The dispatch was produced, and he was informed by the officer sending the answer, of what had been done.

"'Did I do right?' said the officer to the Secretary.

"'Yes, Major,' replied Mr. Stanton, 'I think you have sent the correct reply, but I should hardly have dared to take the responsibility.'

"At this the whole magnitude of the office and the great responsibility he had taken upon himself, seemed to fall upon the officer, and almost overcame him; and he asked Mr. Stanton what he had better do, and was advised to go directly to the President, on his return, and state the case frankly to him. It was a sleepless night to the officer, and at the very earliest hour consistent with propriety he went to the White House."

Here the officer, scarcely even by the accidental interposition of the President's son, was able to reach him, as there were strict orders for his privacy just then. At last, he entered the President's room, and, the story continues,

"The dispatch was shown him, and the action upon it stated frankly and briefly. The President thought a moment and then said, 'Did you consult the Secretary of War, Major?' The absence of the Secretary at the important moment was then related to Mr. Lincoln, with the subsequent remark of Mr. Stanton, that he thought the right answer had been given, but that himself would have shrunk from the responsibility.

"Mr. Lincoln, on hearing the story, rose, crossed the room, and taking the officer by the hand, thanked him cordially, and then spoke of Mr. Stanton as follows:

"'Hereafter, Major, when you have Mr. Stanton's sanction in any matter, you have mine, for so great is my confidence in his judgment and patriotism, that I never wish to take an important step myself without first consulting him.'"

Only a few days before his death, Mr. Lincoln gave a still more striking testimony of the affectionate nature of his regard for Mr. Stanton. This was when Mr. Stanton tendered him his resignation of the War Department, on the ground that the work for whose sake he had taken it, was now done.

"Mr. Lincoln," says a witness, "was greatly moved by the Secretary's words, and tearing in pieces the paper containing the resignation, and throwing his arms about the Secretary, he said, 'Stanton, you have been a good friend and a faithful public servant, and it is not for you to say when you will no longer be needed here.' Several friends of both parties were present on this occasion, and there was not a dry eye that witnessed the scene."

Mr. Stanton occupied a situation of torturing responsibility and distracting cares. He bore burdens of perplexity and doubt and apprehension such as might tax the stoutest nerves. His only mode of meeting and repelling the dashing waves of hourly solicitations and the thousand agencies which beset a man in his position, was to make himself externally as rugged and stern as a rock.

But those who knew him intimately, as did Lincoln, and as did many others who were drawn towards him, interiorly, during the wrench of the great struggle, knew that deep within there was a heart, warm, kind, true and humbly religious—deeply feeling his responsibilities to God, and seeking with honest purpose to fulfil his duties in the awful straits in which he was placed. To a lady for whom he had performed in the way of his office some kindness, and who expressed gratitude, he writes:

"In respect to the matter in which you feel a personal interest and refer to with kind expressions of gratitude towards myself, I am glad that in the discharge of simple duty I have been able to relieve an anxious care in the heart of any one, and much more in the hearts of persons, who although personally unknown to me, I have been accustomed from early youth to reverence.

"In my official station I have tried to do my duty as I shall answer to God at the Great Day, but it is the misfortune of that station—a misfortune that no one else can comprehend the magnitude of, that most of my duties are harsh and painful to some one, so that I rejoice at an opportunity, however rare, of combining duty with kindly offices."

It remains to be seen what further services, if any, Mr. Stanton will render to his country in a public capacity. Should he again be a public servant, it will be as it has been, the United States, and not he, who will be the obliged party.

CHAPTER XII.

FREDERICK DOUGLASS.

The Opportunity for Every Man in a Republic—The Depth Below a White Man's Poverty—The Starting Point whence Fred Douglass Raised Himself—His Mother—Her Noble Traits—Her Self-Denial for the sake of Seeing him—She Defends him against Aunt Katy—Her Death—Col. Loyd's Plantation—The Luxury of his own Mansion—The Organization of his Estate—"Old Master"—How they Punished the Women—How Young Douglass Philosophized on Being a Slave—Plantation Life—The Allowance of Food—The Clothes—An Average Plantation Day—Mr. Douglass' Experience as a Slave Child—The Slave Children's Trough—The Slave Child's Thoughts—The Melancholy of Slave Songs—He Becomes a House Servant—A Kind Mistress Teaches him to Read—How he completed his Education—Effects of Learning to Read—Experiences Religion and Prays for Liberty—Learns to Write—Hires his Time, and Absconds—Becomes a Free Working-Man in New Bedford—Marries—Mr. Douglass on Garrison—Mr. Douglass' Literary Career.

THE reader will perceive, in reading the memoirs which we have collected in the present volume, that although they give a few instances of men who have risen to distinction from comfortable worldly circumstances, by making a good use of the provision afforded them by early competence and leisure, yet by far the greater number have raised themselves by their own unaided efforts, in spite of every disadvantage which circumstances could throw in their way.

It is the pride and the boast of truly republican institutions that they give to every human being an opportunity of thus demonstrating what is in him. If a man *is* a man, no matter in what rank of society he is born, no matter how tied down and weighted by poverty and all its attendant disadvantages, there is nothing in our American institutions to prevent his rising

Eng'd by A H Ritchie

Frederick Douglass

to the very highest offices in the gift of the country. So, though a man like Charles Sumner, coming of an old Boston family, with every advantage of Boston schools and of Cambridge college, becomes distinguished through the country, yet side by side with him we see Abraham Lincoln, the rail splitter, Henry Wilson, from the shoemaker's bench, and Chase, from a New Hampshire farm. But there have been in our country some three or four million of human beings who were born to a depth of poverty below what Henry Wilson or Abraham Lincoln ever dreamed of. Wilson and Lincoln, to begin with, owned nothing but their bare hands, but there have been in this country four or five million men and women who did not own even their bare hands. Wilson and Lincoln, and other brave men like them, owned their own souls and wills—they were free to say, "Thus and thus I will do—I will be educated, I will be intelligent, I will be Christian, I will by honest industry amass property to serve me in my upward aims." But there were four million men and women in America who were decreed by the laws of this country not to own even their own souls. The law said of them—They shall be taken and held as chattels personal to all intents and purposes. This hapless class of human beings might be sold for debt, might be mortgaged for real estate, nay, the unborn babe might be pledged or mortgaged for the debts of a master. There were among these unfortunate millions, in the eye of the law, neither husbands nor wives, nor fathers nor mothers; they were only chattels personal. They could no more contract a legal marriage than a bedstead can marry a cooking-stove, or a plough be wedded to a spinning wheel. They were week after week advertised in public prints to be sold in company with horses, cows, pigs, hens, and other stock of a plantation.

They were forbidden to learn to read. The slave laws imposed the same penalty on the man who should teach a slave to read as on the man who wilfully put out his eyes. They had no legal right to be Christians, or enter the kingdom of heaven, because the law regarded them simply as personal property, subject to the caprice of an owner, and when the owner did not choose to have his property be a Christian, he could shut him out from the light of the gospel as easily as one can close a window shutter.

Now if we think it a great thing that Wilson and Lincoln raised themselves from a state of comparatively early disadvantage to high places in the land, what shall we think of one who started from this immeasureable gulf below them?

Frederick Douglass had as far to climb to get to the spot where the poorest free white boy is born, as that white boy has to climb to be president of the nation, and take rank with kings and judges of the earth.

There are few young men born to competence, carried carefully through all the earlier stages of training, drilled in grammar school, and perfected by a four years' college course, who could stand up on a platform and compete successfully with Frederick Douglass as an orator. Nine out of ten of college educated young men would shrink even from the trial, and yet Frederick Douglass fought his way up from a nameless hovel on a Maryland plantation, where with hundreds of others of the young live stock he shivered in his little tow shirt, the only garment allowed him for summer and winter, kept himself warm by sitting on the sunny side of out buildings, like a little dog, and often was glad to dispute with the pigs for the scraps of what came to them to satisfy his hunger.

From this position he has raised himself to the habits of mind, thought and life of a cultivated gentleman, and from that point of sight has illustrated exactly what slavery WAS, (thank God we write in the past tense,) in an autobiography which most affectingly presents what it is to be born a slave. Every man who struck a stroke in our late great struggle—every man or woman who made a sacrifice for it—every one conscious of inward bleedings and cravings that never shall be healed or assuaged, for what they have rendered up in this great anguish, ought to read this autobiography of a slave man, and give thanks to God that even by the bitterest sufferings they have been permitted to do something to wipe such a disgrace and wrong from the earth.

The first thing that every man remembers is his mother. Americans all have a mother at least that can be named. But it is exceedingly affecting to read the history of a human being who writes that during all his childhood he never saw his mother more than two or three times, and then only in the night. And why? Because she was employed on a plantation twelve miles away. Her only means of seeing her boy were to walk twelve miles over to the place where he was, spend a brief hour, and walk twelve miles back, so as to be ready to go to work at four o'clock in the morning. How many mothers would often visit their children by such an effort? and yet at well remembered intervals the mother of Frederick Douglass did this for the sake of holding her child a little while in her arms, lying down a brief hour with him.

That she was a woman of uncommon energy and strength of affection this sufficiently shows, because as slave mother she could do him no earthly good—she owned not a cent to bring him. She could not buy him clothes. She could not even mend or wash the one garment allotted to him.

Only once in his childhood did he remember his mother's presence as being to him anything of that comfort and protection that it is to ordinary children. He, with all the other little live stock of the plantation, were dependent for a daily allowance of food on a cross old woman whom they called Aunt Katy. For some reason of her own, Aunt Katy had taken a pique against little Fred, and announced to him that she was going to keep him a day without food. At the close of this day, when he crept shivering in among the other children, and was denied even the coarse slice of corn bread which all the rest had, he broke out into loud lamentations. Suddenly his mother appeared behind him—caught him in her arms, poured out volumes of wrathful indignation on Aunt Katy, and threatened to complain to the overseer if she did not give him his share of food—produced from her bosom a sweet cake which she had managed to procure for him, and sat down to wipe away his tears and see him enjoy it. This mother must have been a woman of strong mental characteristics. Though a plantation field hand, she could read, and if we consider against what superhuman difficulties such a knowledge must have been acquired, it is an evidence of wonderful character. Douglass says of her that she was tall and finely proportioned. With affecting simplicity he says: "There is in Pritchard's Natural History of Man, p. 157, the head of a figure the features of which so resemble those of my mother, that I often recur to it with something of the feeling which I suppose others to experience when looking on the pictures of dear departed ones."

The face alluded to is copied from a head of Rameses the great Egyptian king of the nineteenth dynasty. The profile is European in its features, and similar in class to the head of Napoleon. From all these considerations, we have supposed that the mother of Douglass must have been one of that Mandingo tribe of Africans who were distinguished among the slaves for fine features, great energy, intelligence and pride of character. The black population of America is not one race. If slaveholders and kidnappers had been busy for years in Europe stirring up wars in the different countries, and sending all the captives to be sold in America, the mixture of Swedes, Danes, Germans, Russians, Italians, French, might all have gone under the one head of *Whitemen*, but they would have been none the more of the same race. The negroes of this country are a mixture torn from tribes and races quite as dissimilar. The Mandingo has European features, a fine form, wavy, not woolly hair, is intelligent, vigorous, proud and brave. The Guinea negro has a coarse, animal head, is stupid, dirty, cunning. Yet the argument on *negro* powers is generally based on some such sweeping classification as takes the Guinea negro for its type.

The father of Frederick Douglass was a white man, who, he never knew—it would have been of no advantage to him had he known—but there is reason to think that those fine intellectual gifts, that love of liberty, and hatred of slavery which have led him to the position he now occupies among freemen, were due to the blood of his mother. That silent, noble black woman, whose wrongs were borne in such patience, whose soul must so often have burned within her, whose affections were stronger than weariness, and whose mind *would* possess the key of knowledge even though she gained it at such terrible sacrifices and hazards, she is to be honored as the mother of Garrison is, as having lived in her son and being the true author and inspirer of all that is good and just in him.

After a few short interviews the communication between Douglass and his mother ceased. She was taken sick, had a long illness and died without a word or message, or any token passing between her and her child. He running wild, a dirty little animal on the distant plantation, she suffering, wasting, dying in silence—going into the great Invisible where so many helpless mothers have gone to plead for their children before God.

The plantation of Col. Loyd, on which Fred Douglass was raised, was a representative fact illustrating what may be known of slavery. *There* might be seen a large airy elegant house, filled with every luxury and comfort, the abode of hospitality and leisure. Company always coming and going—bountiful tables spread with every delicacy of sea and land—choice cookery, old wines, massive plate, splendid curtains and pictures, all combined to give the impression of a joyous and abundant life. Fifteen well dressed, well trained servants, chosen for good looks and good manners, formed an obsequious army of attendants behind the chairs of guests at the dinner hour, or waited on them in their private apartments.

The shrubbery, the flower gardens, the ample lawns, were laid out with European taste, the stables had studs of the finest blood horses at the disposal of guests—all was cultivation, elegance and refinement.

Col. Loyd was supposed to own a thousand slaves, and what the life was on which all this luxury and elegance was built, the history of Douglass and his mother may show. Col. Loyd owned several contiguous farms or plantations, each one under an overseer, and all were under the general supervision of an agent who lived on the central plantation and went by the name among the slaves of Old Master. Between this man and his family, and Col. Loyd and his family, there was none of the intercourse of equals. No visits were ever exchanged, and no intercourse except of a necessary business character ever took place. The owner and his family had nothing to do with the management of the estates any further than to enjoy and dispense the revenues they brought; in all the rest was left to "Old Master and the Overseers." The estate was as secluded from all influence of public opinion, and the slaves were as completely in the power of the overseers, as the serfs in the feudal ages. Even the vessels which carried the produce of the plantation to Baltimore, were owned by Col. Loyd. Every man and boy by whom these vessels were worked, excepting the captains, were Col. Loyd's property. All the artizans on all the places, the blacksmiths, wheelwrights, shoe makers, weavers and coopers, also were pieces of property belonging to Col. Loyd. What chance was there for laws or for public sentiment, or any other humanizing influence, to restrain absolute power in a district so governed?

One of the earliest lessons in the practical meaning of slavery was taught to the child by hearing the shrieks and groans of a favorite Aunt Esther, under the lash of Old Master. She was a finely formed, handsome woman, and had the presumption to prefer a young slave man to her master, and for this she was made the victim of degradation and torture.

On another occasion he saw a young girl who came from one of the neighboring plantations, with her head cut and bleeding from the brutality of the overseer, to put herself under the protection of Old Master. Though the brutality of her treatment was perfectly evident, he heard her met only with reproaches and oaths and ordered to go back at once or expect even severer treatment. This was a part of an unvarying system. It was a fixed rule, never to listen to complaints of any kind from a slave, and even when they were evidently well founded, to affect to disregard them. That the slave was to have no appeal in any case from the absolute power of the overseer, was a fundamental maxim of the system.

Endowed by his mother with an intelligent and thoughtful organization, young Douglass began early to turn in his mind the dark question, "*Why am I a slave?*" On this subject he pushed enquiries among his little play-fellows and the elderly negroes, but could get no satisfactory solution, except that some remembered that their fathers and mothers were stolen from Africa. When not more than seven or eight years old these thoughts burned in him, whenever he wandered through the woods and fields, and a strong determination to become a freeman in future life took possession of him. It may have been inspired by the invisible guardianship of that poor mother, who, unable to help him in life, may have been permitted higher powers in the world of spirits.

The comments which Douglass makes on many features of slave life, as they affected his childish mind, are very peculiar, and show slavery entirely from an inside point of view.

In regard to the physical comforts of plantation life, he gives the following account:

"It is the boast of slaveholders that their slaves enjoy more of the physical comforts of life than the peasantry of any country in the world. My experience contradicts this. The men and the women slaves on Col. Loyd's plantation received as their monthly allowance, eight pounds of pickled pork or their equivalent in fish. The pork was often tainted and the fish of the poorest quality. With this, they had one bushel of unbolted Indian meal, of which quite fifteen per cent.

was fit only for pigs; with this one pint of salt was given, and this was the entire monthly allowance of a full grown slave, working constantly in the open field, from morning till night, every day of the month, except Sundays. This was living on a fraction more than a quarter of a pound of poor meat per day, and less than a peck of corn meal per week, and there is no work requiring more abundant supply of food to prevent physical exhaustion, than the field work of a slave.

"So much for food. Now as for raiment. The yearly allowance of clothing for slaves on this plantation, consisted of two linen shirts, one pair of tow trowsers for summer, a pair of trowsers and jacket of slazy workmanship for winter, one pair of yarn stockings, and one pair of coarse shoes. The slave's entire apparel could not have cost more than eight dollars a year. Children not yet able to work in the field had neither shoes, stockings, jackets or trowsers given them. Their clothing consisted of two coarse tow linen shirts per year, and when these failed, they went literally naked till next allowance day. Flocks of children from five to ten years old might be seen on Col. Loyd's plantations as destitute of clothing as any little heathen in Africa and this even in the frosty month of March.

"As to beds to sleep on, *none* were given—nothing but a coarse blanket, such as is used in the North to cover horses—and these were not provided for little ones.

"The children cuddled in holes and corners about the quarters, often in the corners of the huge chimneys with their feet in the ashes to keep them warm."

An average day of plantation life is thus given:

"Old and young, male and female, married and single, drop down together on the clay floor of the cabin each evening with his or her blanket. The night however is shortened at both ends. The slaves work often as long as they can see, and are late in cooking and mending for the coming day, and at the first grey streak of morning are summoned to the field by the driver's horn.

"More slaves are whipped for oversleeping than for any other fault. The overseer stands at the quarter door, armed with his cowhide, ready to whip any who may be a few minutes behind time. When the horn is blown, there is a rush for the door, and the hindermost one is sure to get a blow from the overseer. Young mothers working in the field were allowed about ten o'clock to go home and nurse their children. Sometimes they are obliged to take their children with them and leave them in the corners of the fences, to prevent loss of time. The overseer rides round the field on horseback. A cowskin and a hickory stick are his constant companions. The slaves take their breakfast with them and eat it in the field. The dinner of the slave consists of a huge piece of ash cake, that is to say, unbolted corn meal and water, stirred up and baked in the ashes. To this a small slice of pork or a couple of salt herring were added. A few moments of rest is allowed at dinner, which is variously spent. Some lie down on the "turning row" and go to sleep. Others draw together and talk, others are at work with needle and thread mending their tattered garments; but soon the overseer comes dashing in upon them. Tumble up—tumble up is the word, and now from twelve o'clock till dark, the human cattle are in motion, wielding their clumsy hoes, inspired by no hope of reward, no sense of gratitude, no love of children, no prospect of bettering their condition, nothing save the dread and terror of the driver's lash. So goes one day and so comes another." This is slavery as remembered by a cultivated, intelligent man who was born and bred a slave.

In regard to his own peculiar lot as a child on this plantation, he says: "I was seldom whipped, and never severely, by my old master. I suffered little from any treatment I received, except from hunger and cold. I could get enough neither of food or clothing, but suffered more from cold than hunger. In the heat of summer or cold of winter alike I was kept almost in a state of nudity—no shoes, stockings, jacket, trowsers—nothing but a coarse tow linen shirt reaching to the knee. This I wore night and day. In the daytime I could protect myself pretty well by keeping on the sunny side of the house, and in bad weather in the corner of the kitchen chimney. The great difficulty was to keep warm at night. I had no bed. The pigs in the pen had leaves, and horses in the stable had straw, but the children had nothing. In very cold weather I sometimes got down the bag in which corn was carried to the mill, and got into that. My feet have been so cracked by the frost that the pen with which I am writing might be laid in the gashes.

"The manner of taking our meals at old master's, indicated but little refinement. Our corn-meal mush, when sufficiently cooled, was placed in a large wooden tray, or trough, like those used in making maple sugar here in the north. This tray was set down, either on the floor of the kitchen or out of doors on the ground; and the children were called, like so many pigs; and like so many pigs they would come, and literally devour the mush—some with oyster shells, some with pieces of shingles, and none with spoons. He that ate fastest got most, and he that was strongest got the best place; and few left the trough really satisfied. I was the most unlucky of any, for Aunt Katy had no good feeling for me; and if I pushed any of the other children, or if they told her anything unfavorable of me, she always believed the worst, and was sure to whip me."

The effect of all this on his childish mind is thus told:

"As I grew older and more thoughtful, I was more and more filled with a sense of my wretchedness. The cruelty of Aunt Katy, the hunger and cold I suffered, and the terrible reports of wrong and outrage which came to my ear, together with what I almost daily witnessed, led me, when yet but eight or nine years old, to wish I had never been born. I used to contrast my condition with the blackbirds, in whose wild and sweet songs I fancied them so happy! Their apparent joy only deepened the shades of my sorrow. There are thoughtful days in the lives of children—at least there were in mine—when they grapple with all the great primary subjects of knowledge, and reach in a moment, conclusions which no subsequent experience can shake. I was just as well aware of the unjust, unnatural, and murderous character of slavery, when nine years old, as I am now. Without any appeal to books, to laws, or to authorities of any kind, it was enough to accept God as a father, to regard slavery as a crime."

Douglass' remarks on the singing of slaves are very striking. Speaking of certain days of each month when the slaves from the different farms came up to the central plantation to get their monthly allowances of meal and meat, he says that there was always great contention among the slaves as to who should go up with the ox team for this purpose. He says:

"Probably the chief motive of the competitors for the place, was a desire to break the dull monotony of the field, and to get beyond the overseer's eye and lash. Once on the road with an ox team, and seated on the tongue of his cart, with no overseer to look after him, the slave was comparatively free; and, if thoughtful, he had time to think. Slaves are generally expected to sing as well as to work. A silent slave is not liked by masters or overseers. '*Make a noise*,' '*make a noise*,' and '*bear a hand*,' are the words usually addressed to the slaves when there is silence amongst them. This may account for the almost constant singing heard in the southern states. There was generally more or less singing among the teamsters, as it was one means of letting the overseer know where they were, and that they were moving on with the work. But on allowance day, those who visited the great house farm were peculiarly excited and noisy. While on their way, they would make the dense old woods, for miles around, reverberate with their wild notes. These were not always merry because they were wild. On the contrary, they were mostly of a plaintive cast, and told a tale of grief and sorrow. In the most boisterous outbursts of rapturous sentiment, there was ever a tinge of deep melancholy. I have never heard any songs like those anywhere since I left slavery, except when in Ireland. There I heard the same *wailing notes*, and was much affected by them. It was during the famine of 1845–6. In all the songs of the slaves there was ever some expression in praise of the great house farm; something which would flatter the pride of the owner and possibly, draw a favorable glance from him.

"I am going away to the great house farm,
O yea! O yea! O yea!
My old master is a good old master,
O yea! O yea! O yea!

*   *   *   *   *   *

"I did not, when a slave, understand the deep meanings of those rude, and apparently incoherent songs. I was myself within the circle, so that I neither saw nor heard as those without might see and hear. They told a tale which was then altogether beyond my feeble comprehension; they were tones, loud, long and deep, breathing the prayer and complaint of souls boiling over with the bitterest anguish. Every tone was a testimony against slavery, and a prayer to God for deliverance from chains. The hearing of those wild notes always depressed my spirits, and filled my heart with ineffable sadness. The mere recurrence, even now, afflicts my spirit, and while I am writing these lines, my tears are falling. To those songs I trace my first glimmering conceptions of the dehumanizing character of slavery. I can never get rid of that conception. Those songs still follow me, to deepen my hatred of slavery, and quicken my sympathies for my brethren in bonds."

When Douglass was ten years old a great change took place in his circumstances. His old master sent him to Baltimore to be a family servant in the house of a family connection.

He speaks with great affection of his new mistress, Miss Sophia Auld. It is the southern custom for the slave to address a young married lady always by this maiden title. She had never before had to do with a slave child, and seemed to approach him with all the tender feelings of motherhood. He was to have the care of her own little son, some years younger, and she seemed to extend maternal tenderness to him. His clothing, lodging, food were all now those of a favored house boy, and his employment to run of errands and take care of his little charge, of whom he was very fond. The kindness and benignity of his mistress led the little boy to beg her to teach him to read, and the results are thus given:

"The dear woman began the task, and very soon, by her assistance, I was master of the alphabet, and could spell words of three or four letters. My mistress seemed almost as proud of my progress, as if I had been her own child; and supposing that her husband would be as well pleased, she made no secret of what she was doing for me. Indeed, she exultingly told him of the aptness of her pupil, of her intention to persevere in teaching me, and of the duty which she felt it to teach me at least to read *the Bible.* Here arose the first cloud over my Baltimore prospects, the precursor of drenching rains and chilling blasts.

"Master Hugh was amazed at the simplicity of his spouse, and probably for the first time, he unfolded to her the true philosophy of slavery, and the peculiar rules necessary to be observed by masters and mistresses, in the management of their human chattels. Mr. Auld promptly forbade the continuance of her instruction; telling her, in the first place, that the thing itself was unlawful; that it was also unsafe, and could only lead to mischief. To use his own words, further, he said, 'If you give a nigger an inch, he will take an ell; he should know nothing but the will of his master, and learn to obey it. Learning would spoil the best nigger in the world; if you teach that nigger'—speaking of myself—'how to read the Bible, there will be no keeping him; it would forever unfit him for the duties of a slave, and as to himself, learning would do him no good, but probably a great deal of harm—making him disconsolate and unhappy. If you learn him now to read, he'll want to know how to write; and this accomplished, he'll be running away with himself.' Such was the tenor of Master Hugh's oracular exposition of the true philosophy of training a human chattel; and it must be confessed that he very clearly comprehended the nature and the requirements of the relation of master and slave. His discourse was the first decidedly anti-slavery lecture to which it had been my lot to listen. Mrs. Auld evidently felt the force of his remarks; and, like an obedient wife, began to shape her course in the direction indicated by her husband. The effect of his words *on me* was neither slight nor transitory. His iron sentences, cold and harsh, sunk deep into my heart, and stirred up not only my feelings into a sort of rebellion, but awakened within me a slumbering train of vital thought. It was a new and special revelation, dispelling a painful mystery, against which my youthful understanding had struggled, and struggled in vain, to wit: the *white* man's power to perpetuate the enslavement of the *black* man. 'Very well,' thought I, 'knowledge unfits a child to be a slave.' I instinctively assented to the proposition; and from that moment I understood the direct pathway from slavery to freedom."

But the desire of learning, once awakened, could not be hushed, and though Douglass' mistress forebore his teaching, and even became jealously anxious to prevent his making further progress, he found means to continue the instruction. With a spelling-book hid away in his bosom, and a few crackers in his pocket, he continued to get daily lessons from the street boys at intervals when he went back and forth on errands. Sometimes the tuition fee was a cracker, and sometimes the lesson was given in mere boyish good will. At last he made money enough to buy for himself, secretly, a reading book, "The Columbian Orator." This book was prepared for schools during the liberty-loving era succeeding the American revolution, when southern as well as northern men conspired to reprobate slavery. There consequently young Fred found most inspiring documents. There was a long conversation between a master and a slave where a slave defended himself for running away by quoting the language of the Declaration of Independence. Douglass also says of this book:

"This, however, was not all the fanaticism which I found in this Columbian Orator. I met there one of Sheridan's mighty speeches on the subject of Catholic Emancipation, Lord Chatham's speech on the American war, and speeches by the great William Pitt and by Fox. These were all choice documents to me, and I read them over and over again, with an interest that was ever increasing, because it was ever gaining in intelligence; for the more I read them the better I understood them. The reading of these speeches added much to my limited stock of language, and enabled me to give tongue to many interesting thoughts, which had frequently flashed through my soul, and died away for want of utterance."

All this knowledge and expansion of mind, of course produced at first intellectual gloom and misery. All the results of learning to read, predicted by the master, had come to pass. He was so morose, so changed, that his mistress noticed it, and showered reproaches upon him for his ingratitude. "Poor lady," he says, "she did not know my trouble and I dared not tell her—her abuse felt like the blows of Balaam on his poor ass, she did not know that an *angel* stood in the way"

"My feelings were not the result of any marked cruelty in the treatment I received; they sprung from the consideration of my being a slave at all. It was *slavery*—not its mere *incidents*—that I hated. I had been cheated. I saw through the attempt to keep me in ignorance; I saw that slaveholders would have gladly made me believe that they were merely acting under the authority of God, in making a slave of me, and in making slaves of others; and I treated them as robbers and deceivers. The feeding and clothing me well, could not atone for taking my liberty from me."

About this time Douglass became deeply awakened to religious things, by the prayers and exhortations of a pious old colored slave who was a drayman. He could read and his friend could not, but Douglass, now newly awakened to spiritual things, read the Bible to him, and received comfort from him. He says, "He fanned my already intense love of knowledge into a flame by assuring me that I was to be a useful man in the world. When I would say to him, how can these things be, his simple reply was, '*trust in the Lord.*' When I told him that I was *a slave* FOR LIFE, he said: 'The Lord can make you free, my dear. All things are possible with him, only have faith in God. If you want your liberty, ask the Lord for it in faith, and HE WILL GIVE IT TO YOU.'" Cheered by this advice, Douglass began to offer daily and earnest prayers for liberty.

With reference to this he began to turn his thoughts towards acquiring the art of writing. He was employed as waiter in a ship yard, and watching the initial letters by which the carpenters marked the different parts of the ship, and thus in time acquired a large part of the written alphabet. This knowledge he supplemented by getting one and another boy of his acquaintance on one pretence or other, to write words or letters on fences or boards. Then he surreptitiously copied the examples in his little master's copybook at home, when his mistress was safely out of the house, and finally acquired the dangerous and forbidden gift of writing a fluent, handsome current hand.

He had various reverses after this as he grew in age and developed in manliness. He was found difficult to manage, and changed from hand to hand like a vicious intractable horse. Once a celebrated negro breaker had a hand upon him, meaning to break his will and reduce him to the condition of a contented animal, but the old story of Pegasus in harness came to pass. The negro breaker gave him up as a bad case, and finally his master made a virtue of necessity, and allowed him to hire his own time. The bargain was that Douglass should pay him three dollars a week, and make his own bargains, find his own tools, board and clothe himself. The work was that of caulker in a ship yard. This, he says, was a hard bargain; for the wear and tear of clothing, the breakage of tools and expenses of board made it necessary to earn at least six dollars a week, to keep even with the world, and this per centage to the master left him nothing beyond a bare living.

But it was a freeman's experience to be able to come and go unwatched, and before long it enabled him to mature a plan of escape, and the time at last came when he found himself a free colored citizen of New Bedford, seeking employment, with the privilege of keeping his wages for himself. Here, it was that reading for the first time the Lady of the Lake, he gave himself the name of Douglass, and abandoned forever the family name of his old slaveholding employer. Instead of a lazy thriftless young man to be supported by his earnings, he took unto himself an affectionate and thrifty wife, and became a settled family man.

He describes the seeking for freeman's work as rapturous excitement. The thought "I can work, I can earn money, I have no master now to rob me of my earnings," was a perfect joyous stimulus whenever it arose, and he says, "I sawed wood, dug cellars, shoveled coal, rolled oil casks on the wharves, helped to load and unload vessels, worked in candle works and brass foundries, and thus supported myself for three years. I was, he says, now living in a new world, and wide awake to its advantages. I early began to attend meetings of the colored people, in New Bedford, and to take part in them, and was amazed to see colored men making speeches, drawing up resolutions, and offering them for consideration."

His enthusiasm for self-education was constantly stimulated. He appropriated some of his first earnings to subscribing for the Liberator, and was soon after introduced to Mr. Garrison. How Garrison appeared to a liberated slave may be a picture worth preserving, and we give it in Douglass' own words.

"Seventeen years ago, few men possessed a more heavenly countenance than William Lloyd Garrison, and few men evinced a more genuine or a more exalted piety. The Bible was his text book—held sacred, as the word of the Eternal Father—sinless perfection—complete submission to insults and injuries—literal obedience to the injunction, if smitten on one side to turn the other also. Not only was Sunday a Sabbath, but all days were Sabbaths, and to be kept holy. All sectarism false and mischievous—the regenerated, throughout the world, members of one body, and the HEAD Jesus Christ. Prejudice against color was rebellion against God. Of all men beneath the sky, the slaves, because most neglected and despised, were nearest and dearest to his great heart. Those ministers who defended slavery from the Bible, were of their 'father the devil;' and those churches which fellowshipped slaveholders as Christians, were synagogues of Satan, and our nation was a nation of liars. Never loud or noisy—calm and serene as a summer sky, and as pure. 'You are the man, the Moses, raised up by God, to deliver his modern Israel from bondage,' was the spontaneous feeling of my heart, as I sat away back in the hall and listened to his mighty words; mighty in truth—mighty in their simple earnestness."

From this time the course of Douglass is upward. The manifest talents which he possessed, led the friends of the Anti-Slavery cause to feel that he could serve it better in a literary career than by manual labor.

In the year 1841, a great anti-slavery convention was held at Nantucket, where Frederick Douglass appeared on the stage and before a great audience recounted his experiences. Mr. Garrison followed him, and an immense enthusiasm was excited—and Douglass says: ' That night there were at least a thousand Garrisonians in Nantucket." After this the general agent of the Anti-Slavery Society came and offered to Douglass the position of an agent of that society, with a competent support to enable him to lecture through the country. Douglass, continually pursuing the work of self-education, became an accomplished speaker and writer. He visited England, and was received with great enthusiasm. The interest excited in him was so great that several English friends united and paid the sum of one hundred and fifty pounds sterling, for the purchase of his liberty. This enabled him to pursue his work of lecturer in the United States, to travel unmolested, and to make himself every way conspicuous without danger of recapture.

He settled himself in Rochester, and established an Anti-Slavery paper, called Frederick Douglass' Paper, which bore a creditable character for literary execution, and had a good number of subscribers in America and England.

Two of Frederick Douglass' sons were among the first to answer to the call for colored troops, and fought bravely in the good cause. Douglass has succeeded in rearing an intelligent and cultivated family, and in placing himself in the front rank among intelligent and cultivated men. Few orators among us surpass him, and his history from first to last, is a comment on the slavery system which speaks for itself.

Phil. H. Sheridan

CHAPTER XIII.

PHILIP H. SHERIDAN.

Sheridan a Full-Blooded Irishman—The Runaway Horse—Constitutional Fearlessness—Sheridan Goes to West Point—Sheridan's Apprenticeship to War—The Fight with the Apaches at Fort Duncan—He is Transferred to Oregon—Commands at Fort Yamhill in the Yokima Reservation—The Quarrel among the Yokimas—Sheridan Popular with Indians—He thinks he has a Chance to be Major Some Day—Sheridan's Shyness with Ladies—He Employs a Substitute in Waiting on a Lady—Sheridan's Kindness and Efficiency in Office Work—He Becomes a Colonel of Cavalry—His Shrewd Defeat of Gen. Chalmers—Becomes Brigadier—The Kentucky Campaign against Bragg—Sheridan Saves the Battle of Perrysville—Saves the Battle of Murfreesboro—Gen. Rousseau on Sheridan's Fighting—Sheridan at Missionary Ridge—Joins Grant as Chief of Cavalry—His Raids around Lee—His Campaign in the Valley of Virginia—He Moves across and Joins in the Final Operations—His Administration at New Orleans—Grant's Opinion of Sheridan.

MAJOR-GENERAL PHILIP HENRY SHERIDAN is a full-blooded Irishman by descent, though American by birth. He was born in poverty. So large a share of American eminent men have been born poor, that it might almost be said that in our country poverty in youth is the first requisite for success in life.

Sheridan's parents, after remaining a few years at the east, moved to Ohio, where their son grew up with very little schooling, and under the useful necessity of working for a living. There is a story current of his having been put upon a spirited horse when a boy of five, by some mischievous mates, and run away with to a tavern some miles off. He stuck fast to the horse, though without saddle or bridle, and without size or strength to use them if he had them. It was by a mere chance that he arrived safe, and when lifted off by the sympathizing family of the inn, the little fellow admitted that he was shaken and sore with his ride, but he added, "I'll be better to-morrow, *and then I'll ride back home.*" The incident is of no great importance in itself, but it shows that even then the boy was already constitutionally destitute of fear. He seems to have been made without the peculiar faculty which makes people take danger into the account, and try to keep at a distance from it. The full possession of this deficiency (if the phrase is not too direct a contradiction in terms,) is quite uncommon. Admiral Nelson had it, as was shown, very much in Sheridan's own style, in his boyhood. The future victor of Trafalgar had strayed away from home, and got lost. When he had been found and taken home, a relative remarked, "I should have thought that fear would have kept you from going so far away." "Fear?" said the young gentleman quite innocently; "Fear? I don't know him!" He never afterwards made his acquaintance, either; nor, it would seem, has Sheridan.

When young Sheridan received his appointment to a cadetship at West Point, he was driving a water-cart in Zanesville, Ohio. The person who actually procured the appointment was Gen. Thomas P. Ritchey, member of Congress from Sheridan's district. The candidate was very young for the appointment, and very small of his age, insomuch that his friends considered it extremely doubtful whether he would be admitted. He was, however, and passed through the regular West Point course, in the same class with Generals McPherson, Scofield, Terrill, Sill and Tyler, and with the rebel general Hood, who was so fearfully beaten by Thomas at Nashville. His scholarship was not particularly remarkable, and as is often the case with pupils who have no particular want of courage, high health and spirits, or of the bodily and mental qualities for doing things rather than for thinking about it, he experienced various collisions of one and another kind, with the strict military discipline of the institution.

He graduated in June, 1853, and as there was at the moment no vacant second lieutenancy, he was given a brevet appointment, and sent out in the next autumn to Fort Duncan on the Rio Grande, at the western edge of Texas, and in the region haunted by two of the most ferocious and boldest of the tribes sometimes called on the frontier the "horse Indians"—the Apaches and Camanches.

From this time until the rebellion, Lieutenant Sheridan was serving, not exactly his apprenticeship to his trade of war, but what would in Germany be called his *wanderjähre*—his years as wandering journeyman. It was an eight years of training in hardships and dangers more incessant and more extreme than perhaps could be crowded into any life except this of the American Indian-fighter; and doubtless its wild experiences did much to develop the bodily and mental endurance and the coolness and swift energy which have characterized Sheridan as a commander.

For two years Sheridan was at Fort Duncan, and was then promoted to first lieutenant, transferred to the Fourth Regiment, and after some delay in New

York waiting for some recruits, he accompanied them by sea to the Pacific coast, and immediately on reaching San Francisco was placed in command of the escort for a surveying expedition employed on a branch of the Pacific Railroad. On this duty, and afterwards in command of posts or on scouts and expeditions up and down those remote and wild regions, the time passed until the outbreak of the war in 1861.

In the fights and adventures of this rough life, Sheridan's soldierly qualities were often exhibited. While at Fort Duncan, being outside the fort with two men, the three were surprised by a gang of a dozen or more Apaches, whose chief, taking it for granted that the three had surrendered, jumped down from his horse, to tie them up and have them carried off. As he did so, Sheridan, quick as lightning, sprang up in his place, and goaded the wild mustang at full speed to the fort. On reaching it, he called instantly to arms, snatched a pair of pistols, and without dismounting or waiting to see who followed, wheeled and flew back as swiftly as he had come. His two men were fighting stoutly for their lives. Sheridan dashed up and shot the chief. The soldiers, following hard after him, charged the savages, and in a moment the discomfited Apaches were ridden down, dispersed and most of them killed.

During Sheridan's stay in Oregon, his commanding officer, Major Rains, (afterwards the rebel General Rains,) made a campaign against the Yokima Indians, in which Sheridan did right good service, and so conspicuously at the affair of the Cascades on the Columbia, April 28, 1856, as to be mentioned in general orders with high praise. The Indians having been subdued, were placed on a tract called the Yokima Reservation, and Sheridan was appointed to command a detachment of troops posted among them, to act substantially as their governor. He erected a post called Fort Yamhill, and remained there for two or three years, ruling his wild subjects with a good deal of success, and being quite popular with them, as well as praised and trusted by his own superiors. An eye-witness has told the story of an occurrence at Fort Yamhill, a good deal like the affair of the Apaches at Fort Duncan, and which equally illustrates the swift and vehement courage with which Sheridan always does his soldier's work. One day a quarrel arose in the camp of the Yokimas, outside the fort. These turbulent savages have no more self-control than so many tigers, and in a moment their knives were out, and a bloody battle-royal was opened. Sheridan was near enough to see that there was a fight, but happened to be alone. He put spurs to his horse, hurried to the fort, ordered what few soldiers were in sight to follow him, turned, set spurs to his horse again, and dashed off for the Indian camp at the very top of his speed; bare headed, sword in hand, *without once looking round to see if he were followed;* and he charged headlong into the fray, riding through the desperate Indian knife-fight as though it were a field of standing grain. The soldiers felt the powerful magnetism of their leader, just as Sheridan's soldiers have always felt it; and, our informant said, every man of them drove on, just like his leader, without looking behind to see if anybody followed. In they went, striking right and left, and in a moment or two, they had charged once or twice through the fight, and it was quelled.

Sheridan was an efficient manager of these Indians, and was popular with them, too. Their wild, keen instincts appreciate courage and energy, sense and kindness, quite as readily as do civilized men.

When the rebellion broke out, Sheridan was ordered East, and on May 14, 1861, was commissioned captain in the Thirteenth Regular Infantry. He was soon sent to Missouri, where his first actual service in the war was a term of office as president of a board for auditing military claims. He was soon, however, sent into the field as chief quartermaster and commissary under Gen. Curtis, and in that capacity served through the brilliant and victorious, but terribly severe campaign in which the desperate battle of Pea Ridge was fought. At this time his professional ambition was not very high, for he observed one day that "he was the sixty-fourth captain on the list, and with the chances of war might soon be a major."

Sheridan is, however, thoroughly modest, and among ladies is—or was—even excessively bashful. There is an amusing story on this point about this very campaign. It is, that Sheridan, too bashful to seek for himself the company of a certain young lady near Springfield, used to furnish a horse and carriage to a smart young clerk of his, conditionally that the said clerk should take the young lady out to drive and entertain her—very much as Captain Miles Standish is said to have once deputed John Alden on a similar errand. The clerk did so, while Captain Sheridan stood in the door and experienced a shy delight in seeing how well the substitute did duty. No end is known for this story—except, indeed, that Captain Sheridan did not marry the lady.

There are on record some reminiscences of Sheridan's character as an officer in this campaign, which paint him in a very agreeable light, as at once energetic and thorough in duty, and kindly in feeling and manner. It was a fellow-officer who thus wrote:

"The enlisted men on duty at headquarters, or in his own bureau, remember him kindly. Not a clerk or orderly but treasures some act of kindness done by Captain Sheridan. Never forgetting, nor allowing others to forget, the respect due to him and his position, he was yet the most approachable officer at headquarters. His knowledge of the regulations and customs of the army, and of all professional minutiæ, were ever at the disposal of any proper inquirer. Private soldiers are seldom allowed to carry away as pleasant and kindly recollections of a superior as those with which Captain Sheridan endowed us. * * * No man has risen more rapidly with less jealousy, if the feelings entertained by his old associates of the Army of the Southwest are any criterion."

Sheridan's next service was as General Halleck's chief quartermaster in the Corinth campaign. Halleck seems to have thought very well of Sheridan from the first, though apparently rather as a trustworthy organizer and manager, than as such a military son of thunder as he has turned out to be. After a time the nature of the war in those parts occasioned a great demand for cavalry officers, and Sheridan being pitched upon for one, was on May 27, 1862, commissioned colonel of the 2d Michigan Cavalry, and was at once sent into the field to help impede the retreat of the rebels when they should evacuate Corinth.

In this and other similar work of that campaign, Sheridan became at once known to the army and to his superiors as a splendid officer, and from that time forward he rose and rose, up to the very last scene of the Virginia campaign, where he wielded the troops that struck the most telling of the final blows against Lee.

His first important service was to take part in Elliott's Booneville expedition. In June he had a cavalry combat with the butcher Forrest, and beat him, and was made acting brigadier. In July, having two regiments with him, he was attacked by the rebel Chalmers with six thousand men. Sheridan's position was strong enough, but he saw that he would shortly be surrounded and starved out by mere weight of numbers. So he contrived a neat and effective surprise; risky, it is true; but it is exactly the character of an able commander to take risks at the right time, *and not lose.* Sheridan sent round to the enemy's rear, by a long detour, a force of about ninety troopers, with instructions to fall on at a given time, when he would attack in concert with them. This was done; the bold squad fired so fast from their repeating carbines that the rebels, startled and perplexed, could not estimate on the probable number attacking them, and were thrown into confusion. At this moment, Sheridan charged in front with his whole force, and in his own manner, and Chalmers' men, instantly breaking, fled in total rout, and were pursued twenty miles, leaving the whole road strewn with weapons, accoutrements and baggage thrown away in their flight. General Grant, at this time Sheridan's department commander, reported in strong commendation of Sheridan's conduct in this affair, and asked a brigadier's commission for him, which was accordingly given, dated July 15th, the day of Chalmers' first attack. Sheridan seems to like to be attacked. He is sure of himself and of his men, conscious of his own coolness, view of the field, recognition of the "critical five seconds," and promptness in moving, and he prepares a return stroke apparently quite as gladly as he administers a first assault.

When, in the summer of 1862, General Bragg advanced by a line far east of the Union forces in the valley of the Mississippi, with the idea of reaching the Ohio, and carrying the war into the North, Grant sent Sheridan to Buell, commanding in Kentucky, who gave him a division and placed him in command of Louisville. Here Sheridan in one night completed a tolerable line of defence, and waited with confidence for an attack, but Bragg never got so far. On Bragg's retreat was fought the battle of Perrysville, which was given by the rebel leader to gain time for his trains to escape from the rapid pursuit of the Union army. In this battle, Sheridan with his division held the key of the Union position, repulsed several desperate assaults, and twice, charging in his turn, drove the rebels from their positions before him. His division lost heavily, but he inflicted heavier losses on the rebels, and his prompt tactics and keen fighting saved the Union army from defeat.

In the terrible fight of Stone River, or Murfreesboro', Sheridan's part, instead of being merely creditable or handsome, was glorious and decisive. But for him, that great battle would have been a tremendous defeat. How desperate the need of the crisis that Sheridan met there, and how well he met it, may somewhat appear from the terms used by the best historian thus far of that battle, in prefacing the detailed account which he gives of the fighting of Sheridan and his men. Mr. Swinton says:

"The difference between troops is great; the difference between officers is immensely greater. While the two right divisions of McCook were being assailed and brushed away, an equal hostile pressure fell upon his left division (Sheridan's). But here a quite other result attended the enemy's efforts; for not only were the direct attacks repulsed with great slaughter, but when the flank of the division was uncovered by the withdrawal of the troops on its right, its commander effecting a skilful change of front, threw his men into position at right angles with his former line, and having thus made for himself a new flank, buffeted with such determined vigor and such rapid turns of offence, that for two hours he held the Confederates at bay—*hours precious, priceless, wrenched from fate and an exultant foe by the skill and courage of this officer*, and bought by the blood of his valiant men. This officer was Brigadier-General P. H. Sheridan."

Few fights were ever more splendidly soldierly than this of Sheridan's. We cannot detail it; but when left with his flank totally uncovered, and where he would have been perfectly justified in retreating, he changed front under fire—the most difficult of all military manoeuvres, repulsed the triumphant enemy four times, held his ground until all three of his brigade commanders were shot; fought until all his ammunition was gone, and no more to be had; then took to charging with the cold steel; and when at last he had to retreat, he brought off in good order the force that was left, "with compact ranks and empty cartridge boxes," having lost seventeen hundred and ninety-six brave men, and having gained the time which saved the battle; and reporting to Rosecrans, he said with sorrow, "Here is all that are left." The hot blooded Rousseau, who had been sent with his reserves into the dark, close cedar thickets where Sheridan was fighting, described the scene in words that enable the imagination to conceive what must have been the reality of which a soldier spoke thus:

"I knew it was hell in there before I got in, but I was convinced of it when I saw Phil Sheridan, with hat in one hand and sword in the other, fighting as if he were the devil incarnate, or had a fresh indulgence from Father Tracy every five minutes."

Father Tracy was Rosecrans' chaplain—Rosecrans and Sheridan both being Catholics. It may be added that those who know Sheridan's battle manners, may perhaps suspect that he needed indulgence for some offence in words as well as deeds. Gen. Sheridan was made major-general for his services at Murfreesboro'.

We cannot do more than hastily sum up the later and even more brilliant portion of Sheridan's splendid career; and indeed it is so much better known that the task is the less needful. Sheridan was active and useful during Rosecrans' advance on Chattanooga. At the defeat of Chickamauga, his services were so conspicuous in making the best of a bad matter, that Rosecrans in his report, "commended him to his country."

Grant now succeeded Rosecrans, and gained the battle of Chattanooga, Monday, Nov. 23, 1863. In the storming of Missionary Ridge, which was the central glory of that fight, Sheridan and his men bore a conspicuous part. When Grant was made Lieutenant General, he quickly ordered Sheridan to report at Washington. Sheridan went, not knowing whether for praise or blame, and was placed in command of all the cavalry of the Army of the Potomac. When Grant crossed the Rapidan, and began that bloody and toilsome, but shattering and finally decisive series of movements which ended with the surrender of the Rebellion, Sheridan and his horsemen were employed in reconnoitering and guarding trains. May 9th, he set out on a raid around the rear of Lee's army, in which he cut up communications, destroyed supplies, and rescued prisoners; beat the rebel cavalry, killing its leader, J. E. B. Stuart; penetrated within two miles of Richmond, thoroughly frightening the rebel capital; extricated his force from a very difficult position on the Chickahominy, by his peculiar style of swift manoeuvre and furious fighting; and came safe through at last to Butler's headquarters.

On another similar expedition in June, he severely damaged the rebel routes of supply to Richmond from the north and west; and for some time after that, his cavalry were overrunning the country south of Petersburg and Richmond, while Grant was establishing himself in the lines before Petersburg.

Sheridan's great historic campaign in the Valley of Virginia was the crowning glory of his splendid career in the war; a career perhaps more brilliant with the gleams of battles than that of any other commander. This fatal valley had from the very beginning of the war been the opprobrium of the Union armies. From it came General Johnston and those forces that reinforced Beauregard at Bull Run, and turned that hap-hazard fight into a victory for the rebels. Through it, alternating with the ground east of the Blue Ridge, the rebels moved backward and forward, as they chose, like a checker-player in the "whip-row." In it, one Union commander after another had been defeated and made to look ridiculous; and it was the road along which every invasion of the North, east of the mountains, was laid out, as a matter of course.

Sheridan turned this den of disgraces into a theatre all ablaze with victories. He was appointed to the command Aug. 7, 1864; for six or seven weeks simply covered the harvests from the rebel foragers; during September was at last given leave by Grant to deliver battle; September 19th, defeated Early at Winchester; September 22d, defeated him again at Fisher's Hill, whither he had retreated; and when the rebel commander retreated again to the far southern passes of the Blue Ridge, Sheridan laid the southern part of the valley thoroughly waste, to prevent the enemy from finding support in it; on the 19th of October, after his army had been surprised by the persevering Early, defeated, and driven in disorder five miles, Sheridan faced it about, and turned the defeat into the most dramatic, brilliant and famous of all his victories.

In February of the following year, Sheridan took a place in that vast ring of bayonets and sabres with which Grant sought to envelop the remaining armies of the rebellion. On the 27th of that month, he moved rapidly up the valley of his victories, ran over what was left of Early's force, smashed it and captured two-thirds of it almost without stopping, then crossed the Ridge, destroyed the James river canal, and breaking up railroads and bridges as he went, rode across the country to White House, and thence once more joined Grant below Petersburg. Last of all, in the final campaign from March 29th to Lee's surrender on April 9th, Sheridan and his troops were the strong left hand of Grant in all those operations; thrust furthest out around Lee, feeling and feeling after him, clutching him whenever there was a chance, crushing him like a vice at every grasp, and throttling him with relentless force, until the very power of further resistance was gone, and that proposed charge of Sheridan's which was stopped by Lee's flag of truce, would really have been made upon an almost helpless and disorganized mass of starving, worn-out soldiers and disordered wagon-trains.

General Sheridan's administration as military governor at New Orleans, was a surprise to his friends, from its exhibition of broad and high administrative qualities. Yet there is much that is alike in the abilities of a good general and a good ruler. Gen. Grant is a very wise judge of men, and his brief and characteristic record of his estimate of Sheridan might have justified hopes equal to the actual result. To any one remembering also his early days of authority over the Yokimas in Oregon, it would doubtless have done so; for a Yokima community and the community of an "unreconstructed" southern rebel city are a good deal alike in many things. What Grant said of Sheridan was as follows, and was sent to Secretary Stanton just after Cedar Creek, and a little while before Sheridan's appointment as Major-General in the Regular Army, in place of McClellan, resigned:

"City Point, Thursday, Oct. 20, 8 p. m.

Hon. E. M. Stanton, etc.:

I had a salute of one hundred guns from each of the armies here fired in honor of Sheridan's last victory. Turning what bid fair to be a disaster into a glorious victory, stamps Sheridan *what I always thought him, one of the ablest of generals.*

U. S. Grant, Lieutenant-General."

The extraordinary series of popular ovations which have attended Sheridan's recent tour through part of the North, have proved that he is profoundly admired, honored and loved by all good citizens; and unless we except Grant, probably Sheridan is the most popular—and deservedly the most popular—of all the commanders in the war. Such a popularity, and won not by words but by deeds, is an enviable possession.

Eng[d] by A H Ritchie

W. T. Sherman

CHAPTER XIV.

WILLIAM T. SHERMAN.

The Result of Eastern Blood and Western Developments—Lincoln, Grant, Chase and Sherman Specimens of it—The Sherman Family Character—Hon. Thomas Ewing adopts Sherman—Character of the Boy—He Enters West Point—His Peculiar Traits Showing thus Early—How he Treated his "Pleb"—His Early Military Service—His Appearance as First Lieutenant—Marries and Resigns—Banker at San Francisco—Superintendent of Louisiana Military Academy—His Noble Letter Resigning the Superintendency—He Foresees a Great War—Cameron and Lincoln Think not—Sherman at Bull Run—He Goes to Kentucky—Wants Two Hundred Thousand Troops—The False Report of his Insanity—Joins Grant; His Services at Shiloh—Services in the Vicksburg Campaigns—Endurance of Sherman and his Army—Sherman's estimate of Grant—How to live on the enemy—Prepares to move from Atlanta—The Great March—His Courtesy to the Colored People—His Foresight in War—Sherman on Office-Holding.

MANY men of a very lofty grade of power and excellence have arisen in our country, among a class who may be described as of Eastern blood but Western development. They have themselves been born at the East, or else their parents had either lived there or had been trained in the ways of the East. Then, growing up in the freer atmosphere, the more spontaneous life, the larger scale of being, of the West, they have as it were, themselves enlarged in mind, and have seemingly become better fitted to cope with vast executive problems. Thus, President Lincoln was of Eastern Quaker blood; General Grant, of Connecticut blood; Secretary Chase, of New Hampshire blood; General Sherman, of Connecticut blood; but they were all either of Western birth or else trained up in Western habits of thought, sentiment and action. The

West is larger, stronger, freer, than the East, and it affords a better opportunity for great, spontaneous and powerful men.

Perhaps no family in the whole United States was better adapted to supply first-class men by this process than the Shermans'. For generations they have been of strong, practical, thoughtful minds, employed in the highest occupations, laborious and efficient in action, pure and lofty in moral tone and character. Roger Minot Sherman, the Revolutionary statesman, was of this stock, though not in the same direct line with the General. General Sherman's grandfather, Hon. Taylor Sherman, was long a judge in Connecticut, and his father, Hon. Charles R. Sherman, was also a judge, having occupied the bench of the Superior Court of Ohio during the last six years of his life. He died in 1829, leaving his widow in narrow circumstances, with eleven children. Of these, Charles T. Sherman, the eldest, has since been a successful lawyer at Washington; William Tecumseh, the General, was the sixth, and John, the energetic, loyal and useful Senator from Ohio, the seventh. The name of Tecumseh was given in consequence of Judge Sherman's admiration of the noble qualities of that famous chief.

Thomas Ewing, the eminent Whig politician, speaker and statesman, had been an intimate personal friend of Judge Sherman, and when the boy, in those days commonly called by the unlovely nickname of "Cump," from his Indian name of Tecumseh, was about nine years old, Mr. Ewing kindly adopted him and assumed the entire charge of his support and education.

Mr. Ewing, in speaking to one of General Sherman's biographers of his character as a boy, described him as not particularly noticeable otherwise than as a good scholar and a steady, honest, intelligent fellow. He said that he "never knew so young a boy who would do an errand so promptly and correctly as he did. He was transparently honest, faithful, and reliable. Studious and correct in his habits, his progress in education was steady and substantial."

In 1836, Mr. Ewing was a member of Congress from Ohio, and having the right to nominate a cadet at West Point, he offered the appointment to his adopted son, who gladly accepted it, and went successfully through the course of study, graduating in 1840. It is a good illustration of the wholesome stringency of the discipline there, that Sherman's class was a hundred and forty strong when it entered, but only forty-two were left to graduate. The rest had fainted by the way for lack of knowledge or energy, or had been dismissed for some fault. In this "Gideon's band" of forty-two, Sherman stood sixth. A short extract from one of his letters while a cadet shows a curious specimen of the same mixture of peremptory sternness in exacting duties and substantial kindness to those who deserved it *but no others*, which have so often been noted in him since. He writes about the freshman who was according to custom under his particular charge, by the local appellation of a "pleb," as follows:

"As to lording it over the plebs, * * * I had only one, whom I made, of course, tend to a pleb's duty, such as bringing water, policing the tent, cleaning my gun and accoutrements and the like, and repaid in the usual and cheap coin—advice; and since we have commenced studying, I make him *bone* (*i. e.* study,) and explain to him the difficult parts of algebra and the French grammar, since he is a good one and a fine fellow; but should he not carry himself straight I should have him found (*i. e.*, rejected at examination) in January and sent off, that being the usual way in such cases, and then take his bed, table and chair, to pay for the Christmas spree." It is evident that while he was well enough satisfied to help his "fine fellow," he would not have cried much while he saw him turned away if for sufficient cause, or when he proceeded to confiscate his scanty furniture.

Sherman was commissioned at graduating, Second Lieutenant in the third U. S. Artillery; in November 1841 joined his company at Fort Pierce, in East Florida; in January 1842 became First Lieutenant, and served successfully at different points in Florida, at Fort Morgan on Mobile Point, Fort Moultrie in Charleston Harbor, and other posts in the South, for some years. During this time the natural elevation of his character saved him from the frivolous or shameful indulgences too often fallen into by officers on garrison duty; he read and studied works on his profession, acquainted himself with the common law, and amused himself with petting birds and beasts, fishing, hunting and occasionally with visiting.

When the Mexican War broke out he was at first sent on recruiting duty, but he quickly set to work to beg for active service, and on June 29, 1846, he at last received an order to join his company at New York, on the way to California, to meet Kearny's expedition across the plains. He set out the very next day, without waiting to visit even Miss Ewing, his guardian's daughter, to whom he was engaged, and sailed with his company in the storeship Lexington, under the command of Lieut. Theodorus Bailey, now Rear-Admiral. General Ord and General Halleck were fellow lieutenants with Sherman, and sailed with him. An account written by a shipmate during this voyage, thus describes Sherman:

"The first lieutenant was a tall, spare man, apparently about thirty years of age, with sandy hair and whiskers, and a reddish complexion. Grave in his demeanor, erect and soldierly in his bearing, he was especially noticeable for the faded and threadbare appearance of his uniform. * * * He was characterized at this time by entire devotion to his profession in all its details. His care for both the comfort and discipline of his men was constant and unwearied."

His California campaigns were not very adventurous, but he became reputed an excellent business officer in his staff appointment as assistant adjutant-general. Returning in 1850, he married Miss Ewing, May 1st, of that year. In September he was made a commissary of subsistence with the rank of Captain; in March 1851, was commissioned brevet Captain, "for meritorious services in California," and in September 1853, seeing no prospects in the army that satisfied him, he resigned, and became manager of Lucas, Miner & Co's branch banking house at San Francisco.

It is probable that the superintendency of the Louisiana State Military Academy, which with a salary of

$5,000 was offered to him and accepted in 1860, was intended to secure his own co-operation in case of secession, or at least his services in training southern officers. But his term of office was not long; although as has been sarcastically observed, "since then, he has had the opportunity to still further educate his former pupils." He had not been in his new post a half year, when, foreseeing the necessary result of the counsels of the South, and not waiting for the overt act which almost all other good citizens needed to open their eyes, he decided upon his course, and wrote to Governor Moore a letter which has been often printed, but which cannot be too often printed; a noble and simple avowal of patriotic principle and duty. It was as follows:

January 8, 1861.

"Governor THOMAS O. MOORE, Baton Rouge, Louisiana:

"SIR:—As I occupy a *quasi*-military position under this State, I deem it proper to acquaint you that I accepted such position when Louisiana was a State in the Union, and when the motto of the seminary was inserted in marble over the main door, 'By the liberality of the General Government of the United States. The Union: *Esto Perpetua.*'

"Recent events foreshadow a great change, and it becomes all men to choose. If Louisiana withdraws from the Federal Union, I prefer to maintain my allegiance to the old Constitution as long as a fragment of it survives, and my longer stay here would be wrong in every sense of the word. In that event, I beg you will send or appoint some authorized agent to take charge of the arms and munitions of war here belonging to the State, or direct me what disposition should be made of them.

"And furthermore, as President of the Board of Supervisors, I beg you to take immediate steps to relieve me as superintendent the moment the State determines to secede; for on no earthly account will I do any act, or think any thought, hostile to or in defiance of the old Government of the United States.

With great respect, &c.,

(Signed,) W. T. SHERMAN."

The rebels had lost their general. His resignation was at once accepted, and Sherman went to St. Louis, where he had left his family, and impatient of idleness, became superintendent of a street railroad company, and so remained until after the surrender of Sumter.

He now went to Washington and offered his services to Government. Secretary Cameron replied, "The ebullition of feeling will soon subside; we shall not need many troops." Mr. Lincoln replied, "We shall not need many men like you; the storm will soon blow over." In short, Sherman could not make anybody believe him, and he experienced a good deal of the disagreeable fate of prophets of evil; and not for the last time either. But he was totally unmoved in his conviction; he refused to have any thing to do with raising three-months' men, saying, "You might as well attempt to put out the flames of a burning house with a squirt-gun;" and he still vainly urged the government with all his might to fling the whole military power of the country at once upon the rebellion and crush the beginning of it. When, however, the regular army was enlarged, Sherman applied for a command in the new force, and Gen. McDowell readily procured him a commission as Colonel of the 13th Regular Infantry, and in the meanwhile, the regiment not being yet raised, he served as brigadier in the battle of Bull Run, under Gen. Tyler, commanding a division.

In this defeat, Sherman and his brigade did very creditably. His promptitude in going into action, and his good fighting, were of great use in gaining the advantages of the beginning of the battle; he did not retreat until ordered to do so, and retired in comparatively good order. He used his natural freedom and plainness of speech in observing upon the conduct of his own officers and men during the battle, and made enemies thereby; but he had so clearly shown himself a good and ready soldier, that when his brother the Senator and the Ohio delegation urged his appointment as brigadier-general of volunteers it was soon given him, and after remaining in the Army of the Potomac until September, 1861, he was sent to Kentucky, as second in command under Gen. Anderson, commanding the department. A month afterwards, Anderson's health having broken down, Sherman succeeded him.

In a few days, Mr. Secretary Cameron, and Adjutant-General Lorenzo Thomas, came to Louisville, in a hurry to have the new department commander beat the rebels and secure Kentucky to the Union. Sherman knew war, almost intuitively; he knew the resources and the spirit of the rebels, and the military characteristics of Kentucky, and of Tennessee behind it. "How many troops," asked the Secretary of War, "do you require in your department?" "Sixty thousand," answered Sherman, "to drive the enemy out of Kentucky; two hundred thousand to finish the war in this section." This seems to have struck the two inquirers as sheer nonsense; and in the adjutant-general's report, which—as if to help the rebels to as full information as possible—was at once printed in all the newspapers, with full particulars of the state of the armies at the west, Sherman's estimate was barely announced, without explanation or comment. All those persons who understood less of war than Sherman, now at once set him down for a man of no sense or judgment. A disreputable newspaper correspondent, enraged at Sherman for some reason, seized the opportunity to set afloat a story that Sherman was actually crazy, and the lie was really believed by multitudes all over the United States. The war-prophet was misunderstood and despised again, even more remarkably than when he foretold a long war, before Bull Run. Sherman's official superiors so far sympathised with this clamor as to supersede him by Gen. Buell, and to send him to Gen. Halleck, who had faith enough left in him to put him in charge of the recruiting rendezvous at Benton Barracks, St. Louis.

Here he remained, hard at work on mere details, all winter. When Grant, having taken Fort Henry, came down the Tennessee, and turning about, ascended the Cumberland, to attack Donelson, Gen. Sherman was ordered to Paducah, to superintend the sending forward of supplies and reinforcements, a duty which he performed with so much speed and efficiency, that

Gen. Grant reported himself "greatly indebted for his promptness."

After Donelson, Sherman was appointed to the fifth of the six divisions in which Grant organized the army with which he advanced by Nashville to Shiloh; the greenest of all the divisions, no part of it having been under fire, or even under military discipline. At the battle of Shiloh, Sherman's troops, with the magnificent inborn courage of the western men, green as they were, fought like veterans; and his and McClernand's divisions were the only part of Grant's army that at all held their ground, and even this was only done after twice falling back to new positions, in consequence of the giving way of troops on either hand. It was with Sherman that Grant agreed, before he knew of the close approach of reinforcements, to attack in the morning; and after the disappointed Beauregard had retreated next day, it was Sherman who moved his division in pursuit; although the exhausted and disorganized condition of the troops prevented continuing the pursuit. He was severely wounded by a bullet through the left hand on the first day of the fight; bandaged the wound and kept on fighting; was wounded again the next day, and had three horses shot under him, but rode out the battle on the fourth. Though the very first battle in which he had held an independent command—for it was to a great degree such—so thoroughly was he master of the "profession in all its details," to which he had seemed so devoted when a lieutenant on shipboard, that he seems to have found no embarrassment in using all the resources which any commander could have employed in his place. Halleck, a man sparing of compliments, in asking that Sherman should be made major-general of volunteers, said: "It is the unanimous opinion here that Brigadier-General W. T. Sherman saved the fortunes of the day on the 6th, and contributed largely to the glorious victory of the 7th."

And General Grant, whose noble friendship with Sherman, beginning about this time, has continued unbroken ever since, spoke subsequently in still more decided and generous terms, when asking for Sherman a commission as brigadier in the regular service. He wrote to the War Department:

"At the battle of Shiloh, on the first day, he held, with raw troops, the key point of the landing. It is no disparagement to any other officer to say, that I do not believe there was another division commander on the field who had the skill and experience to have done it. To his individual efforts I am indebted for the success of that battle."

During the following operations against and around Corinth, Sherman and his division did most excellent service. He had now received his commission as a major-general of volunteers. When Grant became commander of the Department of the Tennessee, in July, 1862, at the time of Halleck's appointment as general-in-chief, he placed Sherman in command of the bitterly and perseveringly rebel city of Memphis, which Sherman governed sternly, shrewdly, thoroughly and well, under the laws of war, until autumn.

In Grant's first attempt against Vicksburg, Sherman's attack by Chickasaw Bluffs, was an important part of the plan. It failed, because the other parts—Grant's march in consequence of the surrender of Holly Springs, and Banks' movement from New Orleans for other reasons—did not succeed; but Grant, in afterwards examining the ground, said that Sherman's arrangement was "admirable."

The capture of the strong rebel fort at Arkansas Post, January 11, 1863, was a suggestion of General Sherman's, who commanded the land force which carried the fort, after one day's fire, with the hearty help of Admiral Porter's fleet.

In Grant's successive attempts against Vicksburg, Sherman was an indefatigable and most efficient helper. In the final move across the river south of the place, Sherman co-operated by amusing the enemy with a false attack at Haines' Bluff, which was kept up with great ostentation during two days, a large rebel force being thus detained from going down the river to oppose Grant's crossing there. In the series of marches and battles that cut off Johnston from Pemberton, destroyed the military importance for the time being of the city of Jackson, and drove Pemberton into the lines of Vicksburg; and during the siege, in effectually preventing any chance of relief from Johnston, Sherman's services were constant and valuable. Instantly upon the surrender, he moved his army corps against Jackson, where Johnston had halted, and by way of finish to the campaign, drove him out, and thoroughly broke up the railroad lines meeting there. We quote again Grant's frank acknowledgment of the services of his great lieutenant:

"The siege of Vicksburg and last capture of Jackson and dispersion of Johnston's army entitle Gen. Sherman to more credit than generally falls to the lot of one man to earn. His demonstration at Haines' Bluff, * * * his rapid marches to join the army afterwards; his management at Jackson, Mississippi, in the first attack; his almost unequaled march from Jackson to Bridgeport, and passage of Black River; his securing Walnut Hills on the 18th of May, attest his great merit as a soldier."

General Sherman's commission as brigadier in the regular army, dated July 4, 1863, the day of the fall of Vicksburg, reached him August 14th, following; and we quote a passage of his letter to General Grant on the occasion, for the pleasant purpose of recording it near Grant's expressions of obligation to Sherman:

"I had the satisfaction to receive last night the appointment as brigadier-general in the regular army, with a letter from General Halleck, very friendly and complimentary in its terms. I know that I owe this to your favor, and beg to acknowledge it, and add, that I value the commission far less than the fact that this will associate my name with yours and McPherson's in opening the Mississippi, an achievement the importance of which cannot be over-estimated.

"I beg to assure you of my deep personal attachment, and to express the hope that the chances of war will leave me to serve near and under you till the dawn of that peace for which we are contending, with the only purpose that it shall be honorable and lasting."

Rosecrans was defeated at Chickamauga by Bragg, Sept. 19th and 20th, 1863. On this, Grant was placed in command of the whole Military Division of the Mississippi, and Sherman under him over the Department of the Tennessee. He was at once set to march his troops four hundred miles across to Grant at Chattanooga; accomplished it with wonderful energy, skill and speed; commanded Grant's left at the battle of Chattanooga, beginning the fight, and sustaining and drawing the rebel attacks until their center was weakened enough to enable the Union center under Thomas to storm Missionary Ridge, and win the battle. After the victory and the enemy's pursuit, Sherman's force was sent straightway northward a further hundred miles, to relieve Burnside, now perilously beset in Knoxville. Colonel Bowman thus powerfully states the task which this energetic and enduring commander and army performed:

"A large part of Sherman's command had marched from Memphis, had gone into battle immediately on arriving at Chattanooga, and had had no rest since. In the late campaign officers and men had carried no luggage and provisions. The week before, they had left their camps, on the right bank of the Tennessee, with only two days' rations, without a change of clothing, stripped for the fight, each officer and man, from the commanding general down, having but a single blanket or overcoat. They had now no provisions save what had been gathered by the road, and were ill supplied for such a march. Moreover, the weather was intensely cold. But twelve thousand of their fellow-soldiers were beleaguered in a mountain town eighty-four miles distant; they needed relief, and must have it in three days. This was enough. Without a murmur, without waiting for anything, the Army of the Tennessee directed its course upon Knoxville."

This vigorous forced march was entirely successful; Longstreet, after one violent and vain assault against Burnside's works, fled eastward into Virginia, and Sherman, returning and placing his troops in camp to rest and refresh, returned to Memphis. While there, March 10, 1864, he received that simple and noble letter from Grant, acknowledging the latter's obligations to Sherman and McPherson, which we have copied in our chapter on General Grant. We quote Sherman's reply, which is indeed not less interesting than the letter as a display of frank and manly friendship, and which moreover contains one of Sherman's characteristic prophecies, viz., the final allusion to the winding up of the war by the "Great March," and the siege of Richmond, when the West should once more have been made sure:

"DEAR GENERAL:—I have your more than kind and characteristic letter of the 4th inst. I will send a copy to General McPherson at once.

"You do yourself injustice and us too much honor in assigning to us too large a share of the merits which have led to your high advancement. I know you approve the friendship I have ever professed to you, and will permit me to continue, as heretofore, to manifest it on all proper occasions.

"You are now Washington's legitimate successor, and occupy a position of almost dangerous elevation; but if you can continue, as heretofore, to be yourself, simple, honest and unpretending, you will enjoy through life the respect and love of friends, and the homage of millions of human beings, that will award you a large share in securing to them and their descendants a government of law and stability.

"I repeat, you do General McPherson and myself too much honor. At Belmont you manifested your traits—neither of us being near. At Donelson, also, you illustrated your whole character. I was not near, and General McPherson in too subordinate a capacity to influence you.

"Until you had won Donelson, I confess I was almost cowed by the terrible array of anarchical elements that presented themselves at every point; but that admitted a ray of light I have followed since.

"I believe you are as brave, patriotic, and just as the great prototype, Washington—as unselfish, kind-hearted, and honest as a man should be—but the chief characteristic is the simple faith in success you have always manifested, which I can liken to nothing else than the faith a Christian has in the Saviour.

"This faith gave you victory at Shiloh and Vicksburg. Also, when you have completed your preparations, you go into battle without hesitation, as at Chattanooga—no doubts—no reverses; and I tell you it was this that made us act with confidence. I knew, wherever I was, that you thought of me, and if I got in a tight place you would help me out, if alive.

"My only point of doubts was in your knowledge of grand strategy, and of books of science and history; but I confess, your common sense seems to have supplied all these.

"Now, as to the future. Don't stay in Washington. Come West; take to yourself the whole Mississippi Valley. Let us make it dead sure—and I tell you, the Atlantic slopes and Pacific shores will follow its destiny, as sure as the limbs of a tree live or die with the main trunk. We have done much, but still much remains. Time and time's influences are with us. We could almost afford to sit still, and let these influences work.

"Here lies the seat of the coming empire, and from the West, when our task is done, we will make short work of Charleston and Richmond, and the impoverished coast of the Atlantic.

Your sincere friend,

W. T. SHERMAN."

When Grant was appointed Lieutenant-General, Sherman succeeded him in the great command of the Department of the Mississippi; and accompanying Grant from Nashville to Cincinnati on the road of the former to Washington, the two great commanders on the way and at the Burnet House in Cincinnati, agreed together upon the whole main structure of that colossal campaign which during the following thirteen months smote into annihilation all that remained of the military power of the rebellion.

Sherman at once set to work to accumulate stores sufficient for a campaign, and his own statements of his motives and views in so doing, are so comically like his doctrines about his "pleb" when a cadet at West

Point, that we quote a couple of passages. Having put a stop to the government issues of rations to the poor of East Tennessee, he says:

"At first my orders operated very hardly, but * * * no actual suffering resulted, and I trust that those who clamored at the cruelty and hardships of the day have already seen in the result a perfect justification of my course."

Seeing it himself, it is moreover clear that if they did not, it would not particularly distress him. In stating how he proposed to live if he marched into Georgia, he is as independently and rigidly just:

"Georgia has a million of inhabitants. If they can live, we should not starve. If the enemy interrupt my communications, I will be absolved from all obligations to subsist on my own resources, but feel perfectly justified in taking whatever and wherever I can find. I will inspire my command, if successful, with my feelings, and that beef and salt are all that are absolutely necessary to life, and parched corn fed General Jackson's army once, on that very ground."

All things being ready, Sherman moved from Chattanooga on May 6th, 1864, and by a series of laborious marches, skillful manœuvres and well fought battles, flanked or drove Johnston backwards from one strong post to another, until on the 17th of July, Jefferson Davis greatly simplified and shortened Sherman's problem by putting the rash and incompetent Hood in the place of the skillful and persevering soldier who had with less than half Sherman's force, by using the natural advantages of the country, made him take seventy-two days to advance a hundred miles, and at the end of that time actually had more troops than at first, while Sherman had many less. In fact, Johnston was on the very point of making a dangerous attack on Sherman at the right point, when Hood took command, at once attacked on the wrong one, and was defeated. Still advancing, Sherman manœuvred Hood out of Atlanta; saw that mad bull of a general set off some months later, head down and eyes shut, on his way to dash himself against the steady strength of Thomas at Nashville; and turning back to Atlanta, he prepared for his Great March to the Sea.

He had already cleaned Atlanta clean of rebels; exporting all of them within their own military lines, and meeting their own and also Hood's appeals, respectively piteous and enraged, with sarcastic answers in his own inimitable style of cold sharp just reasoning. He made the city nothing but a place of arms; and having almost exactly the force of all arms that he had required for his purpose—for his Cassandra days were over, and his country was by this time glad and prompt to believe him and give him the tools he needed to do its work with—he issued his orders of march on November 9th; sent his last dispatch from the interior to Washington, on the 11th; his army was cut free from its former communications next day; on the 14th it was concentrated at Atlanta; next day two hundred acres of buildings, including all but the private dwellings of the city were burned or blown up; a Massachusetts brigade, its band playing the wonderful "John Brown" folk-song, was the last to leave the city; and with all the railroads effectually ruined behind it, and a parting message to General

Thomas that "All is well," all organized, provisioned, and stripped down to the very last limit of impediments, "the Lost Army" and its great leader set their faces southward and disappeared from the sight of their loyal countrymen for four weeks.

We cannot here repeat the well known and romantic story of that Great March. With scarcely any serious opposition, Sherman, an unsurpassed master in the art of moving great armies, deluded what few opponents there were, with feints and marches on this side and on that, or brushed them away if they stood, and pierced straight through the very heart of the rebellion to Savannah; stormed Fort McAllister, opened communication with the fleet, drove Hardee out of Savannah, and presented the city and 25,000 bales of cotton, a "Christmas present" to President Lincoln; then turning northward, resumed his deadly way along the vitals of the confederacy, doing exactly what he had foretold in his letter to Grant; and sure enough, they did between them, "make short work of Charleston and Richmond and the impoverished coast of the Atlantic." The surrender of Lee was quickly followed by that of Johnston, and except for the small force which for a short time remained in arms beyond the Mississippi, the rebellion was ended.

We cannot even give specimen extracts of the many strongly and clearly worded papers written by General Sherman during his military career, as general orders, directions for the government of captured places or property, or discussions of points of military or civil law. But we must transcribe the noblest compliment which the great soldier ever received; the testimony of the colored clergyman, Rev. Garrison Frazier, at Savannah, during the conferences there for organizing the freedmen, to the merits of General Sherman towards the race. Mr. Frazier said:

"We looked upon General Sherman prior to his arrival as a man in the providence of God specially set apart to accomplish this work, and we unanimously feel inexpressible gratitude to him, looking upon him as a man that should be honored for the faithful performance of his duty. Some of us called on him immediately upon his arrival, and it is probable *he would not meet the Secretary with more courtesy than he met us.* His conduct and deportment towards us characterized him as a friend and a gentleman. We have confidence in General Sherman, and think whatever concerns us could not be under better management."

Of Sherman's characteristics as a general, we shall also give one single trait illustrating the most wonderful of them all—his almost divining foresight. We have more than once showed how he foresaw only too much for his own comfort; but in the present instance he kept the matter to himself. It was, a preparation when the war broke out for that very march which he foretold in his letter to Grant and afterwards made. This preparation consisted in his obtaining from the Census Bureau at Washington a map of the "Cotton States," with a table giving the latest census returns of the cattle, horses and other products of each county in them. On the basis of this he studied the South for three years; and when the time for the march came, he knew substantially the whole resources of the country he was to pass through.

General Sherman's negotiations with Johnston, their disapproval by Government, and his quarrel in consequence with General Halleck and Secretary Stanton were unfortunate; but it would be utterly absurd to admit for a moment that his motives in what he did were other than the very best; and his own explanation of the affair shows that he was following out a policy which would have been in full harmony with President Lincoln's own feelings, as communicated to Sherman on the subject.

Perhaps General Sherman may some day be selected for some high civil office. He is a man perhaps only of too lofty character and too brilliant genius to be harnessed into political traces. He was once nominated for something or other at San Francisco, but when the "committee" came to tell him, he answered sarcastically, "Gentlemen, I am not eligible; I am not properly educated to hold office!" Col. Bowman observes, "This nomination was the commencement of his political career, and his reply was the end of it." It is true in too many cases that a true soldier, like a good citizen, will find his very virtues the insurmountable obstacles to political success. This is perhaps likely to remain the case unless the rule shall come into vogue that nobody shall have an office who lets it be known that he wants it.

O. O. Howard

CHAPTER XV.

OLIVER O. HOWARD.

Can there be a Christian Soldier?—General Howard's Birth—His Military Education—His Life Before the Rebellion—Resigns in Order to get into the Field—Made Brigadier for Good Conduct at Bull Run—Commands the Eleventh Corps and Joins the Army at Chattanooga—His Services in the Army of the Potomac—Extreme Calmness on the Field of Battle—Services with Sherman—Sherman's high Opinion of him—Col. Bowman's Admiration of Howard's Christian Observances—Patriotic Services while Invalided at Home—Reproves the Swearing Teamster—Placed over the Freedmen's Bureau—The Central Historic Fact of the War—The Rise of Societies to Help the Freedmen—The Work of the Freedmen's Bureau—Disadvantages Encountered by it, and by General Howard—Results of the Bureau thus far—Col. Bowman's Description of Gen. Howard's Duties—Gen. Sherman's Letter to Gen. Howard on Assuming the Post—Estimate of Gen. Howard's Abilities.

The spirit of Christ is all love; it seeks only to enhance the highest good of existence, and to give to every being its utmost of happiness. The spirit of war is all wrath. It seeks to destroy by violence, and as fast as possible, whatever and whoever may oppose it. These two principles would seem so diametrically opposed to each other, that no man could be at once a Christian and a soldier, any more than he could ride at once on two horses going in opposite directions, or turn his back on himself, and at once go forward and backward. Indeed, the cases where the two professions have been united are rare, and may probably depend upon some uncommon conjunction of gifts. But there certainly have been such. Colonel Gardiner was one. General Havelock was another; and General Howard, who has been surnamed the Havelock of America, is another.

Oliver Otis Howard was born in Leeds, Maine, Nov. 8th, 1830. His father was a thrifty and independent farmer. The boy lived at home until he was ten, when his father dying, an uncle, Hon. John Otis, of Hallowell, took charge of him. He now attended school, went through Bowdoin College, and then entered the West Point Academy, graduating there in 1854, fourth in general standing of his class. Beginning, as usual, as brevet second lieutenant, he was assigned to the ordnance department; and in 1856 was chief ordnance officer in Florida, during a campaign against the Indians there. He worked steadily on in his profession, and at the beginning of the war was assistant professor of mathematics at West Point, and being desirous to accept the command of a volunteer regiment from his own State, asked leave from the War Department to do so, and was refused. On this he resigned his commission, and the Governor of Maine, in the end of May, 1861, appointed him colonel of the Third Maine Volunteers, which was the first three years' regiment from that State.

At Bull Run, he commanded a brigade, being senior colonel on the field, and for good conduct there, was in the following September commissioned brigadier-general of volunteers. In December he was placed in General Sumner's command; and he remained in the Army of the Potomac until the latter part of September, 1863, when, having risen to the command of the Eleventh Army Corps, that and Slocum's corps, both under Hooker, were sent to reinforce the army at Chattanooga.

During this time General Howard was present in all the chief battles of the Army of the Potomac. At Fair Oaks, on the Peninsula, he was twice wounded in the right arm, and had to have his arm amputated; but he got back in season for the next battle—that of the second Bull Run. At Antietam, at Fredericksburg, at Chancellorsville, he was present and fought his command to the uttermost. At Gettysburg, Howard's troops held the key of the position, the cemetery; and a soldier who was in the field with him in that tremendous fight, in speaking of his extreme calmness and coolness under fire, said, "General Howard stood there as if nothing at all was the matter. He never takes stimulants, either. Most of the officers do, but he never does. He was so calm because he was a Christian." Colonel Bowman, in speaking of this same trait in General Howard, testifies to the same point; observing that he is "careless of exposing his person in battle, to an extent that would be attributable to rashness or fatalism if it were not known to spring from religion."

During his campaigns with Sherman he was a most trustworthy and serviceable commander; singularly cool and fearless in battle, and most prompt and thorough in the performance of whatever duty was imposed upon him. After accompanying Sherman in his march for the relief of Burnside, General Howard served in the Atlanta campaign in command of the Fourth Army Corps; after the death of General McPherson, he succeeded him in the important command of the Army of the Tennessee; and in Sherman's Great March, he was placed in command of the right wing, one of the two into which Sherman's force was divided, and in this position served until the end of the war.

General Sherman quickly liked his trusty and helpful subordinate, and has repeatedly paid high compliments to his soldierly and moral excellence. At the end of the Chattanooga campaign, for instance, in reporting to Gen. Grant, he said, "In General Howard throughout I found a polished and Christian gentleman, exhibiting the highest and most chivalrous traits of the soldier." Colonel Bowman speaks of General Howard's practice of Christian observances in the army with a curious sort of admiration which sufficiently shows how uncommon it was, at least among officers of high grade. He says:

"General Howard, it is well known, has been pious and exemplary from his boyhood, was ever faithful and devoted in the discharge of his religious duties, and this even while a student at West Point. He carried his religious principles with him into the army, and was guided and governed by them in all his relations with his officers and men. No matter who was permitted to share his mess or partake of his repast, whether the lowest subaltern of his command or General Sherman himself, no one thought to partake, if General Howard were present, without first the invocation of the Divine blessing, himself usually leading, like the father of a family. General Sherman seems greatly to have admired the Christian character of General Howard, * * * and not only as a Christian but as a soldier, preferring him and promoting him to the command of one of his armies." President Lincoln also valued him very highly, and was his immovable friend.

General Howard's unconditional devotion to duty was very strongly shown in the use he made of his time while disabled from military duty just after the loss of his arm. One of his companions in the service has described how—

"Weak and fainting from hemorrhage and the severe shock his system had sustained, the next day he started for his home in Maine. He remained there only two months, during which time he was not idle. Visiting various localities in his native State, he made patriotic appeals to the people to come forward and sustain the government. Pale, emaciated, and with one sleeve tenantless, he stood up before them, the embodiment of all that is good and true and noble in manhood. He talked to them as only one truly loyal can talk—as one largely endowed with that patriotism which is a heritage of New England blood. Modesty, sincerity, and earnestness characterized his addresses, and his fervent appeals drew hundreds of recruits around the national standard."

Howard's reply to the swearing teamster was a good instance of kind but decided reproof, of just the sort that will do good if any will. The story is this:

"On one occasion, a wagon-master, whose teams were floundering through the bottomless mud of a Georgia swamp, became exasperated at the unavoidable delay, and indulged in such a torrent of profanity as can only be heard in the army or men of his class.

General Howard quietly approached, unperceived by the offender, and was an unwilling listener to the blasphemous words. The wagon-master, on turning around, saw his general in close proximity, and made haste to apologize for his profane outburst, by saying, 'Excuse me, General, I did not know you were here.' The General, looking a reprimand, replied, 'I would prefer that you abstain from swearing from a higher and better motive than because of my presence.'"

In May, 1865, General Howard was placed at the head of the Freedmen's Bureau; a position for which he was probably the very best man in the United States, one whose extremely noble and benevolent purpose was wholly in harmony with the loftiest traits of his own character, and whose peculiar difficulties were such as he was exactly the man to encounter, by nature, education and official position.

By imagining one's self to have passed forward in history for a century or two centuries, and to be taking such a backward perspective view of the southern rebellion as such an advance would give, any mind of historic qualities will perceive more clearly than in any other way the falling off and disappearance of the minor circumstances of the great struggle, and the few great features that remain—the central facts, the real meanings of the war. Of all these, that which will remain most important is, the escape from their modern Egypt of the nation of the slaves. Lives and deeds of individual men will grow obscure. The gigantic battles, the terrific novelties, the vast campaigning combinations of the successive chapters of the war will lose their present strong colors. Even the fact that part of the white population of the United States sought in vain to sever their political union with the rest, will lose its present foremost place in the story; for it will have assumed the character of an abortive delusion; a temporary struggle, whose pretended reasons were sophistical and false, whose real ones were kept out of sight as much as possible, and which ended in the speedy re-establishment of the power attacked. But the emancipation of the slaves is an eternal epoch; it marks the point where the race of one vast continent, after centuries of exile into another continent and of the most degrading subjection to another race, is all at once let out into civilization; brought forth from the pens of beasts, to take a place among the sons of men. Yet more; they are admitted to take a place among the sons of God; for American slavery, as if with the devil's own cunning and cruel power, did really not only exclude the slave from becoming a citizen, but it actually excluded him from the power of becoming a Christian. The emancipation of the slaves was even more than the organization of a new nation; for it was the birth into humanity of a new race.

This view of the case is naturally even now not accepted by large numbers of persons. It was a matter of course that still larger numbers should fail to understand it in the day of it. President Lincoln himself apparently felt more hope than expectation upon the subject; and all know how long he delayed, how unendurably slow he seemed to far-sighted lovers of humanity, before he issued his great proclamation. But there are a few men, who possess at once a powerful instinct of benevolence and an intuitive comprehension of the present and the future—qualities which naturally go together, because they are alike pure, lofty, dependent upon peculiarly noble organizations. As soon as the progress of the war rendered any considerable number of freedmen accessible for any permanently useful purpose, societies began at once to be organized in the North to help the freedman towards his rightful standing of an intelligent Christian citizenship. The first of them were organized in Boston, New York, and Philadelphia, in consequence of the information given by General Sherman, Commodore Dupont, and the able Treasury Agent, Mr. E. L. Pierce, of the situation of the freedmen on the Sea Islands of Georgia and South Carolina. Several societies or "commissions" were established, all of which—except some ecclesiastical ones—are now operating in conjunction as "The American Freedmen's Union Commission." The "Bureau of Refugees, Freedmen and Abandoned Lands," commonly called the Freedmen's Bureau, was created by an act of Congress passed in March, 1865, and in form received the freedmen into the express protection and care of the Government; and its creation was to a considerable extent if not altogether the result of the efforts of the energetic men who had established the various private commissions. It is possible that the Bureau might have been earlier established, had the right man been found to take charge of it. When General Howard was thought of, at the conclusion of the war, it was felt that he was in every respect most suitable. His lofty views of duty; his habits of orderly obedience and orderly command; the facilities of his high military position for dealing with the body of assistants it was contemplated to secure from the army; and above all, his calm, steady, kindly ways, and his rare characteristic and complete sympathy with the missionary object of securing a real Christian citizenship for the unfortunate colored race, were just the qualities that must have been put together if a man was to have been constructed on purpose for the place.

General Howard has been most earnestly at work in this position ever since, amid great difficulties and obstructions, but with unfailing faith and industry; and although it is easy to see how far more of his great task would have been at this day accomplished had the white people of the South, and the Government itself helped the Bureau earnestly and in good faith, yet very great good has already been done.

Doubtless the freed people have in many things been faulty. It would be strange indeed if a whole race could in the twinkling of an eye, put off the bad habits burned and ingrained into the very texture of their bodies and minds, by a heavy tyranny of two centuries and a half. Generations of freedom must pass before the evils can wholly disappear that generations of slavery have systematically and powerfully cultivated. But already, to a very great degree (to use the words of a recent comprehensive summary of the history of the Bureau,) "labor has been reorganized, justice has been secured, systems of education * * * have been established, the transition period from slavery to liberty has been safely passed, and the freed people have emerged from their state of bondage into that of the liberty of American citizenship."

The operations of the Bureau and of the Commission which works in union with it, as a sort of unofficial counterpart—a draught-horse hitched on outside the thills—have sought four objects for the freedmen, in the following order: 1. To provide for their temporal wants; for if they had no food for to-day, and no clothes nor roofs to shelter them, they would be out of the world before they could learn their letters, earn a dollar, or learn to obey the law; 2. To promote justice; 3. To reorganize labor; 4. To provide education.

In his difficult and laborious position, General Howard has had to act without the help of any public funds, by using temporarily certain species of abandoned property, and by means of details of officers and men from the army, who have done their work in the Bureau as part of their military duty, and without other than their usual pay. The good accomplished has been rather by the use of influence, by forbearance, by the exercise of the minimum of absolute authority. But in spite of the good intentions of Congress, the help of the Government of the United States, which, so far as its action upon the Freedmen'sBureau is concerned, is exclusively the executive, has not in any complete sense been given either to the freedmen themselves, in their toilsome upward road, nor to those who have been striving to aid them in the ascent; but it has rather been felt as a cold, sullen and grudging sufferance, verging even into a pretty distinct manifestation of an enmity like that of the worse class of unfriendly southern whites, and showing more than one token of an intention to destroy the Bureau and leave the freedmen helpless as soon as possible.

General Howard has done all that could be done, against these obstacles. It is easy to see what constant exercise he must need, of the Christian virtues of forbearance, patience, kindness, and the overcoming of evil with good, as well as of the moral qualities of honor and justice, and the soldierly attainments of order, promptitude and industry. With some of these he must meet the angry tricks of white enemies; with some, the pitiful faults—which are misfortunes rather—faults of the freedmen themselves—idleness, falsehood, dishonesty, disorder, incapacity, fickleness; with others still, the inactive resistance of his superiors, and the cumbrous machinery of an organization which the nature of the case prevents from coming into good working shape.

In spite of all obstacles, the Missionary General and his Bureau and the Commission have done much. Up to the first day of 1867, fourteen hundred schools had been established, with sixteen hundred and fifty-eight teachers and over ninety thousand pupils; besides 782 Sabbath Schools with over 70,000 pupils; and the freedmen were then paying towards the support of these schools, out of their own scanty earnings, after the rate of more than eleven thousand dollars a month. Within one year, they had accumulated in their savings bank, $616,802.54. Many of them have bought and possess homesteads of their own. Their universal obedience to law would be remarkable in any community in the world, and under such treatment as they have experienced from their former masters since the war, would have been simply impossible for the body of freemen in the most law-abiding of the Northern States. And above all, they are with one accord most zealous, most diligent and most successful, in laboring to obtain the religious and intellectual culture which alone can fit them for their new position, as self-governing citizens of a free country.

The views of intelligent army officers, of the task which General Howard undertook in accepting this post and of his fitness for it, are not without interest. Col. Bowman thus describes the work:

"He was placed at the head of a species of Poor Law Board, with vague powers to define justice and execute loving kindness between four millions of emancipated slaves and all the rest of mankind. He was to be not exactly a military commander, nor yet a judge of a Court of Chancery; but a sort of combination of the religious missionary and school commissioner, with power to feed and instruct, and this for an empire half as large as Europe. But few officers of the army would have had the moral courage to accept such an appointment, and fewer still were as well fitted to fill it and discharge one-half its complicated and multifarious duties."

When General Howard, on accepting his new post, advised his old commander by letter, General Sherman, in a friendly reply, thus wrote:

"I hardly know whether to congratulate you or not, but of one thing you may rest assured, that you possess my entire confidence, and I cannot imagine that matters that may involve the future of four millions of souls could be put in more charitable and more conscientious hands. So far as man can do, I believe you will, but I fear you have Hercules' task. God has limited the power of man, and though, in the kindness of your heart, you would alleviate all the ills of humanity, it is not in your power; nor is it in your power to fulfill one-tenth part of the expectations of those who framed the bureau for the freedmen, refugees and abandoned estates. It is simply impracticable. Yet you can and will do all the good one man may, and that is all you are called on as a man and a Christian to do; and to that extent count on me as a friend and fellow-soldier for counsel and assistance." General Sherman more than once repeated to others similar testimonies of his faith in General Howard.

General Howard has not the vast intellect and brilliant genius of General Sherman, nor the massive strength and immense tenacious will of General Grant. But he has qualities which are even loftier; namely, those which are the sure basis for such respect and confidence as General Sherman's; which alone have enabled him to accomplish what he has in an enterprise wholly discouraging on any merely human principles. Grant and Sherman, in what they have done, had at their backs a people far more intelligent, resolute and wealthy, than those against whom they warred; but a man like Howard, whose soul opens upward and takes in the unselfish strength and love and faith of Almighty God, can do great things for humanity irrespective of money and majorities.

Wm A Buckingham

CHAPTER XVI.

WILLIAM ALFRED BUCKINGHAM.

The Buckinghams an Original Puritan Family—Rev. Thomas Buckingham—Gov. Buckingham's Father and Mother—Lebanon, the Birthplace of Five Governors—Gov. Buckingham's Education—He Teaches School—His Natural Executive Tendency—His Business Career—His Extreme Punctuality in Payments—His Business and Religious Character—His Interest in the Churches and Schools—His Benefactions in those Directions—His Political Course—He Accepts Municipal but not Legislative Offices—A Member of the Peace Conference—He Himself Equips the First State Militia in the War—His Zealous Co-operation with the Government—Sends Gen. Aiken to Washington—The Isolation of that City from the North—Gov. Buckingham's Policy for the War; Letter to Mr. Lincoln—His Views on Emancipation; Letter to Mr. Lincoln—Anecdote of the Temperance Governor's Staff.

In writing the history of men of our time, we feel that we are only making a selection of a few from among many. We have given the character of one State Governor—we could give many more, but must confine ourselves to only two examples. William Alfred Buckingham, for eight years Governor of Connecticut, and under whose administration the State passed through the war, may be held a worthy representative of the wisdom, energy and patriotism of our state magistracy in the time of the great trials.

Gov. Buckingham is of the strictest old Puritan stock. The first of the name in this country was Thomas Buckingham, one of the colony that planted New Haven, Conn., but who soon removed to Milford in that State, where he was one of the "Seven Pillars" of the church there, as originally organized. His son, Rev. Thos. Buckingham, was minister of Saybrook, one of the founders of Yale College, and one of the moderators of the Synod that framed the "Saybrook Platform." Through this branch of the family, this Governor of Connecticut is descended, his father having been born in Saybrook.

William Alfred Buckingham, the son of Samuel and Joanna (Matson) Buckingham, was born in Lebanon, Conn., May 28, 1804. His father was a thrifty farmer, a deacon in the church, a man of remarkably sound judgment and common sense, and a public spirited man, abounding in hospitality. His mother was one of those women in whom the strong qualities of the Puritan stock come to a flowering and fruitage of a celestial quality, a rare union of strength and soundness. She had a mother's ambition for her children, but always directed to the very highest things. "Whatever else you are, I want you to be Christians," was one of her daily household sayings. Her memory is cherished in the records of many words and deeds of love and beneficence, written not with ink and pen, "but in fleshy tables of the heart," in all the region where she lived.

The little town of Lebanon, like many others of the smaller New England towns, had a fine Academy, which enjoyed the culture of some of those strong and spicy old New England school masters, that were a generation worthy of more praise and celebration than the world knows of. For that reason perhaps, this little town of Lebanon has given to the State of Connecticut five Governors, who have held that State office for 37 years out of the past one hundred—more than one-third of the century.

Governor Buckingham's education was a striking specimen of New England. It was based first on the soil, in the habits and associations of a large, thriving, well conducted farm. It was nourished up at those rural Academies, which are fountain memorials of the enthusiasm for education, of our Puritan fathers. He had a special taste for mathematics, which, united with the promptings of a vigorous and energetic physical nature, and love of enterprise, led him to desire the profession of a practical surveyor, a profession which in those days had some state patronage, and was attractive to young men of that class of character. At the age of eighteen, he taught district school, in Lyme, and gave such satisfaction that his services were earnestly sought for another year. He returned, however, to the practical labors of his father's farm, and for the last three years performed as much work as any of the laborers whom his father hired. His nature seemed to incline him rather to a dealing with the practical and physical forces of the world, and so he wisely forbore that classical career which would have occupied four years of his life in a college, and began the career of a man of business at once, entering a dry goods store in Norwich as clerk, at twenty. After two years spent there, and a short experience in a wholesale store in New York, he established himself in business as a dry goods merchant at Norwich, Conn. From this time his career has been a successful one in the business circles of the country. Enterprise, prudence, thrift, order and exact punctuality and spotless integrity have given him a name worth any amount of money. In 1830 he commenced the manufacture of ingrain carpeting, which he continued for 18 years. In 1848 he closed up his dry goods business, discontinued the manufacturing of carpeting, and engaged in the fabrication of India Rubber, a business then in its infancy.

From that time to the present, he has been the treasurer, and an active business director of the Hayward Rubber Company, a company located in Colchester, which has prosecuted an extensive and successful business. He is now a stockholder in eight or ten manufacturing companies, to the general management of quite a number of which he gives his attention.

An important feature in his character in these relations is his great business accuracy and punctuality. With an extended business running through a period of forty years, only two notes drawn, were protested for non-payment, and these cases occurred when he was wholly disabled from business by sickness. It was his custom always to remit money to meet notes due in New York, three days before their maturity. He has always regarded himself as under obligations to pay his debts *at the time* agreed upon, as much as to pay the amount due.

His unvarying and unfailing accuracy in these respects, had given him a character which enabled him at any time to command the assistance of any bank with which he did business. His name was good for any amount of resources. This particular characteristic made his position as Governor of Connecticut, in the sudden crisis of the war, of vital value to the country.

No man could so soon command those material resources which are the *sine qua non* of war, and it is one of many good Providences that the state of Connecticut at this crisis was so manned. Immediately on the news of the war, the banks of the state, and business men in all parts, sent immediate and prompt word to him that he might command their utmost resources. They were even anxious to have their capital at once made serviceable in the emergency, and they felt sure in doing so that they were putting their resources into the hands of a leader every way fitted to employ them to the best advantage.

Governor Buckingham is well known as an exemplary and laborious Christian, a devoted friend of education, a practical and consistent temperance man, and proverbially generous in his charities towards these, and every other good cause. And it has probably been due to this, as much as to his personal and official integrity, that he has been so popular with his friends, and claimed such respect from his political opponents. Indeed nothing could have been more respectful and generous, during all those excited political canvasses which belonged to his public life, than the treatment his private character received from those who were politically opposed to him.

His own strict attention to the proprieties and courtesy's of life, his bland and urbane manners may go a long way towards accounting for this result.

In 1830 he united with the Second Congregational Church, under the care of Rev. Alfred Mitchell, and in 1838 made a report to the Ecclesiastical Society, to show the necessity of organizing a new church. Such a church was organized four years after, and is now known as the Broadway Congregational Church. From its organization to the present time, he has been one of its deacons, an active member, and a liberal supporter. He gave them a fine organ when their present church building was completed, and has lately erected a beautiful chapel for one of their Mission Sabbath Schools. He has himself been a Sabbath School Teacher for the last thirty-seven years, except during the four years of the Rebellion.

He was moderator of the National Congregational Council held in Boston, in 1865.

As a friend of Education, he earnestly advocated the consolidation of the School Districts of Norwich, and a system of graded schools to be open to all, and supported by a tax on property, and he was permitted to see such a system established with the most beneficial results. He was deeply interested in the effort to establish the Norwich Free Academy, gave his personal efforts to obtain a fund for its endowment, and has contributed an amount to that fund second only to one subscriber.

Having seen the extended and beneficial influence which Yale College has exerted and is exerting over the political and religious interest of the country, he has felt it a privilege and a duty to contribute largely to the pecuniary necessities of that institution.

He has given a permanent fund to the Broadway

Congregational Church in Norwich, and to the Congregational Church in Lebanon, with which his parents and sisters were connected, the income of which is to be used for the pastor's library. Joseph Otis, Esq., who founded a public library in Norwich, selected him for one of the trustees, and he is now President of the Board.

As a politician, he was a Whig. In 1842 he was the candidate of that party for a seat in the lower house of the General Assembly, but was not elected. He was afterwards repeatedly nominated both for the House of Representatives and for the Senate, but declined such nominations, and was never a member of a legislative body. He has, however, frequently accepted municipal offices; was often elected a member of the City Council, sometimes occupying the seat of an alderman, and was elected Mayor of the city of Norwich in 1849 and 1850, and again in the years 1856 and 1857. When the Whig party was broken up, he placed himself with the Republicans, and in 1858 was elected Governor of the State, which position he occupied eight years, and four of them were the years of the Rebellion.

The famous Peace Conference met at Washington one month before the inauguration of Lincoln, wherein were represented thirteen of the free States and seven of the slave States, for the purpose of considering what could be done to pacify the excited feelings of the South, and preserve the existing Union.

Governor Buckingham was not a member of the

conference, but appointed the commissioners from Connecticut. He was in Washington during its session, and in daily intercourse with members of that body from all parts of the country, and understood their views of questions at issue. But from the very first he was of opinion that the state of things had reached a place where further compromise was an impossibility, or in the words of Lincoln, the Union must now become either in effect all for slavery or all for freedom in its general drift. So this peace conference broke up, effecting nothing.

When the news of the fall of Sumter reached Connecticut, attended by the Presidential call for troops, the State Legislature was not in session. Governor Buckingham, however, had such wide financial relations as enabled him immediately to command the funds for equipping the militia for the field.

From every quarter came to him immediate offers both of money and of personal services, from men of the very first standing in the State—and Connecticut, we think, may say with honest pride that no men went into the field better equipped, more thoroughly appointed and cared for. Governor Buckingham gave himself heart and soul to the work. During that perilous week when Washington stood partially isolated from the North, by the uprising of rebellion in Maryland, Governor Buckingham, deeply sympathizing with the President, dispatched his son-in-law, Gen. Aiken, who with great enterprize and zeal found his way through the obstructed lines to Washington, carrying the welcome news to the President that Connecticut was rising as one man, and that all her men and all her wealth to the very last would be at the disposal of the country.

The account of Gen. Aiken's trip to Washington with the dispatches for the government there, brings freshly to mind the intense excitement of those days, and it contains some very striking touches of description of the state of things at Washington. Gen. Aiken left Norwich at 6 A. M., on Monday, April 22d, 1861; on reaching Philadelphia that evening, found that city extremely stirred up, and all regular communication with Washington suspended; met a gentleman who wished to reach Washington, and the two spent most of the night in searching for the means of proceeding. At four next morning they got permission to set out on a special train with a Pennsylvania regiment, and after a very slow journey, in consequence of the danger of finding the track torn up, reached Perryville, on the Susquehanna, at ten. Gen. Butler had carried off the ferry-boats to Annapolis; and after delay and search, our two travellers hired a skiff and crossed to Havre de Grace, where they found, not only that the town was full of reports of railroads and telegraphs broken up in all directions, but that there were plenty of men watching to see how many "d—d Yankees," as they called them, were going towards Washington. Gen. Aiken and his friend, however, after a time, chartered a covered wagon and rode to Baltimore, arriving about 9 1-2 P. M. The streets were brilliantly lighted, and full of people, some of them in uniform, and most of them wearing rebel badges; and even the few words which the travellers heard as they passed along the crowded halls of their hotel, apprized them that no man could avow Unionism there and preserve his life in safety for a moment. They accordingly went at once to their rooms and kept out of sight until morning, when the hotel proprietor, a personal friend of Gen. Aiken's companion, and also of the leading Baltimore rebels, procured them passes signed by Gen. Winder and countersigned by Marshal Kane. Having these, they paid $50 for a carriage which took them to Washington. Reaching Washington at 10 P. M. on Wednesday, Gen. Aiken found its silence and emptiness a startling contrast to the hot-blooded crowd at Baltimore. He says:

"Half a dozen people in the hall of the hotel crowded around *to ask questions about the North.* I then began to realize the isolation of the city." Hurrying to Gen. Scott's head-quarters, the old chief was found with only two of his staff. "Upon reading the Governor's letter, he rose and said excitedly, 'Sir, you are the first man I have seen with a written dispatch for three days. I have sent men out every day to bring intelligence of the northern troops. Not one of them has returned; where *are* the troops?' The number and rapidity of his questions, and his very excited manner, gave me a further realization of the critical nature of the situation."

Calling on Secretary Cameron, Gen. Aiken was received very much in the same manner. A friend in one of the Departments "advised very strongly against a return by the same route, *as my arrival was known*, and the general nature of my business suspected by rebel spies, with whom the city abounded, and in some quarters least suspected.

"How the knowledge of my affairs could have been gained has always been a mystery, for I had realized since leaving Philadelphia, that my personal safety depended entirely upon secrecy and prudence.

"At 10 A. M. I called on the President, and saw him for the first time in my life. It was an interview I can never forget. No office-seekers were about 'the presence' that day—there was no delay in getting an audience. Mr. Lincoln was alone, seated in his business room up stairs, looking toward Arlington Heights through a widely opened window. Against the casement stood a very long spy-glass, which he had obviously just been using. I gave him all the information I could, from what I had seen and heard during my journey.

"He seemed depressed beyond measure, as he asked, slowly, and with great emphasis, 'What *is* the North about? Do they know our condition?' I said, 'No, they certainly did not when I left.' This was true enough.

"He spoke of the non-arrival of the troops under Gen. Butler, and of having had no intelligence from them for two or three days. * * *

"I have referred to the separation of the city from the North. In no one of many ways was it brought home more practically to my mind than in this: The funds in my possession were in New York city bank notes. Their value in Washington had suddenly and totally departed. They were good for their weight in paper, and no more. During my interview with the

President, my financial dilemma was referred to. I remarked that I had not a cent, although my pockets were full. He instantly perceived my meaning, and kindly put me in possession of such an amount of specie as I desired. * * * Having delivered my dispatch, and the Governor's words of encouragement, and enjoyed an interview protracted, by the President's desire, beyond ordinary length, I left."

The New York Seventh Regiment reached the city just as Gen. Aiken had walked from the President's house to the State Department; and when the flag announcing their arrival at the Baltimore station was hoisted, says Gen. Aiken, "such a stampede of humanity, loyal and rebel, as was witnessed that hour in the direction of the Baltimore Railway station, can only be imagined by those who, like myself, took part in it. One glance at the gray jackets of the Seventh put hope in the place of despondency in my breast."

Gen. Aiken returned by taking a private conveyance, and obscure roads, until, north of the Pennsylvania line, he reached a railroad, and at Hanover, the first telegraph station, reported progress to Governor Buckingham, having been unable to communicate with him during four days, and not having seen the United States flag once during the whole trip from Philadelphia around to the Pennsylvania line, except on the Capitol at Washington. Gen. Aiken, in concluding his account, says, undoubtedly with correctness, "There has been no hour since that when messages of sympathy, encouragement and aid from the loyal Governor of a loyal State were more truly needed or more effective upon the mind of our late President, than those I had the honor to deliver."

The views of Governor Buckingham as to the policy to be pursued with the rebellion may best be learned from the following letter, which he addressed to the President, dated June 25th, 1861:

"SIR—The condition of our government is so critical that the people of this State are looking with deep interest to measures which you may recommend to Congress, and to the course which that body may pursue when it shall convene on the 4th day of July next.

"You will not therefore think me presuming if I present for your consideration the views entertained by a large majority of our citizens, especially when I assure you that if they are not approved by your judgment, I shall regard it as evidence that their importance is over-estimated.

"There are to-day probably more than three hundred thousand men organized, armed and in rebellion against the general government. Millions of other citizens, who have been protected by its power, now deny its authority, and refuse obedience to its laws. Multitudes of others, who prize the blessings which they have received under its policy, are so overawed by the manifestations of passionate violence which surround them, that their personal security is found in suppressing their opinions, and floating with the current into the abyss of anarchy. The person and property and liberty of every citizen are in peril. This is no ordinary rebellion. It is a mob on a gigantic scale, and should be met and suppressed by a power corresponding with its magnitude.

"The obligations of the government to the loyal, the principles of equity and justice, the claims of humanity, civilization and religion, unite in demanding a force sufficient to drive the rebels from every rendezvous, to influence them to return to their homes and their lawful employments, to seize their leaders and bring them before the proper tribunals for trial, and to inflict upon them the punishment justly due for their crimes. In your message to Congress I trust you will ask for authority to organize and arm a force of four or five hundred thousand men, for the purpose of quelling the rebellion, and for an appropriation from the public treasury sufficient for their support. Let legislation upon every other subject be regarded as out of time and place, and the one great object of suppressing the rebellion be pursued by the administration with vigor and firmness, without taking counsel of our fears, and without listening to any proposition or suggestion which may emanate from rebels or their representatives, until the authority of the government shall be respected, its laws enforced, and its supremacy acknowledged in every section of our country.

* * * * * *

"To secure such high public interests, the State of Connecticut will bind her destinies more closely to those of the general government, and in adopting the measures suggested she will renewedly pledge all her pecuniary and physical resources, and all her moral power.

"I am, dear sir, yours,
with high consideration,
(signed,) WILLIAM A. BUCKINGHAM.

"To Abraham Lincoln,
President of the United States."

This gallant and spirited letter shows conclusively that if the first one or two years of the war trailed on in irresolution and defeat, it was not for want of decided spirit in Connecticut and her governor.

Still later in the war, we find Governor Buckingham addressing the following to President Lincoln, in view of his projected Emancipation Policy:

"STATE OF CONNECTICUT, EXECUTIVE DEPARTMENT,
HARTFORD, Sept. 26, 1862.

"DEAR SIR:—While my views of your Proclamations issued on the 22d and 24th instants, may be of little or no importance, yet you will permit me to congratulate you and the country that you have so clearly presented the policy which you will hereafter pursue in suppressing the rebellion, and to assure you that it meets my cordial approval, and shall have my unconditional support.

"Not that I think your declaration of freedom will of itself bring liberty to the slave, or restore peace to the nation; but I rejoice that your administration will not be prevented by the clamors of men in sympathy with rebels, from using such measures as you indicate to overpower the rebellion, even if it interferes with and overthrows their much loved system of slavery.

"Have we not too long deluded ourselves with the idea that mild and conciliatory measures would influence them to return to their allegiance? They have appealed to the arbitrament of the sword; why should we hesitate to use the sword, and press the cause to a decision? Have we not undervalued their resources, disbelieved in their deep hatred of our government and its free institutions; and, influenced by erroneous ideas of the principles of humanity and mercy, criminally sent our brave sons down to the grave by thousands, without having given them the coveted honor of falling on the battle-field, or without having changed in the least the purpose of our enemies.

"This little State has already sent into the army, and has now at the rendezvous more than one-half of her able-bodied men between the ages of eighteen and forty-five years, and has more to offer, if wanted, to contend in battle against the enemies of our government.

"I trust we shall press with increased energy and power every war measure, as the most economical, humane and Christian policy which can be adopted to save our national union, as well as to secure permanent peace to those who shall succeed us.

"With sympathy for you in your responsible position, and renewed assurance of my cordial support, believe me, with high regard,

your obedient servant,

WILLIAM A. BUCKINGHAM.

"To President Lincoln,
Washington, D. C.

After eight years of public service, five of which were made arduous by this war, into which, as may be seen by these letters, Governor Buckingham threw his whole heart and soul, and in which he bore equally with our good President, the burdens of the country, he retired at last to that more private sphere which he fills with so many forms of honorable usefulness.

We have but one anecdote in closing, a noble tribbute to the Governor's blameless example in his high station.

The Connecticut Election Day, as it is called, or the day when the Legislature assembles, and the Governor is inaugurated, has always been held in the State as a grand gala day. During the war, especially, the military pomp and parade was often very imposing. The Governor's military staff consists of eight or ten members, and while the war lasted hard work and responsible duties fell to their lot. A friend of the Governor who had usually been with him on these occasions, remarked to one of his staff at the last of them:

"I have often been with you on these occasions, and have never seen any liquor drank. I suppose," he added pleasantly, "you do that privately."

"No, sir;" was the reply. "None of the Governor's staff ever use liquor."

"Is that so?" was the surprised reply.

"Yes," was the answer—"it is so."

Such an example as this, in so high a place, had a value that could not be too highly estimated.

Wendell Phillips

CHAPTER XVII.

WENDELL PHILLIPS

Birth and Ancestry of Wendell Phillips—His Education and Social Advantage—The Lovejoy Murder—Speech in Faneuil Hall—The Murder Justified—Mr. Phillips' First Speech—He Defends the Liberty of the Press—His Ideality—He Joins the Garrisonian Abolitionists'—Gives up the Law and Becomes a Reformer—His Method and Style of Oratory—Abolitionists' Blamed for the Boston Mob—Heroism of the Early Abolitionists'—His Position in Favor of "Woman's Rights"—Anecdote of His Lecturing—His Services in the Cause of Temperance—Extract with His Argument on Prohibition—His Severity towards Human Nature—His Course During and Since the War—AChange of Tone Recommended.

WENDELL PHILLIPS was born in Boston, Mass., Nov. 29, 1811.

He is son of John Phillips, first Mayor of Boston. The Phillips family justly rank among the untitled aristocracy of Massachusetts. Liberal views, noble manners, love of learning and benevolent liberality have become in that state associated with the name.

John Phillips, the grand uncle of Wendell Phillips, was the founder of Exeter Academy, in New Hampshire. Besides this he endowed a professorship in Dartmouth College, and contributed liberally to Princeton College, and gave $31,000 to Phillips Academy in Andover.

His nephew Samuel Phillips, planned, founded and organized Phillips Academy in Andover. He was a member of the provincial Congress during the Revolutionary war—a member of the convention to form the United States Constitution in 1779, and a State Senator for twenty years following the adoption of the constitution, and for fifteen years was president in the Senate, and was from first to last the particular and trusted friend of Gen. Washington. If there be such a thing in America as a just and proper aristocracy it inheres in families in whom public virtues and services have been as eminent as in this case.

Wendell Phillips was a graduate of Harvard College in 1831, and at the Cambridge law school in 1833, and was admitted to the Suffolk bar in 1834.

A precise and elegant scholar, gifted with all possible advantages of family, position, and prestige, Wendell Phillips began life with every advantage. But the very year after his admission to the bar, he was a witness of the mob in which Garrison was dragged disgracefully through Boston, for the crime of speaking his conscientious opinions.

The spirit of his Puritan fathers was strong within him—and he was acting in accordance with all his family traditions when he at once espoused the cause of Liberty.

His earliest public speech was made on an occasion befitting a son of old Massachusetts.

On November 7, 1837, the Rev. E. P. Lovejoy, was shot by a mob at Alton, Illinois, while attempting to defend his printing press from destruction. When news of this event was received in Boston, Dr. Channing headed a petition to the Mayor and Aldermen asking the use of Faneuil Hall for a public meeting. It will scarcely be credited by the present generation that a request so reasonable and so natural, headed by a name so commanding as that of Dr. Channing, should have been flatly refused. The Mayor and Aldermen of Boston in those days trembled before the rod of southern masters, and however well disposed towards their own distinguished citizens, dared not encourage them in the expression of any sentiments which might possibly be disagreeable to the South. It is true that this was the third printing press which Lovejoy had attempted to defend. It is true that he had a perfect legal right in his own state of Illinois to print whatever he chose. It is true also that the rioters who came from Missouri and attacked his house and shot him, were the vilest and profanest scum of society which a slave state can breed; but for all that, the State of Massachusetts at that time could scarcely find a place or a voice to express indignation at the outrage. Dr. Channing, undismayed by the first rebuff, addressed an impressive letter to his fellow citizens which resulted in a meeting of influential gentlemen at the old court room. Here measures were taken to secure a much larger number of names to the petition. This time the Mayor and Aldermen consented.

The meeting was held on the 8th of December, and organized with the Hon. Jonathan Phillips for chairman. Dr. Channing opened the meeting with an eloquent address, and resolutions drawn up by him were read and offered.

The attorney general of Massachusetts appeared now as the advocate of the rioters. He compared the slaves to a menagerie of wild beasts, and the Alton rioters to the orderly mob who threw the tea overboard in 1773—talked of the "conflict of laws" between Missouri and Illinois, declared that Lovejoy was presumptuous and imprudent and died as the fool dieth. Then with direct and insulting reference to Dr. Channing, he asserted that a clergyman with a gun in his hand, or one mingling in the debates of a popular assembly, were equally out of place. This speech produced, as was natural, a sensation in Faneuil Hall, and Wendell Phillips who had come without expecting to speak, rose immediately to his feet and amid the boisterous efforts of the mobocratic party in the house to drown his voice made his first public speech.

Mr. Phillip's style of oratory is peculiarly solemn and impressive. The spirit of whole generations of Puritan ministers seems to give might to it. There is no attempt to propitiate prejudice—none to throw out popular allurements—it is calm, intense, and commanding.

"Sir," he said, in the course of this speech, "when I heard the gentleman lay down principles which place the murderers of Alton side by side with Otis and Hancock, with Quincy and Adams, I thought those precious lips, (pointing to the portraits in the hall) would have broken into voices to rebuke the recreant American; the slanderer of the dead. * * * Sir, for the sentiments that he has uttered, on soil consecrated by the prayers of the Puritans and the blood of patriots, the earth should have yawned and swallowed him up."

A storm of mingled applause and hisses interrupted the bold young orator—with cries of "take that back—take that back." The uproar became so great for a time that he could not be heard. One or two gentlemen came to Mr. Phillips' side while the crowd still continued to shout. "Make him take that back—he sha'nt go on till he takes that back." Mr. Phillips came forward to the edge of the platform, and looking on the excited multitude with that calm, firm, severe bearing-down glance which seems often to have such mesmeric effects, said solemnly:

"Fellow citizens, I cannot take back my words. Surely the attorney general so long and well known here, needs not the aid of your hisses against one so young as I am—my voice, never before heard in your walls." After this the young orator was heard to the end of his speech without interruption. In this first speech, which was wholly unpremeditated, he showed all that clearness, elegance of diction, logical compactness, and above all, that weight of moral conviction which characterized all his subsequent oratory.

In allusion to the speech of the attorney general he said: "*Imprudent!* to defend the liberty of the press! Why? Because the defence was unsuccessful! Does success gild crime into patriotism and the want of it change heroic self-devotion into imprudence? Was Hampden imprudent when he drew the sword and threw away the scabbard? Yet he, judged by that single hour, was unsuccessful. After a short exile the race he hated sat again upon the throne.

"Imagine yourselves present when the first news of Bunker Hill battle reached a New England town. The tale would have run thus: 'The patriots are routed—the red coats victorious—Warren lies dead upon the field.' With what scorn would that Tory have been received who should have charged Warren with imprudence, who should have said that 'bred a physician, he was out of place, and died as the fool dieth.' How would the intimation have been received that Warren and his successors should have waited a better time?'

"*Presumptuous!* to assert the freedom of the press on American ground! Is the assertion of such freedom before the age? So much before the age as to leave no one a right to make it because it displeases the community? Who invented this libel on his country? It is this very thing which entitled Lovejoy to greater praise. The disputed right which provoked the revolution was far beneath that for which he died. (Here was a strong and general expression of disapprobation.) One word, gentlemen. As much as thought is better than money, so much is the cause in which Lovejoy died nobler than a mere question of taxes. James Otis thundered in this hall when the King did but touch his *pocket.* Imagine if you can, his indignant eloquence if England had offered to put a gag on his lips. Mr. Chairman, from the bottom of my heart I thank that brave little band at Alton for resisting. We must remember that Lovejoy had fled from city to city—suffering the destruction of three printing presses patiently. At length he took counsel with friends, men of character, of tried integrity, of wide views of Christian principle. They thought the crisis had come—that it was full time to assert the laws. They saw around them, not a community like our own, of fixed habits and character, but one in the gristle, not yet hardened in the bone of manhood. The people there, children of our older States, seem to have forgotten the blood-tried principles of their fathers, the moment they lost sight of New England hills. Something was to be done to show them the priceless value of freedom of the press, to bring back and set right their wandering and confused ideas. He and his advisers looked on a community, struggling like a drunken man, indifferent to their rights and confused in their feelings. Deaf to argument, haply they might be stunned into sobriety. They saw that of which we cannot judge, the *necessity* of resistance. Insulted law called for it. Public opinion, fast hastening on the downward course, must be arrested. Does not the event show they judged rightly? Absorbed in a thousand trifles, how will the nation all at once come to a stand? Men begin as in 1776 and 1640 to discuss principles and weigh characters, to find out where they are. Haply we may awake before we are borne over the precipice."

From this time Wendell Phillips was identified with the radical abolitionists.

His nature is characterized by an extreme ideality. He is essentially in all things a purist. Had he not thus early in life been absorbed by the exigencies of a moral conflict, Mr. Phillips would have shown himself one of the most thorough and carefully cultivated men of literature in our country. The demand for perfection is one of the most rigorous in his nature, and would have shown itself in an exacting precision in style, orthography, rhetoric and pronunciation. In regard to all these things his standard is that of an idealist. But the moral nature derived from his Puritan ancestry, was stronger than every other portion of him, and his ideality became concentrated upon the existing conflict in American society. His nature led him at once to take the most strenuous and rigorous ground side by side with William Lloyd Garrison.

Tried by his severe standard, the constitution of the United States, by an incidental complicity with slavery, had become a sinful compact: a covenant with death and an agreement with hell—and with the unquestioning consistency which belonged to his Puritan blood, he did not hesitate to sacrifice to this belief his whole professional future.

He abandoned his legal practice and took leave of the Suffolk bar, because he could not conscientiously take the oath to support the Constitution of the United States. What things were gain to him he counted loss.

Henceforth there was no career open to him but that of the agitator and popular reformer. He brought to the despised and unfashionable cause not only the prestige of one of the most honored Massachusetts names, and the traditions of a family which was among orthodox circles as a Hebrew of the Hebrews, but the power of decidedly the first forensic orator that America has ever produced. His style was so dazzling, so brilliant, his oratory so captivating, that even the unpopularity of his sentiments could not prevent the multitudes from flocking to hear him. He had in a peculiar degree that mesmeric power of control which distinguishes the true orator, by which he holds a multitude subject to his will, and carries them whither he pleases.

His speeches were generally extempore, and flowed on with a wonderful correctness, and perfect finish of language, without faltering, without the shadow of an inelegance—his sentences succeeding one another with a poised and rhythmical fullness, and his illustrations happily running through the field of ancient and modern history, and with the greatest apparent ease selecting whatever he needed from thence for the illustration of his subject. In invective no American or English orator has ever surpassed him. At the bar of his fervid oratory he would arraign, try and condemn with a solemn and dignified earnestness that might almost have persuaded the object of his attack of his own guilt. Warren Hastings is said to have judged himself to be the basest of men while he listened to the denunciations of Burke, and something of the same experience may have befallen those who were arraigned by Phillips.

There was need enough at this time for a man thus endowed to come to the help of liberty in America, for the creeping influence of the despotic South, lulling, caressing, patronizing, promising, threatening and commanding, had gone very nigh to take away the right of free inquiry and free speech through the whole Northern States.

The few noble women, who formed the original Boston Anti-Slavery Society, were a mark everywhere spoken against. Even after the stormy and scurrilous attack of the mob which drove them out from their meeting, and which almost took the life of Garrison, there was not a newspaper in Boston, except the Liberator, which did not, in giving an account of the matter, blame the abolitionists instead of the rioters. It was the old story that the lamb had troubled the wolf, and ought to be eaten up forthwith. The Advertiser spoke of the affair, "not so much as a riot, as the prevention of a riot," and "considered the whole matter as the triumph of law over lawless violence, and the love of order over riot and confusion." The Christian Register recommended to the ladies to imitate the early Christians of Trajan's day, and meet in secret, adding, with a sneer, "if the *vanity* of the ladies would allow."

A leading orthodox divine shortly after preached a sermon to illustrate and defend the doctrine that no man has a right to promulgate any opinion distasteful to the majority of society where he lives. All, in short, seemed to be going one way—newspapers, pulpits, bar and bench, and the gay world of fashion, were alike agreed that if discussing the condition and rights and wrongs of the slave, was disagreeable to southern people it ought to be put a stop to at once and everywhere, and that the Abolitionists were a pestilent sect, who turned the world upside down.

In Wendell Phillips, at last, the scornful world met its match, for he was fully capable of meeting scorn with superior scorn, and retorting on contempt with contempt, and he stood as high above the fear of man that bringeth a snare, as any of the most unworldly of his Puritan grandfathers.

The little band of Abolitionists that gathered around him and Garrison, men and women, were every one of them heroes. They were of the old revolutionary stock of Boston, and every way worthy of their lineage, and there was need enough it should be so, for the struggle was no inconsiderable one—it was for life and death. Cast out of society, looked on as the off-scouring of the earth, hemmed in everywhere with slanders, often alienated from friends once the dearest and most admiring, laboring almost alone with an incessant and exhausting zeal, some of more delicate organization sunk under the trial, and may be said to have given their lives to the cause.

Wendell Phillips speaks of them feelingly in one of his later speeches, delivered on the anniversary of the Boston Mob:

"Many of those who met in this hall at that time are gone. They died as Whittier well says—

'Their brave hearts breaking slow,
But self-forgetful to the last,
In words of cheer and bugle glow,
Their breath upon the darkness past.'

"In those days, as we gathered around their graves, and resolved that the narrower the circle became the closer we would draw together, we envied the dead their rest. Men ceased to slander them in that sanctuary; and as we looked forward to the desolate vista of calamity and trial before us, and thought of the temptations which beset us on either side, from worldly prosperity which a slight sacrifice of principle might secure, or social ease so close at hand, by only a little turning aside, we almost envied the dead the quiet sleep to which we left them—the harvest reaped, and the seal set beyond the power of change."

The career of Phillips in those days was often amid threats of personal violence. Assassination, the favorite argument of slavery, was held up before him, and the recent death of Lovejoy showed that the threat was not an empty one. At home, his house, in turn with that of other leading abolitionists, was threatened with incendiary violence, notwithstanding it was the shelter of an invalid wife, whose frail life often seemed to hang on a thread. From that shaded and secluded invalid chamber, however, came no weak prayers or faltering purposes, for a braver, higher heart was never given to human being than the one that beat there. In the darkest and most dangerous hours, from that sick room came words of hope and cheer and inspiration, prompt ever to bid him go where the cause called for him, and strengthening him by buoyant fearlessness and high religious trust. Such women are a true inspiration to men.

It is not wonderful that with such rare experience of how noble a being woman may be, and with such superior women for friends and associates, that Wendell Phillips should have formed a high ideal of womanhood, and become early one of the most enthusiastic supporters of all reforms in which the interest of woman is concerned.

On the 15th and 16th of October, 1857, he offered at a convention held in Worcester a series of resolutions in relation to the political rights of women which cover all the ground contended for by modern reformers. His speech on this subject is one of the most able and eloquent on record, and forms a part of the permanent literature of the movement.

He speaks of womanhood with a solemn and religious earnestness, with the fervor of knightly times, and pleads against all customs and laws which bear hardly upon her delicate organization, which mislead her from following her highest aspirations.

An anecdote in circulation about him shows that he not only held such theories, but that he was helpful in practice. It is so in keeping with his general character as to be extremely probable. Notwithstanding the unpopularity of his abolition sentiments, Mr. Phillips' power as an orator was such that when lecturing on ordinary subjects he commanded the very highest prices in the literary market. On one of his tours he met in the cars a woman who was seeking a self-supporting career as a lecturer. Mr. Phillips inquired into her success, and found that independent of her expenses she made at the rate only of five dollars a time. He declared that such an inequality with his own success was an injustice, and added that he must beg her to allow him to equalize the account for once, by accepting the proceeds of his last lecture.

Mr. Phillips had a way of making his fame and reputation gain him a hearing on the unpopular subject which he had most at heart. Committees from anxious lyceums used to wait on him for his terms, sure of being able to fill a house by his name.

"What are your terms, Mr. Phillips?"

"If I lecture on anti-slavery, nothing. If on any other subject one hundred dollars."

The success of his celebrated lecture on the Lost Arts, which has been perhaps more than a thousand times repeated, is only a chance specimen of what he might have done in this department of lecturing, could he have allowed himself that use of his talent.

Mr. Phillips is far from being a man of one idea. Energetic as was his abolition campaign, he has found time and strength to strike some of the heaviest and most victorious blows for temperance. He has been a vigorous defender of the interests of the Maine Law, endangered in Massachusetts by the continual compliances of rank and fashion. His letter to Judge Shaw and President Walker is a specimen of unfearing and unflinching exposure and rebuke of those practices and concessions of public men, which cast contempt on the execution of law. His oration on Metropolitan Police has powerful arguments in favor of the policy of legislative prevention of intemperance.

We have selected his argument on the subject, both as a good example of his style and manner, and as a powerful presentation of a much needed argument.

"Some men look upon this temperance cause as whining bigotry, narrow asceticism, or a vulgar sentimentality, fit for little minds, weak women, and weaker men. On the contrary, I regard it as second only to one or two others of the primary reforms of this age, and for this reason. Every race has its peculiar temptation; every clime has its specific sin. The tropics and tropical races are tempted to one form of sensuality; the colder and temperate regions, and our Saxon blood, find their peculiar temptation in the stimulus of drink and food. In old times our heaven was a drunken revel. We relieve ourselves from the overweariness of constant and exhaustive toil by intoxication. Science has brought a cheap means of drunkenness within the reach of every individual. National prosperity and free institutions have put into the hands of almost every workman the means of being drunk for a week on the labor of two or three hours. With that blood and that temptation, we have adopted democratic institutions, where the law has no sanction but the purpose and virtue of the masses. The statute-book rests not on bayonets, as in Europe, but on the hearts of the people. A drunken people can never be the basis of a free government. It is the corner-stone neither of virtue, prosperity, nor progress. To us, therefore, the title-deeds of whose estates and the safety of whose lives depend upon the tranquillity of the streets, upon the virtue of the masses, the presence of any vice which brutalizes the average mass of mankind, and tends to make it more readily the tool of intriguing and corrupt leaders, is necessarily a stab at the very life of the nation. Against such a vice is marshalled the Temperance Reformation. That my sketch is no mere fancy picture, every one of you knows. Every one of you can glance back over your own path, and count many and many a one among those who started from the goal at your side, with equal energy and perhaps greater promise, who has found a drunkard's grave long before this. The brightness of the bar, the ornament of the pulpit, the hope and blessing and stay of many a family,—you know, every one of you who has reached middle life, how often on your path you set up the warning, "Fallen before the temptations of the streets!" Hardly one house in this city, whether it be full and warm with all the luxury of wealth, or whether it find hard, cold maintenance by the most earnest economy, no matter which,—hardly a house that does not count, among sons or nephews, some victim of this vice. The skeleton of this warning sits at every board. The whole world is kindred in this suffering. The country mother launches her boy with trembling upon the temptations of city life; the father trusts his daughter anxiously to the young man she has chosen, knowing what a wreck intoxication may make of the house-tree they set up. Alas! how often are their worst forebodings more than fulfilled! I have known a case—and probably many of you can recall some almost equal to it—where one worthy woman could count father, brother, husband, and son-in-law, all drunkards,—no man among her near kindred, except her son, who was not a victim of this vice. Like all other appetites, this finds resolution weak when set against the constant presence of temptation. This is the evil. How are the laws relating to it executed in this city? Let me tell you.

"First, there has been great discussion of this evil,—wide, earnest, patient discussion, for thirty-five years. The whole community has been stirred by the discussion of this question. Finally, after various experiments, the majority of the State decided that the method to stay this evil was to stop the open sale of intoxicating drink. They left moral suasion still to address the individual, and set themselves as a community to close the doors of temptation. Every man acquainted with his own nature or with society knows that weak virtue, walking through our streets, and meeting at every tenth door (for that is the average) the temptation to drink, must fall; that one must be a moral Hercules to stand erect. To prevent the open sale of intoxicating liquor has been the method selected by the State to help its citizens to be virtuous; in other words, the State has enacted what is called the Maine Liquor Law,—the plan of refusing all licenses to sell, to be drunk on the spot or elsewhere, and allowing only an official agent to sell for medicinal purposes and the arts. You may drink in your own parlors, you may make what indulgence you please your daily rule, the State does not touch you there; there you injure only yourself, and those you directly influence; that the State cannot reach. But when you open your door and say to your fellow-citizens, 'Come and indulge,' the State has a right to ask, 'In what do you invite them to indulge? Is it in something that helps, or something that harms, the community?'"

* * * * * * * * * *

In our recent war it is scarcely needful to say that Mr. Phillips has always been a counsellor for the most thorough, the most intrepid and most efficient measures.

During the period of comparative vacillation and uncertainty, when McClellan was the commander-in-chief, and war was being made on political principles, Mr. Phillips did his utmost in speeches and public addresses in the papers, to stir up the people to demand a more efficient policy.

Since the termination of the war and the emancipation of the slave, Mr. Phillips seems to show that the class of gifts and faculties adapted to rouse a stupid community, and to force attention to neglected truths are not those most adapted to the delicate work of reconstruction. The good knight who can cut and hew in battle, cannot always do the surgeon's work of healing and restoring. That exacting ideality which is the leading faculty of Mr. Phillips' nature leads him constantly to undervalue what has been attained, and it is to be regretted that it deprived him of the glow and triumph of a victory in which no man than he better deserved to rejoice.

Garrison hung up his shield and sword at a definite point, and marked the era of victory with devout thankfulness; and we can but regret, that the more exacting mind of Phillips was too much fixed on what yet was wanting to share the well earned joy.

When there is strong light there must be shadow, and the only shadow we discern in the public virtues of Mr. Phillips is the want of a certain power to appreciate and make allowances for the necessary weaknesses and imperfections of human nature.

He has been a teacher of the school of the law rather than that of the Gospel; he has been most especially useful because we have been in a state where such stern unflinching teachings have been indispensable.

Mr. Phillips' methods indeed, of dealing with human nature, savor wholly of the law and remind us forcibly of the pithy and vigorous account which John Bunyan puts into the mouth of his pilgrim.

"I saw one coming after me swift as the wind, and so soon as the man overtook me, it was but a word and a blow, for down he knocked me and laid me for dead. But when I was a little come to myself I asked him wherefore he served me so. He said because of my secret inclining to Adam the first, and with that he struck me another deadly blow on the breast, and beat me down backward, and so I lay at his foot as dead as before. So when I came to myself, I cried him mercy; but he said, I know not how to show mercy, and with that he knocked me down again. He had doubtless made an end of me but that one came by and bid him forbear.

Who was he that bid him forbear? I did not know him at first but as he went by, I perceived the holes in his hands and his side."

There is a time for all things, and this stern work of the land had to be done in our country. Almighty God seconded it by awful providences, and pleaded against the oppressor in the voice of famine and battle, of fire and sword.

The guilty land had been riven and torn, and in the language of scripture, made an astonishment and a desolation!

May we not think now that the task of binding up the wounds of a bruised and shattered country, of reconciling jarring interests thrown into new and delicate relationships, of bringing peace to sore and wearied nerves, and abiding quiet to those who are fated to dwell side by side in close proximity, may require faculties of a wider and more varied adaptation, and a spirit breathing more of Calvary and less of Sinai?

It is no discredit to the good sword gapped with the blows of a hundred battle fields, to hang it up in all honor, as having done its work.

It has made place for a thousand other forces and influences each powerless without it, but each now more powerful and more efficient in their own field.

Those who are so happy as to know Mr. Phillips personally, are fully aware how entirely this unflinching austerity of judgment, this vigorous severity of exaction, belong to his public character alone, how full of genial urbanity they find the private individual. We may be pardoned for expressing the hope that the time may yet come when he shall see his way clear to take counsel in public matters with his own kindly impulses, and that those genial traits which render his private intercourse so agreeable, may be allowed to modify at least his public declarations.

Henry Ward Beecher

CHAPTER XVIII.

HENRY WARD BEECHER.

Mr. Beecher a Younger Child—Death of his Mother—His Step-Mother's Religious Influence—Ma'am Kilbourn's School—The Passing Bell—Unprofitable Schooling—An Inveterate School Joker—Masters the Latin Grammar—Goes to Amherst College—His Love of Flowers—Modes of Study; a Reformer—Mr. Beecher and the Solemn Tutor—His Favorite Poetry—His Introduction to Phrenology—His Mental Philosophy—Doctrine of Spiritual Intuition—Punctuality for Joke's Sake—Old School and New School—Doubts on Entering the Ministry—Settlement at Lawrenceburg—His Studies; First Revival—Large Accessions to the Church—"Tropical Style"—Ministerial Jokes—Slavery in the Pulpit—The Transfer to Brooklyn—Plymouth Church Preaching—Visit to England—Speeches in England—Letters from England—Christian View of England—The Exeter Hall Speech—Preaches an Unpopular Forgiveness.

Henry Ward Beecher was the eighth child of Lyman and Roxana Foote Beecher, born in Litchfield, Connecticut, June 24, 1813. The first child of a family is generally an object of high hope and anxious and careful attention. They are observed, watched—and if the parents are so disposed, carefully educated, and often over-watched and over-educated. But in large families, as time rolls on and children multiply, especially to those in straitened worldly circumstances, all the interest of novelty dies out before the advent of younger children, and they are apt to find their way in early life unwatched and unheralded. Dr. Beecher's salary was eight hundred dollars a year, not always promptly paid. This made the problem of feeding, clothing and educating a family of ten children a dark one. The family was constantly enlarged by boarders, young ladies attending the female academy, and whose board helped somewhat to the support of the domestic establishment, but added greatly to the cares of the head manager. The younger members of the Beecher family therefore came into existence in a great bustling household of older people, all going their separate ways, and having their own grown-up interests to carry. The child, growing up in this busy, active circle, had constantly impressed upon it a sense of personal insignificance as a child, and the absolute need of the virtue of passive obedience and non-resistance as regards all grown-up people. To be statedly washed and dressed and catechised, got to school at regular hours in the morning, and to bed inflexibly at the earliest possible hour at night, comprised about all the attention that children could receive in those days.

The mother of Henry Ward died when he was three years old; his father was immersed in theological investigations and a wide sphere of pastoral labors and great general ecclesiastical interests, his grown-up brothers and sisters in their own separate life history, and the three younger children were therefore left to their mortal pilgrimage, within certain well-defined moral limits, much after their own way. The step-mother, who took the station of mother, was a lady of great personal elegance and attractiveness, of high intellectual and moral culture, who from having been in early life the much admired belle in general society, came at last from an impulse of moral heroism combined with personal attachment, to undertake the austere labors of a poor minister's family. She was a person to make a deep impression on the minds of any children. There was a moral force about her, a dignity of demeanor, an air of elegance and superior breeding, which produced a constant atmosphere of unconscious awe in the minds of little ones. Then her duties were onerous, her conscience inflexible, and under the weight of these her stock of health and animal spirits sunk, so that she was for the most part pensive and depressed. Her nature and habits were too refined and exacting for the bringing up of children of great animal force and vigor, under the strain and pressure of straitened circumstances. The absurdities and crudenesses incident to the early days of such children appeared to her as serious faults, and weighed heavily on her conscience. The most intense positive religious and moral influence the three little ones of the family received was on Sunday night, when it was her custom to take them to her bed-room and read and talk and pray with them. At these times, deep though vague religious yearnings were created; but as she was much of her time an invalid, and had little sympathy with the ordinary feelings of childhood, she gave an impression of religion as being like herself, calm, solemn, inflexible, mysteriously sad and rigorously exacting.

In those days none of the attentions were paid to children that are now usual. The community did not recognize them. There was no child's literature; there were no children's books. The Sunday school was yet an experiment, in a fluctuating, uncertain state of trial. There were no children's days of presents and *fêtes*—no Christmas or New Year's festivals. The annual thanksgiving was only associated with one day's unlimited range of pies of every sort—too much for one day, and too soon things of the past. The childhood of Henry Ward was unmarked by the possession of a single child's toy as a gift from any older person, or a single *fête*. Very early, too, strict duties devolved upon him; a daily portion of the work of the establishment, the care of the domestic animals, the cutting and piling of wood, or tasks in the garden strengthened his muscles and gave vigor and tone to his nerves. From his father and mother he inherited a perfectly solid, healthy organization of brain, muscle and nerves, and the uncaressing, let-alone system under which he was brought up, gave him early habits of vigor and self-reliance.

Litchfield was a mountain town, where the winter was a stern reality for six months of the year, where there were giant winds, and drifting snows of immeasurable depth, and ice and sleet storms of a sublime power and magnitude. Under this rugged nursing he grew outwardly vigorous. At nine years of age, in one of those winter droughts common in New England towns, he harnessed the horse to a sledge with a barrel lashed thereon, and went off alone three miles over the icy top of the town hill, to dip up and bring home a barrel of water from a distant spring. So far from taking this as a hardship, he undertook it with a chivalric pride. His only trial in the case was the humiliation of being positively commanded by his careful step-mother to wear his overcoat; he departed obedient, but with tears of mortification freezing on his cheeks, for he had recorded a heroic vow to go through a whole winter without once wearing an overcoat.

For education, technically so called, there were small advantages. His earliest essay of letters was to walk over to West street, to a widow Kilbourn's, where he sat daily on a bench kicking his heels in idleness, and said his letters twice in the day, and was for so long out of the way of the grown folks, which was a main point in child schooling. There was a tinner's shop hard by, and the big girls, some of them, contrived to saw off some of his long golden curls with tin shears contrived from the fragments cast out of the shop. The child was annoyed, but dared not complain to any purpose, till the annoyance being stated at home, it was concluded that the best way to abate it was to cut off all the curls altogether, and with the loss of these he considered his manhood to commence. Next, a small, unpainted, district school-house being erected within a stone's throw of the parsonage, he graduated from Ma'am Kilbourn's thither. The children of all the farming population in the neighborhood gathered there. The exercises consisted in daily readings of the Bible and the Columbian Orator, in elementary exercises in arithmetic, and hand-writing. The ferule and a long flexible hickory switch were the insignia of office of the school mistress. No very striking early results were the outcome of this teaching. Henry Ward was not marked out by the prophecies of partial friends for any brilliant future. He had precisely the organization which often passes for dullness in early boyhood. He had great deficiency in verbal memory, a deficiency marked in him through life; he was excessively sensitive to praise and blame, extremely diffident, and with a power of yearning, undeveloped emotion, which he neither understood nor could express. His utterance was thick and indistinct, partly from bashfulness and partly from an enlargement of the tonsils of the throat, so that in speaking or reading he was with difficulty understood. In forecasting his horoscope, had any one taken the trouble then to do it, the last success that ever would have been predicted for him would have been that of an orator. "When Henry is sent to me with a message," said a good aunt, "I always have to make him say it three times. The first time I have no manner of an idea more than if he spoke Choctaw; the second, I catch now and then a word; by the third time I begin to understand."

Thus, while Dr. Beecher victoriously demonstrated the consistency of decrees and accountability, and the elder brother was drawing all the hopes of the family as the first in his college class, and his elder sisters were writing poetry and receiving visits, and carrying on the cheerful round of Litchfield society, this bashful, dazed-looking boy pattered barefoot to and from the little unpainted school-house, with a brown towel or a blue checked apron to hem during the intervals between his spelling and reading lessons. Nobody thought much of his future, further than to see that he was safe and healthy, or even troubled themselves to inquire what might be going on in his life.

But the child most let alone, is nevertheless being educated gradually and insensibly. The calm, inflexible, elegant breeding of the step-mother, her intense solemnity of religious responsibility, indicating itself in every chance look or motion, fell on the sensitive child-nature like a constant moral stimulant. When a little fellow, whose small feet could not touch the bottom of the old family chaise, he was once driving with her on an errand. The bell tolled for a death, as was then the custom in rural places. "Henry, what do you think of when you hear a bell tolling like that?" she said. Astonished and awe-struck at having his thoughts inquired into, the child only flushed, and colored and looked abashed, and she went on as in a quiet soliloquy, "*I* think, was that soul prepared? It has gone into *eternity!*" The effect on the child's mind was a shiver of dread, like the being turned out without clothing among the icy winds of Litchfield hills. The vague sense of infinite, inevitable doom underlying all the footsteps of life, added to a natural disposition to yearning and melancholy. The scenery around the parsonage fed the yearning—Chestnut Hill on one side, with its lovely, softly wooded slopes, and waving grain-fields; on the other, Mount Tom, with steel-blue pines and a gleaming lake mirror at its feet. Then there was the piano always going, and the Scotch airs, Roslin Castle, Mary's Dream, and Bonnie Doon, sounding out from the parlor windows, and to which the boy listened in a sort of troublous and dreamy mixture of sadness and joy, and walked humming to himself with tears in his eyes.

The greatest trial of those days was the catechism. Sunday lessons were considered by the mother-in-law as inflexible duty, and the catechism as the *sine qua non.* The other children memorized readily and were brilliant reciters, but Henry, blushing, stammering, confused and hopelessly miserable, stuck fast on some sand-bank of what is required or forbidden by this or that commandment, his mouth choking up with the long words which he hopelessly miscalled; was sure to be accused of idleness or inattention, and to be solemnly talked to, which made him look more stolid and miserable than ever, but appeared to have no effect in quickening his dormant faculties.

When he was ten years old, he was a stocky, strong, well-grown boy, loyal in duty, trained in unquestioning obedience, inured to patient hard work, inured also to the hearing and discussing of all the great theological problems of Calvinism, which were always reverberating in his hearing; but as to any mechanical culture, in an extremely backward state—a poor writer, a miserable speller, with a thick utterance, and a bashful reticence which seemed like stolid stupidity. He was now placed at a private school in the neighboring town of Bethlehem, under the care of the Rev. Mr. Langdon, to commence a somewhat more careful course of study. Here an incident occurred which showed that the boy even at that early age felt a mission to defend opinions. A forward school-boy, among the elder scholars, had got hold of Paine's Age of Reason, and was flourishing largely among the boys with objections to the Bible, drawn therefrom. Henry privately looked up Watson's Apology, studied up the subject, and challenged a debate with the big boy, in which he came off victorious by the acclamation of his school-fellows.

His progress in book-learning, however, was slow, though his year at the place was one of great happiness. One trait of the boy, as it has been with the man, was a peculiar passion for natural scenery, which he found full liberty to indulge in his present surroundings. He boarded with a large-hearted, kindly, motherly woman, in a great comfortable farm-house, where everything was free and unconstrained. The house was backed by a generous old orchard, full of fruits and blossoms in spring and summer, and where the partridges drummed and whirred in winter. Beyond that were dreamy depths of woodland, and Henry's studies were mostly with gun on shoulder, roving the depths of those forests, guiltless of hitting anything, because the time was lost in dreamy contemplation. Thence returning unprepared for school, he would be driven to the expedient of writing out his Latin verb and surreptitiously reading it out of the crown of his hat, an exercise from whence he reaped small profit, either mentally or morally. In short, after a year spent in this way, it began to be perceived by the elders of the family, that as to the outward and visible signs of learning, he was making no progress. His eldest sister was then teaching a young lady's school in Hartford, and it was proposed to take the boy under her care to see what could be made of him.

One boy of eleven in a school of thirty or forty girls has not much chance of making a durable impression, but we question if any of Henry's school mates easily forgot him. If the under stratum of his nature was a dreamy yearning melancholy, its upper manifestation was in constant bubbling, restless effervescence of fun and practical joking. The school room was up a long flight of stairs, and one wet day Henry spent a recess when he was supposed to be studying grammar, in opening every umbrella brought to school, and so disposing them on the stairs that the luckless person who opened the outside door would witness a precipitate rush of the whole series into the street—which feat was successfully accomplished to the dismay of the late comer, and the tittering of the whole school, who had been somewhat prepared for the catastrophe.

The school room was divided into two divisions in grammar, under leaders on either side, and the grammatical reviews were contests for superiority in which it was vitally important that every member should be perfected. Henry was generally the latest choice, and fell on his side as an unlucky accession—being held more amusing than profitable on such occasions.

The fair leader on one of these divisions took the boy aside to a private apartment, to put into him with female tact and insinuation those definitions and distinctions on which the honor of the class depended.

"Now Henry, A is the indefinite article, you see—and must be used only with a singular noun. You can say *a man*—but you can't say *a men*, can you?" "Yes, I can say *Amen* too," was the ready rejoinder. "Father says it always at the end of his prayers."

"Come Henry, now don't be joking; now decline He." "Nominative he, possessive his, objective him." "You see, His is possessive. Now you can say, His book—

but you can't say 'Him book.'" "Yes I do say Hymn book too," said the impracticable scholar with a quizzical twinkle. Each one of these sallies made his young teacher laugh, which was the victory he wanted.

"But now Henry, seriously, just attend to the active and passive voice. Now 'I strike' is active, you see, because if you strike you do something. But 'I am struck,' is passive, because if you are struck you don't do any thing do you?"

"Yes I do—I strike back again!"

Sometimes his views of philosophical subjects were offered gratuitously. Being held rather of a frisky nature, his sister appointed his seat at her elbow, when she heard her classes. A class in Natural Philosophy, not very well prepared, was stumbling through the theory of the tides. "I can explain that," said Henry. "Well, you see, the sun, he catches hold of the moon and pulls her, and she catches hold of the sea and pulls that, and this makes the spring tides.

"But what makes the neap tides?"

"Oh, that's when the sun stops to spit on his hands," was the brisk rejoinder.

After about six months, Henry was returned on his parents' hands with the reputation of being an inveterate joker, and an indifferent scholar. It was the opinion of his class that there was much talent lying about loosely in him if he could only be brought to apply himself.

When he was twelve years of age his father moved to Boston. It was a great change to the two younger boys, from the beautiful rural freedom of a picturesque mountain town to the close, strait limits of a narrow street in Boston.

There was a pure and vigorous atmosphere of moral innocence about the mountain towns of Connecticut in those days, which made the breeding up of children on the let-alone system quite feasible. There was no temptation to vice or immorality. The only associate of doubtful character forbidden to Henry, for whose society he craved, was Ulysses Freeman, a poor, merry, softly giggling negro boy, who inhabited a hut not far off, and who, it was feared, might indiscreetly teach him something that he ought not to know—but otherwise it was safe to let him run unwatched, in the wholesome companionship of bob-o'links and squirrels and birch woods and huckleberry bushes. There was not in all Litchfield in those days any thing to harm a growing boy, or lead him into evil.

But in Boston, the streets, the wharves, the ship yards, were full of temptation—the house, narrow and strait. The boy was put into the Boston Latin School, where the whole educational process was a solid square attempt to smite the Latin grammar into minds of all sorts and sizes, by a pressure like that by which coin is stamped in the mint. Educated in loyal obedience as a religion and a habit, pushed up to make the effort by the entreaties of his father, by appeals to his gallantry in overcoming difficulties, his sense of family honor, and the solemn appeals to conscience of his mother, Henry set himself doggedly to learn lists of prepositions and terminations, and bead-rolls of nouns that found their accusatives or genitives in this way or that, except in the case of two dozen exceptions, when they formed them in some other way, with all the other dry prickly facts of language with which it is deemed expedient to choke the efforts of beginners.

It was to him a grim Sinaitic desert, a land of darkness without order, where he wandered, seeing neither tree or flower; a wilderness of meaningless forms and sounds. His life was a desolation, a blind push to do what was most contrary to his natural faculties, repulsive to his tastes, and in which with utmost stress and strain of effort he could never hope to rise above mediocrity. One year passed in this way, and with the fear of disgrace in the rear and conscience and affection goading him on, Henry had actually mastered the Latin grammar, and could give any form or inflection, rule or exception therein, but at an expense of brain and nerve that began to tell even on his vigorous organization.

The era of fermentation and development was upon him, and the melancholy that had brooded over his childhood waxed more turbulent and formidable. He grew gloomy and moody, restless and irritable. His father, noticing the change, got him on a course of biographical reading, hoping to divert his thoughts. He began to read naval histories, the lives of great sailors and commanders—the voyages of Captain Cook, the biography of Nelson; and immediately, like lightning flashing out of rolling clouds, came the determination not to rest any longer in Boston, learning terminations and prepositions, but to go forth to a life of enterprise. He made up his little bundle, walked the wharf and talked with sailors and captains, hovered irresolute on the verge of voyages, never quite able to grieve his father by a sudden departure. At last he wrote a letter announcing to a brother that he could and would no longer remain at school—that he had made up his mind for the sea; that if not permitted to go, he should go without permission. This letter was designedly dropped where his father picked it up. Dr. Beecher put it in his pocket and said nothing for the moment, but the next day asked Henry to help him saw wood. Now the wood-pile was the Doctor's favorite debating ground, and Henry felt complimented by the invitation, as implying manly companionship.

"Let us see," says the Doctor, "Henry, how old are you?"

"Almost fourteen!"

"Bless me! how boys do grow!—Why it's almost time to be thinking what you are going to do. Have you ever thought?"

"Yes—I want to go to sea."

"To sea! Of all things! Well, well! After all, why not?—Of course you don't want to be a common sailor. You want to get into the navy?"

"Yes sir, that's what I want."

"But not merely as a common sailor, I suppose?"

"No sir, I want to be midshipman, and after that commodore."

"I see," said the Doctor, cheerfully, "Well, Henry, in order for that, you know, you must begin a course of mathematics, and study navigation and all that."

"Yes sir, I am ready."

"Well then, I'll send you up to Amherst next week, to Mount Pleasant, and then you'll begin your preparatory studies, and if you are well prepared, I presume I can make interest to get you an appointment."

And so he went to Mount Pleasant, in Amherst, Mass., and Dr. Beecher said shrewdly, "I shall have that boy in the ministry yet."

The transfer from the confined limits of a city to the congenial atmosphere of a beautiful mountain town brought an immediate favorable change. Here he came under the care of a mathematical teacher, educated at West Point, a bright attractive young man of the name of Fitzgerald, with whom he roomed. Between this young man and the boy, there arose a romantic friendship. Henry had no natural talent or taste for mathematics, but inspired by a desire to please his friend, and high ambition for his future profession, he went into them with energy, and soon did credit to his teacher at the blackboard, laboring perseveringly with his face towards the navy, and Nelson as his beau ideal.

Here also he was put through a strict drill in elocution by Professor John E. Lovell, now residing in New Haven, Conn. Of him, Mr. Beecher cherishes a grateful recollection, and never fails to send him a New Year's token of remembrance. He says of him, that "a better teacher in his department never was made." Mr. Beecher had many natural disabilities for the line of oratory ; and their removal so far as to make him an acceptable speaker he holds due to the persevering drill of Mr. Lovell. His voice, naturally thick and husky, was developed by most persevering, systematic training. His gestures and the management of his body went through a drill corresponding to that which the military youth goes through at West Point, to make his body supple to the exigencies of military evolution. As an orator, this early training was of vital importance to him. He could never have attained success without it.

At the close of the first year, a revival of religion passed through the school, and Henry Ward and many others were powerfully impressed. It was in fact, on the part of the boy, the mere flashing out into visible form of that deep undercurrent of religious sensibility which had been the habit of his life, and the result of his whole home education. His father sent for him home to unite with the church on a great communion season; and the boy, trembling, agitated, awe-struck, full of vague purposes and good resolutions and imperfectly developed ideas, stood up and took on him irrevocable vows, henceforth in his future life to be actively and openly on the side of Christ, in the great life battle.

Of course the naval scheme vanished, and the pulpit opened before him as his natural sphere. With any other father or education, this would not have been an "of course;" but Dr. Beecher was an enthusiast in his profession. Every word of his life, every action or mode of speaking, had held it up before his boys as the goal of all his hopes, that they should preach the gospel, and the boy therefore felt that to be the necessary obligation which came upon him in joining the church. He returned to Amherst, where his classical education was continued for two years longer, with a view to fit him for college.

The love of flowers, which has always formed so marked a branch of his general enthusiasm for nature, developed itself at this time in a friendship with a rather rough man who kept a garden. He was so pleased with the boy's enthusiasm that he set apart a scrap of ground for him which he filled with roses, geraniums and other blooming wonders, and these Henry tended under his instructions.

At that time the love of nature was little cultivated among the community. By very many good people, nature was little spoken of except as the antithesis to grace. It was the tempter, the syren that drew the soul from higher duties. The chaplain of Mount Pleasant Institute, a grave and formal divine, found Henry on his knees in his little flower patch, lost in rapturous contemplations of buds and blossoms. He gave him an indulgent smile, but felt it his duty to improve the occasion.

"Ah, Henry," he said condescendingly, as one who makes a fair admission, "these things are pretty, very pretty, but my boy, do you think that such things are worthy to occupy the attention of a man who has an immortal soul?" Henry answered only by that abashed and stolid look which covered from the eyes of his superiors, so much of what was going on within him, and went on with attentions to his flowers. "I wanted to tell him," he said afterwards, "that since Almighty God has found leisure to make those trifles, it could not be amiss for us to find time to look at them." By the time that Henry had been three years in Amherst he was prepared to enter Sophomore in College. Thanks to his friend and teacher Fitzgerald, his mathematical training had given him the entire mastery of La Croix's Algebra, so that he was prepared to demonstrate at random any proposition as chance selected—not only without aid or prompting from the teacher, but controversially as against the teacher, who would sometimes publicly attack the pupil's method of demonstration, disputing him step by step, when the scholar was expected to know with such positive clearness as to put down and overthrow the teacher. "You must not only know, but you must know that you know," was Fitzgerald's maxim; and Henry Ward attributes much of his subsequent habit of steady antagonistic defence of his own opinions to this early mathematical training.

Though prepared for the Sophomore class, his father however, deemed it best on the whole, that he should enter as freshman, and the advanced state of his preparation therefore gave him leisure the first year to mark out and commence a course of self-education by means of the college libraries, which he afterwards systematically pursued through college life. In fact he gave no more attention to the college course than was absolutely essential to keep his standing, but turned all the power of study and concentrated attention he had acquired in his previous years, upon his own plan of culture. As he himself remarks, "I had acquired by the Latin and mathematics, the power of study. I knew how to study, and I turned it upon things I wanted to know." The Latin and Greek classics did not attract him. The want of social warmth in the remove at which they stood from the living present, alienated them from the sympathies of one who felt his mission to be among the men of to-day, and by its living literature. Oratory and rhetoric he regarded as his appointed weapons, and he began to prepare himself in the department of *how to say*—meanwhile contemplating with uncertain awe, the great future problem of WHAT TO SAY.

For the formation of style he began a course of English classical study; Milton's prose works, Bacon, Shakspeare, and the writers of the Elizabethan period were his classics, read and re-read, and deeply pondered. In common with most of the young men of his period, he was a warm admirer of the writings of Robert Hall, and added him to his list of favorite authors. His habits of study were somewhat peculiar. He had made for himself at the carpenter's, a circular table, with a hole in the middle, where was fixed a seat. Enthroned in this seat with his English classics all around him, he read and pondered, and with never ceasing delight.

The stand he took in college, was from the first that of a reformer. He was always on the side of law and order, and being one of the most popular fellows in his class, threw the whole weight of his popularity in favor of the faculty, rather than against them. He and his associates formed a union of merry good fellows, who were to have glorious fun, but to have it only by honorable and permissible means. They voted down scraping in the lecture rooms, and hazing of students; they voted down gambling and drinking, and every form of secret vice, and made the class rigidly temperate and pure. Mr. Beecher had received from family descent what might be called a strictly temperance organization. In no part of his life did he ever use, or was he ever tempted to use tobacco or ardent spirits in any shape. All his public labors, like those of his father before him, have been performed by the strict legal income of ordinary nervous investment; they have not been those deep ruinous drafts on the reserved principal of vital force, which are drawn by the excitements of extra stimulants.

He also maintained the character of a Christian student, by conscientious attention to the class prayer meetings, in which he took his part, as well as by outside religious and temperance labors in the rural population in the neighborhood. He very early formed an attachment to a beneficiary in the college, a man, as he says, of the Isaiah type, large-souled, and full of devotion, who took the boy round with him on his tour of religious exhortation, insisting with paternal earnestness that it was his immediate duty to begin to practice for the work of the Christian ministry. Having brought him once or twice to read and pray, in a little rural meeting, held in a school-house in the outskirts of the village, he solemnly committed the future care of the meeting to the young disciple, and went himself to look up another fold. This meeting Henry religiously kept up among his others, with varying success, during his college career.

The only thing which prevented him from taking the first rank as a religious young man, was the want of that sobriety and solemnity which was looked upon as essential to the Christian character. Mr. Beecher was like a converted bob-o'link, who should be brought to judgment for short quirks and undignified twitters and tweedles, among the daisy heads, instead of flying in dignified paternal sweeps, like a good swallow of the sanctuary, or sitting in solemnized meditation in the depths of pine trees like the owl.

His commendation from the stricter brethren generally came with the sort of qualification which Shakspeare makes,—

"For the man doth fear God, howbeit it doth not always appear, by reason of some large jests which he will make."

In fact, Mr. Beecher was generally the center of a circle of tempestuous merriment, ever eddying round him in one droll form or another. He was quick in repartee, an excellent mimic, and his stories would set the gravest in a roar. He had the art, when admonished by graver people, of somehow entrapping them into more uproarious laughing than he himself practiced, and then looking innocently surprised. Mr. Beecher on one occasion was informed that the head tutor of the class was about to make him a grave exhortatory visit. The tutor was almost seven feet high, and solemn as an Alpine forest, but Mr. Beecher knew that like most solemn Yankees, he was at heart a deplorable wag, a mere whited sepulchre of conscientious gravity, with measureless depths of unrenewed chuckle hid away in the depths of his heart. When apprised of his approach, he suddenly whisked into the wood-closet the chairs of his room, leaving only a low one which had been sawed off at the second joint, so that it stood about a foot from the floor. Then he crawled through the hole in his table, and seated meekly among his books, awaited the visit.

A grave rap, is heard:—"Come in."

Far up in the air, the solemn dark face appears. Mr. Beecher rose ingenuously, and offered to come out. "No, never mind," says the visitor, "I just came to have a little conversation with you. Don't move."

"Oh," says Beecher innocently, "pray sit down sir," indicating the only chair.

The tutor looked apprehensively, but began the process of sitting down. He went down, down, down, but still no solid ground being gained, straightened himself and looked uneasy.

"I don't know but that chair is too low for you," said Beecher meekly; "do let me get you another."

"Oh no, no, my young friend, don't rise, don't trouble yourself, it is perfectly agreeable to me, in fact I like a low seat," and with these words, the tall man doubled up like a jack-knife, and was seen sitting with his grave face between his knees, like a grass-hopper drawn up for a spring. He heaved a deep sigh, and his eyes met the eyes of Mr. Beecher; the hidden spark of native depravity within him was exploded by one glance at those merry eyes, and he burst into a loud roar of merriment, which the two continued for some time, greatly to the amusement of the boys, who were watching to hear how Beecher would come out with his lecture. The chair was known in college afterwards, by the surname of the "Tutor's Delight." This overflow of the faculty of mirthfulness, has all his life deceived those who had only a shallow acquaintance with him, and men ignorant of the depth of yearning earnestness and profound strength of purpose on which they rippled and sparkled.

But at the time that he passed for the first humorist of college, the marks along his well worn volumes of the old English poets show only appreciation of what is earnest, deep and pathetic. He particularly loved an obscure old poet of whom we scarcely hear in modern days, Daniel, who succeeded Edmund Spenser as poet laureate, and was a friend of Shakspeare.

Some lines addressed by him to the Earl of Southampton, are marked by reiterated lines in Mr. Beecher's copy of the old English poets, which showed enthusiastic reading. He says, "This was about the only piece of poetry I ever committed to memory, but I read it so much I could not help at last knowing it by heart:"

"TO THE EARL OF SOUTHAMPTON.

"He who hath never warred with misery,
Nor ever tugged with fortune in distress,
Hath no occasion and no field to try
The strength and forces of his worthiness.
Those parts of judgment which felicity
Keeps as concealed, affliction must express,
And only men show their abilities
And what they are, in their extremities.

"Mutius the fire, the tortures Regulus,
Did make the miracles of faith and zeal;
Exile renowned and graced Rutilius.
Imprisonment and poison did reveal
The worth of Socrates, Fabricius'
Poverty did grace that common weal
More than all Sylla's riches got with strife,
And Cato's death did vie with Cæsar's life.

"He that endures for what his conscience knows
Not to be ill, doth from a patience high
Look on the only cause whereto he owes
Those sufferings, not on his misery;
The more he endures the more his glory grows,
Which never grows from imbecility;
Only the best composed and worthiest hearts
God sets to act the hardest and constant 'st parts."

Such an enthusiasm shows clearly on what a key the young man had set his life purposes, and what he was looking for in his life battle.

Another poem which bears reiterated marks and dates, is to Lady Margaret, Countess of Cumberland, of which these lines are a sample:

"He that of such a height hath built his mind,
And reared the dwelling of his thoughts so strong
As neither fear nor hope can shake the frame
Of his resolved powers; nor all the wind
Of vanity or malice pierce to wrong
His settled peace, or to disturb the same;
What a fair seat hath he! from whence he may
The boundless wastes and wilds of man survey!

"And while distraught ambition compasses
And is compassed; whilst as craft deceives
And is deceived; while man doth ransack man,
And builds on blood, and rises by distress;
And the inheritance of desolation leaves
To great expecting hopes; he looks thereon,
As from the shore of peace, with unwet eye,
And bears no venture in impiety."

These verses are so marked with Mr. Beecher's life habits of thought, with his modes of expression, that they show strongly the influence which these old poets had in forming both his habits of thought and expression. His mind naturally aspired after heroism, and from the time that he gave up his youthful naval enthusiasm he turned the direction of the heroic faculties into moral things.

In the course of the sophomore year, Mr. Beecher was led, as a mere jovial frolic, to begin a course of investigation which colored his whole after life. A tall, grave, sober fellow had been reading some articles on Phrenology, on which Spurzheim was then lecturing in Boston, and avowed himself a convert. Quick as thought, the wits of college saw in this an occasion for glorious fun. They proposed to him with great apparent earnestness that he should deliver a course of lectures on the subject in Beecher's room.

With all simplicity and solemnity he complied, while the ingenuous young inquirers began busily arming themselves with objections to and puzzles for him, by reading the scoffing articles in Blackwood and the Edinburgh. The fun waxed hearty, and many saw nothing in it but a new pasture ground to be ploughed and seeded down for an endless harvest of college jokes. But one day, one of the clearest headed and most powerful thinkers in the class said to Beecher, "What is your estimate of the real logical validity of these objections to Phrenology?" "Why," said Beecher, "I was thinking that if these objections were all that could be alleged, I could knock them to pieces." "So I think," said the other. In fact, the inanity of the crusade against the theory brought forth converts faster than its direct defence. Mr. Beecher and his associates formed immediately a club for physiological research. He himself commenced reading right and left, in all the works of anatomy and physiology which he could lay hands on, either in the college or village libraries. He sent and bought for his own private use, Magendie's Physiology, Combe's Phrenology, and the works of Gall and Spurzheim. A phrenological union was formed to purchase together charts, models and dissecting tools, for the study of comparative anatomy. It was even planned, in the enthusiasm of young discipleship, to establish a private dissecting room for the club, but the difficulties attending the procuring of proper subjects prevented its being carried into effect. By correspondence with his brother Charles, however, who was then in Bowdoin College, an affiliated phrenological club was formed in that institution, and his letters of this period were all on and about phrenological subjects, and in full phrenological dialect. Mr. Beecher delivered three lectures on the subject in the village lyceum, and did an infinity of private writing and study.

He read the old English dramatists, particularly Ben Jonson, Massinger, Webster, Ford and Shakspeare, and wrote out analyses of their principal characters on phrenological principles. The college text-book of mental philosophy was Browne, and Mr. Beecher's copy of Browne is marked through and through, and interlined with comparative statements of the ideas derived from his physiological investigation. With these also he carefully read and analyzed Locke, Stuart, Reid, and the other writers of the Scotch school. As a writer and debater, Mr. Beecher was acknowledged the first of the class, and was made first president of the Athenian Society, notwithstanding it had been a time-honored precedent that that distinction should belong only to the presumptive valedictorian. The classics and mathematics he had abandoned because of his interest in other things, but that abandonment settled the fact that he could never aspire to high college honors. He however, wrote for one of his papers in a college newspaper a vigorous defence of mathematical studies, which won the approbation and surprise of his teachers. It was a compliment paid by rhetoric to her silent sister.

The phrenological and physiological course thus begun in college was pursued by few of the phrenological club in after life. With many it died out as a boyish enthusiasm; with one or two, as Messrs. Fowler of New York, it became a continuous source of interest and profit. With Mr. Beecher it led to a broad course of physiological study and enquiry, which, collated with metaphysics and theology, has formed his system of thought through life. From that day he has continued the reading and study of all the physiological writers in the English language. In fact, he may be said during his college life to have constructed for himself a physiological mental philosophy out of the writings of the Scotch metaphysical school and that of Combe, Spurzheim, and the other physiologists. Mr. Beecher is far from looking on phrenology as a perfected science. He regards it in relation to real truth as an artist's study towards a completed landscape; a study on right principles and in a right direction, but not as a completed work. In his view, the phrenologists, physiologists and mental philosophers of past days have all been partialists, giving a limited view of the great subject. The true mental philosophy, as he thinks, is yet to arise from a consideration of all the facts and principles evolved by all of them.

Thus much is due for the understanding of Mr. Beecher's style, in which to a great extent he uses the phrenological terminology, a terminology so neat and descriptive, and definite in respect to human beings as they really exist, that it gives a great advantage to any speaker. The terms of phrenology have in fact become accepted as conveniences in treating of human nature, as much as the algebraic signs in numbers.

The depth of Mr. Beecher's religious nature prevented this enthusiasm for material science from degenerating into dry materialism. He was a Calvinist in the earnestness of his intense need of the highest and deepest in religion. In his sophomore year there was a revival of religion in college, in which his mind was powerfully excited. He reviewed the almost childish experiences under which he had joined the church, as possibly deceptive, and tried and disciplined himself by those profound tests with which the Edwardean theology had filled the minds of New England. A blank despair was the result. He applied to Dr. Humphrey, who simply told him that his present feelings were a work of the spirit, and with which he dared not interfere. After days of almost hopeless prayer, there came suddenly into his mind an ineffable and overpowering perception of the Divine love, which seemed to him like a revelation. It dispelled all doubts, all fears; he became buoyant and triumphant, and that buoyancy has been marked in his religious teachings ever since.

Mr. Beecher's doctrine upon the subject is that the truths of the Divine nature are undiscoverable by the mere logical faculties, that they are the province of a still higher class of faculties which belong to human nature, the faculties of *spiritual intuition;* that it is through these *spiritual intuitions* that the Holy Spirit of God communes with man, and directs through them the movements of the lower faculties. In full faith in the dependence of man on the Holy Spirit for these spiritual intuitions, he holds substantially the same ground with Jonathan Edwards, though he believes that Divine influence to be far more widely, constantly and fully given to the children of men than did that old divine.

During his two last college years, Mr. Beecher, like other members of his class, taught rural schools during the long winter vacations. In this way he raised funds of his own to buy that peculiar library which his tastes and studies caused him to accumulate about him. In both these places he performed the work of a religious teacher, preaching and exhorting regularly in stated meetings, giving temperance lectures, or doing any reformatory work that came to hand. In the controversy then arising through the land in relation to slavery, Mr. Beecher from the first took the ground and was willing to bear the name of an abolitionist. It was a part of the heroic element of his nature always to stand for the weak, and he naturally inclined to take that stand in a battle where the few were at odds against the many.

In 1832 Dr. Lyman Beecher moved to Cincinnati, two years before the completion of Henry's college course.

He graduated in 1834, and went out to Cincinnati. The abolition excitement at Lane Seminary had just ended, by the departure of a whole class of some thirty students, with Theodore Weld at their head.

Dr. Beecher was now the central point of a great theological battle. It was a sort of spiritual Armageddon, being the confluence of the forces of the Scotch-Irish Presbyterian Calvinistic fatalism, meeting in battle with the advancing rationalism of New England new school theology. On one side was hard literal interpretation of Bible declarations and the Presbyterian standards, asserting man's utter and absolute natural and moral inability to obey God's commands, and on the other side, the doctrine of man's free agency, and bringing to the rendering of the declarations of the scriptures and of the standards, the lights of modern modes of interpretation.

Dr. Wilson, who headed the attacking party, was a man in many points marvellously resembling General Jackson, both in person and character, and he fought the battle with the same gallant, headlong vigor and sincere unflinching constancy. His habits of thought were those of a western pioneer, accustomed from childhood to battle with Indians and wild beasts, in the frontier life of an early state. His views of mental philosophy, and of the modes of influencing the human mind, were like those of the Emperor Constantine when he commanded a whole synod of bishops to think alike without a day's delay, or those of the Duke of Wellington, when he told the doubting inquirers at Oxford, that "the thing to be done was to sign the thirty-nine articles, and believe them." The party he headed, were vigorous, powerful and with all that immense advantage which positive certainty and a literal, positively expressed belief always gives. With such an army and such a general, the fight of course was a warm one, and Dr. Beecher's sons found themselves at once his armor bearers in the thickest of the battle. The great number of ascending judicatories in the Presbyterian Church gave infinite scope for protracting a contest where every point of doctrine could first be discussed and voted on in Presbytery, then adjourned to Synod, then carried to General Assembly, and in each had to be discussed and decided by majorities. What scope for activity in those times! What racing and chasing along muddy western roads, to obscure towns, each party hoping that the length of the way and the depth of the mud would discourage their opponents, keep them away and so give their own side the majority. Dr. Beecher and his sons, it was soon found could race and chase and ride like born Kentuckians, and that "free agency" on horse-back, would go through mud and fire, and water, as gallantly as ever "natural inability" could. There was something grimly ludicrous in the dismay with which Dr. Wilson, inured from his boyhood to bear-fights, and to days and nights spent in cane-brakes, and dens of wolves, found on his stopping at an obscure log hut in the depth of the wilderness, Dr. Beecher with his sons and his new school delegates, ahead of him, on their way to Synod.

The study of theology at Lane Seminary, under these circumstances, was very largely from the controversial and dialectic point of view. It was, to a great extent, the science of defence of new school as against old school.

Mr. Beecher was enthusiastically devoted to his father, and of course felt interested in his success as a personal matter, but in regard to the whole wide controversy, his interest was more that of a spectator than of a partizan on either side. He had already begun his study of mental and moral philosophy on a broad eclectic basis, taking great account of facts and phenomena which he saw to be wholly ignored by the combatants on both sides. The mental philosophy of Reid and the Scotch school, on which Dr. Beecher based his definitions, he regarded as only partially true, and had set down in his own mind at a definite value. The intense zeal and perfect undoubting faith with which both sides fought their battle, impressed him as only a strange and interesting and curious study in his favorite science of anthropology.

He gave his attention to the system, understood it thoroughly, was master of all its modes of attack, fence and defence, but he did it much as a person nowa days might put on a suit of mediæval armor, and study mediæval tactics.

Mr. Beecher had inherited from his father what has been called a genius for friendship. He was never without the anchor of an enthusiastic personal attachment for somebody, and at Lane Seminary, he formed such an intimacy with Professor C. E. Stowe, whose room-mate for some length of time he was, and in whose society he took great delight. Professor Stowe, a man devoted to scholarly learning and Biblical criticism, was equally with young Beecher standing as a spectator in the great theological contest which was raging around him, and which he surveyed from still another stand-point, of ecclesiastical history and biblical criticism. It was some considerable inconvenience to the scholarly professor, to be pulled up from his darling books, and his interjections were not always strictly edifying when he was raced through muddy lanes, and rattled over corduroy roads, under the vigorous generalship of Dr. Beecher, all that he might give his vote for or against some point of doctrine, which, in his opinion, common sense had decided ages ago. He was also, somewhat of a strict disciplinarian and disposed to be severe on the discursive habits of his young friend, who was quite too apt to neglect or transcend conventional rule. The morning prayers at Lane were at conventual hours, and Henry's devotional propensities, of a dark cold winter morning, were almost impossible to be aroused, while his friend, who was punctuality itself, was always up and away in the gloaming. One morning, when the Professor had indignantly rebuked the lazy young Christian, whom he left tucked in bed, and, shaking the dust from his feet, had departed to his morning duties, Henry took advantage of his own habits of alert motion, sprang from the bed, dressed himself in a twinkling, and taking a cross-lot passage, was found decorously sitting directly under the Professor's desk, waiting for him, when he entered to conduct prayers. The stare of almost frightened amazement with which the Professor met him, was the ample reward of his exertions.

Though Professor Stowe never succeeded in making him an exact linguist, or shaping him into a biblical scholar, yet he was of great service to him in starting his mind in a right general direction in the study of the Bible. The old and the new school were both too much agreed in using the Bible as a carpenter does his nail-box, going to it only to find screws and nails to hold together the framework of a theological system. Professor Stowe inspired him with the idea of surveying the books of the Bible as divinely inspired compositions, yet truly and warmly human, and to be rendered and interpreted by the same rules of reason and common sense which pertain to all human documents.

As the time drew near in which Mr. Beecher was to assume the work of the ministry, he was oppressed by a deep melancholy. He had the most exalted ideas of what ought to be done by a Christian minister. He had transferred to that profession all those ideals of courage, enterprise, zeal and knightly daring which were the dreams of his boyhood, and which he first hoped to realize in the naval profession. He felt that the holy calling stood high above all others, that to enter it from any unholy motive, or to enter and not do a worthy work in it, was a treason to all honor.

His view of the great object of the ministry was sincerely and heartily the same with that of his father; to secure the regeneration of the individual heart by the Divine spirit, and thereby to effect the regeneration of human society. The problem that oppressed him was, how to do this. His father had used certain moral and intellectual weapons, and used them strongly and effectively, because employing them with undoubting faith. So many other considerations had come into his mind to qualify and limit that faith, so many new modes of thought and inquiry, that were partially inconsistent with the received statements of his party, that he felt he could never grasp and wield them with the force which would make them efficient. It was no comfort to him that he could wield the weapons of his theological party, so as to dazzle and confound objectors, while all the time conscious in his own soul of objections more profound and perplexities more bewildering. Like the shepherd boy of old, he saw the giant of sin stalking through the world, defying the armies of the living God, and longed to attack him, but the armor in which he had been equipped for the battle was no help, but only an incumbrance!

His brother, who studied with him, had already become an unbeliever, and thrown up the design of preaching, and he could not bear to think of adding to his father's trials by deserting the standard. Yet his distress and perplexity were so great that at times he seriously contemplated going into some other profession.

What to say to make men Christians,—how to raise man to God really and truly,—was to him an awful question. Nothing short of success in this appeared to him success in the Christian ministry.

Pending these mental conflicts, he performed some public labors. He was for four or five months editor of the Cincinnati Journal, the organ of the N. S. Presbyterian Church, during the absence of Mr. Brainard. While he was holding this post, the pro-slavery riot which destroyed Birney's press occurred, and the editorials of the young editor at this time were copied with high approval by Charles Hammond, of the Cincinnati Gazette, undoubtedly the ablest editor of the West, and the only other editor who dared to utter a word condemnatory of the action of the rioters. Mr. Beecher entered on the defence of the persecuted negroes with all the enthusiasm of his nature. He had always a latent martial enthusiasm, and though his whole life had been a peaceful one, yet a facility in the use of carnal weapons seemed a second nature, and at this time, he, with a number of other young men went to the mayor and were sworn in as a special body of police, who patroled the streets, well armed. Mr. Beecher wore his pistol, and was determined, should occasion arise, to use it. But as usual in such cases, a resolute front once shown dissolved the mob entirely.

In his last theological term he took a Bible class in the city of Cincinnati, and began studying and teaching the evangelists. With the course of this study and teaching came a period of spiritual clairvoyance. His mental perplexities were relieved, and the great question of "what to preach," was solved. The shepherd boy laid aside his cumbrous armor, and found in a clear brook a simple stone that smote down the giant, and so from the clear waters of the gospel narrative, Mr. Beecher drew forth that "white stone with a new name," which was to be the talisman of his ministry. To present Jesus Christ, personally, as the Friend and Helper of Humanity, Christ as God impersonate, eternally and by a necessity of his nature helpful and remedial and restorative; the friend of each individual soul, and thus the friend of all society; this was the one thing which his soul rested on as a worthy object in entering the ministry. He afterward said, in speaking of his feelings at this time: "I was like the man in the story to whom a fairy gave a purse with a single piece of money in it, which he found always came again as soon as he had spent it. I thought I knew at last one thing to preach, I found it included everything."

Immediately on finishing his theological course, Mr. Beecher married and was settled in Lawrenceburg. He made short work of the question of settlement, accepting the very first offer that was made him. It was work that he wanted, and one place he thought about as good as another. His parish was a little town on the Ohio river, not far from Cincinnati. Here he preached in a small church, and did all the work of the parish sexton, making his fires, trimming his lamps, sweeping his house, and ringing his bell. "I did all," he said whimsically, "but come to hear myself preach—that they had to do." The little western villages of those days had none of the attractions of New England rural life. They were more like the back suburbs of a great city, a street of houses without yards or gardens, run up for the most part in a cheap and flimsy manner, and the whole air of society marked with the impress of a population who have no local attachments, and are making a mere temporary sojourn for money-getting purposes. Mr. Beecher was soon invited from Lawrenceburg to Indianapolis, the capital of the State, where he labored for eight years.

His life here was of an Arcadian simplicity. He inhabited a cottage on the outskirts of the town, where he cultivated a garden, and gathered around him horse, cow and pig; all that wholesome suite of domestic animals which he had been accustomed to care for in early life. He was an enthusiast on all these matters, fastidious about breeds and blood, and each domestic animal was a pet and received his own personal attentions. In the note-books of this period, amid hints for sermons, come memoranda respecting his favorite Berkshire pig, or Durham cow. He read on gardening, farming, and stock-raising, all that he could lay hands on; he imported from eastern cultivators all sorts of roses and all sorts of pear trees and grape vines, and edited a horticultural paper, which had quite a circulation.

All this was mainly the amusement of his leisure hours, as he preached always twice on Sunday, and held at an average five other meetings a week in different districts of the city. For three months of every year, by consent of his people, he devoted himself to missionary duty through the State, riding from point to point on horseback, and preaching every day of the week.

In his theological studies he had but just two volumes—the Bible and human nature, which he held to be indispensable to the understanding each of the other. He said to himself, "The Apostles who first preached Christ, made converts who were willing to dare or do anything for him. How did they do this?" He studied all the recorded discourses of the Apostles in the book of Acts, in his analytical method, asking, to what principles of human nature did they appeal? What were their methods of statement? He endeavored to compose sermons on similar principles, and test them by their effects on men. He noticed that the Apostles always based their appeals to men on some common truth, admitted by both parties alike; that they struck at the great facts of moral consciousness, and he imitated them in this. He was an intense observer and student of men as they are. His large social talent, his predominating play of humor and drollery, were the shields under which he was constantly carrying on his inquiries into what man is, and how he can be reached. Seated in the places where men congregate to loaf and talk, he read his newspaper with his eyes and ears open to more than its pages. His preaching began to draw listeners as a new style of thing. Its studies into human nature, its searching analysis of men and their ways, drew constant listeners. His fame spread through the country, and multitudes, wherever he went, flocked to hear him. Still, Mr. Beecher did not satisfy himself. To be a popular preacher, to be well spoken of, to fill up his church, did not after all satisfy his ideal. It was necessary that the signs of an Apostle should be wrought in him by his having the power given to work the great, deep and permanent change which unites the soul to God. It was not till about the third year of his ministry that he found this satisfaction in a great revival of religion in Terre Haute, which was followed by a series of such revivals through the State, in which he was for many months unceasingly active. When he began to see whole communities moving together under a spiritual impulse, the grog-shops abandoned, the votaries of drunkenness, gambling and dissipation reclaimed, reformed, and sitting at the feet of Jesus, clothed and in their right mind, he felt that at last he had attained what his soul thirsted for, and that he could enter into the joy of the Apostles when they returned to Jesus, saying, "Lord, by thy name even the devils were made subject unto us."

His preaching of Christ at this time was spoken of as something very striking in its ceaseless iteration of one theme, made constantly new and various by new applications to human want and sin and sorrow.

A member of his church in Indianapolis, recently, in writing the history of the church with which he was connected, thus gives his recollections of him:

"In the early spring of 1842, a revival began, more noticeable, perhaps, than any that this church or this community has seen. The whole town was pervaded by the influences of religion. For many weeks the work continued with unabated power, and at three communion seasons, held successively in February, March and April, 1842, nearly one hundred persons were added to the church on profession of their faith. This was God's work. It is not improper, however, to speak of the pastor in that revival, as he is remembered by some of the congregation, plunging through the wet streets, his trousers stuffed in his muddy bootlegs, earnest, untiring, swift; with a merry heart, a glowing face, and a helpful word for every one; the whole day preaching Christ to the people where he could find them, and at night preaching still where the people were sure to find him. It is true that in this revival some wood and hay and stubble were gathered with the gold and silver and precious stones. As in all new communities, there was special danger of unhealthy excitement. But in general the results were most happy for the church and for the town. Some of those who have been pillars since, found the Saviour in that memorable time. Nor was the awakening succeeded by an immediate relapse.

"Early in the following year, at the March and April communions, the church had large accessions, and it had also in 1845. There was, indeed, a wholesome and nearly continuous growth up to the time when the first pastor resigned, to accept a call to the Plymouth Congregational church, in Brooklyn, New York. This occurred August 24th, 1847, and on the nineteenth of the following month Mr. Beecher's labors for the congregation ceased.

"The pastorate, thus terminated, had extended through more than eight years. During this time much had been accomplished. The society had built a pleasant house of worship. The membership had advanced from thirty-two to two hundred and seventy-five. What was considered a doubtful enterprise, inaugurated as it had been amidst many prophecies of failure, had risen to an enviable position, not only in the capital but in the State. The attachment between pastor and people had become peculiarly strong. Mutual toils and sufferings and successes had bound them fast together. Only the demands of a wider field, making duty plain, divided them, and a recent letter proves that the pastor's early charge still keeps its hold upon his heart. It is not to be wondered at that the few of his flock who yet remain among us always speak of 'Henry' with beaming eyes and mellowed voices."

One expression in this extract will show a peculiarity which strongly recalls the artless, unconventional freshness of Western life in those days. The young pastor, though deeply and truly respected by all his elders and church members, was always addressed as "Henry," by them with a sort of family intimacy and familiarity. It was partly due to the simple, half woodland habits of the people, and partly to that quality in the pastor that made every elderly man love him as a son and every younger one as a brother.

Henry's tastes, enthusiasms, and fancies, his darling garden, with its prize vegetables and choice roses, whence came bouquets for the æsthetic, and more solid presents of prize onions or squashes for the more literal—all these seemed to be part and parcel of the family stock of his church. His brother Charles, who from intellectual difficulties had abandoned the ministry, and devoted himself to a musical life as a profession, inhabited, with his wife and young family, a little cottage in the same grounds with his own, and shared his garden labors, and led the music of his church. "Henry and Charles" were as familiarly spoken of and known in Indianapolis circles as Castor and Pollux among the astronomers. In one of the revivals in Indianapolis, Charles, like his brother before him, found in an uplift of his moral faculties a tide to carry him over the sunken rocks of his logic. By his brother's advice, he took a Bible class, and began the story of the life of Christ, and the result was that after a while he saw his way clear to offer himself for ordination, and was settled in the ministry in Fort Wayne, Indiana. Thus that simple narrative had power to allay the speculative doubts of both brothers, and to give them an opening into the ministry.

Mr. Beecher has always looked back with peculiar tenderness to that Western life, in the glow of his youthful days, and in that glorious, rich, abundant, unworn Western country. The West, with its wide, rich, exuberant spaces of land, its rolling prairies, garlanded with rainbows of ever-springing flowers, teeming with abundance of food for man, and opening in every direction avenues for youthful enterprise and hope, was to him a morning land. To carry Christ's spotless banner in high triumph through such a land, was a thing worth living for, and as he rode on horseback alone, from day to day, along the rolling prairie lands, sometimes up to his horse's head in grass and waving flowers, he felt himself kindled with a sort of ecstacy. The prairies rolled and blossomed in his sermons, and his style at this time had a tangled luxuriance of poetic imagery, a rush and abundance of words, a sort of rich and heavy involution, that resembled the growth of a tropical forest.

"What sort of a style *am* I forming?" he said to a critical friend, who had come to hear him preach.

"Well, I should call it the 'tropical style,'" was the reply.

The Western people, simple and strong, shrewd as Yankees, and excitable and fervent as Southerners, full of quaint images and peculiar turns of expression derived from a recent experience of back-woods life, were an open page in his great book of human nature, where character revealed itself with an artless freshness. All the habits of society had an unconventional simplicity. People met with the salutation, "How are ye, stranger?" and had no thought of any formal law of society, why one human being might not address another on equal terms, and speak out his mind on all subjects fully. When invited to supper at a thrifty farmer's, the supper board was spread in the best bed-room, the master and mistress stood behind the chairs of their guests and waited on them during the meal, and the table groaned with such an abundance of provision as an eastern imagination fails to conceive of. Every kind of fowl, choicely cooked, noble hams, sausages, cheese, bread, butter, biscuit, corn cakes in every variety, sweet cakes and confections, preserved fruits of every name, with steaming tea and coffee, were all indispensable to a good supper.

Of poverty, properly so called, there was very little. There were none of those distressing, unsolvable social problems which perplex the mind and burden the heart of a pastor in older states of society.

Mr. Beecher's ecclesiastical brethren were companions of whom he never fails to speak with tender respect and enthusiastic regard. Some of them, like Father Dickey, were men who approached as near the apostolic ideal, in poverty, simplicity, childlike sincerity, and unconquerable, persevering labor, as it is possible to do. They were all strong, fearless anti-slavery men, and the resolutions of the Indiana Synod were always a loud, unsparing and never-failing testimony against any complicity with slavery in the Presbyterian church.

As to the great theological controversy that divided the old and new school church, Mr. Beecher dropped it at once and forthwith, being in his whole nature essentially uncontroversial. It came to pass that some of his warmest personal friends were members of the Old School church in Indianapolis, and offspring of the very fiercest combatants who had fought his father in Cincinnati.

Mr. Beecher was on terms of good fellowship with all denominations. There were in Indianapolis, Baptists, Methodists, and an Episcopal minister, but he stood on kindly social terms with all. The spirit of Western society was liberal, and it was deemed edifying by the common sense masses that the clergy of different denominations should meet as equals and brothers. Mr. Beecher's humorous faculty gave to him a sort of universal coin which passed current in all sorts of circles, making every one at ease with him. Human nature longs to laugh, and a laugh, as Shakspeare says, "done in the testimony of a good conscience," will often do more to bring together wrangling theologians than a controversy.

There was a store in Indianapolis, where the ministers of all denominations often dropped in to hear the news, and where the free western nature made it always in rule to try each others metal with a joke. No matter how sharp the joke, it was considered to be all fair and friendly.

On one occasion, Mr. Beecher, riding to one of the stations of his mission, was thrown over his horse's head in crossing the Miami, pitched into the water, and crept out thoroughly immersed. The incident of course furnished occasion for talk in the circles the next day, and his good friend the Baptist minister proceeded to attack him the moment he made his appearance.

"Oh, ho, Beecher, glad to see you! I thought you'd have to come into our ways at last! You've been immersed at last; you are as good as any of us now." A general laugh followed this sally.

"Poh, poh," was the ready response, "my immersion was a different thing from that of your converts. You see, I was immersed by a *horse*, not by an ass."

A chorus of laughter proclaimed that Beecher had got the better of the joke for this time.

A Methodist brother once said to him, "Well now, really, Brother Beecher, what have you against Methodist doctrines?"

"Nothing, only that your converts will practice them."

"Practice them?"

"Yes, you preach falling from grace, and your converts practice it with a vengeance."

One morning as he was sitting at table, word was brought in that his friend, the Episcopal minister, was at the gate, wanting to borrow his horse.

"Stop, stop," said he, with a face of great gravity, "there's something to be attended to first," and rising from table, he ran out to him and took his arm with the air of a man who is about to make a serious proposition.

"Now brother G—, you want my horse for a day? Well, you see, it lies on my mind greatly that you don't admit my ordination. I don't think it's fair. Now if you'll admit that I'm a genuinely ordained minister, you shall have my horse, but if not, I don't know about it."

Mr. Beecher took ground from the first that the pulpit is the place not only for the presentation of those views which tend to unite man's spiritual nature directly with God, but also for the consideration of all those specific reforms which grow out of the doctrine of Christ in society. He preached openly and boldly on specific sins prevailing in society, and dangerous practices which he thought would corrupt or injure.

There was a strong feeling in Indianapolis against introducing slavery into the discussions of the pulpit. Some of his principal men had made vehement declarations that the subject never should be named in the pulpit of any church with which they were connected. Mr. Beecher, among his earliest motions in Synod, however, introduced a resolution that every minister should preach a thorough exposition and condemnation of slavery. He fulfilled his part very characteristically, by preaching three sermons on the life of Moses, the bondage of the children of Israel under Pharaoh and their deliverance. Under this cover he gained the ear of the people, for it has always been held both orthodox and edifying to bombard the vices and crimes of old Testament sinners, and to show no mercy to their iniquities. Before they were aware of it however, his hearers found themselves listening to a hot and heavy attack on the existing system of American slavery, which he exposed in a most thorough, searching manner, and although the oppressor was called Pharaoh and the scene was Egypt, and so nobody could find fault with the matter of the discourse, the end and aim was very manifest.

Nobody was offended, but many were convinced, and from that time, Mr. Beecher preached Anti-Slavery sermons in his church just as often as he thought best, and his church became an efficient bulwark of the cause.

The Western states at this time were the scenes of much open vice. Gambling, drinking, licentiousness were all rife in the community, and against each of these, Mr. Beecher lifted up his testimony. A course of sermons on those subjects preached in Indianapolis and afterwards published under the title of "Lectures to Young Men," excited in the day of their delivery a great sensation. The style is that of fervid, almost tropical fullness, which characterized his Western life. It differs from the sermons of most clergymen to young men, in that free and perfect knowledge it shows of all the details of the evil ways which he names. Mr. Beecher's peculiar social talent, his convivial powers, and his habits of close Shaksperian observation, gave him the key of human nature. Many a gambler or drunkard, in their better hours were attracted towards a man who met them as a brother, and seemed to value and aim for the better parts of their nature. When Mr. Beecher left Indianapolis some of his most touching interviews and parting gifts were from men of this class, whom he had followed in their wanderings and tried to save. Some he could save and some were too far in the whirlpool for his arm to pull them out. One of them said when he heard of his leaving, "Before any thing or any body on earth, I do love Beecher. I know he would have saved me if he could."

Mr. Beecher was so devoted to the West, and so identified with it, that he never would have left what he was wont to call his bishopric of Indiana, for the older and more set and conventional circles of New York, had not the health of his family made a removal indispensable.

He was invited to Brooklyn to take charge of a new enterprise. Plymouth Church was founded by some fifteen or twenty gentlemen as a new Congregational Church.

Mr. Beecher was to be installed there and had to pass an examination before Eastern theologians. He had been, as has been shown, not a bit of a controversialist, and he had been so busy preaching Christ, and trying to save sinners, that he was rather rusty in all the little ins and outs of New England theology. On many points he was forced to answer "I do not know," and sometimes his answer had a whimsical turn that drew a smile.

"Do you believe in the Perseverance of the Saints?" said good Dr. Humphrey, his college father, who thought his son was not doing himself much credit in the theological line, and hoped to put a question where he could not fail to answer right.

"I was brought up to believe that doctrine," said Mr. Beecher, "and I did believe it till I went out West and saw how Eastern Christians lived when they went out there. I confess since then I have had my doubts."

On the whole, as Mr. Beecher's record was clear from the testimony of Western brothers, with whom he had been in labors more abundant, it was thought not on the whole dangerous to let him into the eastern sheep-fold.

Mr. Beecher immediately announced in Plymouth Pulpit the same principles that he had in Indianapolis; namely, his determination to preach Christ among them not as an absolute system of doctrines, not as a by-gone historical personage, but as the living Lord and God, and to bring all the ways and usages of society to the test of his standards. He announced to all whom it might concern, that he considered temperance and anti-slavery a part of the gospel of Christ, and should preach them accordingly.

During the battle inaugurated by Mr. Webster's speech of the 7th of March, and the fugitive slave law, Mr. Beecher labored with his whole soul.

There was, as people will remember, a great Union Saving Committee at Castle Garden, New York, and black lists were made out of merchants, who, if they did not give up their principles, were to be crushed financially, and many were afraid. Mr. Beecher preached, and visited from store to store, holding up the courage of his people to resistance. The advertisement of Bowen & McNamee that they would "sell their silks but not their principles," went all through the country, and as every heroic sentiment does, brought back an instant response.

At this time Mr. Beecher carried this subject through New England and New York, in Lyceum lectures, and began a course of articles in the Independent, under the star signature, which were widely read. It is said that when Calhoun was in his last illness, his secretary was reading him extracts from Northern papers, and among others, one of Mr. Beecher's, entitled "Shall we compromise?" in which he fully set forth the utter impossibility of reconciling the two conflicting powers of freedom and slavery.

"Read that again!" said the old statesman, his eye lighting up. "That fellow understands his subject; he has gone to the bottom of it." Calhoun as well as Garrison understood the utter impossibility of uniting in one nation two states of society founded on exactly opposite social principles.

Through all the warfare of principles, Plymouth Church steadily grew larger. It was an enterprise dependent for support entirely on the sale of the seats, and Mr. Beecher was particularly solicitous to make it understood that the buying of a seat in Plymouth Church would necessitate the holder to hear the gospel of Christ unflinchingly applied to the practical issues of the present hour. Always, as the year came round, when the renting of the pews approached, Mr. Beecher took occasion to preach a sermon in which he swept the whole field of modern reform with particular reference to every disputed and unpopular doctrine, and warned all who were thinking of taking their seats what they must expect for the coming year.

When the battle of the settlement of Kansas was going on, and the East was sending forth her colonies as lambs among wolves, Mr. Beecher fearlessly advocated the necessity of their going out armed, and a subscription was raised in Plymouth Church to supply every family with a Bible and a rifle. A great commotion was then raised and the inconsistency of such a gift from a professedly Christian church was much insisted on. Since then, more than one church in New England has fitted out soldiers and prepared munitions of war, and more than one clergyman has preached warlike sermons. The great battle had even then begun in Kansas. John Brown was our first great commander, who fought single handed for his *country*, when traitors held Washington and used the United States army only as a means to crush and persecute her free citizens and help on the slavery conspiracy. During the war Mr. Beecher's labors were incessant. Plymouth Church took the charge of raising and equipping one regiment, the First Long Island, and many of its young men went out in it. Mr. Beecher often visited their camp during the time of their organization and preached to them. His eldest son was an officer in it, and was afterwards transferred from it to the artillery service of the regular army.

At this time Mr. Beecher took the editorship of the Independent, a paper in which he had long been a contributor. He wished this chance to speak from time to time his views and opinions to the whole country. He was in constant communication with Washington and intimate with the Secretary of War, in whose patriotism, sagacity and wonderful efficiency he had the greatest reliance.

The burden of the war upon his spirit, his multiplied labors in writing, speaking, editorship, and above all in caring for his country, bore down his health. His voice began to fail, and he went to Europe for a temporary respite. On his arrival he was met on the steamer by parties who wished to make arrangements for his speaking in England. He told them that he had come with no such intention, but wholly for purposes of relaxation, and that he must entirely decline speaking in England.

In a private letter to his sister at this time, he said, "This contest is neither more nor less than the conflict between democratic and aristocratic institutions, in which success to one must be defeat to the other. The aristocratic party in England, see this plainly enough, and I do not propose to endeavor to pull the wool over their eyes. I do not expect sympathy from them. No order yet ever had any sympathy with what must prove their own downfall. We have got to settle this question *by our armies* and the opinions of mankind will follow."

He spent but a short time in England, enjoying the hospitality of an American friend and former parishioner, Mr. C. C. Duncan. After a fortnight spent in Wales, he went into Switzerland through Northern Italy and Germany.

Mr. Beecher always had side tracks to his mind, on which his thoughts and interests ran in the intervals of graver duties. When he came to the life of a city, and left his beloved garden and the blooming prairies of the West behind, he began the study of the arts as a recreation, and prosecuted it, as he did every thing else, with that enthusiasm which is the parent of industry. He bought for himself quite an art library, consisting of all the standard English works on the subject, and while up and down the country on his anti-slavery lyceum crusade, usually traveled with some of these works in his pocket, and read them in the cars.

He also made collections of pictures and choice engravings, with all the ardor with which before he collected specimen roses. At intervals he had lectured on these subjects. His lecture on the Uses of the Beautiful, was much called for throughout the country. He was therefore in training to enjoy the art treasures of Europe.

He had a period of great enjoyment at Berlin, where, in the Berlin Museum, under the instructionsof Waagen the director of arts, he examined that historical collection, said to be the richest and most scientifically arranged series to mark the history of art which can be found in Europe. The scenery of Switzerland and the art galleries of Northern Italy also helped to refresh his mind and divert him from the great national affliction that weighed on his spirit.

At Paris, he met the news of the battle of Gettysburg and the taking of Vicksburg, and recognized in them the only style of argument which could carry the cause through Europe. Grant was a logician after his own heart.

Mr. Beecher, on his return to England, was again solicited to speak in public, and again declined. So immutable was his idea that this was a battle that Americans must fight out, and which could not be talked out.

He was at last, however, made to see his duty to that small staunch liberal party who had been maintaining the cause of America against heavy odds in England, and he felt that if they wished him to speak, he owed himself to them; that they were brave defenders hard beset; and that their cause and ours was one. Such men as Baptist Noel, Newman Hall, Francis Newman and others of that class, were applicants not to be resisted.

He therefore prepared himself for what he always has felt to have been the greatest effort and severest labor of his life, to plead the cause of his country at the bar of the civilized world. A series of engagements was formed for him to speak in the principal cities of England and Scotland.

He opened Friday, October 9th, in the Free Trade Hall, in Manchester, to a crowded audience of 6,000 people. The emissaries of the South had made every preparation to excite popular tumult, to drown his voice and prevent his being heard. Here he treated the subject on its merits, as being the great question of the rights of working men, and brought out and exposed the nature of the Southern confederacy as founded in the right of the superior to oppress the inferior race. Notwithstanding the roar and fury and interruptions he persevered and said his say, and the London Times next day, printed it all with a column or two of abuse by way of condiment.

October 13th, he spoke in the city hall at Glasgow, discussing slavery and free labor as comparative systems. The next day, October 14th, he spoke in Edinburgh in a great public meeting in the Free Church Assembly Hall, where he discussed the existing American conflict from the historical point of view.

This was by far the most quiet and uninterrupted meeting of any. But the greatest struggle of all was of course at Liverpool. At Liverpool, where Clarkson was mobbed, and came near being thrown off the wharf and drowned, there was still an abundance of that brutal noisy population which slavery always finds it useful to stir up to bay and bark when she is attacked.

Mr. Beecher has a firmly knit vigorous physical frame, come down from back generations of yeomen, renowned for strength, and it stood him in good service now. In giving an account afterwards, he said, "I had to speak extempore on subjects the most delicate and difficult as between our two nations, where even the shading of my words was of importance, and yet I had to outscream a mob and drown the roar of a multitude. It was like driving a team of runaway horses and making love to a lady at the same time."

The printed record of this speech, as it came from England, has constant parentheses of wild uproars, hootings, howls, cat calls, clamorous denials and interruptions; but by cheerfulness, perfect fearless good humor, intense perseverance, and a powerful voice, Mr. Beecher said all he had to say in spite of the uproar.

Two letters, written about this time, show the state of his mind during this emergency:

SUNDAY, Oct. 18, 1863. LONDON.

MY DEAR FRIEND:

You know why I have not written you from England. I have been so full of work that I could not. God has been with me and prospered me. I have had health, and strength, and courage, and what is of unspeakably more importance, I have had the sweetest experience of love to God and to man, of all my life. I have been enabled *to love our enemies.*

All the needless ignorance, the party perversions, the wilful misrepresentations of many newspapers, the arrogance and obstinacy too often experienced, and yet more the coolness of brethren of our faith and order, and the poisoned prejudices that have been arrayed against me by the propagation of untruths or distorted reports, have not prevented my having a love for old England, an appreciation of the good that is here, and a hearty desire for her whole welfare. This I count a great blessing. God awakened in my breast a desire to be a full and true Christian towards England, the moment I put my foot on her shores, and he has answered the prayers which he inspired. I have spoken at Manchester, Glasgow, Edinburgh, and Liverpool, and am now in London, preparing for Exeter Hall, Tuesday next. I have been buoyant and happy. The streets of Manchester and Liverpool have been filled with placards, in black and white letters, full of all lies and bitterness, but they have seemed to me only the tracery of dreams. For hours I have striven to speak amid interruptions of every kind—yellings, hootings, cat calls, derisive yells, impertinent and insulting questions, and every conceivable annoyance—some personal violence. But God has kept me in perfect peace. I stood in Liverpool and looked on the demoniac scene, almost without a thought that it was *me* that was present. It seemed rather like a storm raging in the trees of the forests, that roared and impeded my progress, but yet had matters personal or wilful in it, against me. You know, dear friend, how, when we are lifted by the inspiration of a great subject, and by the almost visible presence and vivid sympathy with Christ, the mind forgets the sediment and dregs of trouble, and sails serenely in an upper realm of peace, as untouched by the noise below, as is a bird that flies across a battle-field. Just so I had at Liverpool and Glasgow, as sweet an inward peace as ever I did in the loving meetings of dear old Plymouth Church. And again and again, when the uproar raged, and I could not speak, my heart seemed to be taking of the infinite fullness of the Saviour's pity, and breathing it out upon those poor, troubled men. I never had so much the spirit of continuing and unconscious prayer, or rather, of communion with Christ. I felt that I was his dear child, and that his arms were about me continually, and at times that peace that passeth all understanding has descended upon me that I could not keep tears of gratitude from falling for so much tender goodness of my God. For what are outward prosperities compared with these interior intimacies of God? It is not the path *to* the temple, but the *interior* of the temple that shows the goodness and glory of God. And I have been able to commit all to him, myself, my family, my friends, and in an especial manner the cause of my country. Oh, my friend, I have felt an inexpressible wonder that God should give it to me to do something for the dear land. When sometimes the idea of being clothed with power to stand up in this great kingdom, against an inconceivable violence of prejudice and mistake, and clear the name of my dishonored country, and let her brow shine forth, crowned with liberty, glowing with love to man, O, I have seemed unable to live, almost. It almost took my breath away!

"I have not in a single instance gone to the speaking halls without all the way breathing to God unutterable desires for inspiration, guidance, success; and I have had no disturbance of *personality.* I have been willing, yea, with eagerness, to be myself contemptible in men's sight if only my disgrace might be to the honor of that cause which is entrusted to our own thrice dear country. I have asked of God nothing but this—and this with uninterrupted heart-flow of yearning request—"Make me worthy to speak for God and man." I never felt my ignorance so painfully, nor the great want of moral purity and nobility of soul, as when approaching my tasks of *defending liberty* in this her hour of trial. I have an ideal of what a man should be that labors for such a cause, that constantly rebukes my real condition, and makes me feel painfully how little I am. Yet *that* is hardly painful. There passes before me a view of God's glory, so pure, so serene, uplifted, filling the ages, and more and more to be revealed, that I almost wish to lose my own identity, to be like a drop of dew that falls into the sea, and becomes a part of the sublime whole that glows under every line of latitude, and sounds on every shore! '*That God may be all in all,*' —that is not a prayer only, but a personal *experience.* And in all this time I have not had one unkind feeling toward a single human being. Even those who are opposers, I have pitied with undying compassion, and enemies around me have seemed harmless, and objects of charity rather than potent foes to be destroyed.

God be thanked, who giveth us the victory through our Lord Jesus Christ.

"My dear friend, when I sat down to write, I did it under this impulse—that I wanted somebody to know the secret of my life. I am in a noisy spectacle, and seem to thousands as one employing merely worldly implements, and acting under secular motives. But should I die, on sea or land, I wanted to say to you, who have been so near and dear to me, that as God's own very truth, 'the life that I have lived in the flesh, I have lived by faith of the Son of God.' I wanted to leave it with some one to say for me that it was not in natural gifts, nor in great opportunities, nor in personal ambition, that I have been able to endure and labor, but that the secret and spring of my outward life has been an inward, complete, and all-possessing faith of God's truth, and God's own self working in me to will and to do of his own good pleasure!

"There, now I feel better!

"Monday, 19th. I do not know as you will understand the feeling which led to the above outburst. I had spoken four times in seven days to immense audiences, under great excitement, and with every effort of Southern sympathizers, the newspapers, street placards, and in every other way to prevent my being heard. I thought I had been through furnaces before, but this ordeal surpassed all others. I was quite alone in England. I had no one to consult with. I felt the burden of having to stand for my country, in a half hostile land; and yet I never flinched for a moment, nor lost heart. But after resting twenty weeks, to begin so suddenly such a tremendous strain upon my voice, has very much affected it. To-day I am somewhat fearful I shall be unable to speak to-morrow night in Exeter Hall. I *want* to speak there, if the Lord will only let me. I shall be willing to give up all the other openings in the kingdom. I cannot stop to give you any sort of insight into affairs here. One more good victory, and England will be immovable. The best *thinkers* of England will be at any rate.

"I hope my people will feel that I have done my duty. I know that I have tried. I should be glad to feel that my countrymen approved, but above all others I should prize the knowledge that the people of Plymouth Church were satisfied with me.

"I am as ever, yours,

H. W. BEECHER."

"OCT. 21, 1863. LONDON.

"MY DEAR FRIEND:

Last night was the culmination of my labor, in Exeter Hall. It was a very fit close to a series of meetings that have produced a great sensation in England. Even an American would be impressed with the enthusiasm of so much of England as the people of last night represented for the North. It was more than willing, than hearty, than even eager, it was almost wild and fanatical. I was like to have been killed with people pressing to shake my hand; men, women, and children crowded up the platform, and ten and twenty hands held over and stuck through like so many pronged spears. I was shaken, pinched, squeezed, in every way an affectionate enthusiasm could devise, until the police actually came to my rescue, and forced a way, and dragged me down into the retiring room, where a like scene began, from which an inner room gave me refuge, but no relief, for only with more deliberation, the gentlemen brought wives, daughters, sons, and selves for a God bless you! And when Englishmen that had lived in America, or had sons in our army, or had married American wives, took me to witness their devotion to our cause, the chairman of the meeting, Mr. Scott, the Chamberlain of London, said that a few more meetings, and in some other parts of England, and the question would be settled! You will have sent to you abundant accounts, I presume.

"Lastly; England will be enthusiastically right, provided we hold on, and *gain victories.* But England has an intense and yearning sense of *the value of success.*

"Yours, ever lovingly."

Mr. Beecher returned from England much exhausted by the effort. All the strength that he had accumulated he poured out in that battle.

Events after that swept on rapidly, and not long after Mr. Beecher, in company with Lloyd Garrison, and a great party of others, went down to Fort Sumter to raise again the national flag, when Richmond had fallen, and the conflict was over. During his stay at the South, he had some exciting experiences. One of the most touching was his preaching in one of the largest churches in South Carolina to a great congregation of liberated slaves. The sermon, which is in a recently printed volume of sermons, is full of emotion and records of thankfulness.

Returning, he was met by the news of the President's death, at which, like all the land, he bowed as a mourner. Not long after, he felt it his duty to strike another key in his church. The war was over, the victory won. Mr. Beecher came out with a sermon on forgiveness of injuries, expounding the present crisis as a great and rare OPPORTUNITY.

The sermon was not a popular one. The community could not at once change the attitude of war for that of peace; there were heart-burnings that could not at once be assuaged. But whatever may be thought of Mr. Beecher's opinions in the matter of political policy, there is no doubt that the immediate and strong impulse to *forgive*, which came to him at once when his party was triumphant, was from that source in his higher nature whence have come all the best inspirations of his life.

Mr. Beecher's views, hopes, wishes, and the policy he would have wished to have pursued, were very similar to those of Governor Andrew, and the more moderate of the republicans, and he did not hesitate at once to imperil his popularity with his own party, by the free expression of his opinions. Those who have been most offended by him cannot but feel that the man who defied the slaveholder when he was rich, haughty and powerful, had a right to speak a kind word for him now when he is poor, and weak, and defeated. The instinct to defend the weaker side is strongest in generous natures.

Mr. Beecher has met and borne the criticisms of his own party with that tolerance and equanimity with which he once bore rebuke for defending the cause of the slave. In all the objects sought by the most radical republicans, he is a firm believer. He holds to the equal political rights of every human being—men and women, the white man and the negro. He hopes to see this result yet established in the Union, and if it be attained by means different from those he counseled, still *if it be attained*, he will sincerely rejoice.

Though Mr. Beecher has from time to time entered largely into politics, yet he has always contemplated them from the moral and ministerial stand-point. His public and political labors, though they have been widely known, are mere offshoots from his steady and habitual pastoral work in his own parish.

Plymouth Church is to a considerable degree a realization externally of Mr. Beecher's ideal of what a protestant church ought to be—a congregation of faithful men and women, bound together by a mutual covenant of Christian love, to apply the principles of Christianity to society. It has always been *per se*, a temperance and an anti-slavery society. The large revenue raised by the yearly sale of pews, has come in time to afford a generous yearly income. This year it amounts to fifty thousand dollars. This revenue has, besides the pastor's salary and current expenses, been appropriated to extinguishing the debt upon the church, which being at last done, the church will devote its surplus to missionary operations in its vicinity. Two missions have been largely supported by the funds derived from Plymouth Church, and the time and personal labors of its members. A mechanics' reading-room is connected with one of these. No church in the country furnishes a larger body of lay teachers, exhorters, and missionaries in every department of human and Christian labor. A large-minded, tolerant, genial spirit, a cheerful and buoyant style of piety, is characteristic of the men and women to whose support and efficient aid in religious works, Mr. Beecher is largely indebted for his success.

The weekly prayer-meeting of the church is like the reunion of a large family. The pastor, seated in the midst, seems only as an elder brother. The various practical questions of Christian morals are freely discussed, and every member is invited to express an opinion.

In one of these meetings, Mr. Beecher gave an autobiographical account of the growth of his own mind in religious feeling and opinion, which was taken down by a reporter. We shall give it as the fitting close of this sketch.

"If there is any one thing in which I feel that my own Christian experience has developed more than in another, I think it is the all-sided use of the love and worship which I have toward the Lord Jesus Christ. Every man's mind, that acts for itself, has to go through its periods of development and evolution. In the earlier part of my Christian career and ministry, I had but glimpses of Christ, and was eagerly seeking to develop in my own mind, and for my people, a full view of his character, particularly with reference to the conversion of men; to start them, in other words, in the Christian life. And for a great many years I think it was Christ as the wisdom of God unto salvation that filled my mind very much;

and I preached Christ *as a power*, not at all too much, perhaps, but almost exclusively.

"Well, I think there has been going on in me, steadily and gradually, a growing *appropriation* of Christ to all needs; to every side and phase of experience; so that at no period of my life was I ever so conscious of a personal need, so definite, and at so many points of my nature, as now. I do not know that I experience such enthusiasm as I have at some former periods of my life; but I think that at no other period did I ever have such a sense of the fulness of God in Christ, or such a sense of the special point at which this divine all-supply touches the human want.

"A few points I will mention, that are much in my mind.

"The love of Christ, as I recollect it in my childhood, was taught almost entirely from the work of redemption. That work of redemption was itself a historical fact, and it was sought to stir up the heart and the affections by a continual review and iteration of the great facts of Christ's earthly mission, passion, atonement and love. I became conscious, very early in my ministry, that I did not derive—nor could I see that Christians generally derived—from the mere continued presentation of that circle of facts, a perpetual help, to anything like the extent that life needs. There would come to me, as there come to the church, times in which all these facts seemed to be fused and kindled, and to afford great light and consolation; but these were alternative and occasional, whereas the need was perpetual. And it was not until I went beyond these—not disdaining them, but using them rather as a torch, as a means of interpreting Christ in a higher relation—that I entered into a train of thought that revealed to me the intrinsic nature of God. I had an idea that he loved me on account of Calvary and Gethsemane, on account of certain historical facts; but I came, little by little, through glimpses and occasional appreciations, to that which is now a continuous, unbroken certainty, namely, a sense of the EVERLASTING NEED OF GOD, IN CHRIST, TO LOVE. I began to interpret the meaning of love, not by contemplating a few historical facts, but by running through my mind human faculties, exalting them, and imagining them to have infinite scope in the divine mind. I began to apply our ideas of infinity and almightiness to the attributes of God, and to form some conception of what affection must be in a Being who had created, who had sustained in the past, and who was to sustain throughout the endless future, a race of intelligent creatures such as peopled the earth. In that direction my mind grew, and in that direction it grows. And from the inward and everlasting nature of God TO LOVE, I have derived the greatest stimulus, the greatest consolation, and the greatest comfort in preaching to others. I find many persons that speak of loving Christ; but it is only now and then that I meet those who seem to be penetrated deeply with a consciousness of CHRIST'S LOVE TO THEM, or of its boundlessness, its wealth, its fineness, its exceeding delicacy, its transcendency in every line and lineament of possible conception. Once in a while, people have this view break upon them in meeting, or in some sick hour, or in some revival moment. That is a blessed visitation which brings to the soul a realization of the capacity of God to love imperfect beings with infinite love, and which enables a man to adapt this truth to his shame-hours, his sorrow-hours, his love-hours and his selfish hours, and to find all the time that there is in the revelation of the love of God in Christ Jesus all-sufficient food for the soul. It is, indeed, almost to have the gate of heaven opened to you. The treasure is inexhaustible.

Out of that has grown something besides: for it is impossible for me to feel that Christ loves me with such an all-surrounding love, and to feel, as I do every day of my life, that he has to love me with imperfections, that he never loves me because I am symmetrical, never because I am good, never because I deserve his love, never because I am lovely, but always because he has the power of loving erring creatures—it is impossible for me to feel thus, and not get some insight into divine charity. Being conscious that he takes me with all my faults, I cannot but believe that he takes others with their faults—Roman Catholics, Swedenborgians, Unitarians, Universalists, and Christians of all sects and denominations; and of these, not only such as are least exceptionable, but such as are narrow-minded, such as are bigoted, such as are pugnacious, such as are unlovely. I believe that Christ finds much in them that he loves, but whether he finds much in them that he loves or not, he finds much *in himself of capacity to love them.* And so I have the feeling that in all churches, in all denominations, there is an elect, and Christ sees of the travail of his soul, and is satisfied.

That is not all. Aside from this catholicity of love of Christians in all sects and denominations, I have a sense of *ownership* in other people. It may seem rather fanciful, but it has been a source of abiding comfort to me for many years, that I *owned* everybody that was good for anything in life.

I came here, you know, under peculiar circumstances. I came just at the critical period of the anti-slavery movement; and I came without such endorsement as is usually considered necessary in city churches in the East. Owing to those independent personal habits that belonged to me, and that I acquired from my Western training, I never consulted brethren in the ministry as to what course I should pursue, but carried on my work as fast and as far as I could according to the enlightenment of my conscience. For years, as you will recollect, it excited remark, and various states of feeling. And so, I felt, always, as though I was not particularly acceptable to Christians beyond my own flock, with the exception of single individuals here and there in other churches. But I have felt, not resentful, and hardly regretful; for I have always had a sort of minor under-feeling, that when I was at home I was strong and all right, though I was conscious that outside of my own affectionate congregation I was looked upon with suspicion. This acting upon a nature proud enough, and sensitive enough, has wrought a kind of feeling that I never would intrude upon anybody, and never would ask any favor of anybody—as I never have had occasion to do; and I stood very much by myself. But I never felt any bitterness towards those who regarded me with disfavor. And I speak the truth, when I declare that I do not remember to have had towards any minister a feeling that I would have been afraid to have God review in the judgment day, and that I do not remember to have had towards any church or denomination a feeling that Christ would not approve. On the other hand, I have had positively and springing from my sense of the wonderful love with which I am loved, and with which the whole church is loved, the feeling that these very men who did not accept me or my work, were beloved of Christ, and were brethren to me; and I have said to them mentally, "I am your brother. *You do not know it, but I am, and though you do not own me, I own you.* All that is good in you is mine, and I am in sympathy with it. And you cannot keep me out of your church." I belong to the Presbyterian church. I belong to the Methodist church. I belong to the Baptist church. I belong to the Episcopal church. I belong to *any* church that has Christ in it. I go where he goes, and love what he loves. And I insist upon it that though those churches exclude me, they cannot keep me out. All those I have reason to believe Christ loves, I *claim* by virtue of the love that Christ has for me. Hence, I have a great sense of richness. I rejoice in everything that is good in all these denominations, and sorrow for everything that is bad, or that hinders the work of Christ in their hands. And I look, and wait, and long for that day when all Christians shall recognize each other.

I think that people in the church are like persons riding in a stage at night. For hours they sit side by side, and shoulder to shoulder, not being able in the darkness to distinguish one another; but at last, when day breaks, and they look at each other, behold, they discover that they are friends and brothers.

So we are riding, I think, through the night of this earthly state, and do not know that we are brethren, though we sit shoulder to shoulder; but as the millennial dawn comes on, we shall find it out and all will be clear."

THE END.

www.ingramcontent.com/pod-product-compliance
Lightning Source LLC
LaVergne TN
LVHW021219110826
845150LV00002B/202

* 9 7 8 1 4 2 5 5 6 4 6 8 1 *